THE

100

BEST

STOCKS

TO BUY IN

2020

PETER SANDER AND SCOTT BOBO

Adams Media

New York   London   Toronto   Sydney   New Delhi

Aadamsmedia

Adams Media
An Imprint of Simon & Schuster, Inc.
57 Littlefield Street
Avon, Massachusetts 02322

First Adams Media trade paperback edition December 2019

ADAMS MEDIA and colophon are trademarks of Simon & Schuster.

For information about special discounts for bulk purchases, please contact Simon & Schuster Special Sales at 1-866-506-1949 or business@simonandschuster.com.

The Simon & Schuster Speakers Bureau can bring authors to your live event. For more information or to book an event contact the Simon & Schuster Speakers Bureau at 1-866-248-3049 or visit our website at www.simonspeakers.com.

Manufactured in the United States of America

10 9 8 7 6 5 4 3 2 1

Library of Congress Cataloging-in-Publication Data has been applied for.

ISBN 978-1-5072-1204-2
ISBN 978-1-5072-1205-9 (ebook)

Contents

A Note to the Reader

Welcome to a new decade. Welcome to the 2020 edition of *The 100 Best Stocks to Buy*.

This is the eleventh edition of *The 100 Best Stocks to Buy* that we've authored. Many of you have bought this book every year to see what's new, what's changed, and to get fresh investing ideas. If so, you're probably used to a more elaborate introduction focused on how our previous year's picks did. That "deep" introduction is gone this year. We felt that what you repeat readers and especially you *new* readers sought was the picks themselves, their stories, and the reasons why we picked them. In fact, the individual stock narratives have been gradually expanding, and with limited space we felt you would prefer the expanded narratives.

There is wisdom in this decision. The fact of the matter is that we are future focused. All investors should be future focused. Performance metrics—whether ours or those put forth by a company—are measures of the past. As investors, we should not ignore these metrics but rather focus more on what's in store for the company, and those tangible and intangible qualities of a company that shape its story.

After a brief review of the core value–based investing principles that got us here, we take you straight to the journey through *The 100 Best Stocks to Buy in 2020*. As you enjoy that journey, we continue to invite you to send your postcards with questions or suggestions about investing to Peter at ginsander@hotmail.com.

Thanks for your continued support.

Invest long and prosper.

Introduction

- An IPO, Beyond Meat, with a hot new product with high market acceptance.
- An ETF, Real Estate Index Fund Shares, added as an alternative to investing in individual stocks.
- New companies, from shoe purveyor Skechers to a reformed Microsoft to institutional asset manager BlackRock.

These are just a few of *The 100 Best Stocks to Buy in 2020*, each one selected for you by our proven investment methodology, one that uses a forward-looking, value-driven investing philosophy to find stocks that consistently perform.

If you bought this book, you may be an astute and experienced individual investor who invests in individual stocks in individual companies. Or perhaps you're a first-time investor and want some guidance about where in the market you should invest and why. Or you may have long invested through mutual funds or a money manager, and you're ready to make a change. No matter how many stocks you've traded or how successful you've been in the past, the 2020 edition of *The 100 Best Stocks to Buy* can be a core investing tool.

In today's economy, with its trade wars, market fluctuations, and ever-changing technology, this book is an essential guide. Despite market fluctuations, as you'll see in the next chapter, we stick to our basic principles: Look for the underlying value of a company; don't buy stock in a company whose business you don't understand; favor dividend-paying and dividend-*raising* issuing companies. However, we've added some new kinds of stocks for you to consider. We're also increasing our focus on growth and looking at new megatrends such as 5G wireless technology so that we can continue building on our strong record of picking stocks that outperform the S&P 500 index. For each of these carefully selected stocks, which you'll find later in the book, organized alphabetically, you'll learn the following:

- The reward-versus-risk category (aggressive growth, growth and income, etc.)
- Basic attributes (ticker symbol, Value Line financial strength rating, current yield, dividend raises in past ten years, beta (volatility), etc.)

- A concise company profile and "story" describing what the company is, what it does, how it has performed and what's in store for the future
- Financial highlights for the previous year
- Reasons to buy the stock
- Reasons for caution
- Compounded earnings and dividend-growth rates
- Eight years of key facts and figures (revenues, net income, earnings per share, dividends per share, cash flow per share, and the high and low stock prices)

As you'll see, *100 Best Stocks* goes well beyond just being a stock screen or a study of stocks to invest in. After we walk you through our valuation and selection process in the next chapter, you'll have the confidence to follow our leads and the knowledge, with further research, to make your own investment decisions. At the end of the day, *The 100 Best Stocks to Buy in 2020* is your proven source of solid, dependable advice to begin your analysis and to ultimately take to the bank.

Part I
THE ART AND SCIENCE OF INVESTING IN STOCKS

The Art and Science of Investing in Stocks

We start with a basic point: We're enthusiastic advocates for the individual investor. We live by the old adage: "Nobody cares about your money more than you do." The future for a company—and its financial results—is driven by the intangible factors like brand, market presence, management excellence, market growth: all things that might be *interpreted* from information found on the Internet but are not handed down in nicely prepackaged chunks. A human must make sense of it all, must interpret it, to decide whether a company will excel down the road—which becomes the basis for buying the company's stock.

The 100 Best Stocks to Buy is an excellent resource for investing ideas, a place to get investing ideas and get started. Our goal is to help you not just keep up with the markets but to exceed their performance—and to collect some dividend income along the way. We want to help you build a portfolio that you're comfortable with, one that allows you to sleep at night. We want to teach you the method for investments that help you achieve your financial goals. In this chapter, you'll find our explanation of our investing principles and methodology. We'll tell you why we look at numbers when valuing a company but also how we look at intangibles not only of where a company is at right now but where it's going. We also generally describe our 2020 picks and the thought process behind them—why we added 17 new or returning stocks and what each of them brings to the table.

Our Stock-Picking Philosophy

We use a value investing approach throughout the book. What is value investing, you ask? Different folks define it differently, but we think of it as seeking stocks whose price is something less than their true, or intrinsic, value. That is, if you buy shares of one of our picks at a favorable price, you are paying less than what it is actually worth, if you were to drill down to its true worth.

Just to be clear, this is the *general* definition of value investing. Those who practice this form of investing (including Warren Buffett and many others) have different ways of doing it. But at the heart of all of them is the idea of buying stocks at something less than their true value.

They're more likely to earn out in the long run, especially when dividends are included, and they're less likely to be volatile along the way.

It's like playing defense with some offense thrown in for good measure. We like slow, steady, long-term earnings without a big shock every time there's a market "crash" or "correction." We suspect you'd like that too.

What Is "Intrinsic Value"?

At the heart of value investing, therefore, is determining the intrinsic value of the stock so you can determine if it's under- or overvalued at today's price. So look up the price of a stock online, compare it to its intrinsic value, and if it's less, push the buy button. Is that all there is to value investing?

Not so fast. Although the Internet is wonderful, we have yet to find a portal that calculates "intrinsic value" and puts it in front of us in flashing bold type.

Any introductory college finance class will cover the theoretical value of a share of stock, which is nothing more than the "present value" of all cash flows you will receive from the stock. That would include dividends—that part's pretty easy. But it would also include the cash you would receive for the stock someday when you sell it. That one is far less certain, much harder to calculate and subject to *discounting* (a dollar earned years from now is worth less than a dollar earned today). You can sell your share on the market, or you may get a payoff down the road if and when the company is acquired by another company. You can't predict the future, so knowing how much you'll get years down the road is next to impossible.

So intrinsic value is a tricky concept, especially if it's considered in the abstract. By necessity, in the real world value investors look at a lot of other things to try to place a value on a company, and thus, a stock.

Invest Like an Entrepreneur

One of the principles of value investing, as we practice it, is this: Think of yourself as an entrepreneur. Imagine that instead of buying its stock, you're buying the company. Can't decide whether to buy a stock, say, Starbucks or Whirlpool or Target or Beyond Meat? Just sit back and pretend for a moment you're filthy rich. You can buy the whole company.

The "price tag" of the company is the market capitalization, or "market cap," of these companies—the number of shares outstanding times the share price. At the time of this writing, Starbucks would fetch about $109 billion. World appliance leader Whirlpool fetches just over $9 billion, while Target is worth about $43 billion and market star Beyond Meat is still only worth a mere $11 billion. Meanwhile, Facebook is "worth" more than $529 billion according to the market. You could buy a whole lot of good companies for $529 billion!

If you had $529 billion, would you want to buy Facebook? Or the other four companies and have billions left over? I know what I'd do: Facebook looks pretty darned overvalued (or, at least, extremely expensive), while the others look like a bargain.

If you think of buying shares as being just like buying the whole company, you'll do well. Think like an entrepreneur, not just an investor. Where and how would you like to deploy your hard-earned capital?

Valuing a Company—It's More Than Just the Numbers

The next step is to assess a company's value. Just as there is no "formula" for determining intrinsic value, there is also no formula for adding up all the fundamentals and attributes of a business to determine value. First of all, not all of the attributes are quantifiable. You can quantify profit margins, but you can't quantify "management excellence."

Moreover, it isn't just the number, it's often the *trend* that's important. A single figure for net profit margin is interesting, but it is far more interesting if looked at over time, say, a series of years. The trend is your friend—or sometimes, your enemy.

Finally, you can't judge a company just on past numbers. We find this to be the bugaboo in many financial analyses and writings; people make a big deal of revenues, profits, margins, debt levels, all important stats measuring the fundamental performance of a business. But all that is what's already happened! As investors, we are trying to predict the future, not the past! So many analysts focus too much on the past performance, not the future traits like market share, management excellence, marketplace acceptance, brand, and customer loyalty that drive future results. It's like driving by looking in the rearview mirror—okay to do sometimes, but you should keep your eyes on what's in front of you.

SIGNS OF VALUE AND UNVALUE

Following are a few signs of value to look for in any company. This is not an exhaustive list, but it's a good place to start:

Signs of Value
- Rising dividends
- Declining share count
- Gaining market share
- Can control price of product or service
- Loyal customers
- Growing margins

- Producing, not consuming, capital (free cash flow)
- Steady or increasing ROE
- Management forthcoming, honest, understandable

…And Signs of Unvalue

- Declining margins
- No brand or who-cares brand
- Commodity producer, must compete on price
- Losing market dominance or market share
- Can't control costs
- Must acquire other companies to grow
- Management in hiding, off message, making excuses, difficult to understand, or in the news for all the wrong reasons

Putting It Into Practice

Now you know in general terms what we mean by value investing. That's the overall philosophy that guides our picks. So how do we put it into practice? What are the steps we take to value a company?

We break down the attributes of a business into two groups: strategic fundamentals and strategic intangibles. Strategic fundamentals are mostly *quantifiable* attributes that "score" a company's success, while strategic intangibles are usually *nonquantifiable* attributes that predict the future and, in combination with fundamentals, give us insight into value (and unvalue!). Finally, there are some questions we ask ourselves, just to keep us on the right track.

Strategic Fundamentals

Let's start with strategic fundamentals, those elements that can be quantified, and how you can use them to begin to build a picture of the company's value. These can typically be found in a company's financial statements, often going several years back. Different companies report them differently, and often you must do a little math or interpreting to figure out what is really going on, but here's a list of things we look at from a 30,000-foot overview, sometimes in more detail where warranted.

Are Gross and Operating Profit Margins Growing?

We like profitable companies. But what we really like are companies with large and especially growing margins. If a company has a gross margin (sales minus cost of goods sold) exceeding that of its competitors, it's probably doing *something* right with its customers and/or its costs. Net margins are a pretty good indicator too, but they're subject to the vagaries and changes in tax rates. We try to stay away from companies with razor thin margins, as even the slightest hiccup can push them into the red.

DOES A COMPANY CONSUME MORE CAPITAL THAN IT PRODUCES?

Just as you can't spend more than you earn over the long term, neither can a company. At the end of the day, cash generation is the simplest measure of whether a company is being successful.

The best way to determine this is to examine the Statement of Cash Flows, especially over time. The "cash flow from operations"—that is, what the company takes in from the business, should exceed the combined totals "cash used for investing purposes"—that is, invested in the business infrastructure, capital assets, etc.—and "cash used for financing activities": dividends paid plus or minus any cash inflows or outflows for selling or buying back securities (shares, bonds, etc.) to finance the business.

ARE EXPENSES UNDER CONTROL?

The best way to test this is to check whether the "Selling, General, and Administrative" expenses (SG&A) are rising and, more to the point, if they are rising faster than sales—information found in the financial reports. If so, that's a yellow, not necessarily a red, flag, but if it continues, it suggests that something is out of control, and it will catch up with the company sooner or later.

IS WORKING CAPITAL UNDER CONTROL?

Insufficient working capital is one of the biggest causes of death for small businesses, and even for bigger ones *changes* in working capital can signal success or trouble. In its purest sense, it is cash, receivables, and inventory, less short-term debts. It's what you own less what you owe aside from fixed assets like plant, stores, equipment, and long-term debt.

If receivables are increasing, that sounds like a good thing—more people owe you more money. But if receivables are rising and sales aren't, that suggests that people aren't paying their bills or, worse, the business must finance more to achieve the same level of sales. Similarly, a rise in inventory without a rise in sales means that it costs the business more money—more working capital—to do the same amount of business. That costs twice, because unless the firm is lucky, more inventory means more obsolescence and more deep-discount sales or write-offs down the road.

Is Debt In Line with Business Growth?

A simple test of business health is to check to see whether long-term debt is increasing or decreasing, and in particular, whether it is increasing faster than business growth. We especially like companies with little to no debt—less interest cost, more flexibility. It's also worth checking to make sure the company isn't simply issuing debt to buy back shares. This isn't a good strategy; in fact, it isn't a strategy at all, since it doesn't contribute to business growth.

Strategic Intangibles

When you look at any company, perhaps the bottom-line question is: If you had $100 billion in cool cash to spend, could you re-create that company? If the answer is yes, it may still be a great company, but it may not be great enough to fend off competition and keep its customers forever. If the answer is no, the company has something unique to offer in the marketplace, difficult to duplicate at any cost.

That distinctive competence, that sustainable competitive edge—whatever it is, a brand, a patent, a trade secret, a unique customer experience, a lock on distribution or supply channels—may be worth more than all the physical and financial assets a company could ever have.

These strategic intangibles drive the future and are a key part of our stock-picking method. Seven examples follow, although there are others; some industries may have some unique ones, like intellectual property in the technology sector.

Does the Company Have a Moat?

A business moat protects the business from competition and helps it command higher prices and earn higher profits. Moats are usually a combination of brand, product technology, design, marketing and distribution channels, and customer loyalty all working together to protect a company.

Does the Company Have an Excellent Brand?

A strong brand means consistency and a promise to consumers, and consumers sold on a brand will prefer it over any other, almost regardless of price. Good brands command higher prices and foster loyalty, identity, and even customer "love."

Is the Company a Market Leader?

Market leadership usually—but not always—goes hand in hand with brand. The trick is to decide whether a company really leads in its industry.

Often—but not always—that's a factor of size. The market leader usually has the highest market share and calls the shots with regard to price, technology, marketing message, etc.—other companies must play catch-up and often discount their prices to keep up. Excellent companies tend to be market leaders, and market leaders tend to be excellent companies. However, this relationship doesn't always hold true—sometimes the nimble but smaller competitor is the excellent company headed for leadership, like Southwest Airlines.

DOES THE COMPANY HAVE CHANNEL EXCELLENCE?

"Channels" in business parlance means a chain of players to sell and distribute a company's products. It might be stores, it might be other industrial companies, it might be direct to the consumer. If a company is considered a top supplier in a particular channel, or a company has especially good relations with its channel, that's a plus.

DOES THE COMPANY HAVE SUPPLY-CHAIN EXCELLENCE?

Like distribution channels, excellent companies develop excellent and low-cost upstream supply channels. They are seldom caught off guard by supply shortages and tend to get favorable and stable prices for whatever they buy. This is not an easy assessment unless you know something about a particular industry.

DOES THE COMPANY HAVE EXCELLENT MANAGEMENT?

It's not easy for an investor to determine if a management team does a good job or acts in shareholder interests. Clues can include candor and honesty and the ability of company management to speak in accessible, easily understood terms about the company and company performance (it's worth listening to conference calls as a resource). A management team that admits errors and avoids other forms of arrogance and entitlement (i.e., luxury perks, office suites, fancy aircraft) is probably tilting its interests toward shareholders, as is the management team that can cough up some decent dividends.

ARE THERE SIGNS OF INNOVATION EXCELLENCE?

If the company is leading the industry in innovation, that's usually a good thing, for "first to market" offers definite business advantages. The less obvious part of this question is whether the company makes the best use of technology to make its operations and customer interfaces as efficient and effective as possible. Sometimes such innovations mean a lot more than bringing new, fancy products and bells and whistles to the market. Look for companies that have deployed technology and innovative customer interfaces to achieve sustainable competitive advantage. Again, Southwest Airlines serves as an example.

Cutting to the Chase: What Really Puts a Company on the Short List

As you can see, "classic" value investing is research intensive, and it would take forever to put together an exhaustive analysis of even one company, let alone search through a universe of 5,000 companies to find the *100 Best* among them. It is rather like attending a dance or party to find a date or partner: You tend to rely on certain cues to decide if you should proceed further! To find those cues, we ask ourselves a series of questions.

Do We Understand the Business?

Long touted by Mr. Buffett and others, one of the main tenets of value investing is to "invest in companies you understand." We subscribe to this wholeheartedly. Not only do we seek companies we understand, but we also gravitate toward companies that communicate clearly. You'll find that we put very few financial or pharmaceutical companies on our list—we have a hard time understanding their businesses, and in many cases, their investor materials.

Can you describe in a few sentences what a company does? How it makes money? If you can't, you might be best to stay away.

Does It Have Good Growth Prospects?

Much is made by the investment community about the "difference" between growth stocks and value stocks. In our view, growth is *part of* value and something to be factored into the value "equation." A stock with strong growth prospects has greater value all other things being equal. Later when we say that we are bringing more "growth" stocks onto the list, we're really referring to value stocks that *have more growth potential.* We love dividend-paying stocks that also have growth potential, and we typically don't pick growth-oriented stocks that don't make money or meet our other value criteria.

Does the Company Pay a Dividend?

A few years ago we came to the realization that we use two simple and key indicators to suggest a good stock for further analysis: (1) strong and growing yield, and (2) the persistence of share buybacks. Like that pretty face at the party, those two features suggest we should make the effort to learn the rest of the story.

We place great emphasis on dividend-paying stocks and especially those that *grow* their dividends. If a company is paying a good dividend, raising it, and buying back shares, good things are likely going on with fundamentals and intangibles behind the scenes.

DOES THE COMPANY GROW ITS DIVIDEND?

We like companies that reward you, the investor, with a periodic *raise* to recognize the value of your commitment of precious investment capital. In that spirit, in our presentation format we show the number of dividend increases in the past ten years in the header right after Current Yield. We know of no other financial publication that does this; in fact, we count the increases by hand from dividend history furnished by Value Line. Out of our *100 Best Stocks* for 2020, some 58 of them have raised their dividends in each of the past eight, nine, or ten years.

DOES THE COMPANY BUY BACK ITS SHARES?

Share buybacks have come into the limelight recently, as (1) companies, rich with cash from the 2017 Tax Cuts and Jobs Act, have more cash than ever to do them and are using it and (2) some politicians are starting to take companies to task for buying back shares (which serves to make the executives look better as per-share earnings are higher) rather than investing in their business or their workers.

We generally applaud buybacks as a way of returning hard-earned capital to shareholders and as an indicator of internal business health—unless the company is simply racking up more long-term debt to do so.

An Art and a Science

Well, so far, we've outlined most of the factors we consider in selecting a *100 Best* stock, but again, there is no magic formula. It is rather like judging art or buying a car—it is as much about how all the facts and impressions and *gestalt* of the company work together to form a pleasing composite impression on our brains at the end of the day.

We don't always get it right; nobody can. Some stocks will serve your individual preferences more than others. We don't expect you to own—or want to own—all 100 stocks; different stocks for different folks, depending on investment objectives, risk tolerance, industry, and a multitude of other factors too long to list.

After all, for intelligent investors, chasing the latest fad doesn't work; buying something and locking it away forever doesn't work anymore either. Investors must make intelligent choices based on true value and follow those choices through time and change. It all points to a value-oriented approach to investing and to staying modestly active with your investments.

Whether you do it yourself or hire others to manage your investments for you, you owe it to your financial future to at least be familiar with good investments and investment alternatives.

INFORMATION SOURCES

All investors need good information sources. We make extensive use of the Value Line Investment Survey, in our opinion one of the best resources available to the individual investor. The Investment Survey assembles a succinct one-page summary of key statistics and history for 1,700 companies, each company quarterly. You can subscribe or often find it in the reference section of a well-stocked local library.

We also use company-published materials and websites including "10-K" annual reports. We subscribe to *Barron's* and *The Wall Street Journal* and soak up other information online as available. Finally, we keep a keen eye on what's happening in the marketplace.

About the 2020 Edition

This year we felt it necessary to "clean house" a little, and so we did. In fact, we replaced 17 companies, the most since our initial year taking the book over from its previous author in 2010.

Part of this housecleaning was to clear out some old "value traps" we hung onto for too long; part of it was moving toward new trends and technologies such as 5G wireless, stay-at-home shopping, and more generally, a continued shift toward millennials as a population majority and an ever larger driving force in business. We also catered a little more to those of you looking for current income, say, in retirement.

The 2020 Investing Context: Strong but Unsettled Economy

It's been a great year—really, a great decade—for investing. As we exit 2019, one must deal with many moving parts to determine which way the markets are headed. Many indicators—unemployment, jobless claims, consumer spending, consumer sentiment, corporate profits, and the markets themselves—are showing that things are really, really good right now. Certain others, like factory utilization, capital spending, trade and the trade deficit, the strong dollar, oil and commodity prices, the inverted yield curve (that is, younger treasury bonds are yielding more interest than older ones), show that we may not be in such good shape.

TRADE WARS

In an effort to stop unfair trade practices on China's part and, perhaps, motivate US corporations to repatriate factories and supply chains the US government placed tariffs on Chinese goods. Then, of course, the Chinese government retaliated with tariffs of their own, so US factories, farmers, and other producers took a hit on the demand side. If the trade wars were to be halted immediately we think the markets would react favorably. If trade policies and the uncertainties they bring remain in place, we feel the markets could react strongly to the downside.

FOCUS ON THE FUTURE

The stay-at-home economy is growing gangbusters, and we're gradually moving into a new world where the Internet controls and powers everything. That is manifesting itself today in the "Internet of Things (IoT)" which is a convergence of imbedded sensors, connected devices, and analytics, giving rise to the "smart home" and evolving into "smart cars" and "smart" everything, all controlled from the palm of our hands by a device. This new ecosystem is powered by Wi-Fi and today's cellular networks, and we see another shift coming with the implementation of so-called "5G" cellular technology, where everything will be connected to everything else seamlessly: no wires, no fiber, always on.

We've added two companies, Crown Castle and T-Mobile, which we think will be important players in a 5G-powered world, and we've brought back two others dismissed for various reasons over the past two years: AT&T and Qualcomm. Others, including Apple, Microsoft, and even Valmont, should benefit from the widespread use of this new platform.

What's New for the 2020 List

Although we say every year our investing style and presentation has remained essentially the same, the approach evolves as it does with any blend of science and art. Experience matters and is taken into account. Changes in the world investing context and environment factor in. Maybe we see things a little differently than we did ten years ago...and certainly 35 years ago. All of these factors influence the mix; here are a few directions we've taken recently (or have continued with emphasis) with this edition:

THIS YEAR'S INVESTING LESSON: VALUE TRAPS

A value trap is a stock that looks cheap on a fundamentals valuation basis—price to earnings, price to cash flow, price to book, both on a historical basis (i.e., P/E compared to years ago) or on a competitive basis (cheaper than others in the same industry). Investors (including us) grab these "bargains" expecting a fairly quick turnaround as the "discrepancy" normalizes or reverts to the mean.

Problem is…it doesn't happen. There's no turnaround, because there's no real catalyst to turn things around. Company materials and financial reports run the mill of rhetoric and business buzzwords; websites are heavy on marketing spin and promises, but there is little in the way of real change. In addition to the rhetoric, you're likely to see declining profit margins, increased competition, lack of meaningful new products or services, declining markets served, pieces that don't go together (resulting from growth-through-acquisitions strategy). The trap springs when investors buy into the company at low prices and the stock continues to languish or drop further.

The trick, of course, is to decide whether a company can right itself and attain the valuation comparable to its past or its peers. Can it innovate? Can it meaningfully reduce costs? Can it penetrate new markets, such as international markets? Can it find ways to add revenue-producing value to its existing product base? Can it sell into adjacent markets?

The bottom line: When a company looks cheap, look twice. Convince yourself it *isn't* a value trap. If you can't do that, move on.

Two New Types of "Stocks"

For the first time in 2020, we have a stock on the *100 Best* list that isn't really a stock. It's an ETF, or Exchange Traded Fund. For several reasons we take a favorable view of Real Estate Investment Trusts (REITs), and we know that most of you want to "park" some cash somewhere safe but also to earn a moderate return. So we added the Vanguard Real Estate ETF to our list.

We also added our first IPO ("Initial Public Offering") stock, that is newly issued shares in a company. Now typically IPOs go pretty strongly against our grain—no track record, highly volatile, typically overvalued, zero dividends. But the one we picked, Beyond Meat, transcends these concerns because the product is so darned good and market acceptance appears to be exceptional. This one appears to be a gold mine.

A Little More Growth

We've duly noted the resurgence of growth-oriented companies and have once again injected a few new ones into the portfolio. Notably, we have also chucked a couple we added last year as they simply were not panning out as it were. Gone (already) are Craft Brew Alliance and CalAmp in favor of 2019 IPO sensation Beyond Meat (yes, we did pick it before it became a sensation!) and wireless tower provider Crown Castle. While our total portfolio still largely consists of steady, defensive, dividend-paying issues, we think we have given you a decent menu of growth stocks to choose from.

LOW-VOLATILITY BIAS

Steady growth, steady returns, steady dividend increases—that's what we continue to prefer for the majority of our picks. While we present "beta" as a measure of market correlation, we look deeper into the actual patterns and history of earnings, dividends, cash flow, and yes, share price—and the relative statistical stability as reported by Value Line. If it's a wild ride, for the most part we don't get on; we prefer to watch from the sidelines instead (Beyond Meat is this year's exception). We know—as the markets continue to rise through the years, the chances for corrective "volatility" increase—there isn't a whole lot we can do about that. That said, we continue to reach a bit more outside our normal "core" type of holding to pick up a few more aggressive companies that seem at the forefront of change. We continue to add a few smaller companies for the list, to add some energy and reap the benefits of these new companies still coming into their own.

STILL PLAYING DEFENSE

While we look more for up-and-comers, we still stick to the more defensive stance in light of market "exuberance" and in recognition of the fact that in our multiyear tenure at the reins of this book, we still have yet to see a down year! Our lists continue to be constructed to provide enough growth opportunity to beat the market but also to best the market in a down market, that is, to be down only 5 percent if the market dropped 10 percent. Quite honestly, many of our *100 Best Stocks* seem fully valued at this juncture. We were—and still are—nervous about riding them any further.

Our strategy for dealing with this continues to be to evaluate all of our picks carefully using our "sell if there's something better to buy" philosophy and try to visualize how they would do in a sloppy market. And while we are embracing growth-oriented issues, we continue to avoid "momentum" plays, which tend to beat a "mo" path downward at the slightest sign of change.

A Few More High-Yield Choices

As stated earlier, it's nice when good investments return strong current income, particularly when they also have some growth possibilities. We continue to like REITs that are also good businesses; they are generally safe, strongly cash-flow positive, and have some characteristics of a good growth company as well—Welltower, Public Storage, and Prologis fit this bill, and this year we added Crown Castle and the catch-all Vanguard REIT ETF.

Last year we added an energy pipeline Master Limited Partnership (MLP)—another popular vehicle that, like REITs, is required to pay 90 percent of its net income in distributions as they pay no corporate income taxes. This format can produce current distributions as high as 9–10 percent, better than any but the most speculative bonds and again, with a growth kicker. We added Enable Midstream Partners, Macquarie Infrastructure, and small developmental investor Compass Diversified Holdings, all of which pay 9 percent or more in dividends. While we don't recommend putting all of your eggs in these high-income baskets, they can be used to juice up your income and to balance against other picks that pay smaller dividends. Plus, at present, if used in taxable accounts you can deduct 20 percent of the income from many of these issues as a "Section 199" deduction. But also beware that these issues will make your taxes more complicated. Thus, retirement accounts such as traditional and Roth IRAs that allow individual stock investments may be the best place to hold these investments.

Without any further fanfare, here are the 2020 best stocks to buy. For a complete list, see page 348 at the end of the book.

Part II

THE 100 BEST STOCKS TO BUY

`CONSERVATIVE GROWTH`

3M Company

Ticker symbol: MMM (NYSE) ❑ Large Cap ❑ Value Line financial strength rating: A++
❑ Current yield: 2.7% ❑ Dividend raises, past 10 years: 10

Company Profile

"3M Science. Applied to Life" is the core slogan of the 3M Company, originally known as the Minnesota Mining and Manufacturing Co. It is a $33 billion diversified manufacturing technology company with leading positions in industrial, consumer and office, healthcare, safety, electronics, telecommunications, and other markets. The company has 81 manufacturing operations in 29 US states and in total 132 manufacturing operations in more than 36 countries. It serves customers in nearly 200 countries; 61 percent of the company's sales are outside the US (31 percent Asia Pacific, 20 percent EMEA, 9 percent Latin America/Canada). 3M also operates 37 laboratories worldwide and spends about 5.8 percent of revenues on R&D. Due to the breadth of their product line and the global reach of their distribution, the company has long been viewed as a bellwether for the overall health of the world economy.

3M's operations are divided into five business segments (approximate revenue percentages in parentheses):

- The Industrial business (37 percent of 2018 sales) serves a variety of vertical markets, including automotive, automotive aftermarket, electronics, paper and packaging, appliance, food and beverage, and construction. Products include industrial tapes, a wide variety of abrasives, adhesives, specialty materials, filtration products, closure systems for personal hygiene products, advanced ceramics, automotive insulation, filler and paint system components, and products for the separation of fluids and gases.
- The Safety and Graphics business (21 percent) serves a broad range of markets that increase the safety, security, and productivity of workers, facilities, and systems. Major product offerings include personal protection, like respirators and filtering systems, safety and security products such as reflectorized fabrics and tapes, energy control products, traffic control products including reflective sheeting for highway signs, building cleaning and protection products, track and trace solutions, and roofing granules for asphalt shingles.

- The Healthcare business (18 percent) serves markets that include medical clinics and hospitals, pharmaceuticals, dental and orthodontic practitioners, and health information systems. Products and services include medical and surgical supplies, skin health and infection prevention products, drug-delivery systems, dental and orthodontic products, health information systems, and antimicrobial solutions. The Healthcare business is the most profitable, with operating margins of 30.2 percent versus margins in the low 20s for the other four businesses.
- The Electronics and Energy segment (17 percent) serves the electrical, electronics, communications, and renewable energy industries, including electric utilities. Products include electronic and interconnect solutions, microinterconnect systems, high-performance fluids and abrasives for semiconductor and disk drive manufacture, high-temperature and display tapes, telecommunications products, electrical products, and optical film materials that support LCD displays and touch screens for monitors, tablets, mobile phones, and other products.
- The Consumer segment (15 percent) serves markets that include retail, home improvement, building maintenance, office, and other markets. Products in this segment include office supply products such as the familiar Scotch tapes, Post-it notes, Scotch-Brite cleaning abrasives, stationery products, construction and home improvement products, home-care products, protective material products, and consumer healthcare products.

Near-term strategies include streamlining the organization structure, combining 40 businesses into 26, a more general cost-containment effort, and a greater emphasis on leveraging and promoting the brand across all businesses. The company has adjusted its portfolio once again with several small acquisitions and divestitures. The cost containment ("transformation" in company lingo) is intended to save $600–$700 million in costs and $500 million in working capital by 2020. It appears that small acquisitions and an emphasis on "priority growth platforms" and fast-track R&D will continue to be themes going forward.

Financial Highlights, Fiscal Year 2018
Slowing China sales and trade uncertainties were the main culprits in 2018's weaker-than-usual 3.5 percent sales gain, while cost savings initiatives and tax cuts were mainly responsible for a 5.5 percent gain in

net income. Improved energy industry fundamentals helped while higher raw material and supply chain costs hurt the year's performance. By segment organic revenue, Industrial, Safety and Graphics, and Electronics and Energy were strongest, while Consumer lagged a bit. By region, Asia Pacific grew 3.8 percent, weaker than last year's 10.9 percent due to the China slowdowns, while the US grew a healthier 3.2 percent compared to 1.5 percent last year. The outlook for 2019 calls for another modest 2–3 percent sales and net income gain, while 2020 improves a bit with a 6–8 percent earnings rise on a 3–5 percent rise in sales. 3M continues to reward shareholders, with a 16 percent dividend raise and another 2 percent share buyback; the company has raised its dividend 61 years in a row and retired 15 percent of its float since 2011.

Reasons to Buy

For years, 3M has served as a classic example of a "conservative growth" stock and is a classic exercise in brand excellence, marketplace and niche strength, and steady performance. The company makes and distributes many repeat-sale products essential to manufacturing and day-to-day operations of other companies and organizations and seemingly essential to most of us, e.g., Post-it notes, Scotch-Brite sponges and Scotch tape—it is a nice mix of consumer and commercially oriented businesses. The company appears to do better than the markets during strong periods and also holds value better than most during downturns. There is a persistent focus on innovation here, both in its products and in its internal operations and marketing—and it's more the slow, steady variety than a flash in the pan. Cash flows are strong and growing and continue to be shared liberally with shareholders.

Reasons for Caution

3M is, and always will be, vulnerable to economic cycles, but in general the business holds up pretty well in down cycles. Both sales and costs are sensitive to trade policy. There's plenty of pressure from the investment community to get the top line moving forward, and we worry that 3M could go on a larger acquisition rampage to boost growth, but we continue to be comfortable with the types of acquisitions the company has made. Further, profit growth has been good for such a large company, so why the angst about revenue growth? We still think there's value here—once again we suggest placing a Post-it on this page to pick up a few shares when the price is right.

SECTOR: Industrials ❑ Beta coefficient: 0.95 ❑ 10-year compound earnings per-share growth: 5.5% ❑ 10-year compound dividends per-share growth: 9.5%

	2011	2012	2013	2014	2015	2016	2017	2018
Revenues (mil)	29,611	29,904	30,871	31,821	30,274	30,109	31,657	32,765
Net income (mil)	4,283	4,445	4,659	4,956	4,833	5,050	5,620	5,928
Earnings per share	5.96	6.32	6.72	7.49	7.58	8.16	9.17	9.96
Dividends per share	2.20	2.36	2.54	3.42	4.10	4.44	4.70	5.44
Cash flow per share	7.85	8.35	9.09	10.02	10.29	10.93	12.04	12.86
Price: high	98.2	95.5	140.4	168.2	170.5	182.3	244.2	259.8
low	68.6	82.0	94.0	123.6	124.0	134.6	173.5	176.5

Website: www.3m.com

GROWTH AND INCOME

Abbott Laboratories

Ticker symbol: ABT (NYSE) ❑ Large Cap ❑ Value Line financial strength rating: A++ ❑ Current yield: 1.8% ❑ Dividend raises, past 10 years: 10

Company Profile

In 2013 longtime *100 Best* stalwart Abbott Laboratories split itself in two, spinning off their research pharmaceutical firm known as AbbVie, which found its way back onto our list three years ago. The remaining healthcare products maker and distributor Abbott Labs, which kept the original company name, made it back a year later, as the split companies both appeared to be headed in the right direction. Abbott then acquired the successful *100 Best* medical device maker St. Jude Medical, which strengthened its hand as a true *100 Best* pick, and the company remains on the list as a solid choice for 2020.

Today's Abbott engages in the discovery, development, manufacture, and distribution of medicines, diagnostics, nutrition, and vascular products. The business continues to operate in four segments:

- Established Pharmaceuticals (14.5 percent of 2018 revenue) contains a portfolio of over 1,500 established and mostly generic prescription products including flu vaccines, hormone replacements, enzyme replacements, antibiotics, and other routine remedies for common ailments (in contrast to expensive, "sexy" treatments for rare diseases). This group is particularly strong in emerging markets.

- Nutritional Products (24.5 percent of revenue) makes and markets a portfolio of baby formulas under the Similac brand and an assortment of nutritional supplements targeted to adults (Ensure and Glucerna are major brands), electrolyte replenishment (Pedialyte), and other nutritional products and supplements. The company claims a number one market position in adult and pediatric nutritionals.
- Diagnostic Products (25 percent of revenue) makes and markets a broad line of diagnostic systems and tests for blood banks, hospitals, commercial labs, and alternate-care testing sites—this group holds a number one position in standard and advanced blood chemistry testing and monitoring. One exciting breakthrough new product is the "FreeStyle Libre," a continuous electronic glucose monitoring system that eliminates finger pricks. This product now has one million users worldwide. Another breakthrough diagnostic system known as "Alinity" speeds up lab testing results with greater accuracy.
- Medical Devices (formerly Vascular Products), 37 percent of revenue, markets a broad line of coronary, endovascular, structural heart, and other physical and electronic products. Recent product breakthroughs include Confirm Rx, the world's first smartphone-compatible Insertable Cardiac Monitor. Abbott products are sold in about 160 countries, with about 65 percent of total sales occurring overseas and 41 percent from emerging markets.

The acquisition of St. Jude brought a well-established product line of structural heart repair devices, including heart valve repair and replacement technologies, heart failure remedies, cardiac rhythm management devices, cardiovascular care devices including imaging devices and stents, and neuromodulation devices to manage chronic pain and movement disorders. The St. Jude acquisition makes Abbott a number one or number two supplier into these important high-growth markets. Overall, and with the St. Jude acquisition, the company holds a number one position in the following healthcare markets:

- Blood and plasma screening
- Adult nutrition
- Pediatric nutrition in many markets
- Heart pumps
- Remote heart failure monitoring
- Point-of-care testing
- Chronic pain devices

Recognized brands include Similac, FreeStyle, PediaSure, Pedialyte, Alinity, Brufen, i-STAT, CardioMEMS, and many others commonly observed in households and clinical environments. Abbott has also been the number one medical products company from 1984 through 2019 on the *Fortune* Most Admired Companies list.

Financial Highlights, Fiscal Year 2018

Global FY2018 sales rose 11.6 percent; about 7.3 percent organically, that is, without the effects of acquisition. High single-digit organic gains were realized by all product groups. Net income rose 16.6 percent. The numbers are hard to compare looking backward or forward, with the AbbVie split, a 2015 sale of some generic pharmaceuticals businesses to Mylan (N.V., Netherlands), the St. Jude acquisition, and the more recent acquisition of diagnostic products maker Alere. Going forward the company projects a 4–5 percent revenue gain for 2019 and a 9–11 percent rise in net income. For 2020, projections call for a 6–8 percent annual revenue gain but a 12–13 percent net income gain as margins improve. Modest buybacks will boost per-share earnings at a somewhat greater rate, while dividends will grow steadily in the single digits after a 14 percent increase in 2019.

The company raised its dividend modestly in 2018 for a 47th consecutive year of dividend increases (not counting the drop when AbbVie split off). The share count increased about 15 percent with the St. Jude acquisition but will drop 1–2 percent annually thereafter.

Reasons to Buy

Abbott is an established leader in important, stable, and mostly recurring healthcare markets and needs. Most of the product portfolio to date consists of products and diagnostics used over and over, including blood tests, diabetes remedies, cardiovascular devices, and nutritional products. We like that kind of business.

The St. Jude acquisition brought Abbott to a leadership position in key cardiovascular markets, a good position with today's demographics and a relatively higher-margined business. Abbott's net margins had been tracking in the 15–16 percent range; with the St. Jude acquisition, net margins will rise into the 17–18 percent range over the next two years and close to 20 percent further out.

Reasons for Caution

Abbott operates with a solid business base but has been heavily involved in acquisitions since its 2012 split with AbbVie. While much of it makes sense from a strategic standpoint, it is disruptive and carries some risks. The good news is that major acquisitions appear to be over for now. The $23.6 billion acquisition price for St. Jude may have been too high (for a company with $6 billion in annual revenue) and will create some goodwill write-offs down the road. Price competition may emerge in the Established Pharmaceuticals unit, particularly in generics.

SECTOR: Healthcare ❑ Beta coefficient: 1.05 ❑ 10-year compound earnings per-share growth: NM ❑ 10-year compound dividends per-share growth: NM

	2011	2012	2013	2014	2015	2016	2017	2018
Revenues (bil)	38.9	39.9	21.9	22.3	20.4	20.9	27.4	30.6
Net income (bil)	7.3	8.2	3.2	3.5	3.3	3.3	4.4	5.1
Earnings per share	4.66	4.99	2.01	2.28	2.15	2.20	2.50	3.20
Dividends per share	1.88	2.01	0.56	0.88	0.96	1.04	1.06	1.12
Cash flow per share	6.61	6.91	3.17	3.35	3.21	3.20	3.70	4.75
Price: high	56.4	72.5	38.6	46.5	51.7	45.8	57.8	74.8
low	45.1	54.0	31.6	35.7	39.0	36.0	38.3	55.6

Note: Figures before 2013 are for combined company. See AbbVie, another *100 Best* stock.

Website: www.abbott.com

AGGRESSIVE GROWTH

AbbVie, Inc.

Ticker symbol: ABBV (NYSE) ❑ Large Cap ❑ Value Line financial strength rating: A ❑ Current yield: 5.3% ❑ Dividend raises, past 10 years: 5

Company Profile

We like it when a company "owns" a niche, particularly in the lucrative pharmaceutical industry and particularly when access to the market is hard to come by, as potential competitors in this industry face monumental barriers to bring products to market. One of the clearest examples of a company profiting handsomely from niche dominance is AbbVie, with its lucrative and multifaceted Humira franchise. But alas, all good things must come to an end someday; patents for Humira are gradually going away as new uses for the drug sustain the market dominance. A complacent company would simply live off the laurels of the blockbuster drug. But not AbbVie—they see the writing on the wall and are actively pursuing what's next while getting the most out of the current franchise. Bravo, AbbVie.

Spun off from the former combined Abbott Laboratories in 2013, AbbVie is a leading research-based biopharmaceutical company specializing in developing and marketing treatments and therapies for a range of complex diseases. The former Abbott was a perennial *100 Best* stock. The other half of the split, still called Abbott Laboratories, specializes mainly in making and distributing a line of medical supplies. AbbVie's products help treat conditions such as chronic autoimmune diseases in rheumatology, gastroenterology, and dermatology; oncology, including blood cancers; virology, including hepatitis C virus (HCV) and human immunodeficiency virus (HIV); neurological disorders, such as Parkinson's disease and multiple sclerosis; metabolic diseases, including thyroid disease and complications associated with cystic fibrosis, as well as other serious health conditions. AbbVie also has a pipeline of new medicines, including more than 50 compounds or indications (20 in late-stage development), such as immunology, virology/liver disease, oncology, neurological diseases, and women's health. Its product portfolio includes Humira, Imbruvica, and an array of virology, metabolics, and endocrinology products.

Accounting for 60 percent of FY2018 sales (down from 65 percent in 2017) and holding the title as highest-grossing drug in the world at just under $20 billion in annual sales, Humira is by far AbbVie's largest product—really, it's a franchise. An immunological agent initially developed to treat rheumatoid arthritis, the company (and the FDA) have found it quite useful for treating other immunological diseases such as psoriasis, psoriatic arthritis, and other diseases in the rheumatology, gastroenterology, and dermatology space. The patent for the "composition of matter" expired at the end of 2016—and normally with 60 percent of the business this would be a huge red flag—but the company has an extensive "patent estate" of several dozen patents for the product covering other uses, formulations, manufacturing processes, and other patents extending well into the next decade.

Out of necessity and good sense, AbbVie has stepped up its pipeline of non-Humira sales, which it now expects to grow to $35 billion in sales by 2025 (notable because that exceeds the company's total sales today). Other emerging drug platforms include hematology (blood oncology) drugs Imbruvica and Venclexta, late-stage immunology drugs (Upadacitinib and Risankizumab—okay guys, we'd like you to find some simpler names for these things!), Elagolix for endometriosis and uterine fibroids, new neuroscience drugs such as Duopa for Parkinson's, and others. As exemplified by the Humira platform, the company continually looks for ways to extend existing and modified formulations into additional disease categories with new delivery and dosage models added in where feasible (Duopa uses an implant to provide steadier levels of dopamine for advanced Parkinson's patients, for example).

The company markets its products in 170 countries; about 34 percent of sales are overseas (compared to 38 percent in 2017).

In late June 2019, AbbVie launched a $63 billion takeover bid for Allergan, maker of Botox and other pharmaceuticals, in an effort to diversify away from its Humira base.

Financial Highlights, Fiscal Year 2018

Stronger sales in non-Humira drugs Imbruvica, Venclexta, and Mavyret led to a 16 percent gain in 2018 revenues (15 percent on a constant currency basis) while net earnings, helped along by the tax cuts, advanced some 36 percent. However, by year's end, the company was experiencing a sharper-than-expected slowdown in Humira sales overseas as patents expired and competitive formulations hit the market—that shrinkage is reflected in the previously noted decline in total overseas sales. The company expects US Humira sales to remain robust and the new products to gather steam; current projections however call for roughly flat 2019 sales with a 3–5 percent earnings gain with revenue growth once again returning to the 5–7 percent range in 2020. FY2020 earnings are projected to rise in the 6–8 percent range. Dividend growth is very strong with back-to-back increases totaling 65 percent in 2018 and 2019; over 130 million shares have been retired since 2016 as well.

Reasons to Buy

Research pharma companies are quite often too complex for our simple minds and tastes, so we take on this sector with great care, as we also did with diabetes drug specialist Novo Nordisk a few years back. Here, we find a bit more complexity since yes, as stated, AbbVie specializes in the treatment of complex and advanced diseases. We won't pretend to understand how its products actually work.

What we do like and think we understand is the underlying business strategy. AbbVie focuses on a few key drug platforms like Humira and Imbruvica, making the most of them while offering extendable solutions for other complex oncological, immunological, and neurological indications as well. While it's unfortunate that there are so many of these complex diseases around to treat, we like AbbVie's focus on this relatively more profitable, defensible end of the market.

The financial track record speaks for itself—any company with a 37 percent–plus net profit margin that shares its success with its shareholders comes as pretty good medicine for us.

Reasons for Caution

Complexity is probably our number one issue—this company could fail miserably in one or more of its markets, and we laypeople would probably be none the wiser. Naturally, the dependence on Humira is a concern; however, the company appears to position itself quite well to minimize the potential damage from patent expirations, and now the pending Allergan acquisition adds to the story. Healthcare industry consolidation and power shifts may lead to reduced drug prices and margins, which would hurt AbbVie and others in the group. Finally, we do worry a bit about the growth-by-acquisition tendencies, though we do think acquisitions so far make sense and are done on top of a pretty sound and successful business.

SECTOR: Healthcare ❑ Beta coefficient: 1.15 ❑ 10-year compound earnings per-share growth: NM ❑ 10-year compound dividends per-share growth: NM

	2011	2012	2013	2014	2015	2016	2017	2018
Revenues (mil)	—	—	18,790	19,960	22,839	25,638	28,216	32,753
Net income (mil)	—	—	5,066	5,375	7,060	7,904	9,011	12,282
Earnings per share	—	—	3.14	3.32	4.29	4.82	5.60	7.91
Dividends per share	—	—	1.60	1.66	2.02	2.28	2.56	3.59
Cash flow per share	—	—	3.44	3.62	4.64	5.23	5.73	8.62
Price: high	—	—	54.8	70.8	71.2	68.1	99.1	125.9
low	—	—	33.3	45.5	45.4	50.7	59.3	77.8

Website: www.abbvie.com

CONSERVATIVE GROWTH

Allstate Corporation

Ticker symbol: ALL (NASDAQ) ❑ Large Cap ❑ Value Line financial strength rating: A+ ❑ Current yield: 2.1% ❑ Dividend increases, past 10 years: 7

Company Profile

Allstate is the nation's second-largest publicly held, full-line "P/C" (property/casualty) insurance provider, offering the gamut of auto, home, renters, and business insurance, and has become a larger player in life insurance, retirement, and annuity segments as well (although it still is ranked only nineteenth among US life insurers). The company serves 16 million households through a network of 36,000 total agents with almost a billion and a half policies in force in all 50 states plus DC and Canada. It prides itself on its four-tiered brand and channel strategy for delivering choice and advice to customers where, when, and how they want it.

The company sells its own Allstate product through 10,430 exclusive Allstate agencies and its "Encompass" subbrand through independent agencies. It estimates that the Allstate brand alone owns 9 percent of the traditional P/C market, with a 10 percent share of the auto market and an 8 percent share for homeowners. The company owns and operates the e-commerce insurance portal Esurance and also sells its product directly, along with other insurance brands, through its "Answer Financial" phone portal for self-directed consumers looking for choices. That said, the lion's share of premiums ($28.9 billion, or 91 percent of policies in force) is earned through the Allstate brand, while Encompass and Esurance contribute about $1.7 billion, or about 6 percent for Esurance and 3 percent for Encompass. By product line, auto leads the way with about 69 percent of premium dollars, homeowners with 24 percent, with the rest coming from life, commercial, and other business lines. Increasingly, the company is using analytics to "microsegment" and tune the premium/cost mix.

The company reports in five segments:

- Allstate Protection (87 percent of 2018 revenues) includes Allstate, Encompass, Esurance, and Answer Financial brands and includes private auto, homeowner, and other personal lines.
- Services businesses (2 percent) enhance customer value propositions and include SquareTrade and Arity (description follows), Allstate Roadside Services, and Allstate Dealer Services.
- Allstate Life (5 percent) offers traditional and variable life insurance products.
- Allstate Benefits (3 percent) offers workplace disability, accident, and other health products.
- Allstate Annuities (2 percent) offers traditional annuities and services.

Recent acquisitions have brought in Arity, a user of data and analytics to better manage risk, enhancing a broader strategy to deploy analytics across the business, and SquareTrade, an innovative multinational provider of protection plans and support services for the consumer electronics buyer. SquareTrade contracts were up almost 36 percent last year. Allstate is also an innovator among insurers: The company was recognized as one of the "50 Companies Changing the World" by *Fortune* magazine. One innovation known as QuickFoto Claim allows 70 percent of claims to start with a smartphone photo thus speeding up the process considerably. Allstate is also a leader in the development of telematics-based driving assessments ("Drivewise" and "DriveSense" platforms) giving near-real-time feedback to driving safety issues and figuring into rates and "Milewise" mileage-based premiums (in six states so far).

Financial Highlights, Fiscal Year 2018

Hurricane and wildfire losses put a small dent in what would have been a stellar 2018 year. Total revenues ticked up a bit over 1 percent, while per-share earnings rose a healthy 20 percent on the back of stronger pricing, investment income, tax changes, and a 6.5 percent share buyback. As 2019 unfolds, the company expects further price increases (the usual response to past casualties) and investment income to drive the "combined ratio" to 85.6. The "combined ratio," which includes underwriting expenses (claims) and operating expenses, was 93.6 percent, that is, $6.40 in pretax profit is generated for every $100 in premiums received, in 2017. The higher-margin figure would drive per-share net up another 13–15 percent in 2019 and 7–9 percent in 2020. Dividend increases and share buybacks will moderate after a 26 percent dividend increase in 2018, again related to tax changes. Allstate has reduced its share count 53 percent since 2004.

Reasons to Buy

We like the market position, brand strength, channel strategy, increased stability, and upside potential both in underwriting and in investment performance. The company has gained a solid strategic hold on its reputation, brand, and channel strategy. Esurance and other "direct" models are gaining traction, while the company is also offering a better product mix and better cross-selling opportunities through its traditional agencies. Increased investment income will also help. Allstate has all the earmarks of a well-managed company.

The Allstate brand is ever stronger, turning from a slight negative years ago to a solid positive through stronger advertising, product offering, and general branding initiatives. The company now proudly places its name on "adjacent" businesses such as Allstate Roadside Services. Another branding example is the new "Package" policy, combining auto and homeowners into a single policy sold under the Encompass brand. All of this combined with solid shareholder returns continues to make Allstate a solid blue-chip performer in a difficult industry with a pretty decent upside going forward.

Reasons for Caution

Competition is stiff and storms and fires are more intense, although Allstate is more geographically diverse than some of its competitors—and we saw how this helps: 2017 and 2018 did not turn out to be disasters. Higher auto claims rates, driven by smartphone use, greater mileages driven because of cheap gas, and a generally faster pace of life are also a concern but will be covered by price increases going into effect now. For years, the brand suffered from a reputation for poor claims performance and an overly sales-y approach. The company has done something about it; the prior volatility of its results in revenues, earnings, and especially dividends paid is hard to ignore. Finally, we'll admit that we find insurers (as most Financials) difficult to understand because of terminology and somewhat different ways of measuring and reporting financial performance; you may also find this company difficult to understand. Proceed carefully.

SECTOR: Financials ❑ Beta coefficient: 0.80 ❑ 10-year compound earnings per-share growth: 0.0% ❑ 10-year compound dividends per-share growth: 0.0%

		2011	2012	2013	2014	2015	2016	2017	2018
Property/casualty premiums (mil)		25,942	26,737	27,618	28,929	30,309	31,407	32,300	34,038
Net income (mil)		699	2,143	2,756	2,379	2,119	1,785	2,476	3,715
Earnings per share		1.34	4.34	5.70	5.42	5.21	4.69	6.71	8.03
Dividends per share		0.83	1.09	0.75	1.12	1.29	1.29	1.45	1.84
Underwriting inc. per share		(4.19)	2.49	4.95	4.22	4.06	3.34	5.82	6.56
Price:	high	34.4	42.8	54.8	71.5	72.9	74.8	105.4	104.5
	low	22.3	27.0	40.7	49.2	54.1	56.0	73.0	77.0

Website: www.allstate.com

AGGRESSIVE GROWTH

Amazon.com, Inc.

Ticker symbol: AMZN (NASDAQ) ❑ Large Cap ❑ Value Line financial strength rating: A+ ❑ Current yield: Nil ❑ Dividend raises, past 10 years: NA

Company Profile

"Alexa, buy ten shares of Amazon."

Such a fantasy hasn't arrived quite yet—that we know of—but who knows, it may soon be part of this juggernaut's amazing streak of innovations and conveniences destined to transform our shopping world.

Simply put, Amazon.com makes us feel old. We can remember a mere 23 years ago when Amazon was just a retailer—a *book* retailer. A huge one, granted, but the first thought that came to mind at the mention of its name was a great place to buy a book *cheap* without having to drive somewhere to find it.

Then they started selling other stuff. And in the 2018 year just completed, they sold $233 billion of mostly other stuff, and made over $10 billion in profit, more than four times the previous annual record, for doing so. A heck of a performance for something that started out as a bookstore.

Amazon.com has become the world's largest e-commerce retailer powered by a massive and unparalleled logistics and information technology engine. Notably, the company's scope has grown beyond even that in the past several years. Amazon Web Services (AWS) is now the world's largest provider of cloud computing services, with a market share larger than that of the next five largest players combined. Amazon Video is a provider of video on-demand services, competing with both traditional cable providers as well as IP (Internet)-based rivals such as Hulu. They are also producing award-winning original movies and series. Through the recent purchase of Whole Foods, Amazon is expanding its test of grocery pickup and delivery services with 60-minute deliveries available in 60 metro areas. Amazon Prime has now dented the rest of the retail and consumer universe with millions of customers willing to pay $10— no, $12—no, now $13—a month for "Prime" priority shipping services now reaching 10,000 US cities with one-day or same-day service, creating a steady flow of little brown boxes wrapped in black tape to our doorsteps—5 *billion* such packages in 2018 (and oh, by the way, you get access to Amazon Prime video and other stuff too). To support this flow, Amazon has become a world-class logistics juggernaut, now operating 75 fulfillment and 25 sorting centers around the country, 50 aircraft with the addition of 10 this year, and more than 20,000 tractor trailer vans.

On the technology product front, we welcome our new friend "Alexa" with open arms. Alexa is the family of Echo smart voice-recognition technologies products transforming our kitchens and living rooms to on-demand music centers and convenience stations—and oh, by the way, enabling us to order that stuff on Prime with a simple voice command. Alexa technology is blossoming; the handy girl is showing up built into 150 different products from headphones to cars to PCs to smart home devices—we can't wait to have Alexa in our next new cars to chat away with on our way across the Mojave Desert—and to boot there are some 28,000 Alexa-compatible devices from more than 4,500 unique third-party brands. One mustn't forget the rather ancient by comparison Kindle business, and it's also worth noting Amazon's Amazonian presence as a retail shopping mall ("Marketplace") for other companies: During the 2018 holiday shopping season, some 200,000 small and medium businesses sold more than $100,000 in product each through Amazon stores; these sales made up more than 50 percent of the company's unit count through the holiday period and 20 percent of dollar volume through the year. Finally, in an ultimate irony, Amazon is testing several types of brick-and-mortar store concepts, including "Amazon Go" (an urban sort of self-serve convenience store devoid of cashiers), and a new grocery store format that in implementation may be half the size of a traditional grocery store but tied in with online shopping and delivery. With all of these strategic initiatives in the works, the company's quarterly reports have become interesting reads.

Among such a laundry list of superlatives, who can fail to note a stock that has gone from the mid-600s when we first added it to the 2017 *100 Best Stocks* list to over $2,000, though correcting to $1,600 as we compose this narrative today? When else have we had anything to do with a stock that sells for $1,600? Only for an extraordinary company on a relentless, and successful, journey to transform the universe, that continues to be Amazon today.

Financial Highlights, Fiscal Year 2018

Overall, FY2018 produced a 31 percent increase in revenues (on top of a similar 31 percent increase in 2017), with "product" sales up 20 percent to $1,442 billion, and "service" sales up 53 percent to $91 billion. North American sales increased 33 percent while International increased 21 percent, and AWS gained 47 percent. AWS continues to produce the lion's share of operating income, while International continues to operate at a loss, mostly due to increased outlays for increased fulfillment capacity and technology. Net income for 2018 more than quadrupled in part due to a 60 percent reduction in the tax rate. FY2018 projections call for a 22 percent revenue gain and 30 percent gain in net income as scale improves and new revenue streams from Whole Foods and Echo technology become more fully realized.

Reasons to Buy

There are many good reasons to own a piece of AMZN right now, as the company is at the heart of the stay-at-home trend; in fact, it is driving it with services like Amazon Prime and the Amazon Marketplace. The Marketplace makes it possible for vendors and customers around the world to connect and transact business without a physical storefront. And who doesn't know about Amazon Prime's bundle of one-click ordering, free two-day shipping to most places, music, movies, free books, and other goodies? Amazon has been at the very forefront of making Internet shopping safe, secure, convenient, cost-competitive for the seller, and price-competitive for the buyer—and it is disrupting most of the retail industry. It's a safe bet that you, or at least your neighbors, are ordering mundane household items like laundry detergent and Hershey's Kisses using Prime. We do—and no, we're not millennials (although we still struggle with having Alexa do it for us).

Okay, so it's a successful business model and a good place to shop. Does that mean it's a good stock to own? Even at today's prices? Obviously, we think so.

The single best reason to own a piece Amazon is that it continues to deliver on nearly every promise made since its founding. Jeff Bezos predicted the company might take a decade to become profitable. This scared away many investors, but in retrospect, it was a brilliant piece of expectations management, having the additional benefit of being the truth. Fifteen years after making *that* statement, Bezos continued to tell investors that new Amazon projects had a five-to-seven-year horizon, on the theory that very few companies had the patience to take on projects that took that long to develop. In Bezos's view, this meant there was effectively zero competition for these longer-term opportunities. Right again.

At that time, e-commerce was growing five times faster than the overall retail market, and Amazon was growing twice as fast as e-commerce as a whole. Fast-forward five years to today, and Amazon has carved out an enormous chunk of the US (and worldwide) retailing market by being willing to take on projects of enormous scale and complexity and executing on them with a vengeance. Alexa gives us a great example, and more is likely in store as they continue to leverage Whole Foods into an online grocery service and local delivery point. Next may be a headlong foray to transform prescription drug delivery and healthcare in general. "We're very stubborn," Bezos once said.

As another example, Amazon Web Services, the company's on-demand cloud computing platform, launched in 2003 as an Amazon-internal IT project for managing certain aspects of transaction data. A year later, it was launched as a service for public use. Today, AWS accounts for over $25 billion in revenue and $7.3 billion in operating profit, exceeding the rest of the company's profit combined.

The list of accomplishments, new products, and platforms is unparalleled in Corporate America—it's almost two full pages of bullet points just in the most recent quarterly report, and far too much to cover here. Quite simply, Amazon is transforming retail, web services, and the living room at a pace heretofore unknown—and expanding its influence steadily into international markets too. The company is truly living up to its name "Amazon."

Reasons for Caution

As much as we like the company, its customer value proposition and execution excellence, there's no getting around the cost of these shares. With a share price of $1,600 the company is priced at some 80 times earnings in early 2019 (based on 2018 projections, compared to 21 for the S&P 500) and with an earnings projection of $53 per share out to 2023, the P/E would still be over 30 at today's price. Although profitability is growing, and sales are growing dramatically, simply maintaining this kind of stock price may require an almost unimaginable sustained financial performance. Amazon has rewarded the bold and faithful handsomely in the past, but the timid and doubtful among us cannot be faulted for treading gingerly through the stacks of this very special bookstore.

SECTOR: Retail ❑ Beta coefficient: 1.10 ❑ 10-year compound earnings per-share growth: 16.5% ❑ 10-year compound dividends per-share growth: NA

		2011	2012	2013	2014	2015	2016	2017	2018
Revenues (bil)		61.9	74.5	89.0	107.0	130.0	136.0	177.9	232.9
Net income (mil)		130.0	274.0	(241.0)	596.0	2,485	2,371	2,244	10,073
Earnings per share		0.29	0.59	(0.52)	1.25	5.20	4.90	4.55	20.14
Dividends per share		—	—	—	—	—	—	—	—
Cash flow per share		5.04	7.68	9.70	14.60	18.60	21.99	21.60	51.76
Price:	high	264.1	405.6	408.1	696.4	685.5	847.2	1213	2050
	low	172.0	245.8	284.0	285.3	474.0	474.0	747.7	1170

Website: www.amazon.com

AGGRESSIVE GROWTH

Analog Devices, Inc.

Ticker symbol: ADI (NASDAQ) ❑ Large Cap ❑ Value Line financial strength rating: A+ ❑ Current yield: 2.0% ❑ Dividend raises, past 10 years: 10

Company Profile

Analog Devices designs, manufactures, and markets high-performance analog, mixed-signal, and digital signal processing chips used in a multitude of electronic devices. Founded in 1965, they have grown to be one of the largest semiconductor houses in the world by focusing almost exclusively on a segment of electronic design known as signal processing. They do not make large-scale microprocessors, discrete digital logic, or memory. Instead, they concentrate on real-time applications such as signal acquisition, analog/digital conversion, signal conditioning, and amplification. In March 2017 the company completed its acquisition of Linear Technology, another analog semiconductor design house but with a highly complementary product line focused primarily on power devices and associated controllers.

Analog's high-value-add components find their way into products such as medical imaging equipment, cellular base stations, digital cameras and televisions, industrial process controls, defense electronics, factory automation systems, satellites, and automobiles. In all, the company derives nearly half its revenue from the Industrial market, with Communications, Automotive, and Consumer markets accounting for the other half in nearly equal shares. They make thousands of products, with the ten highest revenue products in total accounting for just under 8 percent of revenues.

The company fabricates many of its own analog parts at either of its four fabs, located in Massachusetts, Santa Clara, and Limerick, Ireland. ADI also employs third-party suppliers (primarily TSMC in Taiwan) for fabrication of its sub-micron CMOS die. The company closed its wafer fabrication facility in Massachusetts at the end of fiscal 2009 and now sources its blank wafers from third parties.

Financial Highlights, Fiscal Year 2018

The first full year of results from the combined ADI and LT were very much in line with expectations: Revenue was as promised, with greatly improved gross and net margins and improved cash flow. For FY2018, revenue came in at $6.2 billion, up 20 percent over FY2017. Per-share earnings were $5.95, an increase of 27 percent over the previous year. Largely as a result of the LT acquisition, debt ballooned from $500 million in 2015 to $7.5 billion in 2017, though some $1.2 billion was retired in FY2018. Long-term interest is covered at 6.0 and current liabilities are at $850 million, the lowest in several years. In short, the balance sheet looks solid and deserving of its A+ rating. Sales projections for FY2019 are more or less flat (and first quarter results are in line with that expectation), while earnings are expected to decline 3 percent in the face of uncertainties in the Chinese markets.

Reasons to Buy

Last year we praised the LT acquisition in (we admit) a somewhat long-winded presentation on the wonders of the analog semiconductor. We spoke at length on the movement of computational power to the fringes of our sensory experience: sensors, for example, in our phones, our cars, even our refrigerators. We may have belabored the point. But we're pretty sure we got it right. The LT acquisition, though expensive, has worked out well for ADI, even with only six quarters in the books. The effect of Linear's healthy margins have been nothing short of a step function on ADI's output stage. We had looked at ADI almost every year as a possible *100 Best* stock, and while we liked what we saw, there were always one or two stronger prospects in the technology sector. ADI was always steady, but not necessarily stellar. Over the past year and a half, however, ADI's prospects have begun to look much brighter due in large part to their acquisition of LT.

Linear Technology, founded in 1981, quickly established a reputation for design excellence and unparalleled support. Their customers were more than willing to pay higher premiums for LT's parts that were either on the leading edge of new designs or were simply better than what the competition offered. This led to net margins that were the envy of the industry (35.2 percent in 2015) and helped to support an engineering-driven company culture that boasted remarkable talent retention. LT billed itself as "the company that no one leaves." In short, ADI received (for the fairly high price of ten times LT's 2015 revenues and one quarter of an ADI share for each LT share) not just a catalog of parts and customers, but one of the industry's leading pools of talent and a potent product development environment. The addition of LT's customer base (whose design cycles tend to be longer) will also raise the quality and longevity of ADI's revenue streams. We think we can look forward to having ADI on our list for years to come.

Analog chip suppliers tend to hold design wins and customers for the life of a customer's product. In critical circuits, in particular, products are designed with the characteristics of key components in mind, and a change of suppliers for those key components often necessitates a redesign or a respec of the final product. For this reason, ADI's earnings are already quite a bit more reliable than that of the suppliers of commodity integrated circuits, and the acquisition of LT should only improve this desirable product life cycle profile.

Although the effect on the bottom line may be many quarters away, ADI will most certainly be one of the beneficiaries of the rollout of Fifth Generation (5G) cell phone technologies, as they are an early provider of parts used in the development, testing, and implementation of this fundamentally market-changing environment. The implementation of 5G is hardware intensive, and unit volumes will be significant.

And a fun fact: ADI's logo is a schematic symbol for a gain stage, which takes in a small signal and amplifies it into a larger version of that signal. It's hard to imagine a better parallel for "buy low, sell high."

Reasons for Caution

A moderation in the growth of the Chinese economy is slowing the rise of all boats in the technology sector. Also, a US trade war with one's primary trading partner seems a baffling choice, particularly when this trading partner holds 5 percent of your debt and an estimated $2 trillion in foreign reserves. A trade war that also locks out a supplier of computing electronics (Huawei) is a troubling sign for electronics suppliers everywhere and semiconductor manufacturers in particular. ADI will fare no worse than most, and maybe better than many, but the effects of uncertainty and bluster will definitely be felt in the short term. When those in charge come to their senses we should expect a rapid return to normalcy.

SECTOR: Information Technology ▢ Beta coefficient: 1.15 ▢ 10-year compound earnings per-share growth: 11.5% ▢ 10-year compound dividends per-share growth: 10.5%

		2011	2012	2013	2014	2015	2016	2017	2018
Revenues (mil)		2,993	2,701	2,634	2,865	3,435	3,421	5,108	6,201
Net income (mil)		838.9	651.2	673.5	763.3	1,001	958.7	1,688	2,237
Earnings per share		2.72	2.13	2.14	2.40	3.16	3.07	4.68	5.95
Dividends per share		.97	1.20	1.36	1.48	1.60	1.68	1.80	1.92
Cash flow per share		2.72	2.13	2.14	2.40	3.16	3.07	4.68	5.95
Price:	high	43.3	42.7	51.2	58.0	69.0	74.9	94.0	103.6
	low	29.2	34.3	41.7	42.6	50.6	47.2	71.0	76.6

Website: www.analog.com

AGGRESSIVE GROWTH

Apple, Inc.

Ticker symbol: AAPL (NASDAQ) ❑ Large Cap ❑ Value Line financial strength rating: A++
❑ Current yield: 1.5% ❑ Dividend raises, past 10 years: 7

Company Profile

What?? Just as we tout Apple's meteoric ascent into the stratospheric realm of "easily" the world's most valuable company in last year's narrative, now we find it in a four-horse race for number one position. True, Apple did break through the $1 trillion barrier during 2018 (Amazon is the only other to achieve this) in market capitalization (share price × number of shares outstanding), but fell back as a wee bit of softness in its core smartphone market began to show itself. The other three horses in the race are Amazon, Alphabet (Google parent), and—yes it's true—Microsoft, the perennial market cap leader decades ago.

Why do we bring this up? First, it gives an idea of the perennial excellence of Apple and its unequaled rise from a market cap of perhaps $30 billion fifteen years ago. Second, we'd like to point out that if all they were concerned about was market cap, and didn't retire 1.4 *billion* shares since 2014 to make shareholders happy, they'd still be number one by a long shot. Not only does this suggest that today's shares are more valuable, but we also like their willingness to sacrifice "number one" accolades to create shareholder value. Bravo, Apple!

Apple designs, manufactures, and markets mobile communications and media devices including computers, smartphones, tablets, portable music players, digital watches and related software, peripherals, downloadable content, and services. It sells these products through its own retail stores, online stores, and third-party and value-added resellers. The company also sells digital content through its iTunes store. The company has become a big player in the "digital wallet" mobile payment space, with its Apple Pay apps and network. Finally, although it's still a bit of a secret, the company is likely still investigating large-scale technologies such as the automobile business and is also rumored to be looking at the content business, either to buy a major content house like Disney, or to create one of their own, like Netflix.

The company's products have become household names: The iPhone, iPod, iPad, and MacBook head up the list of hardware products. While the software may be less well known, QuickTime, iOS, MacOS, tvOS, and watchOS are important products. Even more important is Services, which have been growing at a double-digit pace into a profitable $30 billion business, bundling together the iCloud, iTunes, Books, Apple Pay, Apple Music, the Mac App Store and other content delivery, and AppleCare support services. Breaking down sales by product family: Smartphones account for $167 billion of the $266 billion in FY2018 sales—fully 63 percent. Mac (personal computers) accounts for 10 percent, iPad 7 percent, "Other Products" (such as Apple Watch) for 6.5 percent, and, not to be left out, Services now accounts for 14 percent of revenues: $37 billion a year (a substantial business all by itself). Annual growth: Smartphones 3 percent, iPad (–2 percent as competition eroded prices), Mac (–1) percent, Services 24 percent, and "other" 35 percent.

It's hard to imagine the current consumer tech landscape without Apple's presence at the top of the heap. Its product line, while comparatively narrow, is focused on areas where the user interface is highly valued, and, increasingly, where some kind of content or service can be sold after the hardware sale. The company has leveraged this focus to become one of the most profitable companies in history, with net profit margins continuing to exceed 20 percent.

Apple is the flagship case study in creating extraordinary value through innovation, innovative leadership, and marketing excellence. They are broadening product lines such as the iPhone to include more high-end and low-end offerings; the iPhone X is now $1,000+ but that has met some customer resistance; they continue to develop new products and carry forward older ones to offer a variety of price points. It's hard to say where the next big technology breakthrough will occur, but wearable technology could be the next best opportunity.

Financial Highlights, Fiscal Year 2018

Despite a lot of press to the contrary, sales continue their upward march, with 2018 revenues 16 percent ahead of a rather soft 2016. Notable was the continued relative weak growth of smartphones (3 percent) but also a 1.3 percent net margin improvement, some due to taxes, leading to a fully charged 23 percent gain in net profits. At $59 billion the company still generates more profits than most companies do sales! Some customer resistance to higher priced phones and a lagging China business (competition plus tariff effects) have led to softer projections for 2019, including a sales decline of 4–5 percent (yes, you read that right!) and a 10–12 percent drop in net profit. The company feels it can get back half of those drops in 2020; in the meantime, continued aggressive buybacks and 5–10 percent dividend raises will keep shareholders happy.

Reasons to Buy

Innovation. Market leadership. Brand strength. Growth. Profitability. Cash flow. Cash returns. And now, the steady and growing "Services" revenue and profit stream. Best in class across the board. How could Apple not be a *100 Best* stock? We certainly like the results, but mostly we continue to admire (and believe in) the business and innovation excellence that got Apple there in the first place.

Apple's best-known product, the iPhone, seems ubiquitous, and it's easy to think the market has become saturated. It's the gold standard, which is good, but especially at some of its price points, it invites competition, especially in China and other emerging markets. But that said, Apple has improved quality (life expectancy, battery life, water resistance, cameras) and feature sets, and is holding its own if not gaining share in key segments of the market. New services, particularly Apple Pay, cloud storage, and the music service, are growing rapidly—and that's just sales. The profitability and cash-flow story is even better. Net profit margins of 21–23 percent for a company of this size alone are remarkable, suggesting that the company's products are far from becoming commoditized. On the shareholder-return front, the recent emphasis on returning cash to shareholders has plenty of distance to go.

While many are concerned about Apple's ability to innovate, and while there has been something of a slowdown in the creation of whole new businesses, like iPods and tablets, we continue to feel that Apple still has room to create blockbusters in the "wearable" technology space—smartphone technology integrated into clothing, for example, and in flexible display technologies (see Corning, another *100 Best* pick) and even into flexible *phones*, some of which will unfold into tablet-like devices. We foresee more "vertical" applications of iPhone/iPad form and technology in cars (check out CarPlay) and in the healthcare space for remote patient monitoring and such. And who knows—Apple may someday rival Netflix or Amazon Prime in content development and streaming services.

Although Apple shares have increased in value, in part due to scarcity, we feel that among the so-called "FAANG" stocks they present the best short- and long-term value. Recent headlines have given some buying opportunities.

Reasons for Caution

Our biggest concern is simple: Smartphones make up 63 percent of the business. That brings a risk of saturation and competition that has made us uncomfortable in the past, but the current success of the iPhone 8 and X series mitigates the concern. That said, similar concerns prevail in the tablet space, where competition from Microsoft Surface and others is getting stronger. But this segment is only 8 percent of the business—a good thing in this case. In the main, we continue to admire Apple's ability to generate income, and now, to distribute it to shareholders. The franchise is the world's most valuable, but nobody can sit on their laurels, especially when their laurels are this high off the ground and in plain sight of every competitor. Apple must continue to feed the innovation machine.

SECTOR: Consumer Discretionary ❑ Beta coefficient: 1.00 ❑ 10-year compound earnings per-share growth: 33.5% ❑ 10-year compound dividends per-share growth: NM

	2011	2012	2013	2014	2015	2016	2017	2018
Revenues (bil)	108.2	156.5	170.9	182.8	233.7	216.8	229.2	265.6
Net income (bil)	25.9	41.7	37.0	39.5	53.4	45.7	48.4	59.5
Earnings per share	3.95	6.31	5.66	6.45	9.22	8.31	9.21	11.91
Dividends per share	—	0.38	1.63	1.82	1.98	2.18	2.40	2.72
Cash flow per share	4.26	6.85	6.96	8.09	11.59	10.53	11.41	14.81
Price: high	61.0	100.7	82.2	119.8	134.5	118.7	177.2	233.5
low	44.4	58.4	55.0	70.5	92.0	89.5	114.8	146.6

Website: www.apple.com

AGGRESSIVE GROWTH
Aptiv PLC

Ticker symbol: APTV (NYSE) ❑ Large Cap ❑ Value Line financial strength rating: B++ ❑ Current yield: 1.0% ❑ Dividend raises, past 10 years: 4

Company Profile

"Smart Mobility" is the website mantra, and "Safe," "Green," and "Connected" are the key strategic megatrends addressed by Aptiv PLC, a leading maker of automotive electronic architecture components and systems. Once known as Delphi Automotive (and by a few other names as well), Aptiv PLC is a tech-heavy remnant of a once-captive and later spun-off major parts supplier to General Motors. Over the years many lines of business have been either discontinued or disposed of. Most significantly in December 2017, Aptiv spun off its entire Powertrain Systems segment into a new, independent company named Delphi Technologies PLC. They no longer make brake hoses, door handles, air-conditioning parts, batteries, fuel injectors,

wheel bearings, dashboards, suspension components, drivetrain components, or any of dozens of other associated automotive parts—operations
that have all been sold off over the past decade. Today's leaner, more focused
Aptiv now designs and supplies electronic systems ranging from conventional vehicle electronics to electric vehicle components to "autonomous"
(driver-assist and driverless) technology, including all those new gadgets that
stop your car automatically or sense you're drifting into other lanes, and
so forth. The company organizes its businesses into two segments: Signal
and Power Solutions, and Advanced Safety and User Experience. Signal and
Power Solutions (72 percent of 2018 sales) provides hardware and systems
for the complete design, manufacture, and assembly of a vehicle's electrical
architecture. The goal here is to create the vehicle's signal distribution and
computing backbone with particular emphasis on reduced emissions, higher
fuel economy, and an open framework for increased content and future electrical upgrades. The Advanced Safety and User Experience unit provides
components, controls, configured systems, and software development platforms for safety features, security, comfort, and vehicle operation. These
products are the basis for features such as autonomous driving, active safety
systems (airbags and active braking, etc.), heads-up displays, and integrated
infotainment systems. Overall, their charter is to reduce driver distraction,
improve vehicle safety and efficiency, and enhance the driver experience.

Aptiv operates 126 manufacturing sites and 15 technical centers in 44
countries.

Financial Highlights, Fiscal Year 2018

Aptiv's financials are a bit hard to understand over time as it only became
independent in 2011 and has undergone numerous acquisitions and even
more divestitures since. The business seems to have stabilized at about
$14.5 billion in revenue. Order strength in the Advanced Safety and User
Experience segment will likely more than offset a bit of drag in the more
conventional Signal and Power Solutions segment due to slowing worldwide
car production and currency effects; the company forecasts a 3–4 percent
revenue gain in 2019. The phaseout of expenses from restructuring, the
Powertrain spin-off, and a few acquisitions should improve gross and net
margins at least 1 percent, giving rise to a 15–20 percent net income gain
in 2019; Aptiv projects another 12–15 percent earnings gain in 2020 on
a more robust 6–8 percent gain in sales. As part of the restructuring, the
dividend was cut in 2018 but should be on the rise again in 2020.

Reasons to Buy

With 94 percent of all accidents caused by human error, the expansion of the smartphone and IoT devices into the vehicle, and the environmental impact of automotive activity, it's not hard to see a bright future for innovative electronic automotive technology solutions. Automobile manufacturers are eager to adopt these high-value-add features, as drivers seek ubiquitous connectivity to the outside world.

Aptiv is one of the leading competitors in this field and has customized and sold systems to a number of the major automakers, with GM and Volkswagen leading the pack. Automakers prefer to outsource this sort of technology; it's simply more cost competitive to buy versus starting from scratch with an in-house development project. It also provides for the ability to gain from their competitor's experience, assuming they're buying the same systems.

Aptiv's current driver-assist products are doing well in the market with sales to each of the top 25 automakers and a product presence in 86 percent of the top-selling vehicles in the US, the EU, and China.

Reasons for Caution

A more intelligent and efficient vehicle transportation usage model could make for downward pressure on the unit sales of vehicles themselves. Any decline due to this effect is probably several years out, though, and would be preceded by a significant up-tick in unit volumes as part of the rollover. There's always the possibility that autonomous vehicle adoption will be delayed or nixed altogether by accidents and technical problems. In the short run, the company is still pretty dependent on conventional and legacy automotive electrical systems, and is tied closely to automotive production—which is slowing.

SECTOR: Industrials ❑ Beta coefficient: 1.25 ❑ 10-year compound earnings per-share growth: NA ❑ 10-year compound dividends per-share growth: NA

	2011	2012	2013	2014	2015	2016	2017	2018
Revenues (mil)	16,041	15,519	16,463	17,023	15,165	16,661	12,884	14,435
Net income (mil)	1,145	1,077	1,212	1,351	1,176	1,149	990	1,067
Earnings per share	2.72	3.33	3.89	4.48	4.14	4.21	3.81	4.02
Dividends per share	—	—	0.68	1.00	1.00	1.16	1.38	0.88
Cash flow per share	2.72	3.33	3.89	4.48	4.14	4.21	3.81	6.70
Price: high	22.9	38.3	60.4	74.9	90.6	84.8	105	103.2
low	19.2	21.8	37.2	58.2	66.1	55.6	66.6	58.8

Website: www.aptiv.com

Archer Daniels Midland Company

Ticker symbol: ADM (NYSE) ❑ Large Cap ❑ Value Line financial strength rating: A+ ❑ Current yield: 3.3% ❑ Dividend raises, past 10 years: 9

Company Profile

ADM is one of the largest food processors in the world. It buys corn, wheat, oilseeds, and other agricultural products and processes them into food, food ingredients, animal feed and ingredients, and biofuels. It also resells grains on the open market. More recently, it has gotten into more refined food ingredients such as flavorings and "natural" ingredients. Rather than the finished consumer products most food processors are known for, ADM produces and distributes intermediate components for food product manufacture and is by far the largest publicly traded company in this business. "ADM Feeds Your Food Business" is their traditional motto, and, owing to today's trends in health and nutrition, they have added another: "Where nutrition innovation begins."

Among the more important products are vegetable oils, protein meal and components, corn sweeteners, flour, biodiesel, ethanol, other food and animal feed, and now, specialty ingredients. Foreign sales make up about 55 percent of total revenue.

The company is highly vertically integrated and owns and maintains facilities used throughout the production process. It sources, transports, stores, and processes agricultural materials in 76 subsidiary countries on six continents, with 330 food processing and ingredient manufacturing plants, 450 crop procurement facilities, 230 bulk storage terminals, and its own extensive sea/rail/road network. The company owns or leases 2,800 rail cars, 2,300 barges, 31 ocean vessels, and 1,400 semitrailers. There are 62 innovation centers worldwide.

The company has operated in four business segments for years—Agricultural Services, Oilseeds Processing, Corn Processing, and the newer Wild Flavors and Specialty Ingredients. After realigning a few business units within these segments and giving the "upstart" Wild Flavors and Specialty Ingredients a more inclusive name—Nutrition—we end up with the following:

- Origination (39 percent of 2018 sales, 16 percent of operating profit) is the unit that takes in agricultural commodities, that is, buys, sells, stores, cleans, and transports grains to and from ADM facilities and other clients in the animal feed and ag processing industries. The crop procurement, bulk storage facilities, and transportation assets mentioned previously are all managed in this segment.

- Oilseeds (38 percent, 44 percent): The Oilseeds Processing unit processes soybeans, cottonseed, sunflower, canola, peanuts, and flaxseed into vegetable oils and protein meals for the food and feed industries. Crude vegetable oils are sold as is or are further refined into consumer products, while partially refined oils are sold for use in paints, chemicals, and other industrial products. The solids remaining from this processing are sold for a number of applications, including edible soy protein, animal feed, pharmaceuticals, chemicals, and paper.

- Carbohydrate Solutions (16 percent, 28 percent) includes wet and dry corn and wheat-milling operations (primarily in the US) producing food products too numerous to list but include syrup, starch, glucose, dextrose, and other sweeteners. (As ADM puts it, "From a bushel of corn we can create 24 products.") Markets served include animal feeds and the vegetable oil market. Fermentation of the dextrose yields ethanol, amino acids, and other specialty food and feed products. The ethanol is processed for beverage stock or industrial use as the base for ethanol-blended gasoline and other fuels. Within this group, ADM owns a 40 percent interest in the Red Star Yeast Company and just added a 50 percent stake in Russia-based Aston Foods and Food Ingredients.

- Nutrition (6 percent, 10 percent) manufactures and distributes specialty products including natural flavor ingredients, flavor systems, natural colors, proteins, emulsifiers, natural health and nutrition products, and nutrition systems for animals and animal feed. In early 2018 ADM acquired Probiotics International Ltd. and Rodelle, a supplier of vanilla products; in early 2019 it acquired Neovia, a European provider of animal nutrition solutions.

Financial Highlights, Fiscal Year 2018

Acquisitions, spin-offs, currency effects, fluctuating prices, and fluctuating costs of agricultural commodity inputs make any yearly comparison of ADM results challenging. FY2018 once again was no exception. A recovery in the oilseed business, with volumes 5 percent ahead and stronger prices, with moderately stronger results in Origination and Carbohydrate Solutions together drove a 6 percent 2018 revenue increase; higher margins and lower taxes ground out a 49 percent jump in net earnings—albeit just back to levels achieved three years ago. Continued integration of small acquisitions, cost measures, and favorable markets should drive another 5–7 percent earnings increase on top of a 2–4 percent revenue increase for 2019. As the overall strategy moves to get a larger share of the higher-margined Nutrition business while fine-tuning the commodity businesses, the company predicts another 7–9 percent income growth on a continuing 2–4 percent revenue rise. Steady dividend increases and modest share buybacks should continue.

Reasons to Buy

We still like the strong market position and long-term strategy of ADM. Agriculture is still a key strategic business on a global basis, and increased demand for food and especially middle-class Western diets from emerging market customers bodes well. The company is and has been a strong player in the biofuels industry. While uncertainties continue in the ethanol and biofuels segment, the company's experience and scale in ethanol and biodiesel are strong positives, and the company should win as other smaller players exit the market.

There are four major suppliers that dominate the world market for commodity foodstuffs: Archer, Bunge, Cargill, and Dreyfus—the "ABCD" of world foods. ADM continues to grow its presence in the emerging markets of Asia, South America, and Eastern Europe. ADM's presence and extensive transportation capability give it a decided advantage over its smaller competitors, many of which are focused only in certain markets or certain industries. The company is fine-tuning its business mix, disposing of smaller low-margin product lines in favor of a higher value add in the food chain with the addition of small but important Nutrition lines; we like the increasing emphasis on this business. We like the solid track record for growth in dividends and overall shareholder value.

Reasons for Caution

We've seen how agricultural cycles and overproduction can negatively impact this company, and it will try the patience of the most patient investors. Trade is an important component of this business, and the current trade uncertainties aren't helping. The higher-margined, more specialized Nutrition segment flavorings and ingredients is less commoditized but does add some risk—tastes are fickle and it's an area that ADM doesn't have much experience in. ADM is heavily invested in the corn-ethanol-fuel processing chain, which has had its own ups and downs as well as detractors. Federal government policy toward ethanol subsidies bears watching. Finally, the company does produce that nasty-sounding but in fact relatively benign high fructose corn syrup; a pickup in nutritional health sentiment in the food and especially the beverage industry won't help.

SECTOR: Consumer Staples ❏ Beta coefficient: 1.05 ❏ 10-year compound earnings per-share growth: 0.5% ❏ 10-year compound dividends per-share growth: 11.5%

	2011	2012	2013	2014	2015	2016	2017	2018
Revenues (mil)	80,676	89,038	89,804	81,201	67,762	62,346	60,828	64,341
Net income (mil)	2,036	1,496	1,342	2,248	1,849	1,280	1,216	1,810
Earnings per share	3.13	2.26	2.02	3.43	2.98	2.16	2.13	3.19
Dividends per share	0.62	0.69	0.76	0.96	1.12	1.20	1.28	1.34
Cash flow per share	4.54	3.56	3.42	4.80	4.59	3.80	3.84	4.92
Price: high	38.0	34.0	44.0	53.9	53.3	47.9	47.4	52.1
low	23.7	24.2	27.8	37.9	33.8	29.9	38.6	39.2

Website: www.adm.com

GROWTH AND INCOME

RETURNING FOR 2020

AT&T, Inc.

Ticker symbol: T (NYSE) ❏ Large Cap ❏ Value Line financial strength rating: A++ ❏ Current yield: 6.5% ❏ Dividend raises, past 10 years: 10

Company Profile

AT&T is the world's largest telecommunications holding company. Although known for years as the 600-pound gorilla of domestic wireline local and long-distance telecom service, it has evolved to also be the largest provider of wireless, commercial broadband, and Wi-Fi services in the United States. Additionally, it has become a large player in consumer broadband products with its ISP services, DirecTV satellite television service, and U-verse voice/TV/Internet product bundle. AT&T also owns the former Time Warner Communications company (a former *100 Best* stock now known as WarnerMedia), a mass media and entertainment conglomerate with large holdings in content development in film, cable, television, and publishing.

The company is now organized into four operating units: Communications, which includes the consumer and commercial wireline and consumer video services; WarnerMedia, which includes all of the various film and television production studios; AT&T Latin America, for services in Mexico, Latin America, and the Caribbean; and Xandr, an advertising and analytics operation. The Communications segment is by far the largest operating unit, accounting for 84 percent of total revenues, with WarnerMedia coming in at 11 percent.

In mid-2015, AT&T acquired satellite TV provider DirecTV for about $50 billion, allowing it to offer data services and satellite TV to far-flung customers who could not be reached profitably via the company's landline or fiber solutions. In June of 2018, a 20-month ordeal of governmental actions (both actual and threatened) concluded with AT&T's acquisition of TWC for $109 billion. An appeal of the decision in the final federal judgment was denied in March of 2019, so this appears to be well settled.

The company continues to provide wireline services in 13 states via (ironically) ten of the original Bell Operating Companies, companies that were created when AT&T was originally broken up by a US government antitrust action back in 1982.

Financial Highlights, Fiscal Year 2018

Detailed year-over-year comparisons are difficult here for a number of reasons: the acquisition of TWC, the subsequent reorganization of the company into four operating segments from its previous three, adoption of a new revenue accounting standard, and the effects of the 2017 tax changes which led to AT&T reporting a negative 97 percent tax rate in 2017. The top-level numbers, however, bear out part of what brought AT&T to our attention this year: a 6 percent increase in top-line revenue, a 20 percent increase in net margin, and a 17 percent increase in EPS despite an 18 percent increase in share count. Of particular interest is the Communications segment, which saw a 4 percent decrease in revenue but a 2 percent increase in margin contribution. Also worth noting is the highly profitable WarnerMedia segment, where the margin contribution was 30 percent of revenue. Nice buy.

Projections for FY2018 are for revenue growth of 8 percent and earnings growth of 10 percent. Dividends are expected to increase by 2 percent, a pattern the company has held for at least the past 10 years.

Reasons to Buy

Way back when in 2017 we shared our concern about the "vertical" nature of the Time Warner deal. The content developers at TWC were suppliers to AT&T (and others); our concern was that the "others" would no longer be active participants in the bidding for goods now being supplied by a competitor (AT&T). This scenario has not really developed as we had imagined. In fact, vertical mergers have become a trend in the industry, as other content owners (such as Disney) are working to silo their products and, similar to what AT&T has done with TWC, create their own distribution channels. In fact, there are now at least three major conglomerates employing this content/channel model: TWC/AT&T, NBCUniversal/ Comcast, and Disney/Fox (through its direct-broadcast satellite operations in the UK, Europe, and Asia). So far, there are few signs of a negative impact to the availability or profitability of AT&T's acquired properties such as HBO, TBS, and CNN. The growing acceptance of this model and AT&T's early lead in the area, along with a friendly ear at the FCC, are positive signs going forward.

Another positive development: AT&T announced (but has not yet detailed) an over-the-top streaming service, slated to arrive in early 2020. Over-the-top (OTT) streaming is content delivered not through a traditional broadcast television platform, but rather directly via the Internet. Products such as Netflix, Hulu, and Amazon Video are examples of OTT delivery of content, all of which have found great acceptance in the market. Key to this strategy, obviously, is having access to the content, and this is where AT&T shines, with the entire back catalog of Warner Brothers, Turner, TimeWarner, and in-house projects from HBO and others. While this may not seem like a significant product announcement, the fact is that an OTT strategy, relatively easy to implement when you have the wired and wireless infrastructure of an AT&T, is an effective defense against a future of cord cutters and others who simply don't want or need a set-top box. Before long OTT is likely to be the preferred method of receiving content, which bodes well for AT&T, as it simplifies operations tremendously and allows for installing (and charging for) service and bandwidth on mobile devices. Currently, all of AT&T's on-demand services (excepting DirecTV Now and HBO Now) are tied to a set-top box. The service will be a direct competitor to the successful Netflix.

The two big acquisitions send a strong message that AT&T isn't just about phones and text messaging; it is about the consumer experience in all forms of access and entertainment available today. The acquisitions will increasingly bundle all forms of access and at the same time generate growth, higher margins, and thus far higher profits and especially cash flows down the road. To customers, AT&T will be a communications and entertainment machine; to investors it's a cash-flow machine.

Many investors will consider AT&T and will dismiss it as old school—too tied to old wireline operations and other traditional markets and crippled by its own size and reliance on crusty declining markets. In fact, though, AT&T has managed to innovate its way into new markets and succeed against a field of competitors who were thought to be far more nimble. The company is on a growth path that leverages its strength in broadband, mobile communications, satellite, and now, content. Perhaps more than any other *100 Best* company, AT&T has weathered massive changes in its business environment and has formed itself into an agile and forward-looking company with a clear view of its future in the information era. And it has shown that it can manage and reap the benefits of large acquisitions.

Finally, it should be noted that at the current share price of $32, the dividend yield is nearly 6.5 percent, with an 8.8 trailing P/E ratio. There are very few stocks that provide this combination of high return and safety and opportunity for growth.

Reasons for Caution

The two large acquisitions of DirecTV and Time Warner each added a billion shares to an already large pile of 5.2 billion shares. AT&T now has 7.3 billion shares outstanding, and that's a lot of mouths to feed. On the one hand, in an era when nearly every company worth looking at is returning money to shareholders by way of stock buybacks rather than investing in growth, AT&T is digging moats, building catapults, and hammering out swords and shields for the coming battles (our only *Game of Thrones* reference, we promise). On the other hand, you must earn $73 million to add one penny to EPS. Acquisitions are expensive. And even though margins are up nicely, per-share revenues are down 10 percent from just a year ago. If there are efficiencies hiding in these acquisitions, the company would do well to find them.

SECTOR: Telecommunications Services ▫ Beta coefficient: 0.75 ▫ 10-year compound earnings per-share growth: 3.0% ▫ 10-year compound dividends per-share growth: 3.0%

	2011	2012	2013	2014	2015	2016	2017	2018
Revenues (bil)	126.7	127.4	128.8	132.4	146.8	163.8	160.5	170.8
Net income (bil)	13.1	13.7	13.4	13.1	15.1	17.6	18.8	24.0
Earnings per share	2.20	2.33	2.50	2.50	2.69	2.84	3.05	3.52
Dividends per share	1.72	1.76	1.80	1.84	1.88	1.92	1.96	2.00
Cash flow per share	5.31	5.70	6.10	6.04	6.05	7.07	7.04	7.19
Price: high	31.9	38.6	39.0	37.5	36.4	43.9	43.0	39.3
low	27.2	29.0	32.8	31.7	31.0	33.4	32.6	26.8

Website: www.att.com

CONSERVATIVE GROWTH

Becton, Dickinson and Company

Ticker symbol: BDX (NYSE) ❏ Large Cap ❏ Value Line financial strength rating: A++ ❏ Current yield: 1.3% ❏ Dividend raises, past 10 years: 10

Company Profile

Gotten a flu shot or any other "delivery" of medicine lately? Chances are the device used to make the delivery had a prominent B-D logo on the package. "B-D" stands for "Becton, Dickinson," one of the premier medical supply and technology companies on the planet.

Becton, Dickinson is a global healthcare technology player focused on improving drug delivery, enhancing the diagnosis of infectious diseases and cancers, and advancing medical lab work and drug discovery. The company develops, manufactures, and sells medical supplies, devices, laboratory instruments, antibodies, reagents, and diagnostic products through three segments: BD Medical, BD Life Sciences, and the new Interventional segment, which came about with the $25 billion 2017 acquisition of former *100 Best* company C.R. Bard, a major developer and supplier in the vascular, urology, oncology, and surgical spaces. With this and the 2016 acquisition of automated care delivery provider CareFusion, B-D has grown to become one of the world's top five medical suppliers, and is now a bigger player in many vital fields of health such as surgery, cardiology, urology, and critical care.

International sales account for about 46 percent of the total; the company does business in 190+ countries. The B-D brand is found throughout the range of clinics, medical offices, and hospitals and is well recognized in the medical community.

More detail on the three segments:

- BD Medical (54 percent of 2018 sales) provides solutions for medication management and delivery (including the familiar syringes, catheters, IV solutions, and related products), medication management (pumps, dispensing, tracking, and other systems including the CareFusion line), diabetes care delivery systems and devices, and prefillable containers and systems for storing and delivering injectable pharmaceutical products.
- BD Life Sciences (27 percent of sales) provides research tools and reagents to accelerate the pace of biomedical discovery. Clinicians and researchers use BD Life Sciences' tools to study genes, proteins, and cells to understand disease, improve technologies for diagnosis and disease

management, and facilitate the discovery and development of new thera-
peutics. Products include reagents, fluorescence cell-activated sorters and
analyzers, monoclonal antibodies and kits, and cell-imaging and reagent
solutions, among others.

• BD Interventional (19 percent of sales,) formerly Bard, offers some
15,000 products targeted to clinical, surgical, and maintenance applications in biosciences, cancer screening, diabetes care, drug delivery,
genomics, and infection prevention.

Financial Highlights, Fiscal Year 2018

FY2018 reported revenues showed a hefty 32 percent gain, although the
vast majority of that came through the addition of Bard and the Interventional segment. Excluding that, revenue still grew at a healthy 13.5
percent, with growth in China and emerging markets standing out. Net
income advanced some 38 percent with higher-margined products in the
acquisition and with other acquisition synergies. FY2019 will give us the
most "pure" compare year in a while; revenues are expected to grow about
9 percent while earnings are expected to rise almost 20 percent; growth
slows a bit to 5 percent for 2020 revenues and about 10 percent for earnings. Modest dividend increases should continue and share counts rose
some 17 percent with the Bard acquisition—to be bought back gradually
with more emphasis placed on paying off the $10 billion of debt used to
buy Bard before the end of the decade.

Reasons to Buy

Becton, Dickinson continues to be a classic "blue-chip" company, still as
recession-proof as any stock on our list. The steady upward share price
march since 2013 is classic, and the stock has risen faster in the past year
as these acquisitions have been added—all in an environment where some
healthcare stocks have sold off due to uncertainties about drug costs and
business models. Earnings, cash flow, and dividend growth over the years
have been steady, and net profit margins are both healthy and reaching
record levels (17–18 percent) recently and are expected to grow beyond
20 percent in the next few years. The company will benefit from becoming a full-line supplier of a wide variety of mostly consumable medical products and will also continue to benefit through the broadening
of healthcare offerings into developing nations, from the automation of
medicine delivery, and from a greater emphasis on preventative care, e.g.,
flu shots.

Reasons for Caution

B-D has been on an acquisition binge over the past three years. What they have done they have done well, but a grow-by-acquisition strategy always poses some risks. Possible changes in the Affordable Care Act and more recently the ad hoc healthcare delivery consortium started by Amazon, Berkshire Hathaway, and JPMorgan Chase also add some downside and uncertainty. Recent healthcare cost scrutiny may hurt some supplies and testing product lines but should help lines devoted to preventative care and efficient care delivery, like CareFusion. All said, Becton continues to be one of the best, safest, steadiest, and most well-managed players in the industry—and now it's becoming one of the biggest.

SECTOR: Healthcare ❑ Beta coefficient: 1.12 ❑ 10-year compound earnings per-share growth: 9.5% ❑ 10-year compound dividends per-share growth: 12.0%

		2011	2012	2013	2014	2015	2016	2017	2018
Revenues (mil)		7,828	7,708	8,054	8,446	10,282	12,453	12,093	15,983
Net income (mil)		1,272	1,123	1,159	1,236	1,480	1,869	2,072	2,862
Earnings per share		5.61	5.36	5.81	6.25	7.16	8.59	9.48	11.01
Dividends per share		1.64	1.80	1.98	2.18	2.40	2.64	2.92	3.00
Cash flow per share		8.27	8.30	8.79	9.37	11.25	13.99	13.56	17.48
Price:	high	89.4	80.6	110.9	142.6	157.5	181.9	229.7	265.9
	low	72.5	71.6	78.7	105.2	128.9	129.5	161.5	208.8

Website: www.bd.com

AGGRESSIVE GROWTH

Best Buy, Inc.

Ticker symbol: BBY (NYSE) ❑ Large Cap ❑ Value Line financial strength rating: A ❑ Current yield: 2.7% ❑ Dividend raises, past 10 years: 10

Company Profile

Call us "stock environmentalists" if you will. Why? Because every now and then we see it fit to "recycle" an old stock back on to the *100 Best Stocks* list. Sometimes we take a company off the list because its fortunes and/or its business model simply hasn't kept up with the times; markets dry up, competitors take over, and so forth. This is a "slow" denouement from the list. Other "faster" denouements occur when a company is acquired or goes through a sudden change (or the whole industry, for that matter) rendering it unattractive in a hurry and due for replacement. Anyone remember General Electric?

The removal of Best Buy from our list in 2013 was an example of the "slow" denouement, where the competitive pressure of online sales and most particularly Amazon seemed to be taking over Best Buy in the marketplace, to the point where customers didn't "defect" completely but rather used Best Buy's expensive real estate as a "showroom" to observe a product in action and in person—then get the ol' phone out and order it online. Such a business model did not appear destined for long-term success.

So what puts a company like Best Buy back onto our list? What causes us to "recycle" it back into a *100 Best* pick? It's usually one or a combination of two things: (1) a definitive and executable strategy to combat the afflictions that put it out into the heap in the first place, (2) changing market conditions that move toward where the company already is.

Best Buy serves as a good example of recycling a company due to both these merits. They weren't going to take the "showrooming" thing lying down and decided one of the best ways to combat the online threat was to provide service—real service—to customers buying complex technology products to differentiate it from the online offering. "Service" in this case means not only fix-and-repair service, but also help in applying a product to a customer's home needs. What router do I need? What theater sound system works best in my home environment? What home security system do I need, and how do I set it up to work on my smartphone? Secondly, the marketplace moved their way, for with the demise of Circuit City, H.H. Gregg, and other consumer electronics superstores, they found themselves not just at the top of the heap but as the whole heap, in a good position with the addition of Geek Squad, Total Tech Support, and In-Home Advisor offerings. Welcome back, Best Buy!

Best Buy operates a total of 1,415 stores, 1,005 of them the familiar "big-box" yellow-signed retail format stores mostly in suburban locations across all 50 states, D.C., and Puerto Rico, 132 in Canada, 161 in Mexico, 45 Best Buy Mobile each in Mexico and Canada, 21 contractor-oriented Pacific Sales, and six Best Buy Express stores. By product category, 44 percent of 2018 sales were computing and mobile, 33 percent were consumer electronics, appliances 10 percent, entertainment (media, etc.) 8 percent, services 5 percent.

Two years ago, as Amazon and others appeared to be eating all of brick-and-mortar retailers' lunches, Best Buy among many, and perhaps more than most, recognized the need for change. Simply trying to discount their way past Amazon would not get them to the finish line ahead, as Target realized at about the same time in 2016–17. (See Target, another 2020 *100 Best* stock.) In late 2017, Best Buy announced its "Building the New Blue" strategy.

The overarching purpose of "Building the New Blue" was to "enrich our customers' lives through technology." Of course, the internal purpose was to add enough value to the sale through service and assistance before, during, and after the sale to differentiate the offering in the customer's eyes; to get the customer to pay a little bit more and forgo the Amazon opportunity. "Building the New Blue" recognizes that Best Buy is uniquely positioned to deliver this value with its in-store and on-site service offerings. The company is capitalizing through several platforms, including:

- New Technology Solutions: Trained sales floor and acquired Geek Squad and Magnolia Home Theater personnel combine to provide a solution-focused service helping customers identify needs and address those needs with products and services bought throughout the stores.
- Total Tech Support: Customers can buy an enhanced Geek Squad extended warranty contract giving them access to Geek Squad 24/7 break/fix and presales support for all home technology needs.
- Online Experience: An ongoing effort to streamline the online buying process is bringing more customers and offering true value to more valuable customers through loyalty and reward programs; we think it's one of the best in the business.
- In-Home Advisor: This includes free, in-home consultations with one of 350 expert store "personal shoppers" across the store network.
- Supply Chain Improvements: They speed up the pipeline flow and make Amazon-comparable and even Amazon-beating delivery fairly routine.

Financial Highlights, Fiscal Year 2018

FY2018 revenues were up 7 percent on a same-store comp gain of 5.6 percent; net earnings were up 19.4 percent on a 0.3 percent gain in net profit margin (not bad on a 3.2 percent base) and per-share earnings rose over 20 percent on a 6 percent share buyback and a 32 percent dividend increase. While mobile and gaming are slowing down and saturating somewhat, BBY recognizes the opportunity in home theater, security, and other "home" platforms and plans to make the most of the service offerings. Sales are expected to rise about 7.5 percent annually through 2020 with a flat to 2 percent rise in earnings in 2019 as the mobile market matures and continued investments are made and 7–9 percent in 2020 as the "Building the New Blue" strategy takes hold.

Reasons to Buy

Quite simply, we think Best Buy has effectively addressed the strategic gap that had been emerging between it and the online competition. Moreover, other marketplace winds blowing its way include the demise of brick-and-mortar competitors and the impending of the fully integrated "smart" home as a complete electronically driven system with smartphone-driven remote control and 5G and IoT networked devices throughout. We like how Best Buy is evolving their offerings to capitalize on the smart home evolution.

Reasons for Caution

The consumer electronics space is still extremely competitive, and new technologies can cause retailers to run short of the latest and greatest while becoming stuffed to the gills with too much "older" or out of favor items. The current saturation in mobile and gaming devices and to a lesser extent appliances serves as an example.

SECTOR: Retail ❑ Beta coefficient: 1.20 ❑ 10-year compound earnings per-share growth: 3.0% ❑ 10-year compound dividends per-share growth: 11.5%

	2011	2012	2013	2014	2015	2016	2017	2018
Revenues (bil)	50.0	44.0	40.6	40.3	395	39.4	42.1	42.9
Net income (mil)	1,365	863	721	916	973	1,148	1,357	1,498
Earnings per share	3.61	2.54	2.07	2.60	2.78	3.58	4.42	5.32
Dividends per share	0.62	0.66	0.68	0.72	0.92	1.12	1.36	1.80
Cash flow per share	6.68	5.34	4.17	4.47	5.03	5.79	7.21	8.54
Price: high	36.3	28.0	44.7	41.0	42.0	49.4	69.0	84.4
low	21.8	11.2	11.4	22.2	28.3	25.3	41.7	47.7

Website: www.bestbuy.com

AGGRESSIVE GROWTH

NEW FOR 2020

Beyond Meat

Ticker symbol: BYND (NASDAQ) ❑ Mid Cap ❑ Value Line financial strength rating: NA ❑ Current yield: Nil ❑ Dividend raises, past 10 years: NA

Company Profile

We've never done this before. Into deep, uncharted waters we sail our *100 Best Stocks* ship with our first IPO (Initial Public Offering) issue, that is, a fresh and new company very much in its initial phases of proving itself in the marketplace—and in the financial markets. We've strenuously avoided IPOs in the past, for they have little business history. They may be years away from profitability and still more years away from dividends and other shareholder returns. Too, the IPOs seem more designed to make the founders and original shareholders rich than the ones who come on after the offering. All that said, we wish to remind you again that including a stock on the *100 Best* list doesn't mean you should buy it. It just means that you might want to take a look, and if it satisfies your fancies and risk tolerance as an investor, and you can get it for the right price, then you might push the buy button. End of disclaimer.

"A Brand Morphing Into a Movement" and "The Future of Protein" touts the go-public message of vegan meat products producer Beyond Meat. Beyond Meat went public in mid-2019, almost ten years after founder Ethan Brown started formulating plant-based meat substitutes. Ethan Brown's simply stated goal: to evolve out of 12,000 years of humans raising animals for food toward a new animal-free protein-based future to improve human health, combat climate change, conserve natural resources, and improve animal welfare. He wants to make raising animals for food "obsolete."

The main idea is that, in his words, "none of the core elements of meat is exclusive to the animal"; they are abundant in the plant kingdom as well. The animal serves as a "bioreactor," consuming vegetation and water and converting those inputs into meat. The idea behind Beyond Meat is to take those constituent parts from plants, add water, and organize them into the "basic architecture of animal-based meat." In so doing, "we bypass the animal, agriculture's greatest bottleneck."

So what is Beyond Meat? It is the result of a "Manhattan Project" in vegetarian meat creation, where a team of scientists came up with blends of proteins from peas, beans, oils, texturing, and other proprietary ingredients. The mix is fed into a food extrusion machine that cooks it with steam, pressure, and water to form the texture and give it flavor. Beyond Meat started in 2014 with two products: Beyond Chicken and Beyond Beef. A burger patty called "The Beast" was released in 2015 and sold through Whole Foods. That led to the Beyond Burger, a packaged version to be sold alongside regular meat products in grocery stores, starting again with Whole Foods in 2016 and now available at Kroger, Safeway, Albertsons, Wegmans, Ahold, Target, and others. It's to be sold in fast food and other burger eateries as well. Products have expanded to include Beyond Sausage. By July 2018, the Beyond Burger was in all A&W Canadian locations, TGI Fridays, Del Taco,

BurgerFi, and Bareburger, and by January 2019 it was being sold in Carl's Jr. restaurants with plans to "add several prominent restaurant chains in 2019."

That's where your coauthor Peter, a devout Midwestern-born meat eater, got talked into a Beyond Meat burger at his local Carl's by his health-conscious 24-year-old son, Julian. Skeptical of the taste and the two-dollar price premium, he bit and found the taste and texture just as good as the burger it replaced! It was amazing. At that moment he realized that if he could only invest in it somehow…

And Peter isn't the only one. Skeptics included early funder Bill Gates, who in 2013 wrote, "I couldn't tell the difference between Beyond Meat and real chicken." Celebrity food journalist Mark Bittman of *The New York Times* wrote that "you won't know the difference between [Beyond Meat] and real chicken. I didn't, at least, and this is the kind of thing I do for a living."

The "movement" crosses between health-conscious meat avoiders and people concerned about the 80 percent of arable lands that are used to produce animal and meat products to people concerned about the life-styles of the animals themselves. It's a *big* movement; it is said that one-third of all Americans, and 37 percent of millennials in particular, plan to eat more plant-based products next year. According to Brown, plant-based meats create 90 percent fewer greenhouse gas emissions, consume 99 percent less water, use 93 percent less land and 46 percent less energy than their animal source equivalents, and are obviously better for animal welfare—and he is "comfortably aware that Beyond Meat products are free of cholesterol."

Prior to the IPO of Beyond Meat, it has been hard to invest in this type of enterprise. There are few pure plays. Three years ago we picked White-Wave Foods, maker of plant-based and organic dairy products like Silk and Horizon Organic, only to have it be acquired by French dairy and yogurt product producer Danone shortly after it appeared in the book.

Beyond Meat is currently headquartered in Southern California with a production facility in Columbia, Missouri. It is in the process of signing pro-duction agreements with partners in other states to keep up with demand. Currently, the handsomely packaged products are found in 15,000 stores, and "raw" and frozen product is found in 12,000 restaurant and food service out-lets in the US and Canada as well as certain locations in Germany, France, and Israel. Its vegan patties recently outsold Angus and other prepackaged beef patties in Kroger's Ralphs subsidiary in Southern California.

The strategy is obviously to build brand exposure and market share—something that the recent IPO will go a long way to help. There are rumored talks with many fast-food chains and even with legendary meatball supplier IKEA. "I want to be on every plate," reflects Mr. Brown.

Financial Highlights, Fiscal Year 2018

As is always the case in an early-stage enterprise, the financial picture is highly dynamic and lacks the history to make concise financial projections. Total net revenues for the three years 2016–18 were $16.1 million, $32.6 million, and $87.9 million respectively, with a first-quarter 2019 revenue weighing in at $31 million. Retail revenue is $12.3 million, $25.5 million, and $50.8 million for the three years, while restaurant and food-service revenue came in at $3.8 million, $7.1 million, and $37.2 million respectively. Cost of goods sold ran $22.4 million, $34.7 million, and $70.4 million, making the company gross profit positive by $17.5 million for the first time in 2018. For 2018, R&D expense was $9.6 million and SG&A ran $34.4 million, producing a loss from operations of $27.9 million. "Adjusted EBITDA," an approximation of cash flow, stood at ($19.3) for the 2018 year.

The company currently has about $300 million in cash in its coffers, including proceeds from the 9.63 million share IPO. The IPO was set at $25, the stock opened at $46 (which we will use as the basis for annual performance measurement) and closed the first day above $66; with about 57 million total shares outstanding, the company is valued at about $3.6 billion, a hefty premium for a company with $88 million in 2018 sales. We could not find projections for 2019 and 2020, but suffice it to say that if they execute on their strategy to supplant (no pun intended) 13 percent of the $270 billion US meat market ($1.4 trillion globally) with natural and organics as WhiteWave and others did with dairy, there should be plenty of pickings on the table for Beyond Meat shareholders.

Reasons to Buy

Can you say disruptive?

The consumer is changing. People have long said they would switch away from meat for health reasons, and in the case of younger consumers, environmental reasons—but up until Beyond Meat there have been issues with taste, texture, quality, and price. With Beyond Meat, we get a product that really does taste, look, feel, and cook like meat, so the question becomes, "Why *wouldn't* I eat this?" When you have a product that gets that kind of accolade from people of all ages—and we won't hesitate to call out millennials—you've got something big going.

We're glad there's a new way, albeit risky, to invest in this transformative idea, albeit a risky one for the time being. As we said, this isn't for everybody… The best investment advice we can give right now is to try this product, then do your due diligence, then "Go Beyond" carefully if you so choose.

Reasons for Caution

This is by far the riskiest stock we've ever placed on the *100 Best Stocks* list. We vigorously avoid stocks in companies that are good ideas, but not good businesses, like so many of the dot-coms on our investing menu years ago. This one has all the risks of a typical IPO, from market acceptance to capital shortage to production problems to legal vulnerabilities to competition. Well, it appears they've got market acceptance, at least so far; that is a big hurdle in this business. When they pass so many taste tests (including ours) early on, it's a great start. But they still need to prove they can make money.

SECTOR: **Consumer Staples** ❑ Beta coefficient: **NM** ❑ 10-year compound earnings per-share growth: **NM** ❑ 10-year compound dividends per-share growth: **NM**

	2011	2012	2013	2014	2015	2016	2017	2018
Revenues (mil)	—	—	—	—	—	16.2	32.6	87.9
Net income (mil)	—	—	—	—	—	(25.1)	(30.3)	(29.9)
Earnings per share	—	—	—	—	—	(5.51)	(5.57)	(4.75)
Dividends per share	—	—	—	—	—	—	—	—
Adjusted EBITDA	—	—	—	—	—	(22.0)	(17.6)	(19.3)
Price: high	—	—	—	—	—	—	—	—
low	—	—	—	—	—	—	—	—

Website: www.beyondmeat.com

GROWTH AND INCOME   NEW FOR **2020**

BlackRock, Inc.

Ticker symbol: BLK (NYSE) ❑ Large Cap ❑ Value Line financial strength rating: A+ ❑ Current yield: 3.2% ❑ Dividend raises, past 10 years: 9

Company Profile

As a buyer and reader of *The 100 Best Stocks to Buy*, you're most likely an individual investor who has the time, inclination, and interest to make your own investments and build your own investment portfolio with the goal of a financially secure retirement or similar in mind. But, to be sure, as the gamut of investors goes, you're in a minority.

Actually the vast majority of investments are handled and managed by investment professionals on your behalf in large managed institutional funds such as pension funds, insurance funds, retirement plans, and so forth. Another large chunk of investments might be directly managed by you but put into investment products such as mutual funds, index funds, and exchange-traded funds (ETFs)—recent statistics show a substantial increase in the use of ETFs and index funds ("passive" investments) over the years. Anyway, the bottom line is that most of the investment world invests through professional investment managers and/or investment *products*—that is, packaged investments designed to track or slightly beat major stock indexes—and to beat what most folks can do on our own.

Anyhow, for about five years we have had State Street on the *100 Best* list, an investment bank and major provider of custodial and other services to investment product producers (mainly mutual funds), also with the world's first line of ETFs known as "SPDRs." State Street has done fairly well over the years, but we feel they are (1) overly complex because of their banking roots, (2) a little too tied to traditional mutual funds which are gradually falling out of favor to ETFs, and (3) tied in the ETF space to SPDRs, which are losing market share.

We decided to transition to more of a pure play—the premier investment management firm and the largest purveyor of ETFs (its brand is "iShares"): BlackRock, Inc.

BlackRock manages assets on behalf of institutions and individuals worldwide through an assortment of equity; fixed income; cash management; balanced, alternative investment; and advisory products. It is a go-to firm for any institution and for many individuals with large sums to manage. While the largest pension plans such as CalPERS (California Public Employees Retirement System) are large enough to have their own professional advisory staff, the vast majority of such plans do not, and even CalPERS most likely buys BlackRock products and services.

BlackRock has about $6 *trillion* in assets under management (AUM). Of the $6 trillion:

- $2.3 trillion (38 percent) is invested for institutional clients (pension funds, insurers, retirement plan managers) in non-ETF index products
- $1.7 trillion (28 percent) is invested in iShares ETFs (the company does not provide a breakdown as to how much of that is individual versus institutional investors)

- $1.1 trillion (18 percent) is invested in actively managed (nonindex) mutual funds, other products, or individual stocks and bonds
- $425 billion (7 percent) is cash invested in short-term cash management investments

…and the rest is a collection of other smaller investment products and services.

The company estimates that, overall, two-thirds of their AUM base is invested for retirement. Of interest to most of us as individual investors, of course, are the iShares ETFs, which BlackRock didn't even invent (they were acquired from Barclays in 2009) but have grown to lead the market with a 39 percent share, far more than State Street's 17 percent share with their original SPDRs. There are about 800 ETFs to choose from, ranging from the broadest global equity and bond index funds down to very specific products such as the iShares Robotics and Artificial Intelligence ETF.

BlackRock has a track record for innovation in this space both in terms of product and service offerings. "LifePath," the original set of "target date" funds that automatically adjust portfolio balance according to age (mostly between stocks and bonds) is a BlackRock innovation; "Aladdin" (okay, it stands for Asset Liability and Debt and Derivative Investment Network; you had to ask!) is a well-regarded investment-planning and risk-management tool deploying analytics and artificial intelligence.

Financial Highlights, Fiscal Year 2018

BlackRock earns most of its keep through investment product and service fees. While their product fees are among the lowest in the industry, revenues will suffer if the "base" declines with a market reversal, or if clients move away from their products. The strategy is to charge low fees and make it up through scale.

While the 2018 fourth quarter market reversal took a 5 percent bite out of AUM (which is proving to be temporary), total revenues for the year advanced almost 14 percent, while net income rose a slightly more modest 12 percent. The company is currently embarking on a cost-reduction program to help net earnings keep up with revenues and to answer price competition in the industry. Forecasts have been trimmed to reflect a slight decline going forward into 2019 again because of the market reversal, but revenues and earnings should rise in the mid-to-high single digits in 2020 and beyond.

Reasons to Buy

BlackRock is a pure play—and really the 800-pound gorilla—of the investment management and investment products industry. It is relatively easy to see (compared to many financial companies) how they make their money. Their size and scale result in a net profit margin exceeding 30 percent, and their size also protects their market position since competitors would have a hard time matching their assortment of products and services at a reasonable cost. As well, the company sits in the right place to capture the increasing popularity of so-called "passive" investing.

As you read through their marketing and investor relations materials, you'll see a refreshing transparency and clarity for what they do, especially for a financial firm. In fact, they present their actual investment performance records for different types of AUM: For instance, taxable actively managed fixed income AUMs beat their benchmarks 90 percent of the time over a five-year period; equity funds ranged from 73 to 90 percent over five years and 70 to 83 percent over one year, and so forth. They have done well for their clients and they aren't afraid to lay their results on the table. While the markets fell some 20 percent in late 2018, BlackRock's assets declined only 7 percent.

Revenues, earnings, and dividends have grown at an increasing pace and appear on path to continue that trend (the dividend was raised twice in 2018); share buybacks have gradually trimmed the share count.

Reasons for Caution

The obvious risk is that the markets resume a major downturn into a recessionary environment. AUM would decline; revenues and earnings would decline in lockstep.

SECTOR: Financials □ Beta coefficient: 1.30 □ 10-year compound earnings per-share growth: 14.5% □ 10-year compound dividends per-share growth: 17.5%

	2011	2012	2013	2014	2015	2016	2017	2018
Revenues (mil)	9,081	9,337	10,180	11,061	11,401	11,155	12,491	14,198
Net income (mil)	2,337	2,458	2,932	3,294	3,345	3,172	3,694	4,361
Earnings per share	12.37	13.79	16.87	19.29	19.79	19.04	22.47	26.93
Dividends per share	5.50	6.00	6.72	7.72	8.72	9.16	10.00	12.02
Cash flow per share	15.82	17.70	19.10	21.40	21.97	21.05	24.59	28.95
Price: high	209.6	209.9	323.0	368.6	382.8	399.5	520.7	594.5
low	137.0	160.3	208.8	284.8	275.0	280.9	365.8	360.8

Website: www.blackrock.com

AGGRESSIVE GROWTH

Boeing Company

Ticker symbol: BA (NYSE) ❑ Large Cap ❑ Value Line financial strength rating: A++ ❑ Current yield: 1.9% ❑ Dividend raises, past 10 years: 8

Company Profile

What a difference a few years makes: In seven or eight short years, high-flying Boeing has gone from being a maligned corporate misfit striving to keep up with Europe's Airbus and unable to get its brilliant 787 Dreamliner out the door to one of America's corporate superstars—a transformation almost of Apple-ian proportions. The company has blended many tailwinds—lower fuel prices, healthier airline customers, a strong and more fuel-efficient product catalog, higher defense spending, operational efficiencies, and tax policy changes—into a smooth flight trajectory that doesn't look to descend anytime soon.

Boeing has delivered on its new aircraft, including new, larger, and more efficient versions of its ever-popular 737 series, although, as is widely known now, the 737-MAX series was grounded in early 2019 due to two crashes and faulty software that likely caused them. (We expect the planes to be flying again by 2020 with unknown financial and marketplace consequences in the interim. They can carry up to 200 passengers over 4,000 miles on 8 percent less fuel than an older 737; 5,000 are on order since launch.) The company is well positioned in good areas in the defense and space sectors including satellites and unmanned guided weapons that appear to have strategic advantage going forward. The backlog is over $465 *billion* on unfilled orders for some 5,800 aircraft—although the effects of the 737-MAX problems are not known long term and are not factored in. The world-class production capability can now turn out 57 737's a month, up from 52 last year. The company values its potential ten-year market opportunity at $8.1 *trillion*. Boeing clearly exceeded our expectations since we put it on the list two years ago.

Boeing is the world's largest aerospace company. Its leading commercial aircraft lines include the familiar 737, 767, 777, and 787 platforms, but it also produces business jets and a variety of defense aircraft including F-15 and F/A-18 fighters, CH-47 (Chinook) and AH-64 (Apache) helicopters, Osprey vertical landing and takeoff aircraft, and Harpoon guided weapons. The company has delivered over 3,500 new commercial airplanes and 1,000 military aircraft and satellites in the past five years. It also is involved in space and security systems, managing the International Space Station and selling various kinds of satellites.

The company is organized into two principal segments: Commercial Airplanes and Defense, Space & Security. Commercial Airplanes accounts for about 61 percent of 2018 revenues, while the Defense, Space & Security group, which includes Boeing Military Aircraft and Network & Space Systems, brings in about 26 percent; Global Services & Support and Other brings in about 13 percent. The company is the US's largest exporter and has operations in 65 countries, with foreign sales accounting for 56 percent of 2018 revenues.

Financial Highlights, Fiscal Year 2018

Strong product deliveries and a boom in the relatively profitable 737 platform led to a solid 8.4 percent revenue increase in 2018, while per-share earnings, on the back of strong business, operating efficiencies, tax changes, and a 4 percent share buyback, ascended a full 53 percent. Flight conditions remain favorable for the 2019 campaign, with a forecasted 10–12 percent revenue growth and another 20–25 percent rise in per-share earnings. For 2020, Boeing expects things to level off a bit to a 12–15 percent per-share earnings rise on a 5–7 percent revenue increase. Quite a flight, especially for a company this size, indeed! Net profit margins, helped considerably by the new tax law, will approach 12 percent after navigating through the 5–7 percent range for many years. Dividend increases have been substantial—20 percent in FY2017; increases in the 0–25 percent rate going forward appear likely at least for the next two years. The company has repurchased over 24 percent of its shares in the past five years and has returned $40 billion to shareholders overall during that period.

Reasons to Buy

New products, strong execution, and a much healthier "customer" industry have created a good perfect storm for Boeing—and revenues in general and profitability in particular have responded well. Airline fleets are eager to replace aging, less fuel-efficient aircraft. Increased defense spending will also help. The company is reaping the success of massive R&D investments in recent years and is achieving scale, which also improves profitability. It also helps to have such large backlogs, as the company doesn't have to guess on production requirements, product mix, etc. In this kind of business, it's nice to know what you're going to be doing for the next five years. There's a lot to like in the new aircraft—and a lot to like in the generous shareholder returns as well.

Reasons for Caution

Throughout its history, Boeing has been subject to cyclical turbulence as the airline industry and defense spending go through cycles of their own. Some of these cycles have been severe. That said, the current positive cycle seems to have longer legs, and the company's products in our view have a stronger and more sustainable competitive advantage in technology and scale that should help avoid the kinds of sharp downturns seen previously—if the airline business softens, they will still buy new aircraft in an effort to become more efficient. That all said, the 737-MAX is creating a bit of a down cycle on its own, which should prove only temporary. Additionally, new competition has arrived at the gate in the form of new Chinese-built airliners, which have not yet been certified for US carriage but still bear watching. Finally, one cannot ignore the steep share price ascent starting in early 2017—and any pilot knows that such sharp ascents bring with them a greater chance for a stall and fall. We took a hard look at this one and feel the company's current excellence and prospects outweigh share price risk, but do book your flights carefully in this stock.

SECTOR: Industrials ▫ Beta coefficient: 1.16 ▫ 10-year compound earnings per-share growth: 12.5% ▫ 10-year compound dividends per-share growth: 14.5%

		2011	2012	2013	2014	2015	2016	2017	2018
Revenues (bil)		68.7	81.7	86.6	90.8	96.1	94.6	93.9	101.7
Net income (bil)		3.6	3.9	4.6	5.5	5.2	6.9	7.1	10.5
Earnings per share		4.82	5.11	5.96	7.38	7.44	10.84	11.71	17.86
Dividends per share		1.68	1.76	1.94	2.92	3.64	4.36	5.68	6.84
Cash flow per share		7.08	7.56	8.60	10.40	10.51	14.36	15.59	22.15
Price:	high	80.6	77.8	142.0	144.6	158.8	160.1	299.3	394.3
	low	56.0	66.8	72.7	116.3	115.1	102.1	155.2	292.5

Website: www.boeing.com

AGGRESSIVE GROWTH

CarMax, Inc.

Ticker symbol: KMX (NYSE) ▫ Large Cap ▫ Value Line financial strength rating: B+ ▫ Current yield: Nil ▫ Dividend raises, past 10 years: NA

Company Profile

"The Way Car Buying Should Be" is the appropriate slogan used by this clean-cut chain of used vehicle stores and superstores and its new big-box, retail-like model for selling cars. CarMax buys, reconditions, and sells cars and light trucks at 203 retail centers in 100 metropolitan TV markets in 39 states, mainly in the Southeast, Midwest, and California, but is gradually moving to a more nationwide footprint. The company specializes in selling cars that are under six years old with less than 60,000 miles in excellent condition; the cars are sold at a competitive price for their condition, typically in the $10,000 to $34,000 price range in a no-haggle environment. The price is the price; the emphasis is on the selection, condition of the vehicles, and on a helpful and friendly sales and transaction process. Sales representatives are compensated for cars they sell but not in such a way that drives them to push the wrong car on a customer. The company sold some 748,961 used vehicles in 2018, up 3.8 percent from 2017 and up 83 percent from the 408,080 sold in 2011. The average selling price for 2018 was $20,077, up 1.6 percent from the previous year as used car prices have softened a bit—but the average gross margin was $2,175 per vehicle, up slightly from the previous $2,173.

CarMax has now successfully reached most of the country with its format, and continues to expand by adding stores in smaller cities like Fort Wayne, Indiana, and Lubbock, Texas, and adjacent cities and suburbs like Salem, Oregon, Scottsdale, Arizona, and Denton, Texas. Adding stores in these adjacent cities not only brings the CarMax concept closer to large suburban populations but it also serves as a good way to keep more inventory in a metropolitan area, which in turn improves the chance of making a sale. CarMax will in most cases move a car from one suburban location to another free of charge and will handle intercity transfers for a moderate fee. About 34 percent of sales are for vehicles transferred at buyer request, illustrating how store inventories support each other. In all CarMax plans to open 13 more new stores in 2019. From 203 stores total today, they anticipate 225 stores in place by the end of the decade, at which time they will slow capital spending on new stores and change focus to a longer-term strategy, which is to build a national footprint and brand, achieve economies of scale, and make the most of online marketing initiatives.

The health of the economy and consumer spending has swung car buying into a higher gear, but today's more financially prudent consumer is more likely to head straight to the one- to six-year-old used car sector of the business, where prices are 40–60 percent lower than comparable new cars. The new car boom of recent years has led to a large number of lease returns, which, while depressing used car prices somewhat, also provides a major source of low-cost supply for CarMax's inventory. In addition to "retail" used car sales, CarMax is a big player in auto wholesaling, having moved about 447,491 units mostly taken in trade; the company is the world's largest used car buyer. The company also earns income through its financing unit, known as CarMax Auto Finance, or CAF. The unit finances about 43 percent of the company's sales.

CarMax also has service operations and sells extended warranties and other products related to car ownership. The company has state-of-the-art web-based and mobile tools as well as other aids designed to make the car selection, buying, and ownership experience more personalized, more "self-service," and generally easier. As CarMax puts it, customers expect four things when they buy a car:

1. Don't play games
2. Don't waste my time
3. Provide security
4. Make car buying fun

The company's offering is aimed at reducing these concerns and providing the right experience. The offering continues to be largely unique in the industry, and competitors would have a long way to go to catch up.

Financial Highlights, Fiscal Year 2018

A strong finish to a strong 2018 year brought a total sales increase of 6.2 percent on a relatively weak same-store sales gain of 0.3 percent. (The weak same-store sales showing was partly influenced the 2017 Gulf Coast hurricanes, which bumped up the 2017 sales "base" in those areas.) Higher conversion rates, more "omnichannel" sales over the Internet, and lower taxes helped drive earnings some 23 percent forward. A combination of higher store count, continued strength in conversion rates (sales per customer visit), strength in wholesaling and add-on sales (extended warranties, etc.), and financing income is expected to bring a 5–6 percent 2019 sales gain with relatively flat net income; however, aggressive buybacks will produce a 5–6 percent gain in per-share earnings. For 2020, CarMax expects a 7–10 percent per-share earnings gain on a 6–8 percent gain in sales.

As a deliberate alternative to dividends, the company announced its first share buyback program in 2012 and has pursued it aggressively. Every year since then they have retired 30 percent of the float.

Reasons to Buy

CarMax states its purpose clearly: "To drive integrity in the automotive industry by being honest and transparent in every interaction." Quite simply, CarMax is a play on the theme that the traditional dealer model is broken and that people will continue to see value in late-model used vehicles. CarMax as a brand is gaining national recognition as a go-to in the car buying (and selling) process.

Additionally, CarMax brings the latest in business intelligence and analytic models to the car-marketing process, in procurement, merchandising, pricing, and selling the vehicles. Do green Jeep Cherokees sell well in Southern California? Then let's find some, put them on the lot there, and set at a market-based price. KMX is well ahead of the industry in making analysis-based supply and selling decisions and has quite successfully deployed analytic tools to adjust prices and inventories quickly to market conditions. They point out the large amounts of data accumulated through selling 11 million vehicles, hosting 65 million customers in their history, and handling 200 million digital interactions per year—a distinct competitive advantage that bodes well for the future.

CarMax is increasingly a big player in the 42-million vehicle used car market (versus 17 million for new cars), taking market share from traditional used car dealers, but there's fertile ground to capture more. The company estimates that it has only 4.4 percent of the current market for zero-to-ten-year-old used vehicles in markets in which it operates, and only 3.3 percent of the total nationwide—all while being the largest player and twice the size of the nearest competitor.

The company is positioned well both for organic growth through market share and for geographic growth; there is still plenty of fertile ground for new growth, especially in the Northeast and Northwest and smaller metro areas. The footprint is slowly but surely becoming a nationwide one, which will not only help volumes but also brand recognition, pricing power, buying power, and cost absorption.

Reasons for Caution

CarMax will always be somewhat vulnerable to economic cycles, the availability of credit, and the availability of quality used vehicles to resell. Recent concerns about vehicle availability have morphed into concerns about oversupply as lease returns flood the market. Lease returns are an important source of supply for the company, so there is good news in this as well.

A new trend toward longer six- and seven-year new car financing periods may keep people in their cars longer, but it may also incentivize people to buy used to avoid the long financing period in the first place. As this company is still in the growth phase, and new dealerships involve putting lots of new cars on the ground, working capital needs are extensive, long-term debt has risen, and cash returns to shareholders have not met our norms; however, the share repurchase program takes a big step toward fixing that.

SECTOR: Retail ❑ Beta coefficient: 1.20 ❑ 10-year compound earnings per-share growth: 15.0% ❑ 10-year compound dividends per-share growth: NA

	2011	2012	2013	2014	2015	2016	2017	2018
Revenues (mil)	10,004	10,963	12,574	14,269	15,150	15,875	17,120	18,173
Net income (mil)	413.8	425.0	492.6	583.9	628.6	633.8	684.0	842.2
Earnings per share	1.79	1.87	2.16	2.68	3.05	3.30	3.70	4.79
Dividends per share	—	—	—	—	—	—	—	—
Cash flow per share	2.19	2.00	2.70	3.35	3.93	4.30	4.81	6.12
Price: high	37.0	38.2	53.1	68.7	75.4	66.6	77.6	81.7
low	22.8	24.8	38.0	42.5	50.6	41.3	54.3	55.2

Website: www.carmax.com

AGGRESSIVE GROWTH

Carnival Corporation

Ticker symbol: CCL (NYSE) ❑ Large Cap ❑ Value Line financial strength rating: B++ ❑ Current yield: 3.7% ❑ Dividend raises, past 10 years: 6

Company Profile

Carnival Corporation is the world's largest leisure travel company, providing cruises and cruise vacations to destinations throughout the world. The company operates under 11 individual cruise brands or separate cruise lines in two segments—North America, and Europe, Australia & Asia (EAA) segments. The North America segment includes Carnival Cruise Line (25 ships), Princess Cruises (17 ships), Holland America Line (14 ships), and The Yachts of Seabourn (a luxury line of three ships) cruise brands. The EAA segment includes Costa Cruises (serving Italy, France, and Spain), Cunard Cruises (premium UK, including The Queen Elizabeth, Queen Mary 2, and Queen Victoria), AIDA Cruises (Germany), P&O Cruises (UK), and P&O Cruises (Australia). Together, these cruise lines operate 104 modern ships (with 17 more on the way between now and 2022) with more than 237,000 berths visiting over 700 ports around the world, and the company claims about 48 percent of the worldwide cruise market. The company operates a few port facilities, Alaska tours, and some other adjacent travel operations. About 65 percent of revenues come from the North American brands, while about 53 percent of passengers are North American, 32 percent are European, and 13 percent are from Australia and Asia. For those of you who feel from experience that cruise ships must make most of their money selling alcohol on board, indeed about 25 percent of their revenue is classified as "onboard and other."

The ships are modern, really, floating hotels, and the travel experience is all-inclusive and easy for guests. The typical cruise is set up for all age groups, with plenty of varied activities and foods for all, including new specialty restaurants and celebrity chefs on board and big names such as Crosby, Stills & Nash in the entertainment lineup. The *Carnival Vista*, launched in 2016, has an onboard brewery, an IMAX theater, and an aerial "Skyride." The *Carnival Panorama*, a sister ship to launch in 2019, adds a water park, ropes course, a lip sync studio, a full-blown musical theater, and a Cloud 9 Spa to this amusement-park-on-the-waves theme. The *Carnival Mardi Gras*, to be launched in 2020, will have the Ultimate Sea Coaster, the first roller coaster at sea. Shaquille O'Neal will be the new "chief fun officer" on the *Carnival Radiance*, also to launch in 2020. P&O Cruise Lines will launch the new *Iona*, which will be powered entirely by liquefied natural gas (LNG) and have a half-mile-long Lanai deck, all part of Carnival's long-stated objective to reduce fuel consumption by 25 percent—which will be met three years early. In all, the company adds two or three new ships every year and targets an annual 5 percent compounded annual growth rate. About six more LNG ships are in the plans.

Fares are "all-inclusive," but travelers will find plenty of add-ons such as Internet service and alcoholic beverages, which run up an additional tab while on board. Cruises range from short three- and four-day "Love Boat" cruises out of Los Angeles, to three- and four-week and longer passages through entire regions such as the Middle East or Southeast Asia to a six-month around-the-world journey.

Customer service is paramount and has become a recent emphasis of the Carnival lines. Live agents are available before, during, and after the cruise to answer any questions ("Can my 17-year-old bring his skate-board?" "Yes, but he'll have to stow it while on board the ship; he can access it for ports of call."). The experience is turnkey and much simpler than the typical land-based vacation, especially if multiple destinations are involved. The company and its lines have gotten smart about attracting repeat customers through loyalty programs and "perks"—some wealthier retirees might spend half a year on the company's ships as a simpler, less-expensive alternative to owning a large motor home or vacation property. Retirees have always been prime targets—but the offering is becoming more attractive to families and younger customers as well—to a degree, because cruises have become more "hip."

Recent directions include "green cruising," where ships are powered by liquefied natural gas, and more originations and availability from China to serve the growing traveling middle class there. It is estimated that 200 million outbound cruise travelers will hit the waves in 2020, up from 135 million in 2018. To that end, Carnival has created a joint venture with the China State Shipbuilding Corporation to form a local cruise company and, of course, to build ships.

Financial Highlights, Fiscal Year 2018

Fuel costs, which have almost doubled in two years, were the chief bugaboo in an otherwise healthy 2018 cruise campaign. Revenues rose 7.8 percent, while net income, not so heavily impacted because fuel price increases happened toward the end of the year, rose 21 percent. In the first quarter 2019, net income dropped 20 percent, as higher fuel prices and the strong dollar finally started rocking the boat. For the short term, these factors are likely to hamper results, but the company predicts a 5–7 percent annual revenue increase in the years 2019 and 2020 on strong bookings, with a 1–2 percent increase in 2019 net earnings followed by 6–8 percent in 2020 as more efficient ships come on line. The ship definitely isn't sinking, although the stock price has recently; in fact, 10 percent dividend increases and 2–3 percent share buybacks are likely in store after the 2019 headwinds have subsided.

Reasons to Buy

We continue to think cruising has come into its own as a mainstream regular travel alternative, not just a niche business providing a once-in-a-lifetime honeymoon or retirement cruise to Alaska. Cruises are more complete and easier than in past years, and there is something for everyone. The new ships are spectacular.

The marketing story is solid—strong brands, customer service, and customer loyalty leading the way. Millennials, who once probably would never have thought of a cruise, now are attracted to the activities, special meals, and entertainment, and the experience as a whole. It is no longer just for Grandma and Grandpa. As this group is more and more likely to shun material goods for experiences, cruise operators, especially those offering "interesting" itineraries, are in the right dock at the right time. We also think their strategy to capitalize on growing China tourism is on course, as are their efforts to attract other significant national markets such as Germany and the UK. Shareholder returns, too, have been ample.

Reasons for Caution

It's hard not to think about how economic cycles can affect this industry; fancy vacations are usually the first thing to go when times turn tough. We'd counter that cruises don't have to be "exotic," and many are affordable even on a modest family budget—there's something for everyone here. High fixed costs (ships, especially today's ships, are expensive!) present some financial challenges especially in bad times. Fuel prices are the chief concern at the moment, and competition in this industry is fairly intense, but we feel that Carnival has the strongest position, the best brands, and the best overall offering. You should no longer need a life jacket to buy this company, but watching the horizon is important as it is for any stock.

SECTOR: Consumer Discretionary ❑ Beta coefficient: 1.00 ❑ 10-year compound earnings per-share growth: 3.0% ❑ 10-year compound dividends per-share growth: 2.0%

		2011	2012	2013	2014	2015	2016	2017	2018
Revenues (mil)		15,793	15,382	15,456	15,884	15,774	16,389	17,510	18,881
Net income (mil)		1,912	1,464	1,078	1,516	2,103	2,580	2,606	3,152
Earnings per share		2.42	1.88	1.39	1.99	2.70	3.45	3.59	4.44
Dividends per share		1.00	1.00	1.00	1.00	1.10	1.35	1.60	1.95
Cash flow per share		4.36	3.84	3.44	4.06	4.83	5.95	5.99	7.43
Price:	high	48.1	39.9	40.5	46.5	55.8	54.9	69.9	72.7
	low	28.5	29.2	31.4	33.1	42.5	40.5	51.7	45.8

Website: www.carnivalcorp.com

GROWTH AND INCOME

CenterPoint Energy, Inc.

Ticker symbol: CNP (NYSE) ❑ Large Cap ❑ Value Line financial strength rating: B+ ❑ Current yield: 3.8% ❑ Dividend raises, past 10 years: 10

Company Profile

Based in Houston, Texas, CenterPoint Energy is in the electricity delivery (not production, but delivery) business, serving more than 2.6 million customers in a 5,000-square-mile service territory in the greater Houston area and now in southern Indiana and parts of Ohio; it is also in the retail gas delivery business, serving more than 4.4 million metered customers in Louisiana, Arkansas, Minnesota, Mississippi, Oklahoma, and Texas (including Houston) and now Indiana and Ohio. The Indiana and Ohio part of the business came in a $6 billion acquisition of Vectren, completed in early 2019. CenterPoint is also in the natural gas production and distribution business, with a 54 percent interest in a master limited partnership called Enable Midstream Partners, a new *100 Best* stock for 2020, which produces and distributes wholesale gas and some oil mainly from Texas and Oklahoma. Finally, the company operates an unregulated CenterPoint Energy Services arm, which sells gas to commercial, industrial, and wholesale customers in 33 US states and provides an assortment of consulting services for other utilities.

CenterPoint intrigues us because, first, it does not own generating assets but instead distributes electricity to its customers produced by 18 providers, some of whom are "green" and all of whom offer expanded choices to Houston-area residents. It owns the wires, the meters, and the customer contact, while such messy problems as fuel costs and environmental risks are left to someone else. Second, in its distribution business, the company has learned to use technology to drive efficiency and improve the customer experience, with advanced implementations of smart grids, smart metering, and other technologies from companies such as Itron, Inc. (a former *100 Best* pick). The company has installed smart meters for almost all of its customer base—more than 2.4 million "advanced" meters—automating meter reading and frequent readouts on electricity use. Customers are never left in the dark for long—these technologies manage the grid to reduce consumption, access the least expensive source, and keep the lights on more reliably—and when that fails, the company has also learned how to hook up with customer smartphones and media to quickly advise of service interruptions or other important announcements.

Electricity transmission and distribution has historically accounted for about 31 percent of revenues; regulated retail gas distribution accounts for 38 percent, unregulated wholesale gas sales 29 percent, and services 2 percent—but these numbers will change a bit with the incorporation of Vectren and an organizational realignment. The company recognizes no revenue from its Enable investment, but it earned about $485 million pretax in 2018 as "Equity in earnings (losses) of unconsolidated affiliates"—compared to $265 million in 2017 and far better than the $1.6 billion paper loss it took in 2015.

Financial Highlights, Fiscal Year 2018

With the limited partnership interest and the large unregulated sales unit, revenues and earnings can vary more widely than with most large utilities. We had a major hurricane (Harvey) to recover from in 2017, gains from the Tax Cuts and Jobs Act, and integration costs for Vectren, with Vectren revenues not starting until early 2019. All of this added up to a 10 percent revenue gain but a 46 percent mostly one-time drop in net earnings. Vectren will add about 22 percent to revenues; rate relief and a slight customer base increase will add the rest—the total projected increase for 2019 is about 26 percent, while earnings will recover and then some as major cost synergies take effect; the company expects 2019 net income nearly 30 percent higher than 2017 levels.

Depletion and depreciation allowances typically keep cash flows well ahead of earnings for this type of company. As such, cash flows are well ahead of the pace of earnings and nearly four times the indicated dividend, making it secure though significantly higher than the national utility average.

Reasons to Buy

CenterPoint is a progressive-minded utility located in what has been a high-growth market that simply cannot do without electricity. We look at the electricity business as a key business anchor with decent growth prospects, and we like the deployment of leading-edge technologies in that business. We like their positioning as a low-cost producer and wholesaler in the gas business with a built-in outlet in the regulated business for their product. The Enable "pendulum" has swung back from "problem" to "opportunity," and any good news in this sector, including a sale, will only help from this point forward. The dividend is still high compared to peers and appears secure and poised to grow about 4 percent a year; we think they could afford more. CenterPoint combines the safety and yield of a quality utility with a bit of appreciation potential in the energy production and distribution business.

Reasons for Caution

The merger naturally raises some integration issues; it also causes us to ponder whether it was simply done to buy growth, a strategy we don't particularly care for. First indications call for some significant cost savings as CenterPoint has a highly advanced operating platform that would work well at other utilities. That said, southern Indiana is not a high-growth region. Whether eventually sold, or retained, Enable still creates some uncertainty, though most of the bad news seems to be behind CenterPoint. We do worry that another slowdown in the energy economy could temper Houston's growth, creating a soft patch in its own right.

SECTOR: Utilities ❑ Beta coefficient: 0.80 ❑ 10-year compound earnings per-share growth: -1.5% ❑ 10-year compound dividends per-share growth: 5.5%

	2011	2012	2013	2014	2015	2016	2017	2018
Revenues (mil)	8,459	7,452	8,106	9,226	7,386	7,528	9,614	10,589
Net income (mil)	546	581	536	611	465	432	679	368
Earnings per share	1.27	1.35	1.24	1.42	1.08	1.00	1.57	0.74
Dividends per share	0.79	0.81	0.83	0.95	0.99	1.03	1.07	1.12
Cash flow per share	3.43	3.89	3.54	3.85	3.40	3.68	4.03	3.24
Price: high	21.5	21.8	25.7	25.8	23.7	225.0	30.5	29.6
low	15.1	18.1	19.3	21.1	16.0	16.4	24.5	24.8

Website: www.centerpointenergy.com

AGGRESSIVE GROWTH

Chemed Corporation

Ticker symbol: CHE (NYSE) ❑ Large Cap ❑ Value Line financial strength rating: B++ ❑ Current yield: 0.4% ❑ Dividend raises, past 10 years: 10

Company Profile

"Call Roto-Rooter, that's the name, and away go troubles down the drain" is the affable slogan of this well-known "root" business of the two-company conglomerate Chemed. Yes, if Roto-Rooter is the root, then those roots have sprouted a "tree" in an entirely different business: end-of-life health—hospice—care. Today's Chemed is two businesses for the price of one: the VITAS Healthcare Corporation (67 percent of FY2018 revenues) and the original Roto-Rooter, now 33 percent of revenues (up from 29 percent in 2016). Consider this relatively new-to-our-list company a healthcare business, one for your health at the end of life, and one for the health of your home plumbing. Chemed came onto our list as a Mid Cap three years ago, and we're happy to say it has "graduated" to Large Cap status. Always like when that happens…

As the name sounds like one of a chemical company, the name "Chemed" deserves some explanation. Its roots (sorry!) go back to a Cincinnati soap products maker (a familiar theme) known as DuBois

Chemicals, which eventually made a name in the industrial cleaning products business. Chemed Corporation came on to the scene in 1971 when W.R. Grace, which had bought DuBois in 1964, spun it off as "Chemed." Chemed bought and ran Roto-Rooter franchises, and as the saying goes, liked the business so much it bought the entire company in 1980 (it had been founded in 1935). Chemed decided to quit the capital-intensive and environmentally sensitive commodity chemical business in 1991 and sold DuBois. The company bought VITAS in 2004. After a few other acquisitions and divestitures, we arrive at today's Chemed, a parent company of two distinct businesses. Both businesses are operated as wholly autonomous entities; the Chemed ownership or brand does not appear on either subsidiary's website except under a well-subordinated "parent company" tab at the bottom of the VITAS page (www.vitas.com) and a bare mention on Roto-Rooter's "About Us" page.

Founded in 1978 as a volunteer organization by a United Methodist minister and his wife, an oncology nurse, today's VITAS business provides noncurative hospice and palliative care services to its patients through a network of physicians, registered nurses, home health aides, social workers, clergy, and volunteers. Included are spiritual and emotional counseling to both patients and their families. In 2018, VITAS provided over 6 million days of care in 14 states for over 82,000 patients and their families; about 98 percent of that in their home (2 percent in dedicated inpatient units). The median length of stay is about seven days; the average daily census is now about 18,000 patients, up from 15,000 in 2015. They estimate they own about 7 percent of the market. VITAS operates in an industry dominated primarily by small, nonprofit, community-based hospices. About 96 percent of revenue is from Medicare or Medicaid sources.

The name "Roto-Rooter" is probably more familiar to most of us. Roto-Rooter originally was created to offer round-the-clock drain cleaning and maintenance services using the familiar "snake" equipment they pioneered and now manufacture and sell. Today's Roto-Rooter has expanded into providing a full line of on-site, often emergency-based plumbing and water restoration services both to residential and commercial customers; plumbing now accounts for about half of the subsidiary's revenue. The business operates through 1,150 company-owned branches and independent contractors and 400 franchisees. The company covers 90 percent of the US and 40 percent of Canada's population and holds about 15 percent of the drain cleaning market and a 2–3 percent share of the same-day plumbing fix market.

Financial Highlights, Fiscal Year 2018

FY2017 revenues rose almost 7 percent overall, although beneath the surface Roto-Rooter revenues increased 12.8 percent while VITAS, helped by an improved census and by slightly higher reimbursement rates, advanced about 5 percent. Net earnings were up 42 percent on operating efficiencies, tax cuts, and better reimbursement rates. For 2019 the company expects moderate growth in the 4–5 percent range on the hospice front and continued growth in the 9–10 percent range and margin expansion with selective price increases for Roto-Rooter; altogether earnings should increase 4–6 percent and per-share earnings 7–9 percent on a 6–7 percent bump in revenue. FY2020 forecasts call for a little higher growth rate in the VITAS segment (6 percent) and a little lower at Roto-Rooter—9 percent. Total net profit should rise 7–9 percent. Share buybacks in the 2 percent range will drive the already-low (15.5 million) share count lower, while dividend increases in the 10 percent range will sweeten the pot a little.

Reasons to Buy

Although Chemed has performed quite well and the stock price reflects it, we still like the potential here. Chemed offers the opportunity to buy into not one but two good businesses; both have a component of stability with ample growth opportunity. Both are leaders and recognized brands in highly fragmented industries; what other brand of plumbing services do you know aside from Roto-Rooter? Although the 14 states with current operations represent a populous cross section of the US, there is plenty of potential for geographic expansion in the VITAS business toward becoming a nationally recognized name, and possibly international. Also, increased understanding and use of home hospice services over more pricey hospitalization in end-of-life stages will help. The combined business exhibits improving margins, operating leverage, low debt, and strong cash generation and a willingness to return it to shareholders, mainly in the form of share buybacks. The small share count (15.5 million shares) is attractive so long as things are going well; there are relatively few shares to go around for institutional investors as the word gets out about Chemed.

Reasons for Caution

One may always wonder about the merits of managing two such completely disparate, unrelated businesses; as well, there is always a good possibility another (perhaps unrelated) company may be brought into the mix. Two disparate businesses may be manageable but as many learned in the late 1960s and early 1970s conglomerate boom, too many is not.

Chemed has already gained some appeal with the investment community; that and the low share count has driven recent share prices to high levels. The low share count can bring upside but also downside volatility if business conditions deteriorate. Shop carefully—else your investment results may be headed for life support—or worse, down the drain.

SECTOR: Healthcare ◻ Beta coefficient: 1.05 ◻ 10-year compound earnings per-share growth: 12.5% ◻ 10-year compound dividends per-share growth: 16.0%

	2011	2012	2013	2014	2015	2016	2017	2018
Revenues (mil)	1,356	1,430	1,413	1,456	1,543	1,580	1,667	1,783
Net income (mil)	86.0	89.3	77.2	99.3	110.3	108.7	141.1	200.4
Earnings per share	4.10	4.62	4.16	5.57	6.33	6.48	8.43	11.93
Dividends per share	0.60	0.68	0.76	0.84	0.92	1.00	1.08	1.16
Cash flow per share	6.06	6.47	6.23	7.84	8.56	8.86	11.00	15.07
Price: high	72.3	72.1	82.0	112.0	160.1	164.1	251.0	336.0
low	47.7	49.1	61.7	72.5	100.5	124.8	158.8	243.7

Website: www.chemed.com

AGGRESSIVE GROWTH

NEW FOR 2020

Chemours Company

Ticker symbol: CC (NYSE) ◻ Large Cap ◻ Value Line financial strength rating: B+ ◻ Current yield: 2.7% ◻ Dividend raises, past 10 years: 2

Company Profile

Breaking up is hard to do. Beyond that, most of us don't want to be around someone who is going through or who has just gone through a breakup or personal "restructuring." What you see may not be anything close to what you get in the long term, as everything is up in the air. Who knows what you'll end up with when things settle? Well, such is it also for companies and stocks. Those of you who have been with us for a while know that we are reluctant to include companies going through major changes—mergers, breakups, major divestitures, or restructurings. Only if we can see the future pretty clearly will we attempt to keep them around, though we do often put them back on the *100 Best* list once the dust settles.

Such is the case with long-term *100 Best* bellwether DowDuPont. Change is king at DWDP, having first gone through a big proxy fight with

Nelson Peltz's Trian Partners, then a spin-off of its performance chemical division into the independent entity known as Chemours in late 2015, then a megamerger with chemical and plastics maker Dow, upon the completion of which they announced the breakup into three companies, now known as Dow (chemicals and plastics, once again), Corteva Agriscience (agricultural chemicals), and finally, DuPont (specialty chemicals and products).

We generally like the prospects for DowDuPont and all three of its new descendants who came into being in 2019. However, we simply cannot get a good enough grip on prospects, and won't have enough history, to select any one of—or all three—of these descendants. So, at least for the time being, we will "pinch hit" for DWDP with its previous spin-off, Chemours. We do think this company has good prospects itself, and it will give good exposure to a DuPont kind of company until we can evaluate the three new descendants for the 2021 list.

Spun off from DuPont in July 2015, performance chemical provider Chemours produces three primary lines of chemicals and materials:

- Titanium Technologies (48 percent of 2018 sales) produces a line of titanium dioxide ("TiO_2") chemicals, mostly white pigments, for the paint, paper, plastics, and other industries, many of which are marketed under the "Ti-Pure" brand.
- Fluoroproducts (44 percent) produces a large line of fluorocarbon products, some of the more well-known and popular varieties including Teflon resins and coatings, spray-can propellants, and a lengthy list of refrigerants, without which mechanical refrigeration and air-conditioning generally wouldn't work. If you use "Freon-" or "Opteon"-branded refrigerants when you get your car air-conditioner serviced, you're using a Chemours product, though if you use a different brand, it quite possibly could have a Chemours origin.
- Chemical Solutions (9 percent) produces a line of industrial chemicals, including, for you chem buffs, aniline and methylamine monomers, glycolic acid, and other specialty chemicals for semiconductor manufacturing; and for you gold bugs, sodium cyanide for gold and silver mining and extraction.

The company is an innovation leader in these markets and works with customers on developing applications for these materials and revising or refining them as suited for customer processes. About 64 percent of sales are overseas.

Financial Highlights, Fiscal Year 2018

Stronger pricing and modest volume increases helped both the top and bottom line for Chemours in 2016. Revenues rose 7.4 percent with roughly equal contributions across all segments, while net earnings rose a nicely Teflon-coated 33 percent. There were signs that TiO_2 volumes were slowing at the end of the year, and the rather strong dollar wasn't helping this export-fueled company. For 2019 a sales increase of 3–5 percent looks to be in order with a not-too-exciting 1–3 percent earnings increase. Don't get the cyanide out just yet, for we like 2020 prospects better with an 8–10 percent earnings increase on a 4–6 percent increase in revenue. The company has authorized $1 billion for share buybacks—significant for a firm with a market cap just north of $6 billion.

Reasons to Buy

The spin-off from DuPont gave this modestly sized company a chance to focus, spread its wings, and do what it does best: find customer solutions through chemistry for its large stable of manufacturing and mining end customers. After a slow start, they seem to have made good on this focus and have grown into much more than a commodity supplier of certain key industrial chemicals. They are market leaders both in TiO_2 and the very strategic fluorochemical business. From a valuation perspective, Chemours is hard to beat, with a price-to-earnings ratio just above 7.0 and a price-to-cash-flow ratio under 5 at the time of this writing; the market has hardly given them credit for value delivered to shareholders at present, let alone the future. If nothing else, Chemours is a safe and relevant parking place to sit awaiting the DowDuPont split.

Reasons for Caution

Even with the strong focus on applications engineering and with market leadership in many of their key lines, they are still a chemical company, subject to many of the economic burdens of a commodity supplier. Competition, price wars, and sharp up-and-down demand cycles can be plagues in this corner of the chemical industry as with most others; they lack the product breadth of DowDuPont to help play defense against these cycles.

SECTOR: Materials ❑ Beta coefficient: 2.00 ❑ 10-year compound earnings per-share growth: NM ❑ 10-year compound dividends per-share growth: NM

	2011	2012	2013	2014	2015	2016	2017	2018
Revenues (mil)	—	—	—	—	5,717	5,400	6,183	6,638
Net income (mil)	—	—	—	—	(74)	235	747	996
Earnings per share	—	—	—	—	(0.41)	1.29	3.91	5.45
Dividends per share	—	—	—	—	0.03	0.12	0.12	0.84
Cash flow per share	—	—	—	—	1.07	1.70	5.65	7.30
Price:　high	—	—	—	—	16.7	27.3	58.1	54.6
low	—	—	—	—	4.6	3.1	20.8	25.2

Website: www.chemours.com

GROWTH AND INCOME

Chevron Corporation

Ticker symbol: CVX (NYSE) ❑ Large Cap ❑ Value Line financial strength rating: A++ ❑ Current yield: 4.09% ❑ Dividend raises, past 10 years: 10

Company Profile

Over the past four years, Chevron has become a poster child for strong, stable, entrenched businesses in can't-lose industries suddenly rocked out of bed by changes beyond their control—namely the 70 percent drop in the price of its chief product, oil, in 2015 and its rather wide range of fluctuation since then. As a poster child, the company continues as an example of how to deal with marketplace volatility as the price of oil (and gas) continues to swing back and forth.

As with everyone else in the energy and most other commodity industries, the downturn forced tough decisions on cost cutting and "right-sizing," all while maintaining the course for investors. For the most part Chevron stayed the course by selling some assets, issuing debt, and pulling back capital expenditures. They maintained the dividend, and even increased it, albeit by one cent in 2016 and three cents in 2017 to keep their 30-year string of raises intact. A moderate improvement in oil prices to north of $70/barrel and a leaner, meaner cost structure brought the company into the black in 2017 and well beyond in 2018, though not back to the heady days of 2008–14. The dividend was raised 12 cents while earnings more than doubled.

Chevron is the world's third-largest publicly traded, integrated energy company based on oil-equivalent reserves and production. It is engaged in every aspect of the oil and gas industry, including exploration and production, refining, marketing and transportation, chemicals manufacturing and sales, and power generation.

Active in more than 180 countries, Chevron has reserves of about 11.7 billion barrels of oil equivalent (56 percent liquids, 44 percent gas), with a production rate of 1.7 million barrels of oil equivalent (flat from 2016 and 2017), and global refining output of more than 2.7 million barrels per day (also flat) and operates more than 10,000 retail outlets around the world. Oil-equivalent production is concentrated in the US (27 percent), Australia (15 percent), Asia excluding Thailand (13 percent), Thailand (8 percent), Nigeria (8 percent), Indonesia (5 percent), Canada and Bangladesh each 4 percent, and 16 percent other. For the most part, with minimal Middle East exposure, these locations are relatively low risk and high potential compared to many competitors' production holdings. Although it increased the overall exposure to the 2014–15 oil price swoon, Chevron is more concentrated in oil (less in gas) than some of its competitors. That said, it has stepped up its new shale developments, particularly in gas, while reducing development costs substantially. It has invested big in the relatively low-cost Permian Basin in west Texas and in liquefied natural gas (LNG) operations in Australia; these investments led to a 136 percent reserve replacement rate in 2018, one of the best in the industry.

Chevron also has active global downstream businesses in manufactured products including lubricants, specialty chemicals and additives, specialty refining units for aviation and maritime markets, and various logistics activities, including pipelines, shipping, and a global trading unit.

The company's global refining network comprises ten wholly owned and joint-venture facilities. Gasoline and diesel fuel are sold under three well-known consumer brands: Chevron in North America; Texaco in Latin America, Europe, and West Africa; and Caltex in Asia, the Middle East, and southern Africa.

Chevron is the number one jet fuel marketer in the US and third worldwide, marketing 500,000 barrels per day in 80 countries. The company's fuel and marine marketing business is a leading global supplier and marketer of fuels, lubricants, and coolants to the marine and power markets, also with about 500,000 barrels in sales per day.

The company's traditional emphasis in oil hurt the company as prices fell almost 70 percent in 2014–15, severely affecting the bottom line and causing a rare annual net loss in 2016. In 2017 a combination of cost and capital containment, more flexible spend, asset sales, and a return to $50 to

$60 per barrel oil brought the company back to a cash-flow positive state, after increasing borrowings considerably to cover the dip. That continued in 2018 until another dip into the low $50s. Chevron's strategy continues to be to go "lean and mean," to drive down costs and use scale and to rely on strength in downstream refining and marketing to stabilize the business. Chevron should easily break even at $50 oil and bring solid positive cash flow at $60 and $70 oil.

Financial Highlights, Fiscal Year 2018

FY2018 revenues rose 17 percent largely on higher oil and gas pricing. Net profit rose to a full $7.7 billion to $14.8 billion—a far cry from the half a billion loss in 2016. Lower oil prices (who knows what they will actually be!) are expected to dampen revenue growth to less than 2 percent in 2019, with net profits edging lower; in 2020 margins should recover slightly with more efficient production; earnings are projected in the $15 billion range on another 1–2 percent revenue rise. Dividend growth looks to return to a steady mid-single digits annual increase, while modest buybacks and debt reduction will also resume after a four-year hiatus.

Reasons to Buy

We are obviously betting on the long term: long-term strength and cash returns to investors. Chevron is a play on size, strength, and response to business adversity.

For exploration and production strength and geographic and technological diversity, few companies exceed Chevron's strengths. The 138 percent reserve replacement ratio (new finds versus depletion) is among the top in the industry. The company is in some of the best sectors and geographies in the business and has established a good brand and track record for discovery, production, and downstream operations. We like the diversification into refining, which generally benefits from lower input prices. Long term, the company has a solid record and emphasis on cash generation and distribution. We think shareholders will be well rewarded with growing cash returns in the long run—especially as energy prices normalize even to the diminished $60 level. We continue to think CVX is among the best in a difficult industry.

Reasons for Caution

Of course, recent energy price shifts continue to put a dent in CVX's universe. The price shifts have been an opportunity for some of the wiser—and more cash rich—players such as Chevron to streamline operations and to acquire productive assets more cheaply. The biggest long-term negative is an almost doubling of long-term debt to $35 billion to keep the home fires burning; while that debt has already been trimmed to $30 billion it still remains large. This business may never return to its previous glory, but it is still a safe play and likely winner in today's leaner circumstances—and what's wrong with $15 billion in profit, anyhow?

SECTOR: Energy ❑ Beta coefficient: 1.20 ❑ 10-year compound earnings per-share growth: -12.5% ❑ 10-year compound dividends per-share growth: 8.0%

	2011	2012	2013	2014	2015	2016	2017	2018
Revenues (bil)	253.7	241.9	228.8	212.0	138.4	114.5	141.7	166.3
Net income (bil)	26.9	26.2	21.4	8.9	4.6	(0.5)	7.2	14.8
Earnings per share	13.44	13.32	11.09	10.14	2.45	(0.27)	3.79	7.74
Dividends per share	3.09	3.51	3.90	4.21	4.28	4.29	4.32	4.48
Cash flow per share	19.98	20.05	18.61	19.17	13.70	10.05	13.90	18.00
Price: high	111.0	118.5	127.8	135.1	113.0	119.0	126.2	133.9
low	102.1	95.7	108.7	100.1	69.6	75.3	102.6	100.2

Website: www.chevron.com

CONSERVATIVE GROWTH

The Coca-Cola Company

Ticker symbol: KO (NYSE) ❑ Large Cap ❑ Value Line financial strength rating: A++ ❑ Current yield: 3.4% ❑ Dividend raises, past 10 years: 10

Company Profile

The Coca-Cola Company is the world's largest beverage company. For more than 100 years, the company has mainly produced concentrates and syrups, which it then bottles or cans itself or sells to independent bottlers worldwide. Then in 2010 it took a big step to "own" the supply chain with the acquisition of bottler Coca-Cola Enterprises' North American operations; CCE still handles distribution for Europe. Independent bottlers add water (still or carbonated, depending on the product), sugar, and other (often local) ingredients, then bottle and distribute the products to restaurants, retailers, and other distributors. Now it has largely completed another big step—"refranchising"—selling many of these bottlers off to generate cash, to focus on the core businesses, and to dramatically increase profitability. And what are the "core businesses"? Well, in today's more nutrition-conscious, health-conscious world, it reaches way beyond the traditional carbonated soda beverage. The company strives, in its own words, to "evolve as a total beverage company." Yesterday's staid Coke is changing, and for the most part, we applaud the changes.

Coke operates in more than 200 countries and markets nearly 500 brands of concentrate and finished beverages, which are bottled into more than 3,900 different branded products, including Coca-Cola; 21 of those brands bring in over $1 billion annually—a figure that has doubled since 2007. The numbers are staggering: Coke ships over 29 billion cases annually, which works out to 637 billion servings sold per year, 1.9 billion beverages consumed per day—or 21,990 servings per second. Currently it is all processed through 250 bottling partners operating 900 plants moving product through 24 million retail outlets.

As a breakdown of revenue, 64 percent of all sales are overseas—16 percent in Latin America; 29 percent in Europe, the Middle East, and Africa; and 19 percent in the Pacific.

The product line continues to adjust to today's health-conscious, often millennial consumer. New acquisitions and product development have followed a multipoint strategy: (1) leveraging the power of winning brands (the popular smaller 7.5-ounce cans, multiple flavorings for Diet Coke); (2) creating premium experiences (Schweppes 1783 premium flavored tonic mixers); and (3) pursuing on-trend nutrition (AdeS soy-based beverages, smoothies and smoothie-based beverages, vitamin waters). The company has also invested in Monster Beverage and others. In 2018 the company made a large entry into the coffee business with the acquisition of UK coffee shop operator Costa, which operates in 30 countries. Some 19 of their 21 billion-dollar brands have low- or no-calorie alternatives. The new Freestyle machine found in a growing number of fast-food restaurants allows drinkers to customize their drinks. It's fun, and remember—customization is one of today's biggies. The 7.5-ounce "mini-can" has been around for a while, but is very popular among those just looking for a quick refresher or trying to control portions and calories (and it sells for about the same amount as a full-sized can). And how could we not like the new "Smoobucha" line of blended smoothie and kombucha drinks within the Odwalla line—what a trendy product, what a catchy name! And, finally, something we've all awaited: a return to the original Coke bottle shape and format in some markets.

Coke organizes its businesses into the following clusters:

- Sparkling soft drinks: Coke, Sprite, Coke Zero, Diet Coke, Fanta, Schweppes, etc.
- Water, enhanced water, and sports drinks: DASANI, smartwater, vitaminwater, Glacéau, Aquarius, Powerade, Burn, Monster (through 15 percent ownership stake)
- Juice, dairy, and plant-based beverages: AdeS, Del Valle, Minute Maid, Odwalla, Simply (as in Simply Orange), ZICO
- Tea and coffee: Costa, FUZE Tea, Gold Peak, Ayataka, Honest Tea

Notably, while the company didn't disclose percentages of revenue for these clusters, the three non–soft drink clusters in total come pretty close to 50 percent of Coke's revenue; that is, the "nonbubbly" business is almost as big as the bubbly one.

The point is simple: Coke is diversifying into a comprehensive ready-to-drink beverage provider.

As mentioned previously, the company has almost finished the process of spinning off the US distribution channel (bottlers). The resulting Coca-Cola is leaner, meaner, and more profitable; the company took a 10 percent hit in revenues in 2018 but managed to grow net income as we'll see in the next section.

Financial Highlights, Fiscal Year 2018

As mentioned, it is hard to look at Coke over time as the structural changes of refranchising have disrupted the view of financial history. In addition to the revenue and operating income figures mentioned, operating margins have increased a full 7.6 percent and tangible and intangible assets have dropped by a third. So—for all intents—just as much profit on far less revenue and a smaller asset base. As for the "core" business, revenues were largely flat (no pun intended) as modest improvements in price and product/package mix were offset by higher freight costs (mainly in the US) and inflation (mainly in Latin America) and a 1 percent currency headwind. While total revenues dropped 10 percent including the divestitures, net income rose about 8.4 percent on higher margins and lower taxes. For 2019, growth in noncarbonated and certain carbonated beverages and the Costa acquisition will drive revenues forward 8–9 percent (4 percent organic) with earnings rising a more modest 1–2 percent; in 2020 Coke projects a more fizzy 8–10 percent earnings rise on a 3–5 percent pickup in revenue. Cash returns to investors continue to be decent on both the buyback and dividend front.

Reasons to Buy

The well-conceived de-franchising strategy is icing on the cake for this already hugely profitable corporation. Who, besides Apple, makes 27 percent net profit margins? Coke does with this move.

While the traditional fizzy drink business is becoming a bit passé in today's world, Coke is adapting to the change and in our view, continues to be solid. The company has category leadership, especially globally, in soft drinks, juices and juice drinks, and ready-to-drink coffees and teas. They're number two globally in sports and energy drinks, water, and ready-to-drink teas.

The Coca-Cola name is probably the most recognized brand in the world and is almost beyond valuation. Indeed, Mr. Buffett once uttered the classic line about its brand strength and intangibles: "If you gave me $100 billion and said, 'Take away the soft drink leadership of Coca-Cola in the world,' I'd give it back to you and say it can't be done."

That's all pretty old news now; what's important is that Coca-Cola has also shown us, in today's world, that it isn't just going to sit around and go flat while we investors sit around and cry in our beer (wait, kombucha). We see signs that the company "gets it" and will not only adapt but will eventually have a chance to remain the number one brand even with a full new mix of beverages and packages for the modern world. Coca-Cola has traditionally been a steady defensive stock and offers a solid dividend with a constant track record of dividend growth. The company boasts—quite rightly—about having raised dividends in each of the past 56 years. It is also fairly pure play on international business.

Reasons for Caution

Coca-Cola is under our constant scrutiny for relevance in today's increasingly millennial-dominated market. Sales of traditional sparkling beverages in established markets—the US and Europe, and now Latin America—are in a slow decline due to interest in health and reducing obesity. But Smoobucha berry and ginger has promise, to be sure.

For the future, these market changes could provide some speed bumps. One wonders how the Coke culture will resonate with today's millennial beverage requirements—less sugar, fewer artificial ingredients, more customization and transparency—and one wonders further whether the new-age consumer will adapt well to healthy or fun drinks sold by Coca-Cola. Therein lies the 64-ounce question: Can they deliver change? Fast enough? Can they get the message out? In time to make a difference as traditional sugary beverages decline? Right now, our bet is still "yes."

Overall, this is a slow, steady growth story, which may be too slow for many, with new risks the company didn't face when Mr. Buffett bought his 400 million shares years ago.

SECTOR: Consumer Discretionary ❑ Beta coefficient: 0.70 ❑ 10-year compound earnings per-share growth: 4.0% ❑ 10-year compound dividends per-share growth: 8.0%

	2011	2012	2013	2014	2015	2016	2017	2018
Revenues (mil)	46,554	48,017	46,854	45,998	44,294	41,863	35,410	31,856
Net income (mil)	8,932	9,019	9,374	9,091	8,797	8,354	8,340	8,935
Earnings per share	1.92	1.97	2.08	2.04	2.00	1.91	1.91	2.08
Dividends per share	0.94	1.02	1.12	1.22	1.32	1.40	1.43	1.56
Cash flow per share	2.41	2.46	2.58	2.53	2.49	2.37	2.23	2.35
Price: high	35.9	40.7	43.4	45.0	43.9	47.1	47.5	50.8
low	30.6	33.3	36.5	36.9	36.6	39.9	40.2	41.4

Website: www.coca-colacompany.com

AGGRESSIVE GROWTH

Columbia Sportswear Company

Ticker symbol: COLM (NASDAQ) ❑ Mid Cap ❑ Value Line financial strength rating: B++ ❑ Current yield: 1.0% ❑ Dividend raises, past 10 years: 10

Company Profile

We like to read corporate histories. Especially when complete and well written, they provide not only the facts about what happened when along the way, they also offer a lot of insight into the purpose, culture, citizenship, customer sensitivity—and yes, maturity—of an organization. Such is the case with clothing maker Columbia Sportswear, one of our favorites:

"Born and raised in Portland, Oregon, Columbia Sportswear Company has been making gear so that Pacific Northwesterners can enjoy the outdoors for more than 70 years. At the helm for over 40 years has been our Chairman, Gert Boyle. Her Tough Mother persona has grown Columbia into the global sportswear company that it is today—still based in Portland, still making no-nonsense apparel and footwear to keep you WARM, DRY, COOL and PROTECTED no matter what. Our unique Pacific

Northwest heritage and Boyle family irreverence is what sets us apart from the competition."

Typically we don't lift content verbatim from such corporate writings. But this one not only describes Columbia's colorful past; it also quite aptly describes what the company has become today. As described—and still led by the 95-year-old Ms. Boyle (Chairperson of the Board) and her 69-year-old son Timothy (President and COO)—Columbia makes a line of practical, functional, and tastefully styled active wear that is increasingly used in nonactive situations. Most of you have seen a Columbia vest or jacket or two on the streets or in the woods during your daily travels. Rainwear is a specialty—given its Portland roots—but the company makes and distributes high-quality, conservatively designed shirts, pants, hoodies and fleece wear, tops and bottoms for women, shoes, and accessories, among other products. The clothing and shoes are designed for outdoor wear and for skiing/snowboarding and other rugged activities, but they are casual enough and of high-enough quality to fit in well for Casual Friday at work and casual anything outside of work; you won't get turned away at your favorite nice restaurant if you show up wearing Columbia. You probably won't notice Columbia—until you notice it. It's all about one of our favorite themes: "elegant simplicity."

Apparel, accessories, and equipment accounted for about 78 percent of 2018 sales, with footwear making up the rest. The company has expanded its own direct-to-consumer channel through Columbia-branded stores and through its website. US distribution is a mixed wholesale and direct model, with 3,300 wholesale customers on the wholesale side; the DTC (direct-to-consumer) side added 8 stores to reach 113 outlet retail stores, 23 branded retail stores, and 4 brand-specific e-commerce sites (see following for some of the specialty brands). DTC accounted for 42.5 percent of 2018 sales, a gain of 22 percent over 2017. About 38 percent of sales are outside the US, with Asia-Pacific and Latin America accounting for about half of that. Through a joint venture, the company has 86 retail locations and an online sales presence in China. All apparel and footwear are manufactured by contract manufacturers to spec; the company operates no manufacturing facilities.

Columbia has also expanded into more specialty lines, such as yoga clothing. Columbia also owns and distributes Mountain Hardwear, a respected climbing-inspired line of high-end performance outerwear, and other "lifestyle" brands including SOREL (women's wear), prAna ("stylish, sustainable active wear"), and Montrail (high-performance running footwear). SOREL is the largest subbrand, accounting for about 9 percent of

2017 revenues; the others account for less than 5 percent each. The Colum-bia brand itself accounts for just over 81 percent of revenues.

On the innovation front, a new performance technology called "OutDry Extreme," including jackets made from 21 recycled plastic bottles, has received excellent reviews in the rainwear category, and the technology has been extended to gloves and footwear. A new line of performance fishing wear has also recently come to market. Comfort is a major theme; "Clothing that feels as good as it looks" is one of their mottos.

Financial Highlights, Fiscal Year 2018

Columbia had a very good FY2018. Sales rose 14 percent with the Columbia brand, SOREL and DTC sales leading the way. Strong execution across the brands, increased DTC sales, an accounting change, and lower tax rates all drove net margins a full percentage point higher, a big deal in the low-margined cloth-ing industry (Columbia's 10 percent net margins are excellent for the industry), and drove a 28 percent rise in net income. Going forward, international strength, operational improvements, and greater emphasis on direct channels should pro-duce earnings gains in the 10–15 percent range annually on sales gains in the 6–8 percent range. Dividends have been ascending to the summit slowly but surely, while share buybacks have stopped for the moment at the side of the trail.

Reasons to Buy

Four years ago we looked for a company to replace the stumbling Ralph Lauren on our *100 Best* list, and we found it in Columbia Sportswear. The brand has slowly but surely expanded its international reputation for func-tionality, performance, good design, quality, and value. It has the conserva-tive, enduring qualities of Ralph Lauren products without being showy or pretentious; its understated elegance has resonated with millennials much better than Ralph, and its appeal is much wider than just millennials. Go out on a rainy day (or any other) and see what people are wearing.

As the brand has solidified and gone global, the company has woken up from the financial doldrums too. Sales, margins, and profits are all on a decent uptrend in a tough retail market as the products become more stan-dard and are distributed more widely in varying retail channels including direct (you must no longer trek to REI to buy Columbia).

Reasons for Caution

The clothing business is by nature notoriously cyclical and trendy, and we don't pretend to be able to follow these trends, let alone pick the companies that will ride ahead of them. That's why we like Columbia—it is trendy because it isn't trendy. That said, even this strength can fall on its ear as it has with Ralph Lauren, Eddie Bauer, and many of its brethren. (We think those two names experienced other problems, namely Ralph's hoity-toity snob appeal and Eddie's poor quality, which Columbia may not experience if it stays on track.) Competition from the likes of Patagonia and Marmot is also substantial, but neither produces as complete a line nor has achieved as wide a distribution as Columbia. Oh, and about distribution—channel partners can be fickle too—or even go bankrupt as Sports Authority did two years ago. We hope they don't reach too far down market to boost volumes; as any mountain climber knows, it's easy to "fall" in this industry and hard to recover.

SECTOR: **Consumer Staples** ❑ **Beta coefficient: 1.10** ❑ **10-year compound earnings per-share growth: 6.0%** ❑ **10-year compound dividends per-share growth: 13.0%**

	2011	2012	2013	2014	2015	2016	2017	2018
Revenues (mil)	1,694	1,670	1,685	2,100	2,326	2,377	2,466	2,802
Net income (mil)	103	100	94	137	174	192	210	268
Earnings per share	1.52	1.47	1.37	1.94	2.45	2.72	2.98	3.81
Dividends per share	0.43	0.44	0.46	0.57	0.62	0.69	0.73	0.90
Cash flow per share	2.19	2.07	1.95	2.74	3.33	3.61	3.86	4.78
Price: high	35.3	29.2	39.7	45.9	74.7	63.6	72.5	95.7
low	20.6	21.6	23.9	34.3	41.1	43.6	51.6	70.4

Website: www.columbia.com

CONSERVATIVE GROWTH

Comcast Corporation

Ticker symbol: CMCSA (NASDAQ) ❑ Large Cap ❑ Value Line financial strength rating: A ❑ Current yield: 2.2% ❑ Dividend raises, past 10 years: 10

Company Profile

Comcast is one of the nation's leading providers of communications services and information and entertainment content passed through those services. The company is now organized into six businesses: Cable Communications, Cable Networks, Broadcast Television, Filmed Entertainment, Theme Parks, and now SKY, acquired in late 2018, a major European entertainment network, Internet, and phone service provider based in the UK.

- The Cable Communications core business is Comcast Cable, the familiar cable TV delivery network that has evolved into a conduit for delivering bundled "Xfinity X1" high-speed Internet services, phone services, scheduled TV, studio shows and movies, on-demand content, and home security and automation services. This business serves some 30.3 million video subscribers (28 million residential, 2.3 million business customers) and 25.1 million Internet subscribers in 39 states. As described in the following, this segment is the largest at 58 percent of total revenues.
- Cable Networks is an assortment of content properties delivered primarily through cable (not just Comcast Cable) and includes regional sports networks such as Comcast Sports Network Bay Area and national channels such as MSNBC, CNBC, Syfy, Bravo, Oxygen, the Golf Channel, and E! (an entertainment channel) as well as Fandango (a moviegoer's website) and others. Most of the channels just listed have penetrated at least 70 million households.
- The Broadcast Television business is centered on NBCUniversal, which includes the familiar NBC broadcast network, which broadcasts through some 200 affiliated television stations across the US. Included are 11 owned television stations, NBC studios, and also Telemundo and NBC Universo, all acquired in 2013.
- Filmed Entertainment includes Universal Pictures, DreamWorks Animation (acquired in 2016), Focus Features, and Illumination brands of feature-length films and other entertainment. The Theme Parks business includes Universal theme parks in Hollywood, Orlando, and Osaka, Japan. These parks host permanent and periodic attractions, including a new Jurassic World attraction in Hollywood and a Harry Potter–themed roller coaster in Orlando.
- SKY operates in four of the five largest pay television markets in Europe: UK, Germany, Italy, and Spain; the majority of its revenues come from the direct-to-consumer video business, which has 23.6 million customers. It also provides high-speed Internet and phone (wireless and wired) service bundles.
- Finally, "other" business interests include ownership of the Philadelphia Flyers hockey team and the Wells Fargo Center arena in Philadelphia.

With these businesses, Comcast has become one of the largest integrated content development and distribution businesses in the US.

Comcast places a lot of emphasis on connectivity and penetration in its customer base. In 2018, they estimated a total opportunity ("homes and businesses passed") of 57.2 million locations; that is, 57.2 million locations they could serve with currently installed cable lines. Out of that opportunity, they estimate 30.3 million video subscribers (53 percent penetration), 25.1 high-speed Internet subscribers (44 percent), and 11.6 million voice telephone subscribers (20 percent). There are now 2.3 million business subscribers for high-speed Internet, a recent focal area. The company also emphasizes selling multiple products (i.e., cable TV and Internet), much of it through its bundled "Xfinity X1" bundled brand, and estimates about 20 million multiple product customers, or about two-thirds of all subscribers in the US. The SKY acquisition doubles the company's pay TV base.

For management purposes, Comcast breaks down its business into two major segments: Cable Communications and NBCUniversal:

- Cable Communications (58 percent of total revenues and 70 percent of operating income) houses the "delivery" business, including video, high-speed Internet, and voice services (collectively, "cable services") and the Xfinity bundle.
- NBCUniversal (38 percent of revenues, 30 percent of income) houses the content creation and entertainment businesses, including Cable Networks—12 percent of total revenues, Broadcast Television (11 percent), Filmed Entertainment (9 percent), and Theme Parks (7 percent).

Not surprisingly, the Comcast network has long been built on acquisitions, starting with the cable network and continuing more dramatically with the acquisition of NBC, Universal, and DreamWorks properties. SKY, acquired for $30.5 billion, is the largest recent acquisition, and the company is fighting "cord cutters" by launching a new "free" streaming service to its existing customers. Content you want, when and where you want it.

Financial Highlights, Fiscal Year 2018

Strength across all businesses resulted in a roughly 7 percent revenue increase from its core businesses, augmented by another 5 percent from SKY, giving a roughly 12 percent overall increase. NBCUniversal, Broadcast Networks, and Cable Networks turned in revenue increases of 8.9, 19.6, and 12.2 percent while Cable Communications was relatively flatter at 3.9 percent. Earnings rose 20 percent including a good share from SKY.

A 120 million share buyback helped drive per-share earnings up over 24 percent. For 2019 revenues "sky" higher mainly on SKY, up 18–20 percent for the year, while earnings should rise in the 6–8 percent range. FY2020 forecasts call for a 10–12 percent earnings advance on a more moderate 5–6 percent top-line growth.

Reasons to Buy

The addition of Comcast to the 2013 *100 Best* list was one we debated out of concern about cable companies in general. However, it continues to pay off handsomely; the shares have tripled since our decision as Comcast has evolved into a media, not just a cable, company. We like the company's strategic and operational focus—the acquisitions make sense, and the metrics they present truly describe what's important in the business—not just size and volume but also making customer relationships better and more profitable. The different pieces of the company fit together well.

As regular watchers of CNBC, MSNBC, Comcast Sports, and others, and admirers of the DreamWorks and other film platforms, we like the content assortment—it may not be the biggest, but it is one of the best content franchises. As cable cords are cut, we expect content to become a bigger part of the business than the 40 percent it brings today. Comcast (and its competitors) are becoming a larger version of what the big three television networks once were. They own not only the content development and marketing but also the content delivery infrastructure, giving them a step up on most other content providers. There are no franchises or distributors to deal with, and they are free to develop independent content and compete with their own live and streamed content as they see fit. This is an extremely dynamic market model, and Comcast holds a leadership position. AT&T, once again a *100 Best* stock, seems to be pursuing the same path—content (Time Warner) plus delivery (through wireless and DirecTV).

Reasons for Caution

Although Comcast is certainly big enough to survive on its own, the trend toward industry consolidation brings the usual risks associated with acquisitions. Competition has heated up, both from AT&T and other "traditional" providers and from Internet-only services like Hulu, Netflix, and Roku. "Cord cutting" (going Internet-only) is gathering steam, but Comcast's content stable and competing streaming services release some of the pressure.

SECTOR: Telecommunications Services □ Beta coefficient: 0.85 □ 10-year compound earnings per-share growth: 19.5% □ 10-year compound dividends per-share growth: 19.5%

		2011	2012	2013	2014	2015	2016	2017	2018
Revenues (mil)		55,842	62,570	64,657	68,775	74,510	80,403	84,526	94,507
Net income (mil)		4,377	6,203	6,816	8,380	8,171	8,485	9,850	11,017
Earnings per share		0.79	1.14	1.28	1.47	1.63	1.74	2.06	2.55
Dividends per share		0.23	0.33	0.39	0.45	0.50	0.55	0.61	0.76
Cash flow per share		2.22	2.68	2.83	3.24	3.45	3.80	4.33	5.05
Price:	high	13.6	19.2	26.0	29.7	32.5	35.7	42.2	44.0
	low	9.6	12.1	18.6	23.9	25.0	26.2	34.1	30.4

Website: www.comcast.com

GROWTH AND INCOME

NEW FOR 2020

Compass Diversified Holdings, LLC

Ticker symbol: CODI (NYSE) □ Small Cap □ Value Line financial strength rating: B □ Current yield: 9.8% □ Dividend raises, past 10 years: 3

Company Profile

For years, you've been reading about Warren Buffett and his enormously successful holding company Berkshire Hathaway. You want to get on that bandwagon. Is it rocket science, investing other people's capital in solid, simple upfront businesses you've probably never heard of to produce decent, modestly growing returns, year after year? Like Gorshams? See's Candies? RC Willey? We wouldn't call it rocket science, but we don't have the capital in our bank accounts to do it on our own, either (despite what you might think as we are authors of this book!).

So how can we play this game? We can buy mutual funds or exchange-traded funds, but they simply buy shares of big, big companies, not whole smaller companies. And they might hold on to these shares forever, for better or for worse.

What we're really talking about here is "private equity"—equity capital collected from individuals to go out and buy a company—or a group of companies. Private equity is, well, private in most cases, but there are situations where you can put some private equity of your own into a fund and have it invested by professional managers into—well—a group of companies you've never heard of. These companies are usually bought and held for a time, until they get big enough and successful enough to be sold off at a profit after being managed at arm's length during the holding period. As an owner and investor, you collect income from the companies while under ownership, then collect again (hopefully) when they are sold.

We looked at one of the biggest financial firms out there that does this sort of thing, called Blackstone Group (NYSE:BX). Blackstone has several divisions—one that buys and sells companies; one that buys, manages, and sells real estate; one that runs hedge funds; one that runs senior debt and mezzanine funds—hold it, stop right there! What's a mezzanine fund? A little financial engineering? Not for our appetites. When we got to the 430-page 10-K annual report, we knew we'd never understand this company well enough to present it to you.

So we looked for something smaller and simpler, and *voila*, we stumbled upon Compass Diversified. Compass specializes in "middle market" investments in manufacturing, distribution, and consumer products, normally valued between $100 and $500 million, with cash flows between $10 million and $450 million. It will buy a company, develop it or even seek bolt-on acquisitions for it, and sell it up to five years later in most cases.

As of this writing, Compass owns eight companies:

- Sterno Group (22.5 percent of 2018 revenues, 22.4 percent of operating income): Yes, makers of the familiar Sterno portable food warming and creative table lighting products for the food service industry. In 2016 Compass "bolted on" Northern International, a maker of flameless candles, and in 2018, Rimports, a maker of wax cubes and warmer products for home decor and fragrance systems.
- 5.11 (20.6 percent, -10.5 percent): This company designs, makes, and sells purpose-built tactical apparel and gear for law enforcement, EMS, military special ops, and adventure enthusiasts; once a part of the apparel company Royal Robbins.
- Ergobaby (5.4 percent, 9.4 percent): This company offers a broad range of award-winning premium baby carriers, strollers, car seats, nursing pillows, swaddlers, and other "baby handling" equipment.
- Foam Fabricators (6.7 percent, NA): The company makes custom-molded protective packaging foam solutions for a variety of end markets such as appliances and electronics.

- Velocity Outdoor (7.8 percent, 4.0 percent): This is a leading designer, manufacturer, and marketer of air guns, archery products, laser aiming devices, and related accessories; the Crosman brand is one of theirs.
- Advanced Circuits (5.5 percent, 21.5 percent): The company provides small-run, quick-turn, and volume-produced rigid printed circuit boards for small product runs or prototype products.
- Liberty Safe (4.9 percent): It makes and markets a line of office and gun safes.
- Arnold Magnetic Technologies (7.0 percent, 6.1 percent): The company makes specialty magnets and rare earth magnets for an assortment of industries.

Compass just sold Manitoba Harvest, a Canadian cannabis subsidiary, to Canadian cannabis leader Tilray, for a combination of cash and Tilray stock, which will likely be used to make another investment and/or retire debt. As of this writing, Compass owners realized a gain of $110 million plus retain ownership of some of the Tilray stock, an enticing combination if you're into that sort of thing. They also sold environmental cleanup specialist Clean Earth for a $215 million gain in mid-2019.

You get the idea: Compass incubates good, small businesses into larger ones for eventual sale in totally unrelated but profitable niche industries.

Finally, we should mention the management style and approach that Compass uses with these companies. We've all heard of aggressive, arrogant private equity managers swooping in, disrupting the business, firing employees, wiping out cash resources, generally exploiting their newly colonized companies (if you haven't, read *Glass House* [Brian Alexander, Picador, 2018] about the denouement of the Anchor Hocking glassworks at the hands of private equity). Compass has a totally different style, which they go to great lengths to make public by publishing testimonies from each of their business leaders front and center on their website.

Financial Highlights, Fiscal Year 2018

Compass puts more emphasis on managing and reporting results from each of its businesses than on reporting the whole, which makes for interesting reading but is too broad to go into here. For FY2018 total revenues advanced 33.2 percent, much of that due to the acquisition of Foam Fabricators and the Rimports subsidiary of Sterno, and to a lesser extent the acquisition of Velocity Outdoor. Notable sales gains occurred in Clean

Earth, Arnold, and Sterno, while Liberty and Ergobaby reported modest declines. Gross profit declined from 35.3 percent to 33.9 percent, and the implementation of new accounting standards weighed in on the SG&A side leading to a $10 million reported loss. With new acquisitions fully on board, measures to reduce debt, and back-office consolidation effects taking hold, the company projects a 6 percent sales increase but more importantly, a return to profitability with a $120 million profit for 2019 including the Manitoba divestiture and $70 million net profit for 2020, all while paying a steady $1.44 dividend each year, which management has declared a "top priority."

Reasons to Buy

Do you like to watch *Shark Tank*? We do, and we always dream of being Sharks ourselves, investing our precious capital in good, up-and-coming businesses. Compass gives you a chance to play the role of a Shark, albeit with less choice of what business you wish to invest in; that's already been decided for you. Compass's holdings are clean, simple, and apparently glad to be part of the Compass fold; the path to success seems fairly straightforward through developing existing businesses and acquiring (a few) more. Projections through the early decade look solid, as does the rich $1.44 dividend, well covered by cash flow.

Reasons for Caution

Since there are only eight companies, a hiccup in any one of these businesses can derail the gravy train. While these are good businesses and good brands, in most cases they lack the scale to handle large periods of adversity.

SECTOR: Financials ❑ Beta coefficient: 0.70 ❑ 10-year compound earnings per-share growth: NM ❑ 10-year compound dividends per-share growth: 7.5%

	2011	2012	2013	2014	2015	2016	2017	2018
Revenues (mil)	777	885	985	982	805	978	1,269	1,691
Net income (mil)	(32.1)	(2.5)	68.1	14.5	(3.6)	51.9	27.7	(7.0)
Earnings per share	(0.68)	(0.06)	1.05	0.62	(0.43)	0.46	(0.45)	(0.44)
Dividends per share	1.44	1.44	1.44	1.44	1.44	1.44	1.44	1.44
Cash flow per share	0.35	0.97	2.37	1.29	1.01	2.36	2.26	(1.65)
Price: high	18.6	15.7	19.8	19.8	17.5	19.5	18.4	18.3
low	11.2	12.1	14.8	15.4	9.7	13.6	15.9	11.6

Website: www.compasstrust.com

ConocoPhillips Company

Ticker symbol: COP (NYSE) ❑ Large Cap ❑ Value Line financial strength rating: B++ ❑ Current yield: 1.8% ❑ Dividend raises, past 10 years: 8

Company Profile

Like the rest of the industry, ConocoPhillips was hit hard by the 50–70 percent haircut in the price of their main products, namely, oil and gas four years ago. You won't typically find companies that lose money, especially two years in a row, on our *100 Best* list. But we hung on to this one, first of all, because we expected a cyclical recovery in the price of oil (which to an extent has happened) to cover about two-thirds of the dip. Second, and most importantly, we liked the different approach COP took, truly downsizing (or right-sizing) its business and retaining capital instead of borrowing to pay shareholders. COP did not—as many others did—borrow its way through the trough. Although they did cut their dividend substantially in 2016, as the smoke clears, we think COP will be a particularly solid bet on stabilizing and slightly rising energy prices.

Thanks to the 2012 spin-off of refiner Phillips 66, ConocoPhillips is now a pure play in the E&P (exploration and production) sector. Although lower oil and gas prices have turned ConocoPhillips from a $54 billion multinational E&P company into a $39 billion one of late (with the refining unit, it was once a $240 billion company), COP is still one of the world's largest E&P enterprises. Headquartered in Houston, Texas, the company operates in 16 countries (down from 30) with about 11,300 employees (down from over 19,000).

The company's E&P operations are geographically diverse, producing most of its resources in the US, including a large presence in Alaska's Prudhoe Bay. The company also has a large presence in US shale "fracking" regions, including Eagle Ford and Permian regions in Texas and the Bakken region in North Dakota. (Fracking was once "good"; then considered "bad" because of its relatively high cost. It's becoming "good" again as great strides in efficiency are lowering the breakeven cost.) As well, the company produces in western Canada, Australia, offshore Timor-Leste in the Timor Sea, Indonesia, Malaysia, Brunei, China, and Libya (but no longer Vietnam, Senegal, Nigeria, Algeria, or Russia). The top five producing regions in 2018, accounting for 75 percent of oil-equivalent production, are US Lower 48 (31 percent), Alaska (15 percent), Canada (6 percent), Asia Pacific and Middle East (mostly Australia and Indonesia; 30 percent), and Europe and North Africa (18 percent). The company just announced plans to focus on its domestic shale holdings in Eagle Ford and Delaware Basin in Texas and New Mexico and in the Bakken Shale in North Dakota and Montana, growing its production 25 percent in those regions, and funding this activity by divesting its North Sea operations. As such, US production should account for well over 50 percent of production by 2020.

Recently Conoco has been focusing on "shorter cycle," less capital-intensive projects, selling nonproducing gas assets, and has been slowing deepwater exploration and stepping up "unconventional" plays—shale—all to optimize the balance sheet and cash flow. The company sold about 7 percent of its producing assets in 2018.

Financial Highlights, Fiscal Year 2018

Sales, earnings, and per-share earnings finally escaped their three-year funk in 2015, with revenues rising some 33 percent on the back of higher oil prices and a 7.7 percent increase in production, and net profits finished the year eight times higher than 2017 and almost returning to 2014 levels. Strong cash flows and proceeds from asset sales have retired about $12 billion in debt. For 2019, revenues will take a 7.5 percent hit mostly reflecting asset sales, while earnings will drop 30–35 percent as the costs of new fields must be covered and oil prices moderate. In 2020, however, the benefits start to accrue in the form of a 12–15 percent rise in net earnings on a 10–12 percent growth in the top line. As these shale fields come into their own and as production gets more domestic, the company expects far better margins and for net income to roughly double on a 10 percent sales gain in the five years beyond 2020. In 2017, the average realized price for a barrel of crude oil equivalent was $51.96, 27 percent above the $40.86 received in 2016 but still well off pre-2015 levels. This plus a 4 percent production increase led to a 23 percent rise in revenues. Asset sales, many at less than book value, took a hit to reported earnings, which managed a modest positive figure for the first time in three years. Cash flows were healthy and ten times reported earnings, giving evidence to the fact that asset impairments were a big factor in reported earnings; the actual cash intake was fine. Continued energy price recovery and some production gains and asset purchases are expected to drive revenues 18–20 percent higher in 2018 and 8–10 percent higher again in 2019. Per-share earnings should recover dramatically into the $4 to $5 range by 2019 and well beyond that into the early part of the decade. Dividend increases, slow at first, will begin to chip away at the large 2016 cut but won't achieve those levels anytime soon, while the company appears to have used the 2015–16 slump adroitly to repurchase shares—some 5 percent of them—and will proceed with modest buybacks through 2019. The company also retired about $10 billion in debt, some incurred during the crisis, and now has 25 percent less debt than it had before the crisis started. Moderate dividend increases, share repurchases, and debt repayments look to continue as Conoco becomes more profitable in the wake of the 2015–17 disruptions.

Reasons to Buy

As CEO Ryan Lance put it recently, "ConocoPhillips has taken a leadership stance with a new approach to the E&P business, one designed to deliver predictable performance and superior returns across a wide range of commodity prices." The strategy of disposing assets, generating capital through asset sales and dividend cuts while still paying a constant percentage of cash flows to shareholders, reducing long-term debt, and making itself profitable at sub-$50 oil all seems to have paid off and is laying groundwork for a pretty strong future, with per-share earnings estimated north of $7 in a few years. For a company of Conoco's size, we think they're making the right moves.

We like the domestic slant on the production mix; it is lower cost and more stable than most. We don't have to add a measure of geopolitics into the long list of risk factors. Conoco is clearly focused on profitability rather than size, and that's a hard thing to find in the oil patch.

Reasons for Caution

The story of ConocoPhillips has been a story of change over the past five years. The company successfully divested the refining operations to gain focus—only to gain focus on the most volatile part of the business—which became far more volatile in 2015–17. E&P is risky by nature even with a steady oil price (although COP's domestically oriented portfolio reduces this risk); when you add in price volatility it makes for…well, a volatile mix. COP has taken its pain in stride, but the possibility of a continuing glut as more producers come on line with lower-cost production could keep the headwinds blowing.

SECTOR: Energy ❑ Beta coefficient: 1.45 ❑ 10-year compound earnings per-share growth: NM ❑ 10-year compound dividends per-share growth: 1.5%

	2011	2012	2013	2014	2015	2016	2017	2018
Revenues (bil)	244.8	62.0	54.4	52.5	30.7	23.7	29.1	38.7
Net income (bil)	12.1	7.4	8.0	6.2	(1.7)	(3.2)	0.7	6.3
Earnings per share	8.76	5.91	6.43	4.96	(1.39)	(2.52)	0.61	5.32
Dividends per share	2.64	2.64	2.70	2.84	2.94	1.00	1.06	1.16
Cash flow per share	15.63	11.47	12.57	11.79	5.97	4.77	6.44	10.73
Price: high	77.4	78.3	74.6	87.1	70.1	53.2	56.4	80.2
low	68.0	50.6	56.4	60.8	41.1	31.0	42.3	50.2

Website: www.conocophillips.com

AGGRESSIVE GROWTH

Corning Incorporated

Ticker symbol: GLW (NYSE) ❑ Large Cap ❑ Value Line financial strength rating: A ❑ Current yield: 2.3% ❑ Dividend raises, past 10 years: 8

Company Profile

When you think of Corning, you think of glass. The ticker symbol, in fact, reflects the company's name when it joined the NYSE—Glass Works. Although the company may have been best known for some time as a producer of common housewares such as drinking glasses and dinnerware (anyone remember Corelle?), Corning has long been at the cutting edge (ouch) of glass and ceramics research. In 1932 the company produced the enormous mirror for the Palomar Observatory's main telescope, a 102-inch behemoth that required a full year to cool once cast. Corning also developed and produces viewing glass for spacecraft and high-pressure submersibles. And, of course, the company's invention of high-transmissibility fiber-optic cable (and the production techniques required for efficient manufacturing) revolutionized modern telecommunications by providing high-speed, low-power data connections that were immune to electrical interference. Corning is well known today as the producer of Gorilla Glass, the optically clear, mechanically tough, and electrically conductive material that makes smartphones possible. First employed in the original iPhone, Gorilla Glass is now ubiquitous in the smartphone market.

Corning has historically grown organically via internally developed technologies and product development programs. The company continues to spend on R&D (7.1 percent of their top-line revenue last year), and you wouldn't go too far wrong in thinking of Corning as a materials science and research company with several "killer app" businesses that pay the rent, and then some.

Corning operates in five segments, nearly all centered on the glass business. Display Technologies (29 percent of 2018 sales) is the world's largest producer of glass substrates for liquid crystal displays (LCDs) in Japan, China, Taiwan, and South Korea for the television and computer markets. Optical Communications (37 percent) makes fiber-optic cable and an assortment of connectivity and other products related to fiber for telecommunications companies, LAN, and data center applications. Specialty Materials (13 percent) provides a wide assortment of high-tech, glass-based materials, including the well-known Corning Gorilla Glass, so named for its strength and endurance characteristics. This product is even gaining traction in automotive and architectural markets. Also out of this division comes a new bendable display substrate known as Willow Glass and a host of glass and ceramic products and formulations used in the semiconductor industry, precision instruments, and even astronomy and ophthalmology. The Environmental Technologies segment (11 percent) makes ceramic substrates and filters for emission control systems, mostly for gasoline and diesel engines. The Life Sciences segment (9 percent) makes laboratory glass and plastic wares. An "All Other" segment accounts for less than 1 percent.

The company competes with a number of suppliers, mostly Japanese, on a variety of fronts, and has teamed up with and in some cases acquired some of the smaller companies. Promising innovations include the adaptation of its "Willow Glass," thinner than a dollar bill, for ultrathin, ultrasensitive touchscreens to improve size and weight characteristics of mobile devices. Eventually this will evolve into bendable, curved, and curving glass displays, allowing us to literally wear our devices—an exciting prospect in which companies such as Apple, Samsung, and a host of others are investing heavily. Another go-to-market innovation is Valor Glass, a line of specialty glass packaging for sensitive pharmaceuticals. Acquisitions in 2018 include the optical communications business of 3M, which will give the company greater access to international markets especially.

Gorilla Glass continues to find new applications in architectural and automotive designs—such as the company's new "Dynamic Windows," architectural glass panels, which automatically darken, reducing energy consumption, and new lighter windshields, sunroofs, and other glass products for cars. "AutoGrade" glass, introduced in early 2019, applies Gorilla Glass technology to custom shapes and curvature for automotive displays, giving a durable, attractive, functional and potentially electronically active interface; the company has placed it into 58 automotive platforms so far.

Financial Highlights, Fiscal Year 2018

Corning's 2018 results were quite favorable on the revenue front and better than they look on the profitability front. Strength in all segments and particularly the Optical (helped by 3M acquisition) and the Environmental segment drove sales 11.6 percent higher, while some one-time charges related to acquisitions held net earnings back, operating earnings were higher in all segments except Display; per-share core earnings rose 11 percent. Helped along more by the 3M acquisition, 2019 earnings should rise some 60–70 percent above the diminished 2018 levels and 30–35 percent beyond 2017 levels on an 8–10 percent revenue gain; for 2020, earnings settle in for an 8–10 percent gain on a 5 percent top-line advance. Aggressive share buybacks have taken as much as 10 percent annually out of the share count and have reduced it some 44 percent since 2013—five years! The dividend has also doubled since 2015.

Reasons to Buy

It's always great when you develop a product that's accepted in the market as a standard. Even better is when your customers come to you directly and ask you to develop a product that meets their needs. It's so much easier to sell something to someone when they already want to buy it.

Corning seeks out these opportunities, and as a business model it works well. In fact, two of their mainstay products (Gorilla Glass and catalytic cores) were developed in close partnership with end customers in the smartphone business. Valor Glass, which was developed jointly with Merck and Pfizer, and AutoGrade products developed with and for the auto industry, are more contemporary examples.

As Corning puts it, we are now in the "Glass Age"—many promising new technologies are built on a foundation of high-tech glass products, and Corning is the best pure play in this niche. We like companies that stand to benefit no matter how a market plays out. Our CarMax pick benefits whether Ford or Toyota or Hyundai wins; CarMax sells used cars no matter what. At least for glass displays, Corning is in the same position—whether Samsung or Apple or LG wins the smartphone contest, Corning wins. The explosion in smart devices and the new technologies Corning is likely to bring to that space create some excitement down the road. We think the inevitable advent of wearable mobile computing devices will be a big spark for this company.

We expect some of the new technologies like Gorilla Glass and the self-darkening glass products to become core businesses. The advent of 5G wireless will create opportunities for new and clever implementations of fiber optics, and Corning will be at the center of it with their fiber and connector businesses.

Also worth noting is Corning's persistent return of cash to shareholders, both in the form of dividends and the share buybacks.

Reasons for Caution

While its product portfolio is broader than it was 20 years ago, when its customers were dominated by the telecom industry, Corning is still subject to business and inventory cycles. Glass, without the right amount of innovation, is a commodity business with plenty of foreign competition.

SECTOR: **Information Technology** ◻ Beta coefficient: **1.20** ◻ 10-year compound earnings per-share growth: **-1.0%** ◻ 10-year compound dividends per-share growth: **13.5%**

	2011	2012	2013	2014	2015	2016	2017	2018
Revenues (mil)	7,890	8,012	7,819	9,715	9,111	9,390	10,116	11,290
Net income (mil)	2,620	1,728	1,961	2,472	1,339	1,013	1,325	1,066
Earnings per share	1.76	1.15	1.34	1.73	1.00	0.98	1.48	1.13
Dividends per share	0.23	0.32	0.39	0.52	0.36	0.54	0.62	0.72
Cash flow per share	2.49	1.85	2.12	2.79	2.15	2.21	2.81	2.87
Price: high	23.4	14.6	18.1	23.5	25.2	25.3	32.8	36.6
low	11.5	10.6	11.6	16.5	15.4	16.1	24.1	26.1

Website: www.corning.com

AGGRESSIVE GROWTH

Costco Wholesale Corporation

Ticker symbol: COST (NASDAQ) ◻ Large Cap ◻ Value Line financial strength rating: A+ ◻ Current yield: 1.0% ◻ Dividend raises, past 10 years: 10

Company Profile

Costco Wholesale Corporation operates a multinational chain of membership warehouses, mainly under the Costco Wholesale name, that carry brand-name merchandise at substantially lower prices than are typically found at conventional wholesale or retail sources. The warehouse sales model was originally designed to help small- to medium-sized businesses reduce costs in purchasing for resale and for everyday business use, but as we all know, the stores have opened themselves up to the general public in a membership format, and the individual consumer has been their big growth driver. The company capitalizes on size, scale, and operational efficiencies, such as "cross-docking" shipments directly from manufacturers to stores, to deliver attractive pricing to its customers. Based on sales volume, Costco is the largest membership warehouse club chain and third-largest general retailer in the world.

Costco carries a broad line of product categories, including groceries, appliances, television and media, automotive supplies, toys, hardware, sporting goods, jewelry, cameras, books, housewares, apparel, health and beauty aids, tobacco, furniture, office supplies, and office equipment. Approximately 41 percent of sales come from packaged food, beverages, and "sundries"—snack foods, candy, alcohol, and cleaning supplies; 14 percent from "fresh food"; 16 percent from hardlines—electronics, appliances, hardware, automotive, office supplies, and health and beauty aids—and 11 percent from softlines—primarily clothing, housewares, media, jewelry, and domestics. The rest, including gasoline, pharmacy, optical, and other services, form a catchall "other" category. The emergence of Costco as a grocer of choice cannot be missed, with its appeal to the more cost-conscious set of trend-conscious food consumers.

Additionally, Costco Wholesale Industries, a division of the company, operates manufacturing businesses, including special food packaging, optical laboratories, hearing aid centers, and jewelry distribution. The company operates 567 discount gas stations worldwide. Ancillary businesses such as jewelry, optometry, gasoline, and others, of course, are designed to bring people into the stores. A wide and growing variety of products are sold under its Kirkland private label; at $35 billion in sales, the brand accounts for about 27 percent of the business.

Costco is open only to members of its tiered membership plan; the higher "Executive" tier at $120 annually (versus $60 for the standard membership), gains access to reward points and other perks and discounts. Executive members account for about one-third of the base and two-thirds of the sales. In all, there are 96.3 million members (up 6.6 percent), with a 90.7 percent membership renewal rate in the US and Canada (up 0.7 percent).

As of the end of 2018 Costco has 769 locations worldwide (up from 746 in 2017): 534 in the US and Puerto Rico (up from 518), 100 in Canada (versus 98), 39 in Mexico (versus 37), 28 in the UK (unchanged), 26 in Japan (unchanged), 15 in South Korea (13), 13 in Taiwan (unchanged), 10 in Australia (9), 2 in Spain (2), 1 in France, and 1 in Iceland. The company also has a significant and growing e-commerce presence at www.costco.com.

It still accounts for only 4 percent of revenues, and the company is experimenting with same-day delivery through its Costco Grocery service, which hasn't gained much traction to date but may do so as customers seek to avoid crowds at the stores. The point is that—even though the "flatbed" shopper isn't easily lured by e-commerce—the company is investing on future customer experiences.

Finally, Costco is adding more quality name brands to its stable: Sonos, Pendleton, Columbia, Marmot, Kate Somerville, Health-Ade Kombucha, and Isopure, among others, further establishing itself as the go-to suburban retailer.

Financial Highlights, Fiscal Year 2018

Despite a 53-week 2017 base year, same-store sales rose a hefty 9 percent in the US and Canada and 11 percent internationally, giving rise to a 10 percent overall revenue gain for 2018. Gains were noted both for shopping frequency and ticket size but were also positively impacted by gasoline prices. Gross margin slipped a bit from changes in the mix and a one-time legal settlement, but membership revenue increases, lower SG&A, and lower tax rates more than made up for that, ringing up a 22 percent gain in net income for the year. Revenue from membership fees, helped along by a 2017 mid-year price increase, rose 10 percent to $3.14 billion. Not coincidentally this practically matched the year's net income of $3.13 billion. New store openings combined with competitor Sam's Club closings, online sales growth, international expansion, and operational improvements are expected to load Costco's flatbed with 6–8 percent higher sales and 12–14 percent higher net profits in 2019, moderating to 5–7 percent top- and bottom-line gains in 2020. Healthy dividend increases (possibly including a special dividend) and share buybacks look to continue.

Reasons to Buy

Costco is in an attractive best-of-both-worlds niche: It is a price leader consistent with the attitudes of today's more frugal consumer, yet it enjoys a reputation for being more upscale than the competition. We've all heard the boast, "I got it at Costco" from even our most affluent and high-minded friends—and of course, there's everybody else.

We also continue to like the international expansion and think the formula will play well overseas—although their ambitious European and Asian plans may be tempered a bit by local preferences for small package sizes and the general lack of storage space. Any US resident who has hosted a visitor from abroad knows that Costco is a favored destination during the visit. We expect international expansion will be one of the company's primary growth drivers over the next ten years.

In all, Costco also gets high marks for employee pay, satisfaction, and loyalty, and for corporate citizenship in general. The company has a strong brand in a highly competitive sector relatively immune from the Amazon threat and is well managed.

Reasons for Caution

The major concern today is the emergence of e-commerce, although that threat has subsided somewhat as indicated by gains in sales ticket size. Can consumers defect? Will they? True, you can buy much of what you get at Costco online. But is it really more convenient to receive huge packages on your front doorstep than it is to simply make a once-a-week or once-a-month trip? Time will tell, but Costco has the advantage of ease, we think, when it comes to shopping for large quantities of basic, and not so basic, needs. Another concern is the dependence on low-margin food and sundry lines. That said, food does get customers into the store and gets them there more than once a week. More store traffic means more and more regular store sales overall.

We do fret over the high share price, low margins, and dependence on membership fees for profitability. All three bring a measure of vulnerability to the stock—a misstep could be costly. On the flip side, management has shown its ability to navigate through difficult periods, the brand is strong, and the prospects for a global footprint, above all else, are encouraging for the future. There are a lot of headwinds in today's retail space, but we think Costco is unique enough and strong enough to prosper.

SECTOR: Retail ❑ Beta coefficient: 0.85 ❑ 10-year compound earnings per-share growth: 9.0% ❑ 10-year compound dividends per-share growth: 13.5%

	2011	2012	2013	2014	2015	2016	2017	2018
Revenues (bil)	88.9	99.1	105.1	112.6	116.1	118.7	129.0	142.0
Net income (mil)	1,462	1,741	1,977	2,058	2,334	2,350	2,564	3,134
Earnings per share	3.30	3.97	4.49	4.65	5.27	5.33	5.82	7.09
Dividends per share	0.89	1.03	1.17	1.33	1.51	1.70	1.90	2.14
Cash flow per share	5.34	6.13	6.69	7.05	7.90	8.24	9.00	10.42
Price: high	88.7	106.0	126.1	146.8	169.7	169.6	195.4	245.2
low	69.5	78.8	98.6	109.5	117.0	138.5	150.0	175.8

Website: www.costco.com

Crown Castle International

Ticker symbol: CCI (NYSE) ❑ Large Cap ❑ Value Line financial strength rating: B+ ❑ Current yield: 3.8% ❑ Dividend raises, past 10 years: 4

Company Profile

"Life Connects" is the apt slogan of this medium-sized Real Estate Investment Trust (REIT) that owns, leases, and manages 40,000 cell towers in the US and Puerto Rico. Cell towers? Well, as real estate, that may not sound as sexy as the senior living or outpatient care facilities, state-of-the-art e-commerce logistics facilities, or even self-storage units or oil tanks as we have as REITs or REIT-like investments in other parts of our portfolio. Neither does it sound as sexy as the Empire State Building, which was the cornerstone of the REIT we dropped from the list in 2020 due to lackluster returns and to make room for this REIT, right?

Well, if you think about the times we're in, a REIT that specializes in cell towers and has a dense nationwide network of them, a REIT for which 73 percent of revenues come from AT&T, T-Mobile, Verizon, and Sprint, just might be sexier than it appears on the surface.

Why? Not just because of our growing and sometimes overwhelming dependence on smartphones. Not just because of our modern needs to be "tethered" at every waking moment (and now nonwaking moment) of our lives. What we see here is a cornerstone of a larger vision in which a large measure of basic Internet service—not just *mobile* Internet service—is delivered by 5G networks.

As the website reminds us: "We don't go online anymore. We exist there."

If you had a chance to buy the base roadbeds for the Interstate Highway System in 1955 before the 1956 enactment of its enabling Federal Aid Highway Act, you would have done quite well. Such do we think it is with buying and building the cell tower "roadbed" for today's and tomorrow's latest generation of Information Superhighway technologies. With Crown Castle, you have a chance to buy into the base roadbed for the next generation as well as thriving businesses utilizing current technologies. Crown Castle is the nation's largest provider of "shared communications infrastructure." It operates an infrastructure consisting of approximately 40,000 cell towers, 65,000 on-air or under-contract small cell nodes, and 70,000 route miles of fiber. Much of this infrastructure was assembled through the acquisition of sites and improvements from the very carriers (and their predecessors) who are now Crown's clients. Crown typically engages in long-term lease contracts with its tenants; currently the average remaining life of these agreement already in place is about five years and is expected to produce $22 billion in revenue. Site rental revenues by tenant: AT&T 22 percent, T-Mobile 19 percent, Verizon 18 percent, Sprint 14 percent, and all others combined, 27 percent.

Once a site is up and running, it is easy and relatively profitable to add new carriers or to help existing carriers expand capacity at that site; in fact that is one of the stated growth strategies of the REIT. As of the end of 2018, approximately 42 percent of towers had one tenant, 26 percent two tenants, 16 percent three tenants, 9 percent four tenants, 4 percent five tenants, and 3 percent six or greater, indicating both that this growth strategy was already well deployed but also that there is plenty of opportunity going forward.

About 56 percent of Crown's towers are located in the 50 largest US "basic trading areas" (BTAs) and 71 percent are located in the top 100. About 40 percent are located on "owned" land, the other 60 percent on leased or licensed property interests. When leased property interests are involved, the company typically signs long-term contracts for the use of those parcels; the average lease is 35 years.

The company was formed through the merger of Castle Tower, which was established in 1994, and Crown Communications, and went public in 1998. It was converted to a REIT in 2014, meaning that profits and losses flow through directly to investors without taxation at the corporate level, making individual tax planning a bit more difficult (if held outside of retirement accounts) but availing the owners to the new 20 percent deduction for "Section 199" flow-through income.

Financial Highlights, Fiscal Year 2018

FY2018 was a strong year, as growth in wireless networking requirements and the multiple-carrier growth strategy noted previously produced a 25 percent revenue gain and an adjusted funds from operations (AFFO) increase of 20 percent. Conservatively (we think) the company projects forward top-line growth for 2019 and 2020 in the 4–6 percent range, with per-share AFFO running ahead 6–8 percent in each of the two years. Dividend increases in the high single digits look likely, while Crown will likely issue some shares to offset debt expansion as they fund capacity expansion over time.

Reasons to Buy

Okay, we'll admit it—we are infrastructure geeks. We're fascinated by how all those electric transmission lines and water pipes and oil pipelines and oil refineries and rail lines and sewage treatment plants and aviation transponders work, and how they got there in the first place. We see the critical importance of such infrastructure, which most people rarely see (or look at) and tend to take for granted. And Crown Castle provides yet another key form of infrastructure—one that is hard to see (unless we're driving by one of those weird-looking blue spruce cell towers in the middle of a beech/maple forest). But we know that infrastructure's there, working 24/7 to provide something we need, now more than ever.

As cited in other narratives about companies that stand to win no matter who wins the day in the competitive battlefield—like CarMax in the auto industry (it doesn't matter if Toyota or Ford wins; CarMax will sell just as many used cars)—we like Crown Castle not just because of its growth opportunities and its key role in modern communications infrastructure, but because it stands to win no matter which way the winds blow among the major cell and data carriers. But the real win comes when you throw in the opportunity represented by 5G, the next generation of wireless service that has the potential to bring the Internet to all without cables, fiber, or any other infrastructure beyond transmission towers and electromagnetic spectrum; the possibilities for an infrastructure like Crown seem almost without limit.

Reasons for Caution

Technology can change. Who knows whether 5G will be the medium of the future? Maybe the whole network will be somehow superseded or bypassed by Earth-orbit satellites beaming some other technology? One never knows; when investing in new technology or new technology infrastructure, one must always be careful to embrace the fact that no technology prevails forever—as those like Google who invested to put entire cities on fiber cable can tell you by now. Another problem that no technology can fix is the relatively high price of Crown shares, most recently near 25 times AFFO; we tend to put companies on our list because they're good, not because they're cheap, and leave it to you to find the right moment to dial up a few shares.

SECTOR: Real Estate ❑ Beta coefficient: 0.75 ❑ 10-year compound earnings per-share growth: NM ❑ 10-year compound dividends per-share growth: NM

	2011	2012	2013	2014	2015	2016	2017	2018
Revenues (mil)	1,879	2,033	2,433	3,022	3,690	3,664	4,355	5,423
Net income (mil)	127.5	171.1	188.6	90.1	390.5	1,521.2	444.6	671.0
Earnings per share	0.37	0.52	0.64	0.26	1.04	4.42	1.01	1.34
Dividends per share	—	—	—	—	1.87	3.35	3.90	4.28
Cash flow per share	2.23	2.48	2.76	2.59	4.07	4.30	4.58	5.48
Price: high	46.3	72.3	81.2	85.0	89.4	102.8	115.0	117.6
low	36.4	44.6	66.1	68.4	75.8	75.7	84.0	98.9

Website: www.crowncastle.com

CONSERVATIVE GROWTH

CVS Health Corporation

Ticker symbol: CVS (NYSE) ❑ Large Cap ❑ Value Line financial strength rating: A++ ❑ Current yield: 3.6% ❑ Dividend raises, past 10 years: 9

Company Profile

Gulp! That might be the sound emanating from integrated healthcare services provider CVS Health, as they regain their footing after the $70 billion acquisition of health insurer Aetna in 2018. Yes, it was a big deal, and it signals more deals in the offing both for CVS as they round out their complete offering, and for others just to compete. And you thought this was just a drugstore chain. Well, it once was, not so terribly long ago.

Stanley and Sidney Goldstein were distributing health and beauty products in the early 1960s when they decided to branch out into retailing, opening their first Consumer Value Store in Lowell, Massachusetts, in 1963. The CVS chain had grown to 40 outlets by 1969, the year they sold the business to Melville Shoes. Melville underwent a restructuring in the mid-1990s, spinning off CVS and other retail units.

Stan and Sid should be proud. CVS is the largest pharmacy healthcare provider in the US—but it does so much more than distribute pharmaceuticals, greeting cards, and some basic groceries from its ubiquitous corner big-box drugstores. As it started to offer health services in its stores ("Minute Clinics," for example) four years ago, it changed its name from "CVS Caremark" to "CVS Health." The moniker still fits—quite well—after the Aetna acquisition. CVS's flagship Retail Pharmacy domestic drugstore chain operates 9,967 retail and specialty pharmacy stores and 1,134 walk-in healthcare clinics in 49 states, the District of Columbia, Puerto Rico, and Brazil. Over time, it has expanded through acquiring other players in the category—Osco, Sav-on, Eckerd, and Longs Drugs. CVS's purchase of Longs Drugs in 2008 vaulted the company into the lead position in the US drug retail market, ahead of Walgreens.

While pretty far evolved from the bucolic corner drugstore, with its "big-box convenience store" format, the 2007 acquisition of pharmacy benefits manager Caremark, the 2015 acquisition of 1,700 Target pharmacies and 80 health clinics, and the 2016 acquisition of nursing home pharmacy provider Omnicare, the company took its biggest step forward with the 2018 Aetna acquisition. This was a truly disruptive acquisition; the result would be a vertical combination of a payer (Aetna) and a provider (CVS core businesses) leading to a new level or at least a different kind of cooperation between these elements in the healthcare food chain. CVS maintains that the resulting healthcare landscape will be easier to use and less expensive in the long run; that it will transform healthcare. What remains to be seen is how well the vertical combination will work in practice—will insurance competitor UnitedHealthcare push business away from CVS because the latter owns archrival Aetna? Generally, we see good things coming out of the acquisition both for the company and the industry.

The company is organized into three major segments:

- Pharmacy Services (60 percent of 2018 revenues) provides a full range of pharmacy benefit management (PBM) services administering and distributing pharmaceutical products typically under contract to a payer (insurer) or a healthcare provider. Mail order, Medicare Part D, and specialty pharmacy and clinical services fall into this group. Customers include employers, insurance companies, unions, government employee groups, Medicaid managed care plans, and others.
- Retail/LTC (37 percent) operates the traditional drugstores with prescription and over-the-counter drugs, general merchandise, Minute Clinics (description following), and other store services. The company estimates this business to have a 26 percent share of the retail pharmacy market.
- Healthcare Benefits (3 percent), which mainly includes Aetna. Why only 3 percent? Was Aetna that big a deal? Yes—the deal was consummated on November 28, 2018, so it had only one month of sales. This segment will rise to the 30–40 percent range as a percentage of company business, while the other segments will decrease in proportion (not size, but proportion).

Part of the Retail Pharmacy segment, the company's Minute Clinic concept is especially interesting in today's climate of managing healthcare costs. CVS now has 1,134 clinics (including 80 new clinics in Target stores) in 33 states and DC, offering basic health services like flu shots given by 2,200 nurse practitioners and physician's assistants in a convenient retail environment. We see the Minute Clinic concept playing well with Aetna in a joint effort to reduce doctor visits and lower costs.

Financial Highlights, Fiscal Year 2018

FY2018, aside from the Aetna news, was another mixed year. Total revenues (excluding Aetna) rose 5.8 percent; the increase was largely driven by prescription volume and drug price inflation while generics and reimbursement pressure provided headwinds. Same-store retail sales (excluding pharma) advanced 0.5 percent. Net income rose some 22 percent after a poor year in 2017. FY2019 will be a transition year, although $60 billion in Aetna revenue will help gross revenues rise to something north of $250 billion with another 22 percent rise in net profit. Once things settle in 2020, the company expects net income growth in the 7–9 percent range on sales growth in the 2–4 percent range. Debt levels soared with the Aetna acquisition from $22 billion to $71 billion, while share counts rose some 30 percent to almost 1.3 billion. We expect the company to chip away on both fronts.

Reasons to Buy

Clearly the Aetna combination will change the CVS landscape as well as the whole healthcare sector. We expect it to work in CVS's favor, perhaps strongly, but it may take time. The ability to vertically integrate major pieces of the healthcare system to reduce costs and cut friction will be tested in the merger. Cost efficiencies and competitive advantages are the hopeful result; time will tell. Typically, we take companies going through major strategic shifts like this off the *100 Best* list until the dust settles, but in this case, we like the combination enough to stick with it; additionally, the uncertainty has driven the stock price down through much of the past three years, giving a good buying opportunity.

CVS is already a smartly diversified market leader. Cross-selling of prescriptions, retail products, and health services all seems to be working well and is an important part of the strategy. Now Aetna is added to this powerful crucible.

Reasons for Caution

The acquisition is huge. There is execution risk, as well as marketplace risk if rival players (UnitedHealthcare, Walgreens, to name a few) align their stars to compete. Channel conflict, as described earlier, is also a risk. Long-term debt more than tripled to $71 billion, and the share count went up 30 percent, but revenues and profits will rise 50 percent as an offset to these increases. One also cannot ignore Amazon's stated intentions to enter the prescription drug market. Beyond these, old risks still linger: Some of the features of the Trump administration's agenda create new uncertainties for CVS, including drug pricing and the Affordable Care Act. Altogether, the environment CVS is operating in has become less stable than years past, but we think the company has the footprint, the resources, and the management qualities to effectively manage through the change.

SECTOR: Retail ❑ Beta coefficient: 0.95 ❑ 10-year compound earnings per-share growth: 13.0% ❑ 10-year compound dividends per-share growth: 25.5%

	2011	2012	2013	2014	2015	2016	2017	2018
Revenues (bil)	107.2	123.1	126.7	139.4	153.2	177.5	185.8	194.6
Net income (mil)	3,766	4,394	4,902	5,255	5,810	6,332	6,042	7,406
Earnings per share	2.80	3.43	4.00	4.51	5.18	5.84	5.90	7.08
Dividends per share	0.50	0.65	0.90	1.10	1.40	1.70	2.00	2.00
Cash flow per share	4.10	4.99	5.74	6.30	7.18	8.27	8.40	7.82
Price: high	39.5	49.8	72.0	98.6	113.6	106.7	84.7	83.9
low	31.3	41.0	49.9	64.9	81.4	69.3	66.8	60.1

Website: www.cvs.com

AGGRESSIVE GROWTH

Daktronics, Inc.

Ticker symbol: DAKT (NASDAQ) ❑ Small Cap ❑ Value Line financial strength rating: B+ ❑ Current yield: 4.0% ❑ Dividend raises, past 10 years: 4

Company Profile

"Give it time, and it will come." That's what we've been saying for five years about this small, South Dakota–based digital signage company as its side-ways performance continues to fluster us. We almost took it off the list this year, but after some careful thought and visualization of a digital future virtually surrounded by brightly lit high-definition digital signs and canvasses updated with the latest information, eye-catching colors, and artwork, we just weren't ready to walk away from Daktronics.

The storyboard hasn't changed very much. You're driving down the highway. You're thinking about getting rid of a month's worth of grime and dirt and crud from your car. Suddenly, in vivid Technicolor, you see a billboard ahead on your right. Not just any old indifferent and ignorable billboard displaying the same old thing months on end. It's brightly lit. It flashes an offer. Five Star Car Wash, at this exit, has a "Today Only—25 Percent Off" special. Twenty minutes ago, you passed a high-resolution, multicolor electronic sign flashing "Road Work Ahead—Current Delay 30 Minutes" with a colorfully mapped detour and plenty of color emphasizing important street names and route numbers. So, you tap the brakes, hit the right lane, and off the interstate you go. A win-win—you have a clean car, and the car wash, having a lighter day than usual and temporarily pricing its services accordingly, gets another unit through their system.

Like it or not, we think such real-time, highly visual signage is where the puck is going in marketing: real-time visual displays to complement your real-time mobile devices. Give it time, and there will be real-time visual graphic displays on park benches and subway entrances. Give it time, and there will be "digital street furniture" just about everywhere. Give it time, and there will be large video displays in every entertainment venue, gambling casino, and restaurant. Give it time, and vividly colorful video displays will become standard architectural elements on modern office buildings, inside and out.

How do you invest in this looming megatrend? There's a small company located almost literally in the middle of nowhere—Brookings, South Dakota—that makes this stuff. It makes LED-based signs, scoreboards, and displays large and small. "Digital Street Furniture" is actually one of their product lines. Their core and founding business is the large multimedia scoreboards in place in a growing number of sports arenas.

Daktronics—a rare "Small Cap" pick on the *100 Best* list—is the world's leading supplier of digital signs, scoreboards, and other displays for sporting, commercial, and transportation applications. Business segments include Commercial, Live Events, High School Parks and Recreation, Transportation, and International: These groups are organized around customer segments and are all set up to create and sell unique applications of LED-based signage and software. Here is a bit more "color" on the five segments:

- Commercial (22 percent of FY2018 revenue) sells a variety of digital signage to auto dealer, restaurant, gaming, retail petroleum (gas stations), and shopping center markets. Vivid "video walls," "landmark displays," and "message displays" can be used for architectural or commercial purposes as part of the full building design. A large visual sign installed in London's Piccadilly Circus was a highlight this year.
- Live Events (39 percent of revenue) produces the traditional and some highly customized scoreboards, as well as signs for entertainment venues, including programmable displays, parking information signs, and even specialized signs for places of worship.
- High School Parks and Recreation (14 percent) includes not only digital-age marquee signs for theaters and other venues but also for the box office, merchandise sales areas, and others.
- Transportation (10 percent) covers the freeway signs; there is also plenty of digital signage in airports, train stations, public parking areas, and other public transit facilities.
- International (15 percent) sells all applications into international markets.

Overall, Daktronics has about a 30 percent share of the LED video display market, making it the number one player, and as much as 70 percent of the variable message highway sign market in the US. The company works collaboratively with customers to develop custom products.

Daktronics has 2,713 employees—including, somewhat unusually, about 400 interns and students on the payroll mostly from the local South Dakota State University. Retired cofounder and chairman Aelred J. Kurtenbach, a PhD electrical engineer and professor at SDSU, owns 5.1 percent of the shares. His son, Reece A. Kurtenbach, runs the company. The website, at www.daktronics.com, is a fun and instructive ride.

Financial Highlights, Fiscal Year 2018

The pattern of irregular performance seen in Daktronics is not uncommon in Small Cap companies that deliver relatively few but expensive products like scoreboards. There is a strong seasonal component as well. The Commercial, Transportation, and High School Parks and Recreation segments picked up but did not offset declines in the International and Live Events segments—total 2018 revenues declined 5.7 percent while net income dropped 9 percent. The forecasts indicate that 2018 might be a bottoming year, for it expects earnings gains of 30–45 percent in each of 2019 and 2020 on revenue gains in the 5–7 percent range. Results continue to be somewhat variable due to the timing of large project orders and completions. The dividend, which was cut in 2016, may start a return to previous levels in 2019.

Reasons to Buy

Since beaches and surf weren't part of the landscape when we were growing up in the Midwest, like any normal kids we were fascinated with signs of all kinds. Daktronics takes signs to a new level.

We continue to feel that—like it or not—such digital signage is a big part of the future of mass, real-time marketing communications—a "system" including your mobile device plus electronic signage. Overall, we like situations where a core technology is applied successfully to an ever-larger number of end markets. We also think as such digital signage becomes more mainstream, the company will be able to produce in larger volumes, even mass-produce more of their applications, which should drive down unit costs and increase profitability. We see advantages in the South Dakota location too—a dedicated workforce and low cost of doing business. As well, the company has virtually no debt.

All this said, Daktronics hasn't performed as well as hoped for when we added it to our *100 Best* list in 2015 in an attempt to get a bit of niche technology and Small Cap growth "energy" into the mix. Market acceptance of digital signage on a broad scale just hasn't happened yet, and thus the company has yet to hit its stride. We hope to see a significant near-term advance in Transportation and Commercial applications—this is where we think the bulk of future expansion really lies. Our patience is paid for in part by the attractive dividend (though it was cut in mid-2016), and we hope for an eventual "breakout" in this enticing market. Once again we're hoping we're not wrong, just early.

Reasons for Caution

While the company is the top player in most of its markets, there is plenty of product and price competition in the form of major Japanese firms like Mitsubishi (and if you've been to Tokyo, you know how mainstream digital signage can be). We do also wonder if environmental movements will rise up to quell what could easily become overstimulating visual "pollution," but to our knowledge this hasn't happened on a large scale.

More conventionally, Daktronics clearly has a riskier profile than most of our picks. Order flow and delivery timing can vary considerably and margins are thin. But we continue to believe the business will smooth out and prosper once electronic commercial signage becomes more mainstream.

SECTOR: Information Technology ❑ Beta coefficient: 1.19 ❑ 10-year compound earnings per-share growth: 11.5% ❑ 10-year compound dividends per-share growth: 18.0%

	2011	2012	2013	2014	2015	2016	2017	2018
Revenues (mil)	489	518	552	616	570	590	611	575
Net income (mil)	8.5	22.8	22.2	20.9	2.1	10.3	9.9	9.0
Earnings per share	0.20	0.53	0.51	0.47	0.05	0.23	0.22	0.20
Dividends per share	0.10	0.22	0.23	0.39	0.40	0.40	0.28	0.28
Cash flow per share	0.62	0.91	0.85	0.82	0.43	0.85	0.62	0.65
Price: high	16.7	11.9	16.1	15.6	13.2	10.9	11.1	10.1
low	8.0	6.3	9.4	10.8	7.2	5.9	7.6	7.1

Website: www.daktronics.com

AGGRESSIVE GROWTH

Deere & Company

Ticker symbol: DE (NYSE) ❑ Large Cap ❑ Value Line financial strength rating: A++ ❑ Current yield: 1.9% ❑ Dividend raises, past 10 years: 8

Company Profile

We finally got our way with Deere.

As the slogan tells us, "Nothing Runs Like a Deere." And for the past three years, you could also say, "Nothing Runs Like Deere Stock." A pleasant surprise, for sure—we almost gave up on this one back in 2016 as the business, the stock, and farm economy languished through the middle part of the decade. Deere became a severe test of our mettle and our conviction to stay with good businesses for the long term. The brand and business are best in class, but mid-decade business conditions of agricultural surpluses, a strong dollar, declining exports, low farm prices, and low farm incomes had Deere and most other ag-related companies stuck in the knee-deep mud of cyclical lows. Inventories of both new and used product were piling up at dealerships. But due to brand strength, loyalty (ours and its customers'), the propensity of good companies to use downturns to become more efficient, and our long-term belief in agriculture, we hung on to Deere. We're glad we did, and it has become a classic example of why one should hang on to a business strong to its core, its shares having more than doubled since its 2016 lows.

Founded in 1837, Deere & Company grew from a one-man black-smith shop into a worldwide corporation that today does business in more than 160 countries and employs more than 74,000 people around the globe.

Deere has a diverse base of operations reporting into three segments: Agriculture and Turf, Construction and Forestry, and Financial Services.

Deere has been the world's premier producer of agricultural equipment for nearly 50 years. The Agriculture and Turf segment produces and distributes tractors, loaders, combines, harvesters, seeding, mowers, hay baling, tilling, crop care and application, and other equipment. If it's used on a farm and requires an engine, Deere likely offers it.

Additionally, over the years, the company has developed and expanded lines of turf and utility equipment, including riding lawn equipment and walk-behind mowers, golf course equipment, utility vehicles, and commercial mowing and snow-removal equipment. Deere also offers a broad line of associated implements: integrated agricultural management systems technology and solutions; precision agricultural irrigation equipment and supplies; landscape and nursery products; and other outdoor power products.

With the Construction and Forestry segment, Deere is also the world's leading manufacturer of forestry equipment and a major manufacturer of heavy construction machines (Caterpillar is still the market leader in this segment). Major lines include construction, earthmoving, material-handling, and timber-harvesting machines including but not limited to backhoe loaders; crawler dozers and loaders; four-wheel-drive loaders; excavators; motor graders; articulated dump trucks; landscape loaders; skid-steer loaders; and log skidders, feller bunchers, log loaders, log forwarders, log harvesters, and related attachments. This segment, currently about 22 percent of the business, expanded its footprint significantly overseas with the acquisition of German road construction equipment maker Wirtgen Group Holding GMBH. Wirtgen makes paving, compaction, mixing, and rehabilitation machines and sells them in 100 countries and added about $2.9 billion to the Construction and Forestry segment sales and about 8 percent to Deere's sales overall.

As the company reports it, FY2018 revenue for the Agriculture and Turf segment is about 70 percent of the $25.9 billion in FY2018 product revenue; the Construction and Forestry segment makes up the remainder. The Financial Services segment rolls its revenue into the other segments, and only segment profits are reported, but that segment produces about 20 percent of total net profit.

The Financial Services segment includes John Deere Credit, which is one of the largest equipment finance companies in the US, with more than 1.8 million accounts.

Overall, international sales account for 39 percent of the total.

Interestingly, Deere has become almost as much a technology company as an equipment company, analyzing and investigating all manner of farming activities to improve its equipment designs, offer services, and forecast its business. It has become a quant geek's dream, with tools designed to optimize farming based on real-time data, GPS, on-board sensors, and link-ups with Deere operational centers as its customers plan and perform work in the field. "Revolutionizing Agriculture with Technology" is the slogan, and Deere planted their biggest seeds ever with a record 7.5 percent of sales invested in R&D in 2018.

Financial Highlights, Fiscal Year 2018

When fortunes reverse in a cyclical product sector, the results can be dramatic. Strong international markets, a declining dollar, strengthening agricultural economics, infrastructure spending, and recent improvements in energy, mining, and forestry businesses drove a 17 percent increase in organic FY2018 revenues and a bushel-basket sized 42 percent gain in earnings, based mainly on improved scale and product mix and a stronger contribution from the Construction and Forestry segment. Forward projections call for an 8–9 percent revenue gain for 2019 (some of that is still Wirtgen; they were in the books for only 10 months of 2018) and a more modest 2–3 percent gain in 2020. Per-share earnings should rise in the low 20 percent range in 2019 and 8–10 percent in 2020. After a two-year hiatus, Deere has started raising its dividend again; similarly share buybacks are on hold now pending the acquisition.

Reasons to Buy

Deere has become a classic case study in managing—and investing in—a cyclical company. We had placed our bets that the cycle would end and the heavy use of Deere machinery, coupled with the inevitable long-term growth in agriculture, would put the company back on top of its game in just a few short years. Who could argue about the long-term growth in agriculture, as the global population is predicted to increase 30 percent by 2050 and as global standards of living increase on top of that?

We're also big fans of the brand and historic excellence. As far as industrial companies go, Deere continues to be a poster child for US industrial ingenuity and excellence. It has an outstanding brand (and one of the most popular logos for hats, jackets, and so on, worn by people who have barely seen a farm field!) and reputation in the agriculture industry, and we see the ag industry as strong and strategic far into the future as global living standards improve and emerging markets develop.

Longer term, farm incomes should rise worldwide, and the company continues to invest in developing markets and is a best-in-class innovator bringing the Internet and GPS to farming and farming machines.

Beyond its products, Deere has established an almost unassailable brand leadership with its services and customer-centered innovations. Deere, more than others, puts its people in the field (literally) to figure out what agriculture professionals really need, and they work with their customers closely to sell their products through a solid dealer network.

Reasons for Caution

The company plowed through an extraordinarily difficult period, giving us a test of our long-term commitment. Now the stock price has doubled—what to do next, harvest the gains?

Deere is, and always will be, vulnerable to cycles in the farm sector, and some of those cycles might be artificially influenced by recent trade battles. The normal cycle, and in particular indelible memories of 1980s farm difficulties, can cause the farmers who buy this stuff to get cautious pretty quickly. All in all, farming will always be with us, both in the US and overseas, and there will always be a demand for machines and especially smarter, more efficient ones—Deere has an enormous brand and long-term track record.

SECTOR: Industrials ❑ Beta coefficient: 1.05 ❑ 10-year compound earnings per-share growth: 6.0% ❑ 10-year compound dividends per-share growth: 10.5%

	2011	2012	2013	2014	2015	2016	2017	2018
Revenues (mil)	29,466	33,501	34,998	32,961	25,775	23,387	25,885	33,351
Net income (mil)	2,799	3,065	3,533	3,162	1,937	1,524	2,159	3,061
Earnings per share	6.63	7.64	9.08	8.53	5.76	4.81	6.68	9.34
Dividends per share	1.52	1.79	1.99	2.22	2.40	2.40	2.40	2.58
Cash flow per share	8.34	9.56	11.45	11.45	8.62	7.39	9.32	12.67
Price: high	99.8	89.7	95.6	94.9	98.2	104.6	159.4	175.3
low	59.9	69.5	79.5	76.9	71.9	70.2	103.1	126.7

Website: www.deere.com

Dentsply Sirona

Ticker symbol: XRAY (NASDAQ) ❑ Large Cap ❑ Value Line financial strength rating: B++
❑ Current yield: 0.8% ❑ Dividend raises, past 10 years: 9

Company Profile

We've long been fans of the dental supply business, with its high margins and steady demand growth as people like us age and our teeth become decayed and fall out. Good industry, we believe. Two years ago we switched horses from Patterson Dental, which we felt had become too involved in the veterinary business, to Dentsply Sirona, which we felt was better positioned as a bigger player in dental technology. Well, it didn't quite work out—it turns out that Dentsply had problems of its own, some stemming from their recent merger with Sirona Dental Systems, a major technology player.

Dentsply ran into two problems, one apparently of its own making. The first is an apparent consolidation of inventory at distributors of dental supplies, which we feel may result from ups and downs in the retail dentist space going back to the Great Recession. That has hurt sales; it is clear from the revenue numbers, but there are other internal problems at Dentsply having mostly to do with a poor integration and execution. The company has been quite contrite and forthcoming to recognize that it had internal structural problems—too many silos, for example, separate organizational units working on small parts of the puzzle—giving poor R&D efforts, multiple supply chains, disjointed sales efforts, and so forth. As a result they have undertaken a massive reorganization and restructuring, much of which is to be completed according to their documents in 2019.

Why do we hang on? Ordinarily a company that shoots itself in the foot with poor organization and structure—i.e., poor management—doesn't find itself on the *100 Best Stocks* list. In this case, however, we feel that Dentsply has admitted its mistakes and come to grips with the solutions. A well-executed turnaround effort in a good business space can work very well; we believe this to be the case and so are including Dentsply Sirona once again for 2020.

With the 2016 merger of Dentsply and Sirona, the combined company became the world's largest provider of professional dental products and technologies. These words are important—dental products include substantial consumables which must be purchased repeatedly; dental technology paves the way to more advanced dental solutions and dental office automation, both, as in the example of dental implants and digital imaging and X-ray equipment, are major growth markets. Its products are used by more than 600,000 dental professionals in more than 120 countries with 65 percent of sales coming from outside the US.

Financial Highlights, Fiscal Year 2018

FY2018 hasn't brought much of a smile from Dentsply investors, and FY2019 won't be much better. The company expects the restructuring, which will involve laying off 6–8 percent of the workforce, will start having an effect by the end of 2019 and begin to really hit the ground in 2020. FY2018 sales were largely flat; 2019 sales are also projected flat with a 5–7 percent growth finally in the cards for 2020. Net income dropped in excess of 20 percent and probably won't fully recover until after 2020. On the other hand, international business continues to advance as modern dentistry becomes more widespread; we believe this plus an aggressive pursuit of structural improvement could speed up the recovery.

Reasons to Buy

Dentsply Sirona is well positioned to capitalize on several growth vectors in the dental industry. First, there's the international and emerging market opportunity as modern dental health becomes a standard in overseas and especially developing markets. Second is the greater integration of digital technologies in the dental practice, from X-rays to 3-D and CAD/CAM automation of lab work such as crowns to the management of patient records; the company is well positioned to cross-sell all parts of this operational food chain. Third is the increased presence of single-visit outcomes, where a crown can be mapped, created, and installed in one day using the CEREC technologies. Fourth is the stream of licensee revenue other distributors bring in for deploying Dentsply technologies like CEREC. (As an example, Patterson also offered CEREC as a licensee.)

Of course, these geography- and technology-related growth vectors are additional to the growth already slated for the industry coming in the form of an aging population, greater and longer retention of natural teeth, greater acceptance and practice of dental implants, and the gradual automation and digitization of dental practices.

We like the positioning as a one-stop shop for all technology and consumables needed to run any kind of dentistry-related practice, as well as the greater extension into higher-margined technology products and the greater presence overseas.

Reasons for Caution

When it comes to *100 Best* picks, we don't like surprises (bad ones, anyway) and Dentsply Sirona certainly proved to be one. We feel this is a company that made some bad mistakes but still has a good position in a good market. Had they not been so transparent with their errors and their fixes, we would have dropped them from the list immediately. We're putting some faith in management to execute their changes and turn this company around quickly. The plans look good—but investors, beware. There are risks, but there should be rewards too (hopefully something more than a toothbrush and some dental floss) if they get their cavities filled successfully.

SECTOR: Healthcare ❑ Beta coefficient: 0.90 ❑ 10-year compound earnings per-share growth: 6.0% ❑ 10-year compound dividends per-share growth: 8.5%

	2011	2012	2013	2014	2015	2016	2017	2018
Revenues (mil)	2,537	2,928	2,951	2,922	2,674	3,765	3,950	3,925
Net income (mil)	290.9	319.2	340.7	360.4	373.0	616.0	600.0	435.0
Earnings per share	2.02	2.22	2.35	2.50	2.62	2.75	2.65	2.00
Dividends per share	0.21	0.22	0.25	0.27	0.29	0.30	0.33	0.38
Cash flow per share	2.56	3.20	3.33	3.51	3.62	3.40	4.05	3.60
Price: high	40.4	41.4	51.0	56.3	63.4	65.8	69.0	68.5
low	28.3	34.8	39.4	43.0	49.4	53.4	52.5	33.9

Website: www.dentsplysirona.com

AGGRESSIVE GROWTH

Devon Energy

Ticker symbol: DVN (NYSE) ❑ Large Cap ❑ Value Line financial strength rating: B++ ❑ Current yield: 1.3% ❑ Dividend raises, past 10 years: 6

Company Profile

As recently as 2014 we had five major energy stocks on the *100 Best* list. We pruned out Marathon Oil due to a company split and ExxonMobil due to sheer size and difficulty replacing reserves. We held onto Chevron, ConocoPhillips, and Total S.A., which continue on the list today. But for the 2015 list we were left wondering if we were now underexposed to this key cash-producing economically important sector. So, we added a diversified energy company to replace Marathon and ExxonMobil—Devon Energy—to the 2015 *100 Best Stocks* list.

We all know what happened. That "add" was just in time for the rout in oil prices that started in 2015, continued full force in 2016 to a nadir almost 70 percent lower than the peak, and started to recover in 2017. When the price of your chief product drops 70 percent, you're in trouble—especially if you're relatively small and don't have the resources to easily bridge the gap.

We hastily dropped Devon from the 2016 list.

So why are we still talking about Devon? Well, for the simple reason that oil prices rebounded to around $70/barrel, within 30 percent of the $100/barrel norm seen in mid-decade. Inventories were dropping (finally) as the strong economy drove worldwide demand, and natural gas has been taking over as the fuel of choice for utilities and many industrial processes.

As such we wanted to once again expand our exposure to the sector and to find a company that would give the right kind of exposure to the recovering energy industry. We had a few criteria in mind. First, we wanted a company well positioned to take advantage of the "fracking" (hydraulic fracturing) boom producing a bounty of energy right here in North America. In line with that, we wanted a company with less international exposure, one comfortable with new technologies, one expanding its reserves faster than production, one qualifying as a good corporate citizen, and one with a sizeable presence in the natural gas business. The 2018 production mix was 48 percent oil, 32 percent natural gas, and 20 percent natural gas liquids.

Then, in late 2018, the bottom fell out of oil prices again, even after a brief surge in natural gas prices due to a colder than normal winter, leaving us scratching our heads. One thing for sure is that volatility seems to be here to stay. But we think energy prices will eventually stabilize, and rise gradually as world consumption growth continues.

Devon Energy produces almost exclusively in six locations all within North America. In order of size and as of the end of 2018 its six major operations are:

- Barnett Shale in north Texas—28 percent of company total and a particularly strong concentration of gas
- Canada Heavy Oil—from the Athabasca oil sands—24 percent
- STACK in western Oklahoma—20 percent
- Eagle Ford in west Texas—11 percent
- Delaware Basin in southeast New Mexico and west Texas—10 percent
- Rockies Oil—mostly in Wyoming—3 percent

Devon is involved in "upstream" exploration and production and in "midstream" processing, mainly the separation of natural gas liquids (propane, butane, etc.) from the gaseous methane for sale and shipment. Devon owns a 64 percent stake in ENLAKE, a midstream producer and transporter of energy products. The company's strategies include investing in more innovative oil and natural gas liquids (NGL) production techniques, and in keeping critical mass in relatively few areas to reduce operating costs and concentrate on knowledge of those areas.

The company has doubled production since 2011 and is most excited about innovative "multizone" approaches to development especially in the Delaware and STACK areas. This approach, where several taps are placed strategically in a shale formation, can increase output as much as 20 percent while reducing costs 10–30 percent.

In early 2019 the company announced a plan to sell or spin off its Barnett Shale (mostly natural gas) and Canadian assets to concentrate on higher-margin US oil assets, especially STACK, Eagle Ford, and Powder River. These assets are thought to be able to generate free cash flow above $46/barrel, giving a 56 percent increase in "field-level" margins; the company is projecting a 17 percent growth rate on the remaining assets. Higher margins and cost savings projects will increase profitability although the "New Devon" will have a smaller revenue footprint. Proceeds will be used to halve the current $10 billion in debt and to add $1 billion to a $4 billion share buyback authorization. The transition is expected to be complete by the end of 2019.

Financial Highlights, Fiscal Year 2018

The recovery in energy prices continued throughout most of 2018, only to be nipped in the bud at the end of the year. That may have been a blessing in disguise, as it may have helped trigger the "New Devon" strategic shift just mentioned. Revenues and earnings dropped a full 23 percent on lower volumes and prices. Going forward, comparisons will be difficult, but the company expects in 2019 to earn about the same net profit as in 2018 on another 19 percent drop in revenue; that gives some idea of the anticipated increased profitability. In 2020, the first full year of the new alignment, Devon expects a 25–27 percent increase in earnings on a 5 percent revenue increase; that would further confirm the strategic shift. Proceeds from the assets sales will retire some 16 percent of outstanding shares and fund double-digit dividend hikes over the next few years.

Reasons to Buy

Last year Devon regained its spot on the list as an innovative and efficient energy exploration and production machine right in our own backyard, devoid of the international political risks that face most producers. They had made more of both "fracking" and conventional methods than most. We like their balanced mix of oil, natural gas, and natural gas liquids. Now the company is reinventing its footprint, we feel for the best as it becomes more focused on more profitable assets. We applaud the willingness to change and the ability to become a lean, mean player in a difficult industry; we like the size, scope, and speed of this change in an industry not known for rapid strategic shifts.

Reasons for Caution

Energy prices continue to be the wild card. Devon does well and better than most when prices are firm or higher and can generate red ink (although very little of it in this last go-around) when energy prices falter.

As Devon and other producers become more efficient, the glut of oil and gas can not only drive down prices and drive up storage costs; it can also cause transportation bottlenecks in getting crude and gas to refiners and to market. Shifting markets and shifting prices make this business more difficult than in years past; the good news is that Devon seems to be nimble enough to manage these changes.

SECTOR: Energy ❑ Beta coefficient: 2.16 ❑ 10-year compound earnings per-share growth: -15.0% ❑ 10-year compound dividends per-share growth: 2.0%

	2011	2012	2013	2014	2015	2016	2017	2018
Revenues (mil)	11,494	9,502	10,407	19,566	13,145	12,197	13,949	10,734
Net income (mil)	2,485	1,285	1,727	2,014	1,044	(38)	835	649
Earnings per share	5.94	3.26	4.29	4.91	2.52	(0.13)	1.59	1.29
Dividends per share	0.67	0.80	0.86	0.94	0.96	0.42	0.24	0.30
Cash flow per share	11.71	10.09	11.15	13.04	9.95	3.35	5.54	4.62
Price: high	93.6	76.3	66.9	80.6	70.6	50.7	49.4	46.5
low	50.7	50.9	50.8	41.8	28.0	18.1	28.8	20.4

Website: www.devonenergy.com

Eastman Chemical Company

Ticker symbol: EMN (NYSE) ◻ Large Cap ◻ Value Line financial strength rating: A ◻ Current yield: 3.0% ◻ Dividend raises, past 10 years: 9

Company Profile

Spun off in 1993 from the now-bankrupt Eastman Kodak, Eastman Chemical is one of those "better living through chemistry" companies with a history of solving problems and providing standard, high-tech, and high-precision materials to industries ranging from food and beverage to toys to medical equipment to computers and electronics. The Eastman mission could almost be refined into "better living through polymer chemistry"— the chemical building blocks, mostly sourced from petroleum and other feedstocks known as hydrocarbons, that turn into all things useful such as plastics, paints, coatings, inks, and the like. Many of their products are "intermediaries," used to manufacture other chemicals and products. When speaking the language of the company you quickly pick up expressions like "olefin cycle" and "phthalate," among the more difficult concepts and spelling challenges, like "ophthalmology." We aren't chemists but have enough understanding of basic chemistry to feel comfortable reading their reports; if you don't, you may want to look elsewhere.

The company is organized into four product segments, all of which have something more or less to do with petrochemicals:

- Additives & Functional Products (36 percent of 2018 sales, up 9 percent versus 2017) produces chemical products for the coatings industry and for tires, paints, inks, building materials, durable goods, and consumables markets. Key technology platforms include rubber additives, cellulosic polymers, ketones, coalescents, polyester polymers olefins, and hydrocarbon resins.
- Advanced Materials (27 percent, up 7 percent) produces and markets specialty plastics, interlayers, and films, including copolyesters, cellulose esters, and safety glass, plastic, and solar-protecting window film products for the automotive, building, transportation, LCD and display manufacturing, health and wellness, and durable goods industries.
- Chemical Intermediates (28 percent, up 4 percent) is a catchall for other chemical products that don't fall into the other segments, including

new or custom-made polymer-based products for key customers. Acetic acid, ethylene, paint and building materials intermediaries, agrichemicals, adhesive resins, plasticizers, and aviation hydraulic fluid are among the many products in this group.

- Fibers (9 percent, up 8 percent) produces acetate tow, triacetin, and solution-dyed acetate yarns for the apparel, filtration, tobacco (filters), fabric, home furnishings, medical tape, and other industries.

Obviously, there could be considerably more detail in these descriptions, but it would only engage those with a strong chemistry or materials background. A trip through their "Products" page on their website is fascinating. Bottom line: Eastman makes a lot of strategically important materials that support a lot of manufacturing processes for common and fairly high-volume items, such as beer bottles, automotive glass, and LCD displays. By end-use market, sales divide into Transportation (20 percent), Consumables (17 percent), Building & Construction (14 percent), Industrial Chemicals & Processing (11 percent), Filter Media (8 percent), Consumer Durables (7 percent), Food, Feed, and Agriculture (7 percent), Personal Care/Health (6 percent), Energy, Fuels, & Water (5 percent), Electronics (3 percent), and Other (2 percent). Additionally, these materials are used in considerable amounts in overseas manufacturing. Eastman has adapted by setting up plants in 16 countries and driving foreign sales to 58 percent of the total. By region, sales are 42 percent from North America, 25 percent Asia-Pacific, 27 percent EMEA, and 5 percent Latin America.

Acquisitions of adjacent or related technologies are an important part of Eastman's strategy. More recently the company has divulged a new strategy to become a leader in innovation, to become known as a "materials innovation" company introducing new, more specialized, higher-margin and sometimes branded products into the mix, such as Tritan copolyester, specialty ketones for low volatile organic compound (VOC) coatings, Impera performance resins for tires, and Saflex windshield coatings to enable nonglare "head-up displays" projected on windshields.

Financial Highlights, Fiscal Year 2018

Despite the ambiguities of trade and the strong dollar Eastman managed a 6 percent revenue increase across the board, with strength in most business areas except Chemical Intermediaries. Net earnings were up 8 percent for the year. But as the year progressed, dollar strength and slowdowns in international manufacturing particularly in Europe and China caused Eastman to reduce its forecasts in 2019. Currently revenue is predicted to be roughly flat with earnings up in the 2–3 percent range as higher input costs also come into play. For 2020, the company expects a return to growth with a 16–18 percent rise in earnings on a 5–6 percent growth in revenues, as mix and margin improvements come into play. Cash flows will remain strong and should fund dividend raises in the 10 percent range as well as bolt-on acquisitions and modest share buybacks.

Reasons to Buy

Although Eastman lies on the edge of the "buy businesses you understand" test, this well-managed company really does produce things vitally important to manufacturing mainstream and advanced products. Successful product development has always been a key strength for Eastman, and now that gains more emphasis. Eastman will benefit from the continued strength in domestic manufacturing, although its international operations, particularly in Asia, are traditionally a source of strength. Eastman continues to position itself for continued moderate organic growth with a strong base of repeat business, a more favorable cost structure, and excellent cash flow.

Reasons for Caution

Eastman's fortunes will follow those of the larger manufacturing sector in general and, to a lesser extent, the feedstock (petroleum) market more specifically. Feedstock costs are increasing, although they are able to pass some increases on. An unknown is the competitive strength of the descendants of the DowDuPont split slated to happen in late 2019.

There is always headline risk with chemical companies. Environmental and health risks can pop up in the headlines any time, as well as production risks such as a 2017 explosion in a coal gasification plant. Another example: There is some concern about the health effects of phthalates, one of their key plasticizer products, although they do sell a line of nonphthalate plasticizers.

The prospect of acquisitions does add some risk. That all said, Eastman has all the earmarks of a well-managed and well-positioned company.

SECTOR: Materials ◻ Beta coefficient: 1.26 ◻ 10-year compound earnings per-share growth: 11.0% ◻ 10-year compound dividends per-share growth: 9.0%

	2011	2012	2013	2014	2015	2016	2017	2018
Revenues (mil)	7,178	8,102	9,350	9,527	9,648	9,008	9,549	10,151
Net income (mil)	653	802	1,008	751	848	854	1,001	1,080
Earnings per share	4.56	5.38	6.45	4.95	5.66	5.75	7.22	7.56
Dividends per share	0.99	1.08	1.25	1.40	1.60	1.84	2.04	2.24
Cash flow per share	6.76	7.55	9.45	8.08	9.60	9.79	11.11	12.05
Price: high	55.4	68.2	83.0	90.6	83.9	78.8	95.0	112.4
low	32.4	39.2	63.5	70.4	62.8	56.0	74.8	97.4

Website: www.eastman.com

GROWTH AND INCOME   NEW FOR 2020

Enable Midstream Partners

Ticker symbol: ENBL (NYSE) ◻ Mid Cap ◻ Value Line financial strength rating: B+ ◻ Current yield: 8.3% ◻ Dividend raises, past 10 years: 3

Company Profile

As demand for energy products steadily grows, particularly for clean-burning and efficient natural gas, the supply of these products also grows—and it has been growing rapidly on the domestic front ever since the advent of "fracking" shale recovery technologies ten years ago. Fracking has opened up (or more accurately, reopened) vast domestic energy resources in areas once thought largely exhausted in Texas, Oklahoma, Arkansas, Louisiana, North Dakota, and other shale-rich regions of the country.

As world demand and supply shift to the new realities of clean burning and efficient US production, there will always be a need—regardless of who takes the production risks and where it is refined and ultimately sold—to *move* energy products to market. E&P (exploration and production) is a risky game—some win, some lose. Refining is less risky but can also have hiccups if the price of crude rises or the price of gasoline drops. What will always be in demand, relatively steady demand at that, is the ability to move energy products from the wellhead once developed to the processing facilities and ultimately to market. Due to the sheer volumes involved, and in part also to safety, most of that movement occurs through the tens of thousands of miles of gathering and transport pipelines already existing and under construction in the US.

As the energy industry goes, the pipeline business is relatively less risky and produces steadier, richer cash flows than almost any other part of the industry. Yes, it is capital intensive, but once the pipeline is in the ground, turn on the spigots and out flows the cash. Plenty of cash. Rich and steady.

Last year we added the largest pipeline network to the *100 Best Stocks* list: Enterprise Products Partners. This year we thought we'd add another smaller, strategically located mid-cap partnership enterprise called Enable Midstream Partners. We stumbled onto Enable because it was formed by and is 54 percent owned by Houston-based utility CenterPoint Energy (another *100 Best* pick), which uses it as a minor supplier and a cash flow generator, as does OGE (formerly Oklahoma Gas & Electric), which owns another 25 percent. We thought there must be a good reason why a smallish gas mover and processor was owned by two big and successful utilities; indeed there was.

Formed in 2013, Enable Midstream is a publicly traded master limited partnership that owns, operates, and develops natural gas and crude oil infrastructure assets. These assets typically move energy products from their source to a destination with some key value-add processing along the way. As part of its Gathering and Processing operations, Enable owns 13,300 miles of densely networked gathering pipelines mostly in four major producing areas including the Bakken Shale area in North Dakota and the Anadarko, Arkoma, and Ark-La-Tex Basins in Oklahoma, Texas, Arkansas, and Louisiana for natural gas and to a lesser extent, for oil. The largest and richest of these, by far, is Anadarko, with 65 percent of the gathering pipeline miles and 87 percent of the natural gas equivalent liquid production.

Enable also owns 14 major processing plants that process 2.5 billion cubic feet of gas per day, 7,800 miles of strategically located interstate pipelines, 2,200 miles of intrastate pipelines, and eight storage facilities with 85 billion cubic feet of storage capacity. Eleven of the 14 processing plants are in the Anadarko region. On the Transportation and Storage side of the business, the two intrastate pipeline systems and one interstate system primarily move liquefied natural gas and petroleum products to markets and connecting pipelines in the Oklahoma/Texas/Arkansas/Louisiana region, while one major interstate pipeline moves energy to the Midwest with a gateway at St. Louis; the other, a joint venture with Enbridge, moves energy to port and storage in Mobile, Alabama.

Financial Highlights, Fiscal Year 2018

Measuring business results can be complex in the energy pipeline business, for some business is done as a purchase and sale of energy products, where the pipeline operator takes title to the assets; some is done as a service, where Enable moves someone else's product from one place to another (and/or stores it or processes it, etc.) under contract. About 62 percent of Enable's business is selling product, while the remaining 38 percent is "service." Business results are thus driven by price and throughput.

Favorable energy pricing conditions, especially in late 2018, and strong natural gas demand and throughput made for a good year in 2018, with revenues up 22 percent from 2017. Net income rose about 20 percent, and per-unit cashflow, a closely watched measure in this industry, also rose 20 percent to $2.12 and more than adequately covers the annual distribution of $1.28 per unit. Revenues are expected to rise in the 6–9 percent range annually through 2020, with net profits roughly flat to 2 percent higher as the partnership completes some investments. Enable expects a large step up in profitability, from 14 to 22 percent net margins, when these investments are complete.

Reasons to Buy

With an 8.5 percent distribution rate, the main attraction here is steady, relatively risk-free income. We say relatively because such a dividend rate in a typical manufacturing or service corporation would be looked at with skepticism, as it is much higher than the going dividend rate. With a limited partnership, you skip a level of taxation, which helps, and further, the steadiness of the revenue and cash flow stream allows the operator to pay its investors more generously. We also see some price appreciation potential as domestic energy independence and volumes from the new fracking boom create more throughput to the system. We also feel that the substantial CenterPoint and OGE ownership provides something of a backstop here; these two major investors would not easily let this operation fail or decline.

Reasons for Caution

There have been rumors that CenterPoint might want to sell its interest, although that seems to be off the table for now. Rather than flood the market with units, we suspect they would find a private equity buyer or some such. The recent volatility of energy prices and markets could make one with large unchangeable fixed assets in the (and on the) ground a little nervous—markets change, even the direction of flow can change, and more nimble carriers like railroads can occasionally grab share. Pipelines are pretty good sleep-at-night investments, but not as good as they used to be.

SECTOR: Energy ❑ Beta coefficient: 1.20 ❑ 10-year compound earnings per-share growth: NA ❑ 10-year compound dividends per-share growth: NA

	2011	2012	2013	2014	2015	2016	2017	2018
Revenues (mil)	—	—	—	3,367	2,418	2,272	2,803	3,431
Net income (mil)	—	—	—	530	382	312	436	521
Earnings per unit	—	—	—	1.28	0.91	0.68	0.92	1.11
Distributions per unit	—	—	—	0.55	1.27	1.28	1.28	1.28
Cash flow per unit	—	—	—	1.91	1.66	1.45	1.77	2.12
Price: high	—	—	—	27.5	20.0	16.8	17.4	19.3
low	—	—	—	17.1	6.5	5.4	13.8	12.3

Website: www.enablemidstream.com

GROWTH AND INCOME

Enterprise Products Partners, L.P.

Ticker symbol: EPD (NYSE) ❑ Large Cap ❑ Value Line financial strength rating: B++ ❑ Current yield: 6.3% ❑ Dividend raises, past 10 years: 10

Company Profile

It's no secret that our nation uses enormous amounts of petroleum products—oil and natural gas—for everything from transportation fuels to plastics to feedstocks to pharmaceuticals. But when's the last time you actually physically saw a gallon of gasoline? A cubic foot of natural gas? Other than inside rail tank cars or trucks, when have you seen these vast quantities move from Point A to Point B?

The simple fact is that most of these products move underground, out of sight and largely out of mind. The US consumption of barrels of oil is somewhere around 20 million *a day*; one of those big black rail tank cars you often see carries about 800 barrels, so it would take almost 25,000 cars to carry a day's consumption of oil, and this doesn't even include natural gas or other chemicals and liquids. At 60 feet per tank car, that 25,000-car freight train would be 284 miles long (hope you don't get stuck behind that one!). Put simply: Pipelines are vital to moving today's energy needs.

That's where Enterprise Products Partners comes in as one of the leading "midstream" networks of pipelines, natural gas–processing plants, and storage facilities vital to moving today's energy needs from "upstream"—production or in many cases import—to "downstream"—filling stations, natural gas utilities, airports, chemical plants—the end user.

Since being formed in 1998, Enterprise has assembled, through construction and acquisition, a network of 50,000 miles of pipelines carrying crude oil, raw natural gas, natural gas liquids (NGL), which is essentially compressed natural gas ready for delivery to utilities and the end customer, refined products, and petrochemicals. It has salt dome storage facilities for 260 million barrels of liquid capacity and 14 billion cubic feet of natural gas. The company also operates 26 natural gas–processing plants and 22 NGL and propylene fractionators, which refine NGL into basic petrochemical substrates. Enterprise also runs a large import and export terminal in the Houston Ship Channel.

Much of Enterprise's network is where you might expect it to be. Crude oil and natural gas sourcing pipelines crisscross Texas, Oklahoma, and Louisiana, while NGL, petrochemical, and refined product pipelines head north into the Northeast, Midwest, and Rocky Mountain states. Most gas processing plants are in Texas and Louisiana, but there are several in Colorado, New Mexico, and Wyoming. Typically, the larger the pipeline network, the stronger the offering to petroleum products shippers, because they can reach a destination from a source location without transfer, delays, or additional costs. The combination of transport, storage, and some processing also provides an advantage.

Enterprise Products Partners, like many others in the pipeline business, is technically a limited partnership, which is run by a corporate general partner called Enterprise GP; you don't buy shares but rather limited partnership units. There are no taxes at the corporate level, so all profits are passed on to partnership holders as "distributions," not dividends, and certain other expenses like depreciation are allocated among the partners as well. This can cause some headaches at tax time, so we advise using this type of security in a tax-deferred retirement account if feasible.

Financial Highlights, Fiscal Year 2018

The resurgence of the US shale resource industry in 2017 spearheaded another very good year. Revenues for 2018 rose almost 25 percent mostly driven by across-the-board volume increases, while net income rose almost a full 50 percent as construction costs held 2017 net income figures back a bit. For 2019 Enterprise sees a further 7–8 percent growth in earnings on a 4–5 percent revenue growth; things slow a bit in 2020 to a 3–4 percent earnings rise on a 4–6 percent revenue increase. The company is aggressively building new pipeline capacity to serve fracking sites; the capital budget is $4.5 billion; as well, there's a bit of a drag on earnings. Relatively modest dividend increases are offset by gradual unit buybacks, a rarity for this type of investment.

Reasons to Buy

Pipeline and processing systems typically represent a high-fixed-cost structure, and with Enterprise, most of that infrastructure is already in place, so throughput is relatively profitable and is getting more so as more of the network is finished. Profit margins increase as more of the infrastructure is completed and get better yet if there is volume growth. EPD's margins have increased from the mid-single digits to over 11 percent recently.

Enterprise's network serves many of the key shale resource–producing areas in the southern US and is well positioned to tap the growth in store for this particular source.

Pipeline systems, while affected by energy price fluctuations, are relatively less affected than most other parts of the industry—the stuff still has to get to market, regardless of price. That said, volatility can cause demand and supply shifts, which can destabilize flows and create periods of excess capacity and undercapacity in certain pipeline lanes. Pipeline businesses bring in relatively steady income, and because of the limited partnership setup and no taxes at the corporate level, they pay relatively high and consistent dividends. Enterprise is basically a cross between an unregulated utility and a transportation company, with the steady base and modest growth potential one might expect from such a combination.

Finally, the yield is enticing and—we think—relatively safe, and the share price is relatively steady.

Reasons for Caution

High-fixed-cost businesses are vulnerable to slowdowns and shifts in the geography of production and consumption. These systems are funded with large amounts of debt, which can get expensive in times of higher interest rates—although EPD is thought to be capitalized at largely favorable interest rates. All pipelines are susceptible to safety hazards and fires. The limited partnership structure is difficult to understand, especially at tax time if you use these investments in non-tax-deferred accounts.

SECTOR: Energy ▫ Beta coefficient: 1.30 ▫ 10-year compound earnings per-share growth: 9.5% ▫ 10-year compound distributions per-share growth: 5.5%

	2011	2012	2013	2014	2015	2016	2017	2018
Revenues (mil)	44,313	42,583	47,727	47,951	27,028	23,022	29,242	36,535
Net income (mil)	2,047	2,419	2,597	2,787	2,521	2,513	2,799	4,172
Earnings per unit	1.19	1.36	1.41	1.47	1.26	1.20	1.30	1.91
Distributions per unit	1.21	1.27	1.35	1.43	1.51	1.59	1.67	1.72
Cash flow per unit	1.73	1.96	2.00	2.14	2.01	1.92	2.02	2.70
Price: high	23.3	27.7	33.5	41.4	37.0	30.1	30.3	30.0
low	13.9	22.8	25.5	30.7	20.8	19.0	23.6	23.1

Website: www.enterpriseproducts.com

AGGRESSIVE GROWTH

Fair Isaac Corporation

Ticker symbol: FICO (NYSE) ▫ Mid Cap ▫ Value Line financial strength rating: B++ ▫ Current yield: Nil ▫ Dividend raises, past 10 years: 0

Company Profile

Last year we called out FICO onto the carpet for quadrupling its share price in four years while not even quite doubling sales and earnings over that time. Such a pattern routinely rings alarms in the value investor camp. It can hardly be sustained. Or can it?

Obviously we thought "maybe so" given what FICO does, how well it does it, and how it leads its market. In fact, with 2018 in the books, FICO stock has quintupled, and earnings are up by more than 25 percent, closing the gap at least somewhat between stock price growth and earnings growth. While we're still not sure the momentum will continue at this pace, we do know that we're talking about the 800-pound gorilla in today's lucrative Big Data and analytics space. And we want a piece of that action. Fair Isaac continues to be the Apple, the Google, the Amazon of this key space, a pure play in this ever-expanding and lucrative niche. We think the compounded growth of the company's native market—analytics—plus the growth of the company's business *within* the market will continue to make this company stand out. We also see substantial overseas opportunity, as well as growth opportunities in new add-ons and refinements of its tools. FICO remains a contender for 2020—not because it's a bargain, but because it continues to dominate its healthy niche.

We like it when companies can explain what they do in three sentences or less. FICO has a neat entry in this category (and we quote): "FICO transforms business by making every decision count. FICO's Decision Management solutions combine trusted advice, world-class analytics and innovative applications to give organizations the power to automate, improve and connect decisions across their business." More specifically, FICO provides decision support analytics, software, and solutions to help businesses improve and automate decision-making and risk management. The most well-known and best example of these solutions is the FICO score—an analytic single-figure estimate of a consumer's creditworthiness used mainly in the credit industry but also for other purposes such as employment and insurance. More recently, the FICO score has been more widely distributed to consumers free of charge by financial institutions wishing to give customers insight into their own credit and, by proxy, financial health. As an illustration of its ubiquity, some even use it in dating to assess the responsibility of a potential partner!

FICO provides its analytic solutions and services to a variety of financial and other service organizations, including banks, credit-reporting agencies, credit card–processing agencies, insurers, telecommunications providers, retailers, marketers, and healthcare organizations. It operates in three segments: Applications, Scores, and Decision Management Software. The Applications segment provides decision and risk management tools, market targeting and customer analytics tools, and fraud detection tools and associated professional services, all now under an umbrella called Enterprise Fraud Management. (If you've had a credit card fraud alert recently, it probably came from FICO's "Falcon" suite of fraud prediction and protection services, which are currently deployed to protect some 2.5 billion credit cards.) The Scores segment includes the business-to-business scoring solutions; myFICO solutions, delivering FICO scores for consumers; and associated professional services. The Decision Management Software segment provides software products and consulting services to help organizations build their own analytic tools. Many of these analytics and scores are now delivered through their "Analytic Cloud" as SaaS—Software as a Service—applications, providing an ongoing revenue stream tied to their use.

The company actively works with customers in a variety of vertical markets to identify and apply their tools and applications; these analytics go beyond traditional financial applications into marketing and operational optimization. FICO's analytics are not only used to manage risk and fraud but also to build more profitable customer relationships, optimize operations, and meet government regulations. The company promotes its vertical applications in the grocery, retail, pharmaceutical and life sciences, insurance, financial services, consumer packaged goods industries, and in education and public sector applications as well.

Financial Highlights, Fiscal Year 2018

Led by the Scores segment, total revenues advanced a healthy 11 percent in FY2018. The largest segment, Applications (steady at 57 percent of the business) grew about 6 percent. The Scores segment, which now contributes 33 percent of the business, grew some 29 percent, while the Decision Management Software business, accounting for 10 percent of the business, moved forward at a 8 percent rate. International now accounts for 36 percent of the business, up from 34 percent in 2017. Earnings jumped ahead 20 percent on higher margins related to tax cuts and improved mix and efficiencies. Expectations call for a 12 percent rise in FY2019 per-share earnings on a 9 percent rise in revenues as the company profits from a broadening base of applications outside the financial services industry, and as the transformation to a cloud-based SaaS model becomes more complete.

As promised, the company cut its almost-negligible 8 cent annual dividend. Normally we hate to see any dividend cut; however, in this case it is offset by aggressive share buybacks—2 million shares in 2018 or about 8 percent of the float, bringing the share count reduction to more than 50 percent since 2006. Share count reductions should be in the 2–3 percent range annually over the next few years.

Reasons to Buy

"Big data" and related analytics are gaining strength right now as more vertical industries (banking, retail, utilities, pharma, medical devices, health insurers, etc.) learn how to use them more efficiently and effectively to manage different parts of their business. The market is growing both deeper (more analytics being used) and wider (more companies in more industries in more geographies using them)—a very good scenario as previously pointed out.

There are a number of companies, large and small, in the analytics business, but few have the brand reputation, product packaging, and leadership enjoyed by FICO, which serves more than 95 percent of the largest financial institutions in the US. The company is a pure play and is considered to be the gold standard for this type of product. It is more turnkey and easy for customers who don't have advanced mathematicians and software engineering staffs. As a consequence, and with the brand recognition of the FICO score, the company has attained a large moat on its brand and is a good example of how branding, packaging, and market definition can be as important as the product.

FICO's modeling approaches are now being used to analyze customer behavior and provide decision support for insurability, employability, acceptance into schools, and even customer behaviors in stores or online, other areas well beyond a consumer's ability to repay extended credit. Its analytics predict risks of insurance fraud, cyber security debt default and resolution potential, and a host of other very abstract but also very real risks. As mentioned, the FICO "score" is more and more becoming a household term and feature. International demand for FICO's products continues to grow, too, notably in China, where fraud protection continues to be a big business.

The dividend is history, but we appreciate the company's policy of providing shareholder returns in the form of share buybacks.

Reasons for Caution

There continues to be some competition on the scoring front, but the forefront FICO brand keeps serious competition at bay. Software companies always run a certain amount of technology risk. The ability to sell in a "cloud" environment and to maintain or increase margins by selling the right mix of products and channels will be key. There is some public concern that scoring models oversimplify lending and insurability decisions and should not be used or relied on so heavily.

But mainly we're concerned about how much investors have already loved this stock and have priced FICO's excellent market position to perfection. This not only creates downside price risk but also makes the company's share buybacks expensive. "Score" your purchases carefully—buy when the price is right.

SECTOR: **Business Services** ❑ **Beta coefficient: 1.15** ❑ **10-year compound earnings per-share growth: 9.5%** ❑ **10-year compound distributions per-share growth: NM**

	2011	2012	2013	2014	2015	2016	2017	2018
Revenues (mil)	619.7	676.4	743.4	789.0	839.0	881.4	932.2	1032.5
Net income (mil)	71.6	92.0	90.1	94.9	86.5	109.4	128.3	154.2
Earnings per share	1.79	2.55	2.48	2.72	2.65	3.39	3.98	4.94
Dividends per share	0.08	0.08	0.08	0.08	0.08	0.08	0.04	0
Cash flow per share	2.58	3.20	3.54	3.98	3.85	4.56	5.44	6.36
Price: high	38.5	47.9	63.5	74.4	97.6	133.0	159.9	241.1
low	20.0	34.6	41.3	50.3	69.4	80.2	118.9	152.9

Website: www.fico.com

AGGRESSIVE GROWTH

FedEx Corporation

Ticker symbol: FDX (NYSE) ❏ Large Cap ❏ Value Line financial strength rating: A++ ❏ Current yield: 1.6% ❏ Dividend raises, past 10 years: 9

Company Profile

FedEx Corporation is the world's leading provider of guaranteed express delivery services and a major player in the overall small shipment and small-package logistics market. The corporation is organized as a holding company, with four individual businesses that compete collectively and operate independently under the FedEx brand, offering a wide range of express delivery services for the time-definite transportation of documents, packages, and freight: These services, as a whole, reach 60,000 drop-off locations in 220 countries, operating 678 aircraft through ten air express hubs and approximately 180,000 ground vehicles, operates in some 650 airports and 5,000 facilities overall, sorts and processes some 15 million shipments a day, and estimates that it reaches markets that comprise more than 99 percent of global GDP. The four businesses include:

- FedEx Express (55 percent of FY2018 revenues) offers the familiar overnight and deferred air service through hubs to most of the 650 airports mentioned earlier, with customs clearance services, critical delivery services from centralized "banks," e.g., "Partsbank" and other express logistics services. The 2016 acquisition of TNT Worldwide provided a major step function upward in revenues overall (12 percent) and number of airports served and international markets in general; the integration won't be 100 percent complete until 2020.
- FedEx Ground (28 percent of revenues) offers overnight service from 575 pickup/delivery terminals for up to 400 miles anywhere in the US for packages weighing up to 150 pounds. Ground serves 100 percent of US residences and now features the so-called "SmartPost" operation, where small and less urgent packages are delivered "last mile" to local addresses by the US Postal Service and newly acquired reverse logistics provider GENCO—both key offerings for the e-commerce business. The unit now includes ground services of TNT mainly in Europe and has gained revenue share with double-digit margins—the latter especially notable in the relatively low-margin ground transport business.

- FedEx Freight (10 percent of revenues) offers standard and priority LTL (less than truckload) service across North America mainly for business supply-chain operations with 370 terminals and service centers.
- FedEx Services (3 percent of revenues), which includes 1,800 former Kinkos copy and office centers, now operates under the FedEx Office brand, and FedEx TechConnect provides solutions to integrate supply-chain management IT tools with FedEx's systems.
- Other (3 percent of revenues) now includes FedEx Trade Networks, which designs and manages specialty logistics networks and supply chains using all FedEx services and outside suppliers.

A key part of FedEx's strategy is to provide integrated logistics solutions, that is, encourage customers to use all services (Express, Ground, Freight) according to need rather than just a single service. The company estimates that over 96 percent (up 1 percent from last year) of its customers use two or more of these services; 79 percent use all three (up 2 percent from last year), attesting to the fact that FedEx's business is increasingly tuned to providing a total and flexible logistics solution.

The company just entered into an agreement with Walmart to place 500 new FedEx Office locations in select stores during 2019 and 2020; this is on top of similar agreements to offer pickup and drop-off services at some 7,500 Walgreens store locations and many Kroger, Albertsons, and Office Depot & OfficeMax locations, pickup being especially important in this modern era of "porch piracy" of e-commerce shipments. The company is also implementing a FedEx Returns Technology solution to help e-tailers with reverse logistics, i.e., returns. Recently the company has focused on its competitive advantages, promoting its Ground service as faster than UPS in 28 percent of major shipping lanes and its flexible but more time-definite home-delivery services with heavier allowed weights as compared to UPS.

Financial Highlights, Fiscal Year 2018

Stronger e-commerce, favorable business conditions and a greater degree of automation (96 percent automatic sorting for Ground shipments versus 70 percent for UPS), and a new emphasis on yield management (increasing capacity utilization; select price increases) led to a banner year in 2018, with net income advancing some 25 percent on an 8.5 percent revenue gain in the US. But for 2019 trade uncertainties, TNT integration, Brexit, and a shift from parcels to freight after a TNT cyberattack all are weighing on the international sector; the company has guided lower to a 2 percent earnings advance on a 9 percent revenue increase for 2019 improving somewhat to an 8–10 percent earnings advance on a 10–12 percent revenue increase for 2020. The rise in home-delivered e-commerce has also hurt operating margins somewhat (it takes more resources to deliver many one-off small packages to individual residential addresses). Price increases, scale in home e-commerce delivery, and TNT integration should bring a rise in margins beyond pre-TNT levels in 2020 and beyond, especially if fuel prices continue to moderate. Cash flows continue strong, making moderate buybacks and dividend hikes likely. The company raised the dividend 60 percent in 2017, another 25 percent in 2018, and plans another 45 percent rise by the end of 2020.

Reasons to Buy

FedEx has several tailwinds now—a broad product offering, best-in-class cost structure, customer-driven logistics fine-tuning, and the growth of e-commerce. But trade uncertainties are starting to become an offsetting headwind.

The growing e-commerce business and greater need for a complete, economical, and partially time-sensitive logistics mix makes FedEx the right place to be as American manufacturing activity and local sourcing increase—although this could dampen international shipments. With SmartPost and other business expansions, the Ground segment has reached a 30 percent market share for such services, a position from which it can start to call the shots in the marketplace for lucrative e-commerce and time-sensitive ground business. Indeed, of late, the company has been able to raise prices while also gaining market share. While the shares lost some altitude in 2019 and were trading at a very attractive valuation for this type of company (P/E of 10), we feel that volumes will continue to clearly benefit from the rise in e-commerce and from the economy in general, while profitability will benefit from scale and innovation—a solid success story.

Reasons for Caution

The company is always vulnerable to economic downturns and fuel price increases, particularly if cost increases come faster than they can be recovered in rates and fuel surcharges—as is often the case. While it has already started, it remains to be seen how much the Trump administration's trade policies will affect international trade, which could hurt international volumes and pricing with some offsetting gains in domestic business. Amazon's entry into the shipping business (for its own account) may cause some concern, but no single customer, including Amazon, accounts for more than 3 percent of the business. While the company has done a good job of carving out its "full service" niche, it is always vulnerable to competition in both domestic and overseas markets; that said, its size, scale, and innovation give it advantage.

SECTOR: Transportation ❑ Beta coefficient: 1.20 ❑ 10-year compound earnings per-share growth: 7.5% ❑ 10-year compound dividends per-share growth: 15.5%

	2011	2012	2013	2014	2015	2016	2017	2018
Revenues (mil)	39,204	42,680	44,287	45,567	47,453	50,365	60,319	65,450
Net income (mil)	1,452	2,032	1,561	2,097	2,572	3,016	3,330	4,169
Earnings per share	4.90	6.41	6.23	6.75	8.95	10.80	12.30	15.31
Dividends per share	0.48	0.52	0.56	0.60	0.80	1.00	1.60	2.00
Cash flow per share	11.13	13.08	12.41	16.32	18.35	21.27	23.58	27.32
Price: high	98.7	97.2	144.1	183.5	185.2	201.6	255.1	274.7
low	64.1	82.8	90.6	128.2	130.0	119.7	182.9	150.9

Website: www.fedex.com

First Solar, Inc.

Ticker symbol: FSLR (NASDAQ) ❑ Large Cap ❑ Value Line financial strength rating: A ❑ Current yield: Nil ❑ Dividend raises, past 10 years: NA

Company Profile

"Leading the World's Sustainable Energy Future" harkens the first line on solar provider and operator First Solar's website. First Solar is the largest US-based provider of photovoltaic (solar) energy solutions for both residential and commercial solar markets. It is a vertically integrated business, producing the core building-block solar panels ("Modules" segment) as well as large-scale generation systems that utilize these same panels ("Systems" segment). They also provide Operations and Management (O&M) services for utility-scale installations and sell these O&M and EPC—Engineering, Procurement, and Construction—services for any installation worldwide. They are the world's largest O&M provider, with over 4 percent of the global market under their management. They develop, finance, engineer, build, and operate many of the world's largest grid-connected photovoltaic power plants. They are also entering the field of battery storage solutions on a plant scale to balance loads and deliver electricity around the clock. These plants are built to customer specifications and then turned over when complete or are managed and run by FSLR. Modules account for about 22 percent of 2018 sales; Systems the other 78 percent.

The company's panels employ a proprietary thin-film cadmium-telluride chemistry, which, while less efficient than the highest-grade monocrystalline silicon, is 8 percent more efficient than polycrystalline, the most commonly used crystalline material for energy generation. First Solar's technology also has certain other advantages in production and application.

Founded in 1990 as an R&D-focused endeavor and renamed in 1999, FSLR began commercial operations in 2002 and now designs, manufactures, operates, and maintains all elements of the solar power chain across residential, commercial, and utility-scale applications. They manufacture panels in Perrysburg, Ohio, Ho Chi Minh City, Vietnam, and Kulim, Malaysia. About 66 percent of their sales are in the US, and they continue to be among the industry leaders in R&D spend at 3.8 percent of sales.

Financial Highlights, Fiscal Year 2018

Evolving technology, competitive pressures, government giveaways and take-aways, and ever-changing policies toward and demand for alternative energy, particularly solar, make this a highly dynamic business. The company has had two uncharacteristically slow years: first in 2016 as they essentially skipped a technology evolution, going from "Series 4" to "Series 6" modules, skipping Series 5 altogether at a great short-term cost but a better long-term future getting Series 6 to market sooner. The effects of this carried into 2017, and the company also sold some plants it had been operating—both factors and some effects of tariffs and lower China demand all swirling into a 23 percent sales decline for 2018—however, with Series 6 in full production with a new Vietnam plant and more stability in the Systems marketplace, net income returned to the black with a $155 million profit.

Revenues for FY2018 are expected to grow substantially (50 percent) and return to some of their best past levels in 2019; then only 4–6 percent in 2020. Net income is expected to double again in 2019 with an 18–20 percent follow-on gain in 2020; forecasts for the early 2020s look especially rosy as both businesses hit stride with improved operating leverage and substantially higher margins.

Reasons to Buy

Clearly differentiated from the "pack" of other solar companies, First Solar has (1) a clearly preferred technology for its solar panels; and (2) almost 80 percent of its business comes from building and managing solar systems, where there is far less competition and a steady demand as utilities look (or in many states, are mandated) to add solar to the mix. As solar matures and the number of these plants grow, First Solar should evolve into a much more stable and predictable business.

FSLR's proprietary photovoltaic cell technology requires very little silicon; instead of polysilicon or monocrystalline silicon as a photoelectric core it uses a thin cadmium-telluride film over glass. FSLR is thus not exposed to the vagaries of the worldwide market for polycrystalline silicon. The volatility of this "poly" market played a large role in the unpredictable pricing for panels in the late 2000s and was a major factor in the elimination of many of FSLR's early competitors.

Rather than living on the edge of thin margins and low capitalization, First Solar's balance sheet stands out in the industry with long-term debt as a percent of total capital under 10 percent.

Reasons for Caution

Offshore producers of silicon-based panels have historically been extremely aggressive in pricing their panels, and we anticipate the downward trend will continue. FSLR brings several cost-of-ownership advantages to the table, but pricing pressure on panels is expected to continue as a factor, even with tariffs in place on the "low" tech polycrystalline varieties (thin film is currently exempt from tariffs). Tariffs, of course, bear watching; they can distort the market in a hurry. Tax credits and incentives are also very important to solar sales; for now the 30 percent project tax credits (which affect both residential and plant installations) have been extended through projects started in 2019 but are scheduled to taper off starting with 26 percent in 2020, 22 percent for 2021, and 10 percent for projects commencing thereafter. We would be surprised, however, if these credits aren't extended at the 30 percent level.

SECTOR: Energy ❑ Beta coefficient: 1.35 ❑ 10-year compound earnings per-share growth: NA ❑ 10-year compound dividends per-share growth: NA

	2011	2012	2013	2014	2015	2016	2017	2018
Revenues (mil)	2,766	3,369	3,309	3,392	3,579	2,951	2,941	2,244
Net income (mil)	484	430	353	397	546	(358)	(165)	144
Earnings per share	5.55	4.90	3.70	3.91	5.37	(3.48)	(1.59)	1.36
Dividends per share	—	—	—	—	—	—	—	—
Cash flow per share	8.31	7.95	5.90	6.40	7.90	(1.22)	(0.48)	2.62
Price: high	175.4	50.2	66.0	74.8	67.8	74.3	71.8	81.7
low	29.9	11.4	24.5	40.5	39.2	28.6	25.6	36.5

Website: www.firstsolar.com

AGGRESSIVE GROWTH

Home Depot

Ticker symbol: HD (NYSE) ❑ Large Cap ❑ Value Line financial strength rating: A++ ❑ Current yield: 3.0% ❑ Dividend raises, past 10 years: 9

Company Profile

Admittedly, we were late to the party with Wall Street and Main Street favorite Home Depot, adding it to the *100 Best* list just last year. We explained our skepticism as a matter of languishing performance, too many stores, competition, and less-than-robust service—all of which indeed were a cause for concern for this company ten years ago. We finally climbed on board last year, and, given current performance, we're glad we did.

Founded in 1978, Home Depot overlaid a big-box retail format on lumber yards and other specialty building materials stores essentially set up to sell to the trades, not to end customers. It brought in one-stop shopping, low prices, and a wide assortment of merchandise covering all facets of mostly residential building materials, all with convenient suburban locations and extended retail hours. The formula gained traction, first with an ever-growing base of consumer do-it-yourselfers, then with the contractors that serve the consumer base.

Today's Home Depot operates 2,287 retail stores (up from 2,284 last year—overly rapid expansion and cannibalization is a thing of the past) across the US, with stores in Canada, Guam, Mexico, and Puerto Rico as well. The stores average 104,000 square feet with about 24,000 square feet of additional garden area. In addition to consumer-accessible merchandising in a warehouse environment, the stores have customer service representatives throughout the store to give advice and help shoppers, many of whom are former contractors themselves. Most have a contractor service "PRO" desk for handling contractor business. The stores carry 35,000 SKUs of lumber, floor and wall coverings, plumbing, electrical, paint, furniture, storage, and seasonal items. The primary market has been consumer, but more recently stores are catering to the MRO—maintenance, repair, and operations—facilities in business, government, and others. The company is also investing heavily in customer experience and online sales, for example, $1.2 billion being invested in logistics networks to reach 90 percent of the population with same-day/next-day delivery.

Financial Highlights, Fiscal Year 2018

A strong 5.2 percent increase in same-store sales (albeit somewhat weaker than 2017's 6.5 percent), combined with a healthy average ticket increase drove a 7.2 percent overall increase in the 2018 top line. Higher throughput, minimal new store expenses, and lower tax rates, even with higher logistics costs, rang up a 28 percent gain in net income. A second 4 percent buyback in a row led to an even stronger 32 percent gain in per-share earnings. Forecasts for 2019 and 2020 call for 3–5 percent top-line gains with some one-time items keeping earnings flat for 2019 but resuming growth in the 6–8 percent range in 2020. Aggressive buybacks, which have retired 37 percent of outstanding shares in the past ten years and half its shares since 2005, look to continue, and Home Depot is on a tear with its dividend, raising it 32 percent in 2019 and another 15–20 percent projected in 2020.

Reasons to Buy

Home Depot has been on a roll for almost ten years (and sadly, we missed the first eight of them!). Sales and profits have risen steadily—while share counts have fallen dramatically at the same time. Over that time, dating back to 2011, sales are up 50 percent, and net profit margins have doubled to a retail nirvana of 10 percent, thanks to scale and other efficiencies and the new tax code; annual net profits in total have doubled. The company has amply shared its success with its shareholders as previously described; we like that.

Clearly, beyond these stellar financial results—or more to the point, in advance of them—Home Depot has found a retail sweet spot as more consumers are able and willing to take on do-it-yourself projects (which itself can be attributed in part to HD's existence), and more contractors rely on it as a primary material source. Perhaps most to the point is that Amazon cannot match or duplicate its offering—4 × 8 sheets of plywood just don't go well with Amazon Prime. While Amazon does sell some of the same items, it cannot offer HD's depth, breadth, convenience, and recently, in-store service. The company has achieved scale sufficient to become a powerful buyer in its markets, often dictating or heavily influencing supplier prices. With that size and scale, it can pretty much set the selling price for many of its products. The resulting 10 percent net profit margins are exceptional for a large retailer. Finally, while the stock price has risen steadily, one can take comfort in the fact that much of it has been driven by actual results—earnings growth and share buybacks—rather than reliance on future expectations.

Reasons for Caution

The big fly in the ointment for Home Depot over the years has been economic downturns, which slow the building supply market both for new and remodel home materials. The possibility of rising interest rates is always a concern, as are less favorable property tax and interest deduction treatments, which may attenuate demand in some markets. Home Depot will move with new and existing home sales reports, but we believe their "real" business is with people who aren't moving and instead choose to better up their current place. We think the overall strength in the economy and a greater stay-at-home tendency among today's population will make home—and Home Depot—where the improvements will be.

SECTOR: Retail ❏ Beta coefficient: 1.05 ❏ 10-year compound earnings per-share growth: 9.5% ❏ 10-year compound dividends per-share growth: 16.0%

	2011	2012	2013	2014	2015	2016	2017	2018
Revenues (bil)	70.4	74.8	78.8	83.2	88.5	94.6	100.9	108.2
Net income (bil)	3.9	4.7	5.4	6.1	6.8	8.0	8.8	11.3
Earnings per share	2.47	3.10	3.76	4.56	5.34	6.45	7.49	9.89
Dividends per share	1.04	1.16	1.56	1.88	2.36	2.76	3.56	4.16
Cash flow per share	3.55	4.21	5.08	5.96	6.82	8.07	9.25	11.80
Price: high	42.5	65.9	82.5	106.0	135.5	139.0	191.5	215.4
low	28.1	41.9	62.4	74.0	92.2	109.6	133.0	158.1

Website: www.homedepot.com

AGGRESSIVE GROWTH
Honeywell International

Ticker symbol: HON (NYSE) ❏ Large Cap ❏ Value Line financial strength rating: A++ ❏ Current yield: 2.0% ❏ Dividend raises, past 10 years: 9

Company Profile
Honeywell is a diversified international technology and manufacturing company engaged in the development, manufacturing, and marketing of aerospace products and services; control technologies for buildings and industry; and specialty and safety materials. The company continues to group these activities into four segments: Aerospace (37 percent of FY2018 sales), Honeywell Building Technologies (22 percent), Performance Materials and Technologies (26 percent), and Safety and Productivity (15 percent). In 2019 the company completed the divestiture of the homes and transportation systems business, which made and distributed items such as home thermostats (the new spin-off is called Resideo) and turbochargers (Garrett

Motion Inc.). The company also acquired Transnorm, a maker of warehouse automation equipment. This continues a simplification trend started in 2014 with the disposal of many of its automotive businesses, including "friction materials"—brakes.

The Aerospace businesses produce and market products, software, and services including avionics, cockpit controls, power-generation equipment, satellite and space components, and wheels and brakes for commercial and military aircraft and for airports and ground operations. It also makes jet engines for regional and business jet manufacturers. Products include avionics, auxiliary power units (APUs), aircraft lighting, and landing systems.

The Performance Materials and Technologies operation makes a wide assortment of specialty chemicals and fibers, plastics, coatings, and semiconductor and electronics materials, which are sold primarily to the food, pharmaceutical, petroleum-refining, and electronic packaging industries. Carbon fiber materials are among the more important and fastest-growing products in this segment. Safety and Productivity Solutions markets supply-chain and warehouse automation equipment, portable data collection devices, gas detection equipment, and an assortment of other solutions and components.

The Safety and Productivity Solutions segment is a leading global provider of products, software, and connected solutions that improve productivity, workplace safety, and asset performance. Safety products include personal protection equipment and footwear designed for work, play, and outdoor activities. Productivity Solutions products and services include gas detection technology; mobile devices and software for computing, data collection, and thermal printing; supply-chain and warehouse automation equipment; software and solutions; custom-engineered sensors, switches, and controls for sensing and productivity solutions; and software-based data and asset management productivity solutions.

The Honeywell Building Technologies segment makes hardware and software products and systems that enable building owners and occupants to ensure safety, energy efficiency, productivity, and connectivity, including sensors, switches, control systems, video surveillance, fire suppression, remote monitoring, lighting controls, etc. This segment produces most of the components of what is known in the trade and advertising lingo as a "smart building," along with devices that play well with the new data analytics, and "Internet of Things" concepts.

The company has a considerable international footprint, with technology and manufacturing centers located outside the US; five such centers are located in China along with a similar number in India. Before the homes divestiture, about 57 percent of its business came from outside the US. US government sales, mainly from the Aerospace segment, account for about 8 percent of total sales.

Financial Highlights, Fiscal Year 2018

FY2018 sales moved ahead a modest 3 percent in total, but the previously mentioned divestures took away about 4 percent. Stronger than that average were the remaining Aerospace businesses, particularly commercial aviation, and some of the "productivity solutions" in the Safety and Productivity Solutions group. The Performance Materials segment generally lagged. Net income rose almost 10 percent mainly on tax changes; gross margins were actually slightly lower than 2017 at 7.6 percent. For 2019, revenues will decrease about 10 percent reflecting the spin-offs, but will resume a 5–8 percent upward trajectory in 2020. Net profits will likewise settle 2–4 percent lower but pick up to a 9–11 percent growth in 2020. Annual dividend increases should continue in the 10 percent range with very modest share buybacks for the moment.

Reasons to Buy

A bet on Honeywell is a bet on a well-managed "best in class" producer of a wide variety of business and consumer products with an underlying technology theme—not really "high tech" but using advanced technologies to deliver a solution. The company shows many of the traditional signs of being well managed, with a strong and strategic focus on profitability, cash flow, and operational efficiency and a healthy respect for transparency, as evidenced by its informative annual reports, investor presentations, and other corporate materials. The company's profit margins are notably higher than others in this type of business—and growing. In this case, one doesn't care so much about anemic revenue growth. In the grand scheme, Honeywell has clearly outperformed GE, Siemens, and other rivals—but is not content to rest on its laurels as it seeks to reposition itself in the wake of GE's problems. We approve of their efforts to focus the business.

The company is investing more in providing software products to complete the automation cycle started by its hardware products. It is now expanding its focus to complete solutions through "connectivity" and "adjacency" opportunities, many being software driven, within many of their platforms; software sales are expected to grow by a factor of four over the next five years. Honeywell has a solid balance sheet and participates almost exclusively in high-margin businesses.

Reasons for Caution

There's a fair amount of change, and change can be painful. While the organizational alignment has begun to settle, it's a long way from done, and there is plenty of work to do to educate customers exactly what Honeywell does do and doesn't do these days. Especially given some of these uncertainties, Honeywell shares seem plenty expensive these days—shop carefully. Many of the industries Honeywell sells to can be cyclical and/or low-growth businesses. However, as we've seen, the focus on efficiency and profitability will make the most of cyclically sensitive businesses.

SECTOR: Industrials □ Beta coefficient: 1.05 □ 10-year compound earnings per-share growth: 8.5% □ 10-year compound dividends per-share growth: 10.5%

	2011	2012	2013	2014	2015	2016	2017	2018
Revenues (mil)	36,500	37,665	39,055	40,306	38,581	39,302	40,634	41,802
Net income (mil)	2,998	3,552	3,965	4,422	4,768	5,104	5,492	6,035
Earnings per share	3.79	4.48	4.97	5.56	6.04	6.59	7.11	8.01
Dividends per share	1.37	1.53	1.68	1.87	2.15	2.45	2.74	3.06
Cash flow per share	5.11	5.72	6.32	6.83	7.34	8.06	8.80	9.81
Price: high	62.3	64.5	91.6	102.4	107.4	120.0	158.7	167.6
low	41.2	52.2	64.2	82.9	87.0	93.7	113.6	123.5

Website: www.honeywell.com

CONSERVATIVE GROWTH

Illinois Tool Works, Inc.

Ticker symbol: ITW (NYSE) □ Large Cap □ Value Line financial strength rating: A++ □ Current yield: 2.8% □ Dividend raises, past 10 years: 10

Company Profile

Illinois Tool Works is a multinational conglomerate involved in the manufacture of a diversified range of mostly industrial intermediary and end products. Customers include the automotive, machinery, construction, food and beverage, and general industrial markets. The company currently operates some 85 businesses in seven segments in 55 countries, employing approximately 48,000 people. Some of the products are branded and familiar, like Wolf and Hobart kitchen equipment and Paslode air power tools; most are obscure and only known to others in their industries. Sales outside North America account for 48 percent of the total.

The seven segments are presented here with approximate revenue percentages:

- Automotive OEM (23 percent of 2018 revenues, 21 percent of operating income) includes transportation-related components, fasteners, and polymers, as well as truck remanufacturing and related parts and service for the automotive manufacturer market. Important brands include Drawform ("high volume, highly toleranced deep-drawn metal stampings") and Deltar Interior Components, which makes things like interior door handles.

- Test & Measurement/Electronics (15 percent, 14 percent) supplies equipment and software for testing and measuring of materials and structures, solder, and other materials for PC board manufacturing and microelectronics assembly. Brands include Brooks Instrument, Buehler, Chemtronics, Instron, Magnaflux, and Speedline Technologies.

- Food Equipment (15 percent, 16 percent) produces commercial food equipment and related services, including professional kitchen ovens, refrigeration, mixers, and exhaust and ventilation systems. Major brands include Hobart, Traulsen, Vulcan, and Wolf.

- Polymers & Fluids (12 percent, 10 percent) businesses produce adhesives, sealants, lubrication and cutting fluids, and hygiene products for an assortment of markets. Their primary brands include Futura, Krafft, Devcon, Rocol, and Permatex and such brands as Rain-X and Wynn's for the automotive aftermarket.

- Construction Products (12 percent, 11 percent) concentrates on tools, fasteners, and other products for construction applications. Their major end markets are residential, commercial, and renovation construction. Brands include Ramset, Paslode, Buildex, Proline, and others.

- The Welding segment (11 percent, 13 percent) produces equipment and consumables associated with specialty power conversion, metallurgy, and electronics. Their primary products include arc-welding equipment and consumables, solder materials, equipment and services for electronics assembly, and airport ground support equipment. Primary brands include AXA Power, Hobart, and Weldcraft.

- Specialty Products (13 percent) is a hodgepodge of brands and businesses that includes Diagraph (industrial marking and coding systems), Fastex (engineered components for the appliance industry), and Zip-Pak reclosable plastic packaging.

In 2012, the company embarked on a five-year "Enterprise Strategy" program aimed at simplifying the business and applying sound customer-driven operating principles to fine-tune its base of customers, markets, products, facilities, and supply chains. Emphasis is placed on removing customer pain points, reducing complexity by applying the "80–20" rule (focusing on the 20 percent of customers, products, and processes that deliver 80 percent of the results), customer-driven innovation, and fine-tuning the relationships between headquarters and the operating entities. Growing organically (instead of by acquisition) and improving margins are the chief business objectives; the main strategy is to focus on businesses with strong sustainable differentiation. The company closely monitors operating margin improvements in each of its seven segments. We normally don't bring too many such strategic initiatives to light, but we will in this case because (1) it's working, and (2) such focus is needed in a company with such size and operating complexity; otherwise, it quickly becomes an uncoordinated conglomerate jumble, as many others before it have. ITW has divested 30-plus businesses and two segments, simplified the rest from 800 business units to 85 businesses ("divisions"), achieved a 1.1 percentage-point gain in operating margins in 2018 alone, and identified specific growth drivers in each of the seven segments.

These efficiency measures and "80–20" thinking have not only improved profitability of continuing operations but have also guided the company's thinking in terms of acquiring and selling businesses and in strategically managing the fundamentals within those businesses. The net result can be no better demonstrated than by the fact that in the five years since 2012, per-share earnings have increased *109 percent* while revenues have *decreased* 18 percent in that time. In our view, good management has had no finer hour, and we continue to appreciate ITW's efforts and look forward to the ongoing benefits of this initiative into 2020.

Financial Highlights, Fiscal Year 2018

FY2018 was another year of solid profit gains exceeding revenue gains, fueled both by strong end markets and customer relationships and internal improvements built on the Enterprise strategy. FY2018 net sales advanced 3.2 percent as some slowness crept into the Automotive, Construction, and Specialty Products businesses, while net earnings managed a 9.3 percent increase. Projections call for a 3–5 percent earnings gain on relatively flat sales in 2019, followed by a 4–6 percent earnings gain on a 2–4 percent sales gain in 2020, as many of the end markets level off a bit. The company commits half its profits each year to shareholder returns through dividends and buybacks and plans to increase its payout ratio (dividends to free cash flow) from 43 to 50 percent in the coming years, which will probably bump the dividend as much as 25 percent over that time. ITW bought back about 2.5 percent of its shares in 2018.

Reasons to Buy

Buying shares of ITW continues to be like buying a fund of medium-sized manufacturing businesses you've probably never heard of but would definitely like to own. Indeed, think of it as the Berkshire Hathaway of manufacturing companies if you will—we do. We much admire this management team, with its solid strategic focus and drive to benefit shareholders. Headquarters prescribes the strategies such as margin focus and the 80–20 mindset; managers of the subsidiary businesses have the autonomy to figure out how to deliver results. The model works. We enjoy doing this presentation every year; it's a good tour through how to run a modern conglomerate effectively in an era where many have stumbled, and the company presents itself well to investors.

ITW is well diversified and serves many markets, some with end products, some with components, some in cyclical industries such as automotive and construction, some in steady-state industries like food processing. The businesses balance each other out. The company has solid models for making acquisitions and seems to do better than most conglomerates historically in choosing candidates and then managing them once they're in the fold. The "Enterprise" initiative is turning opportunity into cash flow and using that cash flow to enhance shareholder returns.

Reasons for Caution

ITW is, by its nature, tied to some of the more volatile elements of the business cycle, so it may not be the best pick for investors living in fear of the next downturn. In particular, we worry a bit about the Automotive segment going forward, although recently the unit has been gaining share in the automotive market. Indeed, it does seem that things are leveling off a bit, but the 80–20 focus and attention to profits should keep them headed in the right direction through this period. Conglomerates are notoriously difficult to manage (it's hard enough to manage one business, let alone 85 of them); that said, the company has made a conscious decision to downshift its acquisitions for now.

SECTOR: Industrials ❑ Beta coefficient: 1.10 ❑ 10-year compound earnings per-share growth: 7.0% ❑ 10-year compound dividends per-share growth: 12.5%

	2011	2012	2013	2014	2015	2016	2017	2018
Revenues (mil)	17,787	17,924	14,135	14,484	13,405	13,599	14,314	14,768
Net income (mil)	1,852	1,921	1,629	1,890	1,886	2,036	2,302	2,563
Earnings per share	3.74	4.06	3.63	4.67	5.13	5.70	6.78	7.60
Dividends per share	1.38	1.46	1.60	1.75	2.07	2.40	2.73	3.56
Cash flow per share	5.06	5.55	5.20	6.25	7.17	7.22	8.09	9.21
Price: high	59.3	63.3	84.3	97.8	100.1	128.0	169.7	179.1
low	39.1	47.4	59.7	76.3	78.8	79.1	120.1	117.8

Website: www.itwinc.com

AGGRESSIVE GROWTH

International Flavors & Fragrances, Inc.

Ticker symbol: IFF (NYSE) ❑ Large Cap ❑ Value Line financial strength rating: A+ ❑ Current yield: 2.4% ❑ Dividend raises, past 10 years: 10

Company Profile

"Pioneering sensorial experiences that move the world" crows the well-crafted website for International Flavors & Fragrances—a company that continues to pass our smell and taste tests. IFF is a leading manufacturer of such "sensorial experiences"—natural and artificial flavoring and fragrance chemicals for the food and beverage and consumer products industry, including cosmetics, perfumes, soap and detergents, hair care, pharmaceuticals, and a wide variety of other products. Fragrances accounted for about 48 percent of 2018 sales; flavorings 44 percent; and sales from the newly acquired Frutarom, a leader in natural flavorings, scents, nutrition, and food protection acquired in late 2018, 6 percent. But Frutarom is a sizeable business: On a full-year basis the sales mix is anticipated to be 36 percent "scent" (fragrance), 34 percent "taste" (flavorings), and 30 percent Frutarom.

Not surprisingly, the company's value proposition and strategy are to create a differentiated and high value add for its customers by providing critical, unique, and highly researched ingredients. Many of the approximately 100,000 flavorings and fragrances offered are custom made for clients. For the food and beverage industry, the company estimates that its flavorings cost only 1–5 percent of the product's total cost but generate 45 percent of the motivation to purchase it and to purchase it repeatedly. With the Frutarom acquisition, IFF now positions itself as "a global leader in taste, scent and nutrition."

Indeed, the company holds a number two global market position, with 110 manufacturing facilities, 100 R&D centers, and 33,000 customers around the world. The IFF footprint is truly "international," with 80 percent of sales originating outside North America; in fact, nearly 50 percent of sales originate in emerging markets. Recognizing that flavor and fragrance preferences are very local in nature, the company has established an operational presence in 32 countries and lab facilities in 13 of them, including the US. Still, it estimates only a 16 percent share of the global flavorings and fragrances market and holds the number two position behind Swiss flavorings maker Givaudan. For US investors, it is by far the largest pure play available in this niche.

Research and development—at 8 percent of sales—is a big part of what IFF does. The company does extensive research on consumer tastes and preferences, how flavors and aromas work and hold up in different environments, and how to manufacture their products and develop the best delivery system to make them work over the desired life cycle. Research includes things like study of the "psychophysics of sensory perception" and the genetic basis for preferences in flavor and fragrance. Among successful new products are recently introduced encapsulation technologies that coat fragrance droplets with polymeric shells to enhance life cycle performance and shelf life and "PolyIFF" embedding scent into molded plastic. Through acquisitions the company now offers "PowderPure" natural food drying and powdering technology and a new "Tastepoint" line of middle-market products as a subbrand—with another clever slogan "the perfect blend of heart and science." There is a new "Digital Nose" flavor and fragrance sensing platform designed for use by customers to perfect their product "olfaction." The strategy: Grow business with small and mid-tier clients by providing a small-company look and feel when working with these clients. The company collaborates regularly with chefs, fashion designers, filmmakers, and other trendsetters to evolve new ideas.

Financial Highlights, Fiscal Year 2018

IFF projects that the $20 billion market for flavors and fragrances will grow about 2–3 percent annually, with fully 75 percent of the growth coming from emerging markets, as taste and aroma become more important as product components in China, Latin America, Africa, and the Middle East. FY2018 was a dynamic year with the Frutarom acquisition. Sales grew about 6 percent organically and about 11 percent overall, while net earnings jumped ahead 13 percent mainly on volume leverage and productivity initiatives. The company projects total revenue growth in the 35 percent revenue range including Frutarom, mid-single digits without, for 2019, followed by a 6–8 growth rate in 2020. Similarly, net income should rise about 40 percent in 2019 followed by a 5–7 percent gain in 2020. Dividend growth should be in the high single digits with modest steady share buybacks.

Reasons to Buy

IFF made a transformative, "all in" bet on natural tastes, scents, nutrition, and preservation with the acquisition of Frutarom, which will become 30 percent of the business. Given today's food trends and millennial preferences, this smells like a good move.

IFF has a strong niche and produces elements critical in differentiating products in the fairly undifferentiated food and consumer products businesses. That should play better over time as people's tastes become more trained and more demanding—both in the rich world and especially in developing nations, which is an important trend right now. Not only does the company produce many of the world's leading flavorings and fragrances; it also has the market research and know-how to give it a competitive advantage—a moat—both with its customer insights and knowing how to make and deliver the stuff. We also like the relatively recession-proof nature of this business; we doubt that they will take the flavoring out of your favorite foods anytime soon. Flavorings only account for 1–5 percent of the cost of your favorite beverage, but we Coke drinkers all know what happens when a company monkeys with that.

Reasons for Caution

The cost and availability of key ingredients like vanilla (a large portion of which comes from unstable regions in West Africa) can affect IFF adversely. The strong overseas footprint is probably an advantage most of the time, but strong dollar environments and volatile emerging markets like China and Brazil attenuate that advantage; also, it's hard to keep up with changing consumer tastes in so many places. At mid-single-digit percent growth, the flavorings and fragrances business is low growth; growth has to come from market-share gains and acquisitions, always a challenge. As large as it is, integration of Frutarom could create an occasional stink. Intellectual property protection is also a challenge; many try and some succeed in reverse engineering key ingredients.

SECTOR: Consumer Staples ❑ Beta coefficient: 0.90 ❑ 10-year compound earnings per-share growth: 9.0% ❑ 10-year compound dividends per-share growth: 12.0%

	2011	2012	2013	2014	2015	2016	2017	2018
Revenues (mil)	2,788	2,821	2,953	3,089	3,023	3,116	3,399	3,957
Net income (mil)	306	328	368	416	427	441	468	530
Earnings per share	3.74	3.98	4.47	5.08	5.25	5.51	5.89	6.01
Dividends per share	1.16	1.30	1.46	1.72	2.06	2.40	2.61	2.84
Cash flow per share	4.71	4.95	5.54	6.25	6.45	6.70	7.40	5.90
Price: high	66.3	67.8	90.3	105.8	123.1	143.6	156.6	157.4
low	51.2	52.1	67.5	82.9	97.6	97.2	113.2	122.1

Website: www.iff.com

AGGRESSIVE GROWTH

Intuitive Surgical, Inc.

Ticker symbol: ISRG (NASDAQ) ❑ Large Cap ❑ Value Line financial strength rating: A+ ❑ Current yield: Nil ❑ Dividend raises, past 10 years: NA

Company Profile

Intuitive Surgical designs, manufactures, and markets da Vinci surgical systems and their related instruments and accessories and provides training and support in their use. The da Vinci system combines the benefits of minimally invasive surgery with the precision and ease of use of traditional open surgery. Confused?

Have you ever had to replace the timing belt on your car? You probably didn't do it yourself, since the belt is buried deep in the innards of your engine and is hard to get to. You might need special model-specific tools, you will need a lot of time, and if you set the timing cogs incorrectly when reassembling, you just might destroy your engine the first time you turn the key.

Such was the state of abdominal and thoracic surgeries before the development of endoscopic surgical techniques. Even though the actual area or object of surgical interest in a procedure might have been very small and the surgical act itself trivial, getting in there was anything but. Why? Because even a small surgical tool had to be in the hands of a skilled surgeon, and the surgeon's hands were (comparatively) huge. The hands had to be deep in the patient, and so did all of the tools that were there just to make access possible. Like the timing belt procedure, removing a gall bladder meant moving aside lots of other stuff—abdominal wall, stomach, pancreas—and holding it all in place during the procedure.

Endoscopic surgical techniques, on the other hand, eliminate nearly all of these complications by putting the surgical tool on the business end of a narrow rod or rods, which are inserted through *small* holes in the patient. The surgeon then manipulates these tools from outside the patient's body cavity.

Intuitive Surgical did not invent what has come to be known as "minimally invasive" surgery. Rather, it has refined the methods by using electro-mechanical devices to perform most of the required movements under the control of a trained surgeon. Benefits include reduced risk of infection, reduced blood loss, reduced time spent in the hospital, and generally faster recovery periods. A faster surgical process also means more patients can be attended to with reduced waiting periods. And, in some cases, patients for whom open surgical procedures might not be practical at all can be treated effectively using Intuitive's products.

One of the big da Vinci "aha's" is its ability to work in a remote surgical theater. The surgeon's console, with its controls and imaging systems, and the patient-side cart, with its cameras and robotic arms, can be far apart, allowing the surgeon to perform procedures on patients thousands of miles away, requiring only a solid data link and a local support staff for patient interactions and technical support. Healthcare providers can (theoretically) thus provide expert surgical care in a plurality of locations without the need to staff surgical theaters at every facility.

The company was founded in 1995, went public in 2000, and is now the world leader in robotic-assisted surgery. Its products have been approved for use in abdominal, thoracic, cardiac, urological, gynecological, pediatric, and other procedures.

Financial Highlights, Fiscal Year 2018

FY2018 sales advanced at a decent 19 percent clip while earnings tacked on a little over 15 percent as margins dipped slightly. Procedure growth was also 19 percent. Management feels that the system is gaining traction as a de facto standard rather than a novelty, and expects procedure volume to increase. Add to that healthy penetration overseas and one gets continued revenue growth in the 15–20 percent range for both 2019 and 2020. Net income growth is a bit softer at 12–15 percent as overseas sales are typically less profitable. Overseas sales run 28 percent today. Services and consumables revenue should rise as more systems are in place.

Reasons to Buy

The da Vinci system is proving to be not only a boon for experienced operators but also a powerful training tool for those learning new procedures. It has shown to be successful in reducing the time required to achieve competence in complicated procedures. It is rapidly becoming the preferred surgical treatment for localized prostate cancer and allows surgical procedures to be offered to high-BMI (obese) patients for whom open surgery may not have been an option.

The disciplines of medicine are, often appropriately, slow to change. Given that, it's safe to say that the da Vinci system has made surprising progress in the last decade in advancing the state of the art in surgical technique, safety, and availability. The development of new techniques takes time and the surgical community's support, but Intuitive has made believers of their users, and the company continues to develop procedures and new hardware for the current platform.

Finally, Intuitive is far and away the market leader and operates (pun intended!) with little in the way of pricing pressure. We feel their forecasts might be conservative; it may simply be a case of under-promising with a plan to over-deliver.

Reasons for Caution

Intuitive is a young company and the hardware equivalent of a pharmaceutical business: massive R&D costs and a long wait for uncertain success. The platform holds great promise, but many of the da Vinci's potential applications are yet to be developed, tested, and approved. Any new procedures will take time to perfect, and their final approvals are not guaranteed. There's no question that the company is an exciting prospect, but it's also trading at 45 times earnings, so bear that in mind when deciding if this is the right stock for your portfolio. It could put your portfolio under the knife.

SECTOR: Healthcare ❑ Beta coefficient: 1.00 ❑ 10-year compound earnings per-share growth: 22.0% ❑ 10-year compound dividends per-share growth: NA

		2011	2012	2013	2014	2015	2016	2017	2018
Revenues (mil)		1,757	2,179	2,265	2,132	2,384	2,704	3,129	3,724
Net income (mil)		495	657	671	419	589	736	978	1,127
Earnings per share		4.11	5.33	5.58	3.70	5.18	6.24	8.50	9.49
Dividends per share		—	—	—	—	—	—	—	—
Cash flow per share		4.44	5.73	6.26	4.29	5.83	6.96	9.48	10.80
Price:	high	156.4	198.3	195.2	180.4	188.3	242.4	405.0	581.1
	low	87.3	143.1	117.0	115.5	149.0	167.3	208.2	365.1

Website: www.intuitivesurgical.com

Johnson & Johnson

Ticker symbol: JNJ (NYSE) ❑ Large Cap ❑ Value Line financial strength rating: A++ ❑ Current yield: 2.8 percent ❑ Dividend raises, past 10 years: 10

Company Profile

Johnson & Johnson offers a broad line of consumer products, over-the-counter drugs, prescription drugs, and various other medical devices and diagnostic equipment. It is—or at least has been—one of the most solid and steady names in an ever-changing medical and pharmaceutical field.

With total FY2018 sales of over $81 billion, the company has three reporting segments: Pharmaceuticals (about 50 percent of revenues), Medical Devices and Diagnostics (about 33 percent), and Consumer Healthcare (surprisingly, since it is so recognizable, only about 17 percent). Across those segments, Johnson & Johnson has more than 260 operating companies in 60 countries, selling some 50,000 products in more than 175 countries. Among Johnson & Johnson's premier assets are its well-entrenched brand names, which are widely known in the US as well as abroad. As a marketer, JNJ's reputation for quality has enabled it to build strong ties to commercial healthcare providers. North America accounts for 47 percent of sales, 26 percent EMEA, 18 percent Asia Pacific, and 9 percent Latin America.

In the Consumer segment, the company operates in six broad categories: beauty, over-the-counter drugs, baby care, oral care, wound care, and women's health. The vast portfolio of well-known trade names includes Band-Aid adhesive bandages; Tylenol; Stayfree, Carefree, and Sure & Natural feminine hygiene products; Mylanta; Pepcid AC; Motrin; Sudafed; Zyrtec; Neosporin; Neutrogena; Johnson's baby powder shampoo and oil; Aveeno; Listerine; and Reach toothbrushes. Names in the Pharmaceutical segment are less well-known but include major entries in the areas of antiseptics, antipsychotics, gastroenterology, immunology, neurology and mood disorders, hematology, contraceptives, oncology, pain management, metabolics, and many others distributed both through consumer and healthcare professional channels. Leading diseases addressed include rheumatoid and psoriatic arthritis, inflammatory bowel disease, Alzheimer's, HIV, schizophrenia, prostate cancer, diabetes, and many others. XARELTO (vascular health), STELARA, and REMICADE (inflammatory diseases, plaque psoriasis, Crohn's disease), SYMTUZA and the recently approved JULUCA (HIV-1 infection), and CONCERTA (ADHD) are among the more prominent pharmaceutical names.

Medical Devices and Diagnostics products include professionally used cardiovascular, orthopedic, diabetic, neurologic, and surgical products, ACUVUE contact lenses and other vision care products, and others.

Although most perceive J & J as kind of a "steady Eddie" in the health industry, the company does have an active innovation machine that invests some 10.8 percent of sales with a solid pipeline of new drugs and such enhancements of consumer products as "Oasys," a light-sensitive line of ACU-VUE contact lenses that darken to provide sun protection; "Ready! Tabs," a new line of convenient single-dose Listerine capsules; and a new smartphone-based personalized skin analyzer and 3-D mask printer known as Neutrogena MaskiD. The company is typically fairly active with acquisitions, acquiring mostly small niche players to strengthen its overall product offering.

One recent development worth tracking: The company has been implicated in thousands of lawsuits over the presence of asbestos in its talc-based products. Plaintiffs have won in a few cases, sending the share price lower in late 2018. It has recovered, but the future of this litigation activity presents a risk and bears watching.

Financial Highlights, Fiscal Year 2018

Johnson & Johnson continues to own a dominant and stable franchise in a secure and lucrative industry. The basic model is to have steady, recurring income from solid consumer brands such as Tylenol combined with more aggressive and profitable ventures into pharmaceuticals and surgical products. FY2018 revenues rose 6.7 despite competitive pricing pressure; volumes were up 8.5 percent; acquisitions accounted for only 0.8 percent of this figure. Pharma was the big gainer with a 12.4 percent gain, while Consumer and Devices lagged with gains under 3 percent. A combination of increased R&D and mostly one-time expenses, including litigation, acquisition expenses, and investment losses, bled earnings to the tune of a 10 percent drop from last year. A few divestitures will hold sales pretty much in check in 2019, with 2–3 percent growth forecast for 2020. Net income gets back on track to the tune of a 25 percent recovery in 2019 and another 10–12 percent gain in 2020. Dividend increases should continue in the 5–7 percent annually; the company has raised its dividend for 56 straight years. Buyback capital will be saved for acquisitions.

Reasons to Buy

JNJ continues to be a conservatively run company whose growth prospects have traditionally been on the lower end of this book's scale; that said, growth prospects for sales and especially profits appear to be on the rise as new products gain traction especially in the Pharma segment. The business model mixes reliable, branded performers with more lucrative pharma and medical device products bringing steady earnings and cash flow combined with healthy dividend growth. The 23–25 percent net profit margins are enviable. It's a "sleep at night" stock with a decent growth component and track record for shareholder "raises."

Reasons for Caution

While we still think JNJ is a good, steady horse for a relatively long race, it has picked up some speed of late through increased emphasis on pharma and acquisitions, both of which increase the chance of getting winded somewhere along the way. The asbestos/talc lawsuits could also create a sudden sloppy track to deal with. All in all it's one of our most solid entries in the healthcare space, but it isn't immune from risk and could wind up giving your portfolio bad breath.

SECTOR: Healthcare ▢ Beta coefficient: 0.85 ▢ 10-year compound earnings per-share growth: 4.0% ▢ 10-year compound dividends per-share growth: 9.5%

	2011	2012	2013	2014	2015	2016	2017	2018
Revenues (mil)	65,030	67,224	71,312	74,311	70,074	71,890	76,450	81,581
Net income (mil)	13,867	14,345	15,576	16,323	15,409	16,540	16,680	15,045
Earnings per share	5.00	5.10	5.52	5.70	5.50	5.93	6.20	5.61
Dividends per share	2.25	2.40	2.59	2.76	2.97	3.15	3.32	3.54
Cash flow per share	6.25	6.45	7.10	7.26	6.90	7.45	8.32	8.20
Price: high	66.3	72.7	96.0	109.5	106.5	126.1	144.4	149.0
low	64.3	61.7	70.3	86.1	81.8	94.3	110.8	118.6

Website: www.jnj.com

GROWTH AND INCOME

Kimberly-Clark

RETURNING FOR 2020

Ticker symbol: KMB (NYSE) ▢ Large Cap ▢ Value Line financial strength rating: A+ ▢ Current yield: 3.5% ▢ Dividend raises, past 10 years: 10

Company Profile

For the 2020 *100 Best Stocks* list, admittedly we have gone on a bit of a recycling campaign; that is, we have "recycled" five companies that, for one reason or another, fell off the list during the past few years—AT&T, Best Buy, Devon Energy, Qualcomm, and now, Kimberly-Clark. Does this reflect on the fact that we have simply run out of ideas for new companies to include on the list? Were we wrong with our past "sell when there is something better to buy" appraisals? Or did something change for the worse, then change back for the better, with the fundamentals of said companies?

Well, as you might expect, it is a combination of "all of the above." We have watched the fundamentals or strategic premises of certain companies deteriorate, only to be mended quickly (Best Buy, Target last year). We just plain have misappraised some companies, focusing too much on the bad stuff and not the good stuff, and fortunately, we're willing to change— change *back*—one of the hardest things for most investors to do (AT&T). We have assumed some companies to be goners through mergers or acquisitions, only to have the deal fall through (Qualcomm). We have at times been too aggressive in cutting certain companies from the list in a lust to find some "grass is greener" companies with higher growth rates or in more attractive, "sexy" sectors. In that last category, we find Kimberly-Clark.

We cut Kimberly from our list in 2018. Not that it was doing that poorly or was strategically "broken" in any way. We just saw no real path to growth, and we felt that we had too many household products firms on our list. There was already plenty for a dividend-oriented defensive investor to choose from. We were worried that Kimberly would go on an acquisition binge, picking up companies that were either unrelated or were stuck in an anemic growth mode themselves, so we saw little risk in jettisoning Kimberly and some risk in keeping it. Off to the dustbin it went.

Now, in hindsight, we were right about some of our concerns. Top-line growth has indeed been anemic, even negative, including the spin-off of some of its healthcare line. With currency headwinds, sales have been exactly flat since 2015. The stock price has been flat too—even slightly lower. But earnings have risen substantially. Why? Because of one of the more successful restructuring and business optimizing programs we've seen. It's called "project FORCE," the acronymic code name for the rather clumsily named "Focused on Reducing Costs Everywhere" initiative. Clumsy the name might be, but the company wrung a cool $3.4 *billion* in costs out of its tissues and wipes and other stuff in ten years, and net profits have skied about $500 million a year. Net profit margins have nearly doubled as share count has fallen some 13 percent, and dividends have risen a third in the past six years. Defensive Kimberly-Clark might be, but they're doing okay, albeit quietly, on the offensive end as well.

Kimberly-Clark develops, manufactures, and markets a wide assortment of branded products mainly sourced from wood fiber—that is, paper. The 150-year-old company, now based in Dallas, Texas, with deep roots in the papermaking region of the Fox River Valley in Wisconsin, markets its brands in 175 countries with manufacturing operations in 35 of them, generating 51 percent of its sales overseas. The company is divided into three segments:

- Personal Care (49 percent of 2018 revenues) includes diapers, baby wipes, feminine care products, incontinence care products, and training/youth swim pants marketed under such familiar names as Huggies, Kotex, Poise, Depends, Pull-Ups, GoodNites, and others.
- Consumer Tissue (33 percent) markets facial tissue, bathroom tissue, and paper towels, under the iconic Kleenex brand as well as Scott, Cottonelle, Viva, and others.
- K-C Professional (18 percent) markets facial tissue, paper towels, wipes and bathroom tissue, and cleaning and safety products for "away-from-home" use—that is, mainly, the workplace, public institutions, restaurants, entertainment venues, and so forth. Brands include KleenGuard, Kimtech, WypAll, and others.

Kimberly-Clark, as we like to say, is a "branded house"—more people know and identify with the brands than they do the company (have you blown your nose with a Kimberly-Clark lately?). Five of the brands—Huggies, Scott, Kleenex, Cottonelle, and Kotex—are billion-dollar-plus brands, and K-C brands hold a number one or number two share position in 80 countries worldwide.

Financial Highlights, Fiscal Year 2018

As mentioned earlier, top-line growth, especially net of currency effects, is nothing to write home about—in fact, it is virtually nothing at all. For 2018, sales grew 1.2 percent. Organic growth was "slightly higher" than 1 percent. K-C Professional was a slight bright spot, with organic growth of 3 percent. D&E—Developing and Emerging—markets, a strategic focus, grew 2 percent. Input costs rose but were somewhat offset by "FORCE" cost savings, producing a 4.2 percent growth in earnings and 6.1 percent in per-share earnings with a 2 percent buyback. Shareholders benefitted from the 46th consecutive annual dividend increase and strong cash flows in general. For 2019, sales growth is projected at less than 1 percent, with earnings projected flat due mostly to input cost increases. For 2020, the company expects to gain some traction in D&E markets toward a 2 percent growth expectation; net profits will gain 0–2 percent with per-share earnings up 3 percent. Prospects look more promising for years beyond 2020 as growth gradually returns against an optimized cost structure.

Reasons to Buy

Pure and simple, this is a defensive, sleep-at-night stock with decent growth prospects based on margin improvement and profitability going forward. It will not make you the toast of your next party, unless everybody else's investments happen to be tanking at the time. Over the past ten years, K-C has surprisingly held its own against the S&P 500, rising some 222 percent over the period versus 243 percent for the S&P; what is more notable is that K-C has beaten the S&P Consumer Staples index rather handily: 222 percent versus 183 percent. Welcome back, Kimberly.

Reasons for Caution

Once again we must hope that management doesn't reach too far for growth that isn't really there, either within its core businesses or through acquisitions. For a company with little to no growth, the valuation is a bit rich recently, with a market multiple (price-to-earnings) of 17.8. We would hope the "E" would rise a bit before the "P" came down, and that earnings growth resumes its steady upward track.

SECTOR: Consumer Staples ❑ Beta coefficient: 0.75 ❑ 10-year compound earnings per-share growth: 4.5% ❑ 10-year compound dividends per-share growth: 6.0%

	2011	2012	2013	2014	2015	2016	2017	2018
Revenues (mil)	20,846	21,603	21,152	19,724	18,591	18,202	18,259	18,486
Net income (mil)	1,591	1,750	2,142	1,476	1,013	2,016	2,217	2,310
Earnings per share	3.99	4.42	5.53	3.91	2.77	5.99	6.23	6.61
Dividends per share	2.76	2.96	3.24	3.36	3.52	3.68	3.88	4.00
Cash flow per share	6.78	6.70	7.89	6.40	4.87	8.05	8.38	9.25
Price: high	74.1	88.3	111.7	118.8	129.9	138.9	136.2	123.5
low	61.0	70.5	83.9	102.8	103.0	111.3	109.7	97.1

Website: www.kimberly-clark.com

NEW FOR
2020

Linde PLC

Ticker symbol: LIN (NYSE) ❑ Large Cap ❑ Value Line financial strength rating: B++ ❑ Current
yield: 2.0% ❑ Dividend raises, past 10 years: NM

Company Profile

When companies on our *100 Best* list go through big changes—acquisitions,
mergers, spin-offs—it is our policy and habit to take a hard look at the
"before and after"(that which we can clearly see anyhow) to make sure we
understand the resulting business or businesses as well as we do the original
one(s). Such is the case with industrial gas supplier Praxair, Inc. We knew
it was coming last year; the $11 billion Praxair had agreed to merge with
the much larger and Europe-dominant German-based Linde AG to form
a "new" $29 billion dollar combined entity, which took the Linde name.
It wasn't hard to see the outcome; basically Linde was in much the same
business in Europe and other major international markets, so the combined
entity gained size, scale, and a much larger international footprint. Not too
many complexities to dig through here; we welcome the transitioned Linde
PLC, headquartered in Great Britain, to the 2020 *100 Best Stocks* list.

The merger was presented as a merger of equals, although Linde had a larger
revenue base. The combined Linde is one of the largest suppliers of industrial
gases in the world. It consists of the old Praxair, which was spun off to Union
Carbide shareholders in June 1992 and supplies a broad range of atmospheric,
process, and specialty gases; high-performance coatings; and related services and
technologies. The former Linde supplied much the same assortment of industrial gases with a complement of engineering services and hardgoods such as
welding equipment. The combined company operates in over 100 countries.

The combined Linde's primary products are atmospheric gases—
oxygen, nitrogen, argon, and rare gases (produced when atmospheric air
is purified, compressed, cooled, distilled, and condensed)—and process
and specialty gases—carbon dioxide, helium, hydrogen, and acetylene
(produced as by-products of chemical production or recovered from natural
gas). Customers include makers of primary metals, metal fabricators,
petroleum refiners, and producers of chemicals, healthcare products,
pharmaceuticals, biotech, food and beverage, electronics, glass, pulp and
paper, and environmental products. We don't yet have a breakdown of end
markets for the combined company; the most recent full-year figures for
Praxair are as follows: manufacturing, metals, and energy producers, 51

percent of 2017 sales (energy alone is 12 percent); chemicals, electronics, and aerospace another 22 percent; and healthcare and food/beverage the next 17 percent; with the remaining 11 percent to "other" industries.

For both companies, the gas products are sold into the packaged-gas market and the merchant market. In the packaged-gas market, bulk gases are packaged into high-pressure cylinders and either delivered to the customer or to distributors. In the merchant market, bulk gases are liquefied and transported by tanker truck to the customer's facility.

The combined company also designs, engineers, and constructs cryogenic and noncryogenic gas supply systems for customers who choose to produce their own atmospheric gases on-site. This is obviously a capital-intensive delivery solution but results in lower delivered cost to the customer and higher returns for Linde, as all operational costs are paid by the customer. Contracts for these installations can run to 20 years. Again, for Praxair in 2017, 28 percent of volume was packaged, 34 percent was "merchant," and 28 percent was generated on-site (8 percent is "other").

About 48 percent of Praxair's sales came from outside North America. Once combined with Linde, that number is expected to rise to 62 percent.

Financial Highlights, Fiscal Year 2018

As a new combined entity with little in the way of combined history, this part of the presentation will be necessarily brief. The combined entity reported about $28.5 billion in 2018 sales, which is expected to grow in the 7–9 percent range in each of the next two years. The combined company delivered $3.3 billion in net profit. As the merger will bring substantial cost synergies, as much as $1 billion annually, margins are expected to grow and net profits will grow in the 12–15 percent range in 2019 and 7–9 percent thereafter. The dividend was just raised 6 percent and a $6 billion share buyback program was authorized.

Reasons to Buy

The big story is the Linde merger, which took effect in late 2018. There's still a lot we don't know, but we do know that the combined company will be much larger, more diversified, and more cost efficient.

Aside from soft years in 2015 and 2016 due to energy and manufacturing weakness and a strong dollar, Praxair had a steady history of high margins, growth, and few to no surprises. It had a strong franchise and efficient operations; the Linde merger brings that formula into world markets with a stronger, more cost-efficient offering with divestitures of some

lower-margined businesses. Tailwinds in energy, metals, electronics manufacturing, emerging markets, and currency will continue to help. Much of
its business is delivered on a contract basis, providing a bit of extra stability.
So far, the combined company seems to be taking a shareholder-friendly
approach to returning cash to shareholders.

Reasons for Caution

Mergers of this size aren't simple, and even though the businesses mesh
together well, there are still cultural differences, turf wars, and other issues
to work through, and there may be supply disruptions and unexpected costs.
As hydrocarbon energy products are feedstock for many of Linde's products,
the company has enjoyed recent trends but could take a minor hit if energy
prices rise—although at least for now it has been able to pass on those
increases. The strong international presence means that results are sensitive
to currency fluctuations and weakness in important markets like China.

SECTOR: Materials ❑ Beta coefficient: NM ❑ 10-year compound earnings per-share growth:
NM ❑ 10-year compound dividends per-share growth: NM

	2011	2012	2013	2014	2015	2016	2017	2018
Revenues (mil)	—	—	—	—	—	—	—	28,500
Net income (mil)	—	—	—	—	—	—	—	3,300
Earnings per share	—	—	—	—	—	—	—	6.00
Dividends per share	—	—	—	—	—	—	—	3.30
Cash flow per share	—	—	—	—	—	—	—	11.35
Price: high	—	—	—	—	—	—	—	166.9
low	—	—	—	—	—	—	—	146.0

Website: www.lindeplc.com

GROWTH AND INCOME   NEW FOR 2020

Macquarie Infrastructure

Ticker symbol: MIC (NYSE) ❑ Large Cap ❑ Value Line financial strength rating: B ❑ Current
yield: 9.4% ❑ Dividend raises, past 10 years: 7

Company Profile

Over the years we have tried to bring you an assortment of solid, well-managed
businesses in good industries that are safe and better than average. We seek

current returns through dividends, potential returns through growth, and growing returns through increased dividends. Our style is not to try to hit home runs in the first inning; rather, we try to score runs through the innings by creating baserunners and driving them in over and over. And we don't like to strike out.

So how does this baseball analogy get us to a US transportation and logistics infrastructure company that descended from an Australian conglomerate? We like transportation and logistics infrastructure, and we like 9 percent dividends, especially when they come with a possibility of growth. For this year's list, where we are a little more leery than usual of the typical "growth" stock, Macquarie seems to be a good place to be.

Macquarie Infrastructure owns, operates, and invests in an assortment of logistics assets in the US. Currently they own a network of energy and liquid terminals (tank farms, if you want an image), an airport services business targeted at general and business aviation, and an assortment of energy distribution services in Hawaii. They recently disposed of a wind and solar assets business. Oil tanks? Business jet services? Windmills? These aren't things you'd typically want in your own backyard, but they are important, difficult to copy, and they earn steady income. By operation:

- International-Matex Tank Terminals (IMTT: 31 percent of revenue, 47 percent of free cash flow) is one of the largest independent, third-party providers of bulk liquid terminal services in the US. It handles and stores bulk liquid products—mostly petroleum products, derivatives, and chemicals but also vegetable and tropical oils for "downstream" refiners, manufacturers, and commodities traders. There are 17 terminal facilities in the US and two in Canada, all of which have access to relevant transportation facilities including deepwater ports where appropriate. Customers retain title to the product (less risk for Macquarie) and often purchase storage space by long-term agreement. Total storage capacity is about 49 million barrels, with about 39 percent set up for heavy and residual oils, 34 percent for gasoline and distillates, and 26 percent for chemicals, vegetable and tropical oils, and renewables. The unit is currently repurposing about 3 million in capacity from heavy and residual oils to gasoline and distillates and is also developing new dock and transportation connection facilities to meet customer demand and diversify the mix of products handled. Capacity utilization is about 88 percent, but ran as high as 95 percent in 2015 during the oil production boom.
- Atlantic Aviation (58 percent of revenue, 48 percent of free cash flow) operates one of the largest Fixed Based Operations (FBO) networks in

the country, serving private jet and general aviation owners with fuel, de-icing, aircraft parking, hangar rental, catering, and other services. There are 70 locations operating under long-dated leases (most 20 years or more) in some large and many smaller, strategically located airports across the country such as Teterboro, New Jersey, Santa Monica, California, and Aspen, Colorado. Atlantic plans to grow by acquisition and also by adding facilities; they just opened a 37,000-square-foot hangar at Los Angeles International Airport.

- MIC Hawaii (12 percent of revenue, 5 percent of free cash flow) operates several businesses collectively engaged to provide for Hawaii's energy needs. Included are Hawaii Gas, a regulated utility; an unregulated LPG gas distribution business; and a gas-from-renewables business.

As mentioned previously, they sold the wind and solar energy production assets and used the proceeds to pay down long-term debt.

Financial Highlights, Fiscal Year 2018

FY2018 was a bit of an adventure; Macquarie, much to the surprise of the markets, announced the strategic repositioning of some of the IMTT assets as mentioned previously to higher-value commodity storage—and cut its dividend from $5.43 per share to $4.00 to fund the transition and mitigate the effects of temporarily lost revenue. This surprised the markets, and the stock plunged about a third to a level maintained for most of the last year. Fears that the company couldn't maintain its current dividend were somewhat exaggerated; cash flows and free cash flows, while declining slightly in the 2019 period, are more than adequate to cover.

Revenues were roughly flat compared to 2018, and will stay flat through 2020, which is pretty good considering the divestiture. The repurposed IMTT tanks, new Atlantic assets, and a repositioning of certain assets at MIC Hawaii will increase profits and cash flows, modestly in 2019 and then more aggressively, in the 10–15 percent range, in 2020. The dividend should continue with modest raises.

Reasons to Buy

We like strategic infrastructure assets, and tank farms are important in today's world of high energy production and storage. The surplus of US oil and gas production is a relatively new thing; logistics assets are having to handle flows in many different directions (import, export, etc.), which has increased the demand for flexible storage solutions. When oil prices go up, production goes up too, requiring more storage. When oil prices go down, it's usually due to a demand drop or a supply surge—both of which drive an increased need for storage—in other words, in most scenarios characteristic of today's oil markets, there is a greater need for storage.

Atlantic is one of those vital yet unsung businesses that keeps chugging along; the strong economy has helped increase the overall number of flights. Finally, MIC Hawaii qualifies as another "strategic" asset: in a good location and hard to compete with. The separation of the alternative energy business should help with management focus and strengthen the balance sheet. For investors, the well-covered dividend is the obvious attraction, and once the dust settles and it's clear that the dividend will remain in place, the share price should return to previous levels if for no other reason than to bring the yield in line with comparable yielding assets. Finally, while we like REITs and other asset-based investment trusts, they do provide some tax challenges for after-tax accounts. Macquarie is not a REIT and trades and is taxed like an ordinary equity.

Reasons for Caution

Diversification is good, but diversification across such disparate businesses leaves a few question marks (although Chemed, another *100 Best* stock, pulls it off quite well). The continued generation of sufficient cash flow to pay the dividend is always a concern and should be watched carefully. We would hope for no more "swing and a miss" surprises from Macquarie and would imagine they will work hard to avoid them as well.

SECTOR: Real Estate ❑ Beta coefficient: 1.05 ❑ 10-year compound earnings per-share growth: 2.0% ❑ 10-year compound dividends per-share growth: 8.5%

		2011	2012	2013	2014	2015	2016	2017	2018
Revenues (mil)		989	1,034	1,041	1,350	1,639	1,652	1,814	1,900
Net income (mil)		27.3	13.3	31.3	68.3	(106.5)	156.4	126.0	175
Earnings per share		0.59	0.29	0.61	1.05	(1.39)	1.85	1.56	2.00
Dividends per share		0.60	2.40	2.44	3.78	4.33	4.89	5.43	4.00
Cash flow per share		2.37	1.82	1.87	2.95	2.60	5.46	5.06	5.65
Price:	high	28.6	46.2	59.9	73.5	87.9	85.4	83.5	67.8
	low	19.8	27.3	45.7	51.5	64.1	51.8	63.1	33.7

Website: www.macquarie.com/mic

McCormick & Company, Inc.

Ticker symbol: MKC (NYSE) ❑ Large Cap ❑ Value Line financial strength rating: A+ ❑ Current yield: 1.5% ❑ Dividend raises, past 10 years: 10

Company Profile

"To Make Every Meal and Moment Better" is spice-maker and marketer McCormick & Co.'s tasty slogan. The company manufactures, markets, and distributes spices, herbs, condiments, seasonings, flavors, and flavor enhancers to consumers and to the global food industry. It is the largest such supplier in the world. Customers range from retail outlets and food manufacturers to foodservice businesses.

McCormick's Consumer business (about 61 percent of sales), its oldest and largest, manufactures consumer spices, herbs, extracts, proprietary seasoning blends, sauces, and marinades. Spices are sold under an assortment of recognizable brand names: McCormick, Lawry's, Zatarain's, Thai Kitchen, Simply Asia, Club House, Kohinoor, Stubb's, Golden Dipt, Old Bay, Mojave, and more recently, French's mustard and Frank's RedHot sauces. The company estimates its retail market share to be four times the nearest competitor.

Flavor Solutions (formerly known rather coldly as "Industrial") accounts for 39 percent of the business and markets to foodservice, food-processing businesses, and retail outlets. Brands include most of the previously mentioned plus Flavor Solutions, McCormick for Chefs, and FlavorCell and Giotti natural flavors.

Many of the spices and herbs purchased by the company, such as black pepper, vanilla beans, cinnamon, and herbs and seeds, must be imported from countries such as India, Indonesia, Malaysia, Brazil, and Madagascar. Other ingredients such as paprika, dehydrated vegetables, onion, garlic, and food ingredients other than spices and herbs originate in the US.

The company was founded in 1889 and has approximately 11,600 full-time employees in facilities located around the world. The company has brands for sale in about 150 countries, and tapping into local tastes is a priority—there are innovation centers in 14 countries. The biggest sales components are Americas Consumer (42 percent), Americas Industrial (27 percent), EMEA Consumer (11 percent), EMEA Industrial (8 percent), and Asia-Pacific Consumer (8 percent).

McCormick has been innovating both on the product and on web and media fronts, including more informative print and web content with recipes and other information to spur cooking with spices. The website is fun and full of ideas—recently the theme was Chinese cooking—complete with recipes, flavorings, and ideas. The company has converted 75 percent of their premium spice line to organic and is now number one in the US for organic spices and seasonings, and major US retail chains have expanded the presence of these lines in response. A unique "Flavor Forecast" platform anticipates culinary trends in flavorings and flavor preferences and guides innovation both at McCormick and at downstream food processing companies. One innovation we especially like: Within the "Frank's RedHot" hot sauce subsidiary they plan to add frozen prespiced chicken wings to the product lineup! Overall, 8 percent of 2018 sales came from products introduced in the past three years.

McCormick's website continues to be a case study in how to enhance a brand and "customer intimacy" through a website to ultimately drive more sales. Features include an initiative to map your spice tastes by giving you a personalized flavor profile—then emailing you weekly recipes with spice recommendations tailored to that map. You can enter in a singular spice, one that you might like and/or have an abundance of in your pantry; they shoot back recipes for that spice (something we amateur hash slingers have longed for in cookbooks; give me a selection of recipes that use allspice, for instance). All of these initiatives broaden the market to reach the millions of plain folks like us who weren't born with a wooden spoon in our mouths. For those who were born with such a spoon, or who acquired one through years of training and experience, there is also a "McCormick for Chefs" page. In short, we like this recipe: dominant brand, effective digital marketing to spice it up.

Financial Highlights, Fiscal Year 2018

A combination of continued interest in home cooking, less eating out, and effective cost-savings initiatives spiced up some pretty good results for 2018. Net sales rose 12 percent before currency effects, with the French's and Frank's acquisitions adding 8 of that 12 percent, still a strong performance. The "Comprehensive Continuous Improvement" efficiency program brought $118 million in savings, growing operating margins some 2 percent and guiding a 21 percent earnings increase. For 2019, sales growth slows to a 2–3 percent gain as earnings are expected to rise 8–10 percent; with a 5–7 percent earnings gain expected in 2020 on another 2–3 percent rise in sales. Dividend increases, which have occurred for 33 straight years now, should continue, while buybacks have stopped for the moment as the company invests in innovation and product marketing.

Reasons to Buy

Simply put, McCormick dominates its food business niche and it's an important one—some 90 percent of food flavor is delivered with 10 percent of its cost, and flavor is the biggest determinant of choice. As a strong pure play in the seasonings business, McCormick is the largest branded producer of seasonings in North America and one of the largest in the world. McCormick is not just a producer; it is also an innovator and a marketer, and we feel they've done the right things to build interest in their products and in their brand. They also do well in specialized niche markets such as Mexico and China. They're in the right place as new, fresher, and more tailored, customized, interesting, and international food trends all emerge. We also think they're in a pretty good place with millennials, who want new, different, healthy, and customizable approaches to almost everything—including food—and who want to source their information about food and culinary excellence from the Internet.

On the consumer side, the website and its recipe offerings and the pre-packaged Recipe Inspirations meal kits will get the less-experienced cooks using spices more effectively in their own cooking. In general, the company has recognized that people will use more spices if they know how to use them. These initiatives, combined with continuing of fat flavoring with spice flavoring will add a solid increment to McCormick's business base. It's profitability, stability, and defensive nature represent an attractive combination for investors.

Reasons for Caution

Downsides include the rising cost of ingredients and the sourcing of many of these ingredients in geopolitically unstable regions. There is also increasing competition from private-label products. While earnings and share-price growth have been steady, the price of the stock has been spiced up quite a bit by its success. All that said, we don't see people's tastes in taste diminishing anytime soon.

SECTOR: Consumer Staples ❑ Beta coefficient: 0.75 ❑ 10-year compound earnings per-share growth: 8.5% ❑ 10-year compound dividends per-share growth: 9.0%

	2011	2012	2013	2014	2015	2016	2017	2018
Revenues (mil)	3,650	4,014	4,123	4,243	4,396	4,411	4,834	5,408
Net income (mil)	380	408	418	442	450	479	547	663
Earnings per share	2.80	3.04	3.13	3.37	3.48	3.78	4.26	4.97
Dividends per share	1.12	1.24	1.36	1.48	1.60	1.72	1.88	2.08
Cash flow per share	3.55	3.85	4.00	4.24	4.36	4.64	5.13	6.16
Price: high	51.3	66.4	75.3	77.1	87.5	107.8	106.5	156.0
low	43.4	49.9	60.8	52.6	70.7	78.4	89.6	98.3

Website: www.mccormick.com

CONSERVATIVE GROWTH

McKesson Corporation

Ticker symbol: MCK (NYSE) ❑ Large Cap ❑ Value Line financial strength rating: A++ ❑ Current yield: 1.2% ❑ Dividend raises, past 10 years: 8

Company Profile

Sometimes even your surest and steadiest bets—like our bets on healthcare—hit a rough patch—one that's seemingly even rougher on the stock price than it is on the business. Such is the case with McKesson, once one of our steadiest healthcare performers, and winners, over the years. The malaise in the share price continues, with almost a 50 percent drop from its peak in mid-2015. But is the business really broken? No. Sales have marched along, although at a slower 2 percent annual increase, since that time. Net profit margins are roughly the same at 1.2 percent. So why the drop in price? Why the drop in P/E from over 20 to 9.6 as we write this? Yes, there has been some pricing weakness in generic and prescription pharma lines, weakness in the international sector, uncertainty about the Affordable Care Act, and—yes—Amazon has its eyes on this business. Add to that the new consortium formed by Amazon, Berkshire Hathaway, and JPMorgan Chase to address the health care infrastructure, delivery models, and costs—and a few mergers such as CVS–Aetna—and you can see how a little more uncertainty has crept into this staid business. But we think this business and McKesson's market leadership will remain largely intact. Remember that in emotional markets, often the business is just fine; the pricing of the stock gets out of whack. McKesson stays on the 2020 *100 Best* list once again.

McKesson Corporation is America's oldest and largest healthcare services company and engages in two distinct businesses to support the healthcare industry. Pharmaceutical and medical-surgical supply distribution is the first and by far the biggest business: The company is the largest such distributor in North America, delivering about a third of all medications used daily to 50 percent of US hospitals and all but one of the top 25 health plans. The company delivers to approximately 40,000 pharmaceutical outlets as well as hospitals and clinics throughout North America from 27 domestic and 13 Canadian distribution facilities, and recently added a major distribution stronghold for Europe from which it serves 13 countries. The company has also been adding company-owned pharmacies and has about 4,800 Health Mart outlets in the US with 450 more in Canada from the acquisition of Rexall Health in that country. The distribution business, known as McKesson Distribution Solutions, had accounted for about 99 percent of sales; the McKesson Technology Solutions business, with clinical facility systems, analytics, decision support tools, electronic medical records, supply-chain management and other similar products—1 percent of McKesson but a $2.6 billion business in all—was sold to a couple of third parties. By the end of 2019 the company will reorganize into three operating units: Pharmaceutical and Specialty Solutions, European Pharmaceutical Solutions, and Medical-Surgical Solutions.

The company offers products and services covering most aspects of pharmacy and drug distribution, including not only physical distribution and supply-chain services but also a line of proprietary generics and automated dispensing systems, record-keeping systems, and outsourcing services used in retail and hospital pharmacy operations. The central strategies are to provide a one-stop distribution solution for pharmaceuticals, generics, and surgical supplies and to provide technology solutions to deliver higher-quality and more cost-effective care at the hospital and clinical levels.

Financial Highlights, Fiscal Year 2018

Once again you'd think that with a 50 percent drop in the share price since the 2015 peak, revenues and earnings would be marching backward at a rapid rate. That's not really the case: FY2017 revenues were up 3.7 percent; earnings were up a more modest 3 percent, but per-share earnings were down about 1 percent. FY2019 revenues are projected to rise in the 5–7 percent range, with earnings rising pretty much in step. FY2020 is forecast to bring revenue and profit growth in the 2–3 percent range—rather anemic but again, not bad in light of what's happened to the shares. McKesson will continue with moderate dividend increases; share buybacks appear to be on hold (we'd like to see them buy back more at today's depressed share prices), but some cash has been deployed to pay off long-term debt from recent acquisitions.

Reasons to Buy

Although product price reductions do hurt in such a low-margin business, the distribution business continues to be solid and relatively recession-proof. Demographics and the addition of millions to the insured healthcare rolls have kept demand moving in the right direction, and acquisitions have strengthened that position in domestic and especially international markets. McKesson dominates its niches and is a go-to provider of much of what hospitals and clinics need to operate. It holds market-leader position in several important market categories, including number one in pharmaceutical and generic pharmaceutical distribution in the United States and Canada.

The company has a strong track record of stability and operational excellence and is well managed; for long-term investors, the recent share-price weakness would seem to signal a buying opportunity; a recent P/E under 10 seems too low for a company of this strength and track record, especially with steady earnings growth projected ahead.

Reasons for Caution

We were a bit disappointed to see McKesson jettison the technology business; we feel it is vital in today's environment of increased cost scrutiny, and although only 1 percent of the business, it was an important growth vector. The company does operate on thin margins and as such has a low tolerance for mistakes or major changes in the healthcare space, changes that could be brought on by legislation, regulation, or competition including the aforementioned Amazon/Berkshire/Morgan effort. Hospital censuses are low these days as patients and payers find other ways to get things done and to shorten visits. Amazon itself may turn up the competitive pressure as they have announced their intent to get into the hospital supply distribution business. Changes in the ACA could hurt some, as well as new efforts to reduce drug pricing, and other healthcare changes present more of a wild card than the company has faced in the past. We'd like to see a bit more return to shareholders in the form of cash dividends and share buybacks. They have bought back about 10 percent of their float since the price tanked, but more at these prices would be welcomed.

SECTOR: Healthcare ◻ Beta coefficient: 1.15 ◻ 10-year compound earnings per-share growth: 14.5% ◻ 10-year compound dividends per-share growth: 17.0%

		2011	2012	2013	2014	2015	2016	2017	2018
Revenues (bil)		122.7	122.5	137.6	179.5	190.1	198.5	208.3	216.0
Net income (mil)		1,463	1,516	1,947	2,614	2,290	2,589	2,644	2,600
Earnings per share		6.05	6.33	8.35	11.11	9.84	11.61	12.62	13.50
Dividends per share		0.76	0.80	0.88	1.04	1.08	1.28	1.35	1.46
Cash flow per share		8.40	9.30	11.50	15.68	14.11	16.58	17.80	19.20
Price:	high	87.3	100.0	166.6	214.4	243.6	199.4	169.3	178.9
	low	66.6	74.9	96.7	96.7	160.1	114.5	133.8	106.1

Website: www.mckesson.com

AGGRESSIVE GROWTH

Medtronic PLC

Ticker symbol: MDT (NYSE) ◻ Large Cap ◻ Value Line financial strength rating: A++ ◻ Current yield: 2.4% ◻ Dividend raises, past 10 years: 10

Company Profile

Medtronic is the world's largest manufacturer of implantable medical devices and is a leading medical technology company, providing lifelong solutions to "alleviate pain, restore health, and extend life," primarily for people with chronic diseases. The company stepped up its game markedly in 2015 with the $50 billion acquisition of "rival" device maker Covidien, expanding sales by almost 40 percent mostly by gaining market share internationally and in three key segments: Surgical Solutions, Vascular Therapies, and Respiratory and Monitoring Solutions. Through the acquisition of Covidien, Medtronic also acquired an offshore headquarters in Dublin, Ireland, resulting in some tax savings but not as much as seemed likely at the time; due to the passage of the 2017 Tax Cuts and Jobs Act, much of this saving would have occurred anyway.

Since that acquisition, and with the more recent divestiture of a few small businesses, a more focused Medtronic continues to operate mainly in the areas of cardiovascular, neurological, and other surgeries and therapies and in diabetes management. There are four business segments:

- Cardiac and Vascular Group (38 percent of FY2018 sales). Businesses include Cardiac Rhythm & Heart Failure, Coronary & Structural Heart, and Aortic & Peripheral Vascular. This group as a whole develops products that restore and regulate a patient's heart rhythm as well as improve the heart's pumping function. This segment markets implantable pacemakers, defibrillators, Internet- and non-Internet–based monitoring and diagnostic devices, and cardiac resynchronization devices. Micra, a new implantable cardiac monitor about a third the size of an AAA battery and 80 percent smaller than competing products—about the size of a medicine capsule—exemplifies the company's R&D leadership in this industry, as do new efforts to automate remote monitoring and management of heart rhythm patients, a promising expansion of the "Internet of Things" concept into healthcare. Products also include therapies to treat coronary artery disease and hypertension, including balloon angioplasty catheters, guide catheters, diagnostic catheters, guidewires, and accessories. Another line of products and therapies treats heart valve disorders and repairs/replaces heart valves, some through catheters without chest incisions. The unit also markets tools to assist heart surgeons during surgery, including circulatory support systems, heart positioners and tissue stabilizers, ablation tools, stent graft, and angioplasty solutions.

- The Minimally Invasive Therapies Group (29 percent of sales) produces an assortment of products under its Surgical Solutions and Patient Monitoring and Recovery business units. The majority of Covidien's products fell into this group.
- The Restorative Therapies Group (26 percent of sales) includes Spine, Biologics, Neuromodulation, Surgical Technologies, and Neurovascular business units. The Spine unit develops and manufactures products that treat a variety of disorders of the cranium and spine, including traumatically induced conditions, deformities, herniated discs and other disc diseases, osteoporosis, and tumors. This unit recently rolled out "Intellis"—the world's smallest implantable spinal cord stimulator for chronic pain. The Biologics business is the global leader in biologics regeneration and pain therapies across a variety of musculoskeletal applications including spine, orthopedic trauma, and dental. The Neuromodulation unit employs many technologies used in heart electrical stimulation to treat diseases of the central nervous system. It offers therapies for movement disorders; chronic pain; urological and gastroenterological disorders, including incontinence, benign prostatic hyperplasia (BPH), enlarged prostate, and gastroesophageal reflux disease (GERD); and psychological diseases. The Surgical Technologies unit develops and markets products and therapies for ear, nose, and throat–related diseases and certain neurological disorders; among them are precision image-guided surgical systems.

- The Diabetes Group (7 percent of sales, but still totaling $2.1 billion, a good-sized business) offers advanced diabetes management solutions, including insulin pump therapy, glucose monitoring systems, and treatment management software.

Overseas sales represent about 47 percent of the total; R&D is 7.5 percent of sales.

Financial Highlights, Fiscal Year 2018

The Covidien acquisition, completed in early 2015, created a steep step up in sales, profits, and margins, which Medtronic continued to enjoy into FY2018. Revenues rose about 4 percent, with operational leverage and acquisition synergies bringing a stronger earnings gain at about 7.5 percent. For FY2019 Medtronic estimates a 5–6 percent organic revenue gain with continued modest margin improvement and another 7–8 percent gain in per-share earnings. Revenue and earnings gains look to remain in the 4–5 percent range through 2020, then rise a little faster than that as a rather large assortment of new products come on line. Steady mid-single-digit dividend raises appear to be on order, while the company has curtailed buybacks for the moment to pursue debt reduction.

Reasons to Buy

The name Medtronic continues to be synonymous with medical technology; the company remains one of the pure plays in the healthcare technology space. The company was already a "best in class" player in the markets and technologies it was engaged in, and over time its technologies have become more mainstream. We are also big supporters of its investments in remote medicine, its investments in emerging markets, and its involvement with new products and breakthroughs, especially in neuromodulation and diabetes management. The Covidien merger appears to be working both as a product-line expansion and as an entry ticket into overseas markets. While the merger added both shares and long-term debt, it has retired about half the $20 billion in debt and 20 percent of the nearly 400 million shares issued during the past three years. Finally, the company continues to make strategic acquisitions, most recently for spinal surgery robotic maker Mazor Robotics and another for Nutrino Health in the Diabetes segment; their acquisition track record remains favorable.

Reasons for Caution

The healthcare landscape is changing, with new emphasis on reducing hospital stays, cutting cost, and managing and rewarding patient outcomes. As a consequence, the healthcare "food chain" is changing with new mergers, alliances, and agreements—and where Medtronic fits into this all remains to be seen. Some might find the company's growth rates to be a little shy of the mark, which of course suggests more acquisitions may be forthcoming—another risk factor. Still, that all said, Medtronic continues to be a strong, entrenched leader in medical technology, and well positioned to get stronger still.

SECTOR: Healthcare ❑ Beta coefficient: 0.90 ❑ 10-year compound earnings per-share growth: 6.5% ❑ 10-year compound dividends per-share growth: 15.0%

		2011	2012	2013	2014	2015	2016	2017	2018
Revenues (mil)		16,184	16,590	17,005	20,261	26,833	29,715	29,500	30,750
Net income (mil)		3,447	3,857	3,878	4,750	6,233	6,408	6,254	6,950
Earnings per share		3.46	3.75	3.82	4.26	4.34	4.60	4.77	5.15
Dividends per share		0.97	1.04	1.12	1.22	1.52	1.72	1.84	2.00
Cash flow per share		4.13	4.60	4.73	4.26	6.47	6.81	6.77	7.40
Price:	high	43.3	44.6	58.8	75.7	79.5	89.3	89.7	100.1
	low	30.2	35.7	41.2	53.3	55.5	71.0	69.4	76.4

Website: www.medtronic.com

AGGRESSIVE GROWTH

Microchip Technology, Inc.

Ticker symbol: MCHP (NASDAQ) ❑ Large Cap ❑ Value Line financial strength rating: A ❑ Current yield: 1.8% ❑ Dividend raises, past 10 years: 9

Company Profile

Your washing machine senses the load, adjusts the wash time and temperature accordingly, and texts you when it's done. Your refrigerator expands or contracts its power cycle according to outside temperature and the time of day to save on peak power costs—and it keeps track of what you run out of and provides a list—or better yet, orders it outright. You tell your Alexa-enabled device to play a song, record a shopping list, or tell you the weather in St. Louis in advance of a business trip. Internet-enabled security systems show you what's happening in all parts of your home—whether you're there or not—and in other homes, such as that of your aging elders. Asset monitors keep track of inventory and key business equipment. It's all connected, always on, all the time.

The "Internet of Things" describes a world in which the devices we rely on for some pretty mundane tasks (making coffee, for example) can be connected to other devices in clever ways to compound their utility. We like the fact that when we do finally stumble into the kitchen in the morning wee hours, the coffee is brewed, the lights are dimmed a bit, the temperature is appropriate for the hour, and the morning news briefing is playing with our selected feeds. The prospect of all of our stuff connected to all our other stuff and doing our thinking for us opens up a world of possibilities, and this "bolt-on" intelligence, making "dumb" devices into "smart" tools, is a large part of what Microchip Technology is about.

Interestingly, this "local intelligence" concept is nothing new to MCHP. They've been building low-power microcontrollers (and the tools to integrate them) for over thirty years. The advent of zippy wireless local networking and other enabling technologies has played right into MCHP's strengths as a known quantity in the processor business.

Microchip Technology is a leading manufacturer and supplier of specialized semiconductor products primarily embedded as controllers, processors, or memory products other than what are generally thought of as computers. The company's devices, many of which are customizable, custom made, or programmable, sense motion, temperature, touch, proximity, and other environmental conditions, process the information, and control the device accordingly. Applications number literally in the thousands but are concentrated in automotive, communications, consumer product, appliance, lighting, medical, safety and security, and power and energy management products. The 2018 acquisition of chipmaker Microsemi has expanded their markets considerably to include defense, aerospace, and communications applications. The company offers a full suite of design assistance, tools, and consulting services to help customers, usually OEMs, develop the best applications. They position these services as "low-risk product development" resources for their customers.

Microchip owns most of its manufacturing capability in five plants: two in Arizona, one in Oregon, one in California, and one in Thailand, as part of a deliberate strategy to increase process yields and shorten cycle times (about 60 percent of their sales derive from internal wafer fabs). Most but not all products are shipped "off the shelf" with short cycle times or as a scheduled production. R&D accounts for about 13 percent of revenues. As the company sells primarily to other OEM electronic product manufacturers, about 81 percent of sales are to international customers; about 30 percent are to China. The full breakdown: Asia 58 percent, Europe 24 percent, and the Americas 18 percent. Technology licensing accounts for about 4 percent of revenues.

Microchip has more clearly aligned itself and its branding behind the concept of embedded control solutions and now calls itself "The Embedded Control Solutions Company"—a clear and well-defined business position. The company continues to be an active acquirer as the semiconductor industry consolidates; the two most recent acquisitions include the 2016 purchase of microcontroller and touch technology supplier Atmel for $3.4 billion and the $8.4 billion acquisition of broadly diversified chipmaker Microsemi last year.

Financial Highlights, Fiscal Year 2018

Driven in large part by the two acquisitions just mentioned, FY2018 revenue charged ahead some 38 percent, and net earnings rose an even more robust 47 percent. Business started to taper a bit in early 2019 as seen by other semiconductor businesses; the Microsemi business in particular suffered from excess inventory in the channel, and the slowdown in China and trade wars also provided some headwinds; yet revenues were forecast ahead 8–10 percent with earnings ahead only 4–6 percent driven in part by interest expense associated with the Microsemi purchase. (Long-term debt was used to finance most of this purchase; repayment will start in earnest in 2019 but will leave a lot of interest expense on the income statement.) For 2020 forecasts call for a more aggressive 25–30 percent net income gain on a 10–12 percent revenue advance.

Reasons to Buy

We like companies that make the things that make things work, and Microchip seems well positioned as a leading supplier of all this intelligence as "smart" moves far beyond the "smartphone." There is plenty of competition everywhere for most products, much of it from lower-cost producers in Asia. Inventory cycles can also play havoc with semiconductor producers, who do best by producing in large quantities. Microchip, in our view, has overcome a lot of that by playing in high-value-add niches and by offering plenty of design and technical support "value add" to go along with the product—and now with its acquisitions, by becoming a more dominant player in its niche.

Another differentiator employed by Microchip is a long-standing policy of keeping older parts in their catalog. The nature of their customers' markets (and thus, Microchip's market) often calls for the development of a pervasive architecture over time. Industrial users rarely need the latest in CPU speeds and features, but they do have a large investment in software that's been developed and customized for their application over perhaps decades. If Microchip were to discontinue a line of older, low-volume products, their customers would have to undergo an expensive redesign just to keep their existing product line going. MCHP probably doesn't make a lot of money selling 20-year-old controllers, but their customers do, and keeping their customers in the money makes for a loyal customer base, and a loyal customer base has been very good for business.

Recent consumer technology trends include the concept of the "throwaway" device; smartphones become obsolete, memory requirements grow exponentially, and everything shrinks. MCHP certainly participates in this space, and the addition of Microsemi gives them significant new inroads there, but MCHP, with its tremendous product line breadth and unique customer base might be the most conservative play in a very nonconservative industry.

It has become a tradition for capital-intensive semiconductor companies not to pay dividends or much else in the way of cash returns to shareholders. Capital is gobbled up internally for what seems to be endless new investments in fab capacity, design tools, and ever more expensive materials and supplies. Microchip has also bucked *that* trend with their approach to shareholder value—how many semiconductor firms have paid a dividend, let alone raised it, for nine out of ten years? This is a very profitable, rapidly growing semiconductor manufacturer at the heart of some very hot markets trading at less than 15 times earnings—far less than the S&P multiple at the time of writing.

Reasons for Caution

The Microsemi integration brought $8 billion in debt and some headaches, both of which have been a little slower to go away than hoped. On the other hand, Microsemi brings a broad and deep catalog of parts and an extensive customer base. We hope that acquisitions—at least big ones—are done for now and that Microchip can focus on what it does best: owning a big piece of this trendy, lucrative IoT niche.

SECTOR: Information Technology ❑ Beta coefficient: 1.20 ❑ 10-year compound earnings per-share growth: 11.5% ❑ 10-year compound dividends per-share growth: 4.5%

	2011	2012	2013	2014	2015	2016	2017	2018
Revenues (mil)	1,383	1,606	1,920	2,150	2,180	3,401	3,965	5,500
Net income (mil)	337	389	531	594	590	910	1,340	1,620
Earnings per share	1.65	1.89	2.45	2.65	2.65	3.90	5.42	6.48
Dividends per share	1.39	1.41	1.42	1.43	1.43	1.44	1.45	1.46
Cash flow per share	2.26	3.02	3.60	4.32	4.25	6.30	8.30	10.40
Price: high	41.5	38.9	44.9	50.0	52.4	66.8	95.9	104.2
low	29.3	28.9	32.4	36.9	37.8	39.0	62.2	60.7

Website: www.microchip.com

CONSERVATIVE GROWTH

NEW FOR 2020

Microsoft, Inc.

Ticker symbol: MSFT (NASDAQ) ❑ Large Cap ❑ Value Line financial strength rating: A++ ❑ Current yield: 1.4% ❑ Dividend raises, past 10 years: 9

Company Profile

Microsoft is the world's largest developer of computer software. Its software products are used in both the consumer and enterprise environments, where its operating systems and user-facing software are predominant in many applications. In particular, its Office suite is the de facto standard worldwide for word processing, spreadsheets, and presentations. The company also develops and markets hardware products, including the Xbox video game console, the Surface laptop and accessories, and a new "mixed reality" headset designed for commercial applications.

The company has three reporting segments. Productivity and Business Processes (largely the Office 365 suite of products, but also including LinkedIn, Skype, Microsoft Exchange, SharePoint, Outlook.com, One-Drive, and other subscription-based businesses), the Intelligent Cloud Segment (focused on server products, cloud services, and Enterprise Services, including Enterprise Support), and the thoughtfully named More Personal Computing segment, which includes everything else, including Windows and its OEM licensing, Windows cloud services, hardware devices, and the Gaming business (Xbox, Xbox Live, software, and accessories). The company's revenues and earnings are almost equally split among all three segments.

In 2012 the company released the first in a series of touchscreen-based laptops named Surface. The line has grown over the years to include tablets, sketchpads, hubs, and other configurations, all running Windows and other Microsoft-developed software. The product line is well-regarded as a premium brand in what is largely a commodity market, and is a solid contributor to the company's bottom line.

Anyone reading this is almost certainly familiar with the company's history and the reason for its early pre-eminence in personal computing. And while many decry the near monopoly that the Windows OS has become, the truth is that the Intel x86 architecture and the Microsoft operating system chosen by IBM for the first personal computers have grown, hand-in-hand, to become one of the greatest tools in the histories of commerce, science, education, and the arts. Over the past ten years the company has engaged in the necessary transformation from monopoly supplier to competing in markets where it started at a distinct disadvantage—and has been largely successful.

Financial Highlights, Fiscal Year 2018

Microsoft continued its recent run of noteworthy financials, a welcome change from the prior three years of relatively flat growth. Revenue increased $13.8 billion or 14 percent, driven by growth across each of the company's segments. Productivity and Business Processes revenue increased, driven by LinkedIn and higher revenue from Office. Intelligent Cloud revenue increased, primarily due to higher revenue from server products and cloud services. More Personal Computing revenue increased, driven by higher revenue from Gaming, Windows, search advertising, and Surface, offset in part by lower revenue from Windows Phone. Gross margin increased 16 percent, also due to growth across each segment. Overall gross margins increased slightly, driven by a favorable sales mix and margin improvement in More Personal Computing. Operating income grew 21 percent, again with growth in each segment. LinkedIn operating loss increased $63 million to $987 million, primarily due to increases in SG&A expenses.

Reasons to Buy

In the ten-plus years that we've been watching Microsoft, we've had them on the short list for at least half of those years, but they've never quite made the cut. Our reluctance to include them in our list was not due to the company's reputation as being too big to be effective (although that's quite possible), but rather that the company seemed to lack a sense of direction and focus. The thought was that they would forever be relegated to the position of "supplier of the operating system for other people's barely profitable products." Not an enviable future, in our view.

Obviously things have changed, especially in the direction and focus arena. For example, the company is no longer trying to sell devices like phones and fitness trackers through ties to a Windows environment—the Windows Device Group is being disbanded after two rounds of uninspiring results. Second, it has begun to move the bulk of its OS licensing to a more profitable subscription model, as opposed to a one-time sale. This model has worked very well for the Office suite (Office 365 has a 35 percent compound annual growth rate (CAGR) since inception) and expectations are high for similar results in Windows. Finally, the new CEO has taken a strong position that, near-term, the growth of the company will be in their "Azure" cloud initiative.

Microsoft's early commitment to cloud initiatives have paid off handsomely in exactly the same way that their late entry into mobile phones did not. Analogous to Amazon Web Services, Microsoft Azure is a collection of over 600 cloud computing services with a focus on compute, storage, data management, machine learning, and messaging. Azure provides an environment for building, testing, deploying, and managing applications that allows a single developer access to virtual resources at Microsoft-managed data centers in nearly fifty regions around the world. Over its lifetime, Azure revenue has been growing at a 70 percent CAGR. In 2018, Azure-driven revenue was up 91 percent as part of an overall growth of $4.8 billion in the Intelligent Cloud segment.

The recent acquisition of LinkedIn is going well. Revenues for Q3 '18 were up 23 percent over the prior year and subscriptions are growing at nearly the same rate.

Reasons for Caution

Intel and NVIDIA, hardware suppliers for cloud computing environments (among other things), have recently issued some cautionary releases regarding slowing demand in the CPU and GPU market due to global macroeconomic uncertainties. These are likely to be short-term policy concerns, but if the warnings are solid, it may be an indicator that Microsoft (and others) are cooling somewhat on cloud development projects. It's worth watching. Also, MSFT is trading at something of a premium as of late due to its promising financials and so has a trailing P/E ratio of 29. That's not horribly high in this market, but it might be worth waiting for a bad news day to buy in.

SECTOR: Information Technology ❑ Beta coefficient: 1.10 ❑ 10-year compound earnings per-share growth: 8.0% ❑ 10-year compound dividends per-share growth: 15.0%

	2011	2012	2013	2014	2015	2016	2017	2018
Revenues (bil)	69.9	73.7	77.8	86.8	93.6	92.0	96.7	110.4
Net income (bil)	23.1	23.2	22.4	22.1	21.9	22.3	24.1	30.3
Earnings per share	2.69	2.72	2.65	2.63	2.65	2.79	3.08	3.88
Dividends per share	0.64	0.80	0.89	1.12	1.24	1.44	1.56	1.68
Cash flow per share	3.09	3.12	3.15	3.31	3.47	3.71	4.26	5.28
Price: high	29.5	32.9	39.0	50.0	56.8	64.1	87.5	116.2
low	23.7	26.3	34.6	39.7	48.0	61.9	83.8	97.2

Website: www.microsoft.com

AGGRESSIVE GROWTH

Myriad Genetics

Ticker symbol: MYGN (NASDAQ) ❑ Mid Cap ❑ Value Line financial strength rating: B++ ❑ Current yield: Nil ❑ Dividend raises, past 10 years: NA

Company Profile

Molecular diagnostics. That's the intriguing and somewhat scary-sounding phrase appearing prominently in the website and marketing materials of genetic testing pioneer Myriad Genetics. And we don't use the word "pioneer" loosely—much of their genetic and hereditary analysis comes from the well-developed genetic and genealogical databases of the Latter-day Saint community in northern Utah, where Myriad is based.

What are these "molecular diagnostics"? What do they do for us, and what products and services does Myriad provide? Put simply—and there's a lot of science behind it—Myriad develops and markets tests that predict predispositions to certain diseases and syndromes—originally hereditary cancers such as breast, uterine, colon, prostate, and others—by examining biomarkers on DNA, RNA, and other proteins. Patients who may suspect a high risk of certain cancers based on their family history can have a test run to see if in fact these markers exist, leading to increased scrutiny or even a removal of a uterus or similar procedure in a suspect patient.

The company is now moving toward other kinds of biomarkers to (1) detect a wider variety of diseases beyond cancer, such as immune system deficiencies, rheumatoid arthritis, neurological and urological disorders, and depression, and (2) evaluate whether certain treatments will work before they are administered, saving lives but also thousands of dollars in treatment costs. It is known in the trade as *personalized medicine*, where treatments are specific to one's genetic and biological makeup. Generally speaking, these diagnostics and treatments, while pricey, are thought to reduce overall healthcare costs.

Myriad's stated goal is to provide physicians with critical information to guide patient healthcare management by addressing four key questions:

- What is my likelihood of getting a disease? (Risk)
- Do I have a disease? (Diagnosis/Screening)
- How aggressively should my disease be treated? (Prognosis)
- Which therapy will work best to treat my disease? (Therapy)

You can construct a Product Portfolio table, putting the purpose (Risk, Diagnosis/Screening, Prognosis, Therapy) on the x-axis and the medical specialty (Women's Health, Oncology, Urology, Dermatology, Neuroscience, and Autoimmune) on the y-axis—as they have very effectively on their corporate fact sheet (https://myriad.com/about-myriad/inside-myriad/myriad-fact-sheet/). Key products include the legacy myRisk Hereditary Cancer testing kit for testing for overall cancer risk and BRACAnalysis for assessing the risk of breast and ovarian cancer (Women's Health), with newer versions of myRisk available for prostate and general cancers; and myRisk tests for elevated risk for eight hereditary cancers in all. Foresight and Prelude products help with diagnostic screening. EndoPredict assesses the aggressiveness of breast cancer, while a newer product called Gene-Sight was originally released to help figure out what neuropsychiatric medicines will work to resolve depressive disorders (Neurology). Other products include COLARIS and COLARIS AP for colorectal cancer; Prolaris, which assesses prostate cancer type and measures severity; Vectra DA, which measures rheumatoid arthritis severity; myPath Melanoma, which helps to diagnose melanoma; and myChoice HRD, which assesses potential treatments for certain types of tumors. The myRisk Hereditary Cancer test accounted for some 69 percent of the business in 2018 and is declining as other more specific tests take over; it accounted for 74 percent last year. Most of the other products have been released in the past few years and are still gaining traction with the medical community (and insurers, who must cut the checks to pay for them).

Financial Highlights, Fiscal Year 2018

Myriad has gone through something of a product shift from the declining legacy myRisk Hereditary Cancer test to the more specific tests that are gaining traction today. The company is working to grow international markets, broaden insurance coverage, sign long-term contracts with insurers, and take other measures to build volume and strengthen realized prices. Revenues have been somewhat stuck in the $770 million annual range, with a near flat FY2018 sales performance as new product growth only matched the gradual decline of the legacy myRisk products. Net earnings advanced 46 percent from a price-reduction softened 2017; they still haven't reached the level of the myRisk heyday years of 2013–2016 but are on the right track. Volumes are on the rise, and currently the company is forecasting a 50 percent rise in net earnings for 2020 on revenues in the $900–$950 million range, about 20 percent ahead of 2018. We continue to think these figures could be low as the cost savings benefits of these products become more visible to providers and payers (insurers) in the healthcare space.

Reasons to Buy

There is plenty of wisdom to the idea of personalized medicine, where treatments can be handcrafted to the individual to have the most effect for the least cost. Myriad is an early mover in this space, has broadened their product line into an "industry-leading portfolio" of molecular diagnostic tests, and, importantly and unlike many others in the biotech and this "avant-garde" medical space, they make money doing it. (We like that the best—it's not just a good idea; it's a profitable business.) These tests are becoming more of a standard procedure, which is good, but they have a long way to go before truly becoming mainstream, providing a good "runway" for long-term growth. The concept and products are just now gaining traction in the international space. We don't usually like to make this kind of prediction, but Myriad would seem ripe as a takeover candidate for a larger pharma or medical supplier.

Reasons for Caution

Although Myriad has an early mover advantage, this space is becoming more crowded, especially as consumer genetic analysis provider 23andMe has announced some direct-to-consumer cancer detection products in the breast cancer space, and there are others. Myriad's success depends on adoption by both provider and payer at price points that bring profitability, success against competition, and the successful defense of patents. These factors have caused some distress in the form of relatively weak 20 percent operating margins of late (which are predicted to improve to 30 percent by the next decade). The transition from the more generalized legacy myRisk Hereditary Cancer product to the more specific newer products has been a bit painful and has led to fluctuations in financial performance, but as these new products gain traction and as more are developed and released, financials should improve.

SECTOR: Healthcare ❑ Beta coefficient: 0.85 ❑ 10-year compound earnings per-share growth: NA ❑ 10-year compound dividends per-share growth: NA

	2011	2012	2013	2014	2015	2016	2017	2018
Revenues (mil)	402	496	613	778	723	754	771	773
Net income (mil)	101	112	147	176	80	125	59	87
Earnings per share	1.10	1.30	1.77	2.25	1.08	1.71	0.87	1.20
Dividends per share	—	—	—	—	—	—	—	—
Cash flow per share	1.10	1.47	1.94	2.59	1.53	2.20	1.57	2.00
Price: high	25.9	31.8	38.3	42.5	46.2	43.7	37.3	50.4
low	17.5	20.0	20.0	20.5	30.3	15.9	15.1	26.8

Website: www.myriad.com

GROWTH AND INCOME

NextEra Energy, Inc.

Ticker symbol: NEE (NYSE) ❑ Large Cap ❑ Value Line financial strength rating: A+ ❑ Current yield: 2.8% ❑ Dividend raises, past 10 years: 10

Company Profile

Who would have thought that a utility company would have been one of our better performing stocks over the years, regularly lighting us up for 10, even 15 percent gains annually? Hard to imagine, yes, but NextEra Energy, the world's largest producer of solar and wind energy, is hardly an ordinary utility company.

NextEra is a full-service retail utility, wholesale power-generating operation, and utility services holding company. It is built around the utility stalwart Florida Power & Light; the name "NextEra" was adopted in 2010 telling us how the company sees itself now and in the future. Headquartered in Juno Beach, Florida, NextEra Energy's principal operating subsidiaries are NextEra Energy Resources, LLC, and the original Florida Power & Light Company, the third-largest rate-regulated electric utility in the country. FP&L serves 8.9 million people and 5.5 million customer accounts in eastern and southern Florida. FP&L accounts for about two-thirds of NEE's total revenues.

Through its subsidiaries, NextEra collectively operates the third-largest US nuclear power generation fleet and is the world's largest user of wind and sun resources to generate electricity. As proof that such leadership works, customer electricity rates in its operating territories are 30 percent below the national average, and the company estimates that it has saved its customers almost $10 *billion* in fuel costs over the past 15 years.

As a nonregulated subsidiary, NextEra Energy Resources, LLC (or NEER), was formed in 1998 as a wholesale energy provider (a "diversified clean energy company" in their parlance) and is the world's largest generator of electricity from the wind and the sun. Unlike many other alternative energy–driven businesses, it is a viable stand-alone business entity. About 90 percent of NEER's generation comes from clean or renewable fuels—wind (67 percent), nuclear (12 percent), solar (11 percent), and oil and natural gas (10 percent).

NEER operates well beyond Florida. It has 120 wind farm facilities in 21 US states and Canada, with 16 solar and 3 nuclear energy facilities, and gas infrastructure operations in most of those locations. NEER's energy-producing portfolio includes more than 10,000 wind turbines, which is estimated to comprise 16 percent of the entire wind power–generating capacity in the US, 11 percent of utility-scale solar power production, and 6 percent of total US nuclear power production. All told, the combined fuel mix of alternative energy and natural gas not only reduces NEE's overall fuel costs (24 percent of revenues, compared to 40s and 50s in much of the industry); it also produces levels of sulfur dioxide (the cause of acid rain) some 97 percent below the average for the US electric industry, a nitrous oxide emission rate 79 percent below the industry, and a carbon dioxide (CO_2) emission rate 55 percent below industry averages—these numbers are still improving. Recently the company began to test large-scale battery storage technologies to level out solar and wind production and consumption differences. A 20 megawatt solar plant in Arizona is now paired with a lithium-ion battery storage unit to completely power 5,000 homes in the largest such installation in the US. The NEER subsidiary accounts for nearly a third of NextEra's total revenue—most of it is generated and delivered under long-term contracts—and nearly half of its profits, a healthy return for an alternative energy–based operation.

The company has a few small but promising nonregulated subsidiaries, offering design and consulting services for other alternative and conventional utility providers, and it also operates a fiber-optic network. NextEra is a regular winner of awards for most green, most ethical, and most admired companies—in fact, it made a Top 10 position on 2018 *Fortune*'s list of World's Most Admired Companies and was number one in the Utility industry category for the 12th year out of the last 13.

Financial Highlights, Fiscal Year 2018

NextEra's FPL took a hit from Hurricane Irma in late 2017, and the renewable energy business was hit by somewhat diminished energy tax credits, so FY2018 reported numbers are a bit soft—revenues actually dropped 2.7 percent, although earnings managed a modest 3.5 percent gain in part due to tax cuts. This is business as usual in the utility business, so it had little effect on the share price. Not surprisingly, revenues and profits are expected to resume their upward march in 2019 and 2020 with an 18–20 percent revenue gain in 2019 against a soft comparison and a 38 percent profit recovery and gain. The lights stay on bright into 2020, with an 11 percent net income gain on an 8 percent rise in revenues.

The company expects to raise its dividend 12–14 percent annually.

Reasons to Buy

Every year we look forward to evaluating and writing about NextEra; they are leading so many initiatives in what's otherwise a pretty boring industry.

For those who believe that alternative energy is the future for large-scale power generation (as we do), NextEra continues to be the best play available. The company continues to grow alternative energy capacity on all fronts, particularly wind and solar, and, importantly, continues to make good money on these efforts. All of this adds to the solid and traditional FP&L regulated utility base; this company has the steady feel of a traditional utility blended with a leading-edge alternative energy platform and leading-edge power utility technology. NextEra will lead the way into figuring out the grid of the future, utilizing an optimized mix of centralized and distributed (as in "rooftop") alternative and conventional generating resources. Cash flow is very strong and supports both hearty dividend increases and continued investments in alternative energy production but hasn't been used to reduce share counts (much has been used to reduce debt instead).

Reasons for Caution

The company's FP&L subsidiary is still a regulated utility and may not always receive the most accommodating treatment. Additionally, alternative energy tax credits are likely to diminish over time. Alternative energy innovations and nuclear power carry some risk, and there are those pesky hurricanes. In addition, the low price of natural gas makes some of the alternative energy offerings less attractive in the short run. Growth prospects lead to a relatively high share price and low yield for the industry—this is not your grandma's utility stock—but NEE also is a clear leader in the industry, a trendsetter, a model utility for others to follow.

SECTOR: Utilities ⬝ Beta coefficient: 0.60 ⬝ 10-year compound earnings per-share growth: 7.5% ⬝ 10-year compound dividends per-share growth: 8.5%

	2011	2012	2013	2014	2015	2016	2017	2018
Revenues (mil)	15,341	14,256	15,136	17,021	17,465	16,155	17,195	16,727
Net income (mil)	2,021	1,911	2,062	2,469	2,761	2,687	3,074	3,186
Earnings per share	4.82	4.56	4.83	5.60	6.06	5.78	6.50	6.68
Dividends per share	2.20	2.40	2.64	2.90	3.08	3.48	3.93	4.44
Cash flow per share	9.29	8.70	10.65	12.10	12.90	12.60	12.11	14.65
Price: high	61.2	72.2	89.8	110.8	112.6	132.0	159.4	184.2
low	49.0	58.6	69.8	84.0	93.7	102.2	117.3	145.1

Website: www.nexteraenergy.com

AGGRESSIVE GROWTH

Nike, Inc.

Ticker symbol: NKE (NYSE) ⬝ Large Cap ⬝ Value Line financial strength rating: A++ ⬝ Current yield: 1.0% ⬝ Dividend raises, past 10 years: 10

Company Profile

From a company known the world over as a champion of branding, from its famous "swoosh" logo to the use of "branded" sports figures to garnish its wares with image and images, there's another new brand in the house: "Triple Double." Funny thing is, you as a consumer won't see this brand—it is an internal branding of a new initiative called "Consumer Direct Offense," and the triple double in this case isn't about basketball stats, it's "2X Innovation, 2X Speed, and 2X Direct." It describes Nike's new initiative into the "next phase of sustained long-term growth and profitability." The platform includes new investments in digitally driven innovation, personalization, manufacturing, and supply chain. If all goes according to plan, Nike will once again and in a new way demonstrate its superior use of branding to achieve performance.

Nike is the world's largest designer, developer, and marketer of athletic footwear, apparel, and related equipment and accessory products. Products are sold through a mix of traditional and direct retail, including Nike-owned retail outlets (of which there are 392 in the US and 790 overseas, and include Converse and Hurley stores), its website, and a mix of independent distributors and licensees in more than 190 countries around the world. Recently, the company has added specialized destination "Running Stores" and has expanded reach with more Direct-to-Consumer (DTC) or factory outlets carrying its traditionally strong product innovation to the channel and retail marketplace. In North America, DTC sales now account for 32 percent of Nike brand revenues, up from 29 percent last year.

Nike does no manufacturing; virtually all of its footwear and apparel items are fashioned by independent contractors outside the United States, while equipment products are produced both in the United States and abroad. In total, there are 124 footwear and 328 apparel factories in 37 countries.

Nike's shoes are designed primarily for athletic use, although a large percentage of them are worn for casual or leisure purposes. Shoes are designed for men, women, and children for running, training, basketball, and soccer use, although the company also carries brands for casual wear. The company has been very successful with its offerings for the women's market.

Nike sells apparel and accessories for most of the sports addressed by its shoe lines, as well as athletic bags and accessory items. Nike apparel and accessories are designed to complement its athletic footwear products, feature the same trademarks, and are sold through the same marketing and distribution channels. The buzzword is "athleisure," and Nike is there front and center.

Nike has a number of wholly owned subsidiaries, or affiliate brands, including Converse, Hurley, Jordan, and Nike Golf, which variously design, distribute, and license dress, athletic, and casual footwear, sports apparel, and accessories, some targeted to specific audiences, such as Hurley to a youth audience.

Nike-branded products account for about 95 percent of 2018 revenues. Of the total $34.5 billion in Nike-branded revenues (excluding subsidiaries), about 65 percent of it comes from footwear, 31 percent from apparel, and the remainder from equipment. Apparel has taken over as the fastest-growing segment at 11 percent. The much smaller Converse subsidiary accounts for the remaining 5 percent of the total business and was down about 8 percent for the year.

In total, 59 percent of FY2018 total sales came from outside the US. Approximately 41 percent of sales come from North America, 25 percent from EMEA, 14 percent from China, and another 14 percent from Asia Pacific and Latin America. FY2018 growth came from China (18 percent in constant currency), Asia Pacific and Latin America (10 percent), EMEA (9 percent)—and a decline in North America (–2 percent).

And lest we leave behind the new Consumer Direct Offense "Triple Double" too soon, it is fascinating to consider the possibilities of digital, real-time, personalized manufacturing, and delivery of Nike products. A custom-made shoe built to fit your specs, size, and colors, using 3-D-printed uppers, right in front of you in a Nike store? Or online? It will happen. And when it does, Nike's fortunes will run faster than ever.

Financial Highlights, Fiscal Year 2018

FY2018 revenues hit a bit of an uphill segment on the treadmill due to declines in North America, the equipment category, and certain subbrands such as the Jordan Brand. Even with a 2 percent decline across North America, however, revenues finished the year up 6 percent on strength in apparel, which increased 9 percent, and China, which, as noted, rose 18 percent. However gross margins dropped 0.8 percent on account of currency, lower Nike Direct margins, and off-price discounting; higher "demand creation" expenses and investments under Triple Double; leading to a 6.3 percent drop in net income.

For 2019 and 2020, the company predicts revenue gains in the 6–8 percent range, as new initiatives hit the market and new pitchmen (and some old ones, like Tiger Woods) enjoy new success in their worlds. Net income will recover slowly at first, as tech investments continue and currency effects and competition remain strong; net income should rise 2–3 percent in 2019 followed by a more robust 15–18 percent in 2020 as millennial-friendly personalization becomes a bigger factor. Moderate dividend increases and share buybacks will continue.

Reasons to Buy

Why buy Nike? In a word, brand; in another word, innovation. The Nike brand and its corresponding swoosh continues to be one of the most recognized—and sought after—brands in the world. It's a lesson in simplicity and image congruence with the product behind it. The company continues to invest in innovation in all of its segments, including new fabrics, colors, uniform materials, and digital design linkages to make active lifestyles more individual, productive, and fun—and it is now extending this innovation further into marketing and retail. Today's "fast fashion" context requires fast time-to-market, and the innovation cycle at Nike has been turned into more of a sprint in response. As well, Nike doesn't just limit the brand appeal to athletes: Slogans such as "Just Do It!" and "If you have a body, you're an athlete" emphasize the appeal and lifestyle across all segments of the population. We continue to think this is drop-dead smart.

We also think it's drop-dead smart to be investing in the DTC channel now, as traditional retail struggles and as millennials take over center stage in this market. We continue to like the combination of protected profitability through brand excellence, operational excellence, and a clean conservative balance sheet, all providing a good combination of safety and growth potential.

Reasons for Caution

Our biggest source of caution last year and again this year, as sales growth slowed somewhat, was whether the Nike brand resonates as well with the upcoming millennial generation as it did with us for so many years since the company's inception in the early eighties. The jury is still out on whether Nike is losing market share or is simply suffering from market maturity, but it appears that competitors like Adidas and Under Armour in particular are encountering some of the same difficulties. It may take some tweaks—and some digitally based personalization Nike is already developing—to win the millennials over. We think, but can't be sure, that Nike will remain the best pair of shoes in this race; millennial acceptance can be a very difficult race to predict. Other risks come from the rollout of the DTC channel in keeping the right balance between DTC and traditional wholesale and in avoiding channel conflicts, as well as the usual labor and commodity input price risks. Finally when a stock runs ever faster in the same direction as Nike has for years now, the probability of needing a breather rises—best to buy Nike when it slows down for a curve.

SECTOR: Consumer Discretionary ❑ **Beta coefficient: 0.65** ❑ **10-year compound earnings per-share growth: 13.0%** ❑ **10-year compound dividends per-share growth: 15.5%**

	2011	2012	2013	2014	2015	2016	2017	2018
Revenues (mil)	20,862	24,128	25,313	27,799	30,601	32,376	34,350	36,397
Net income (mil)	2,133	2,223	2,464	2,693	3,273	3,750	4,240	3,974
Earnings per share	1.10	1.18	1.35	1.49	1.85	2.16	2.51	2.40
Dividends per share	0.30	0.35	0.41	0.47	0.52	0.62	0.70	0.78
Cash flow per share	1.30	1.42	1.62	1.85	2.26	2.62	3.01	2.95
Price: high	24.6	28.7	40.1	49.9	68.2	65.4	65.2	86.0
low	17.4	21.3	25.7	34.9	45.3	49.0	50.3	62.1

Website: www.nikeinc.com

Norfolk Southern Corporation

Ticker symbol: NSC (NYSE) ❑ Large Cap ❑ Value Line financial strength rating: A+ ❑ Current yield: 1.9% ❑ Dividend raises, past 10 years: 9

Company Profile

Norfolk Southern Corporation was formed in 1982 as a holding company when the Norfolk and Western Railway merged with the Southern Railway. Including lines received in the split takeover (with CSX) of Conrail, the current railroad operates 19,500 route miles of track in 22 eastern and southern states. It serves every major port on the East Coast of the United States and has the most extensive intermodal network in the east.

Company business in FY2018 was about 13 percent coal (down from the high teens and low 20s in previous years), 63 percent carload industrial, agricultural, chemical, automotive, and basic materials products, and 24 percent intermodal. Major gateways include ports in the eastern half of the US, Great Lakes ports, and major interchange points with the two major western systems: Union Pacific (another *100 Best* stock) and Burlington Northern Santa Fe. The company estimates that its networks reach 65 percent of US manufacturing and 55 percent of US energy consumption. In the late 1990s, the company split the acquisition of northeastern rail heavyweight Conrail with rival CSX Corporation, so it has considerable operations in the Northeast and Midwest in addition to its traditional southern base; it currently owns 58 percent of the old Conrail. The heaviest traffic corridors are New York–Chicago, Chicago–Atlanta, and Cleveland–Kansas City. The company has a diverse base of large Midwestern factories and large and smaller southern factories and basic materials producers in the coal, chemical, automotive, and lumber industry, giving a well-diversified traffic base.

The company provides a number of logistics services and has substantial traffic to and from ports and overseas destinations. The opening of the widened Panama Canal is giving some lift to southern and East Coast ports, which NSC serves well. The company has an active program to attract lineside customers to build freight volumes, and it interchanges with some 250 short-line railroads, adding thousands of carloads to the traffic base at relatively low cost.

NSC is in the midst of major strategic and operational changes to improve traffic flow, asset utilization and efficiency, and customer service.

These initiatives, which include the new "Precision Scheduled Railroad" operating strategy, will increase train speed, reduce car dwell time, increase labor efficiency, and make customer service more predictable.

Financial Highlights, Fiscal Year 2018

Continued shifts in the energy market, which first reduced coal and now oil shipments, are still affecting NSC. Coal revenues are still decreasing but are stabilizing as domestic and overseas users work down inventory. Intermodal traffic was up, reflecting a generally stronger economy and shortages in the trucking industry. Oil shipments have been up and down with oil prices and inventories, and have been up recently as exports have disrupted normal supply chain patterns and as pipelines have become bottlenecks in some markets. Overall, 2018 freight volumes were up 4 percent and revenues were up 9 percent, reflecting rate increases and fuel surcharges. Net income was up a full 40 percent, 17 percent of that from railway operations; the rest from tax cuts and other sources. Per-share earnings rose a solid 52 percent. As the US industrial economy strengthens and commodity markets improve, the company projects continued revenue gains in the 4–5 percent range through FY2020, with continued productivity gains and share buybacks giving a green light to per-share earnings gains 7–9 percent range in 2019 and 11–13 percent range 2020. The key "operating ratio" measure— the ratio of variable to total costs—dropped to a record low 65.4 from 67.4 in 2017, 68.9 in 2016, and 72.6 in 2015. The goal, outlined in the operational and strategy update, is to reach 60 by 2021.

Reasons to Buy

A green light for the economy and significant operational and customer-service improvements for the railroad are all working together to line up the tracks for high-speed growth, especially in net income. During the Great Recession, NSC, like other companies, became more efficient and is well positioned to perform even better as freight volumes grow. It remains to be seen how much the trade policies of the Trump administration will affect domestic business, but a renewed emphasis on US manufacturing will help NSC, as will the Panama Canal widening. We should note that the new tax law is benefitting NSC and other such capital-intensive domestic industries more than most.

Additionally, NSC serves some of the more dynamic and up-and-coming manufacturing markets in the United States, namely, Asian and other foreign-owned manufacturing facilities found particularly in the Southeast. We like the strength and diversity coming from serving the domestic and especially the foreign-owned auto industry—the company serves plants for (in alphabetical order) BMW, Chrysler, Ford, General Motors, Honda, Isuzu, Mazda, Mercedes-Benz, Mitsubishi, Nissan, Subaru, Suzuki, Toyota, and Volkswagen.

Finally, cash flow continues to be strong, with a 25 percent dividend raise in 2018 and an otherwise strong record of share buybacks and dividend increases.

Reasons for Caution

The decline in coal traffic, which mostly supports electric utilities, also exposed the company more to general economic downturns as the remaining mix is more economically sensitive. But that said, current merchandise and intermodal traffic is very strong and appears to be gaining market share from over-the-road trucks; service improvements are likely to make that shift permanent.

The railroad industry in general, by its nature and like other capital-intensive, high-fixed-cost industries, finds it difficult to have just the right amount of capacity. Too much volume can actually be a bad thing as it over-taxes the physical plant and causes service disruptions. For the most part we think NSC has made the right investments and has proven agile overall in managing business cycles, and the new operations and strategies will make the most of it. As well, bad news headlines, such as derailments, will always attract public scrutiny and cries to accelerate expensive safety measures such as Positive Train Control. Finally, the stock price continues to rise sharply with the improved economy and performance; it would be wise to stop, look, and listen before investing.

SECTOR: Transportation ❑ Beta coefficient: 1.15 ❑ 10-year compound earnings per-share growth: 5.5% ❑ 10-year compound dividends per-share growth: 13.0%

	2011	2012	2013	2014	2015	2016	2017	2018
Revenues (mil)	11,172	11,040	11,245	11,624	10,513	9,888	10,551	11,458
Net income (mil)	1,853	1,749	1,850	2,000	1,556	1,668	1,896	2,666
Earnings per share	5.27	5.37	5.85	6.39	5.11	5.62	6.54	9.52
Dividends per share	1.68	1.94	2.04	2.22	2.36	2.36	2.44	3.04
Cash flow per share	8.22	8.49	8.96	9.57	8.76	9.25	10.15	13.95
Price: high	78.4	78.5	93.2	117.6	112.1.	111.4	146.3	186.9
low	57.6	56.1	62.7	87.1	72.1	64.5	105.9	127.8

Website: www.nscorp.com

AGGRESSIVE GROWTH

Novo Nordisk A/S

Ticker symbol: NVO (NYSE) ❑ Large Cap ❑ Value Line financial strength rating: A++ ❑ Current yield: 2.5% ❑ Dividend raises, past 10 years: 8

Company Profile

Unfortunately, diabetes is a widespread and growing disease as more people around the world live to an older age and eat higher-calorie diets. Novo Nordisk, which started out in the early 1920s as two separate diabetes medicine producers, merged in 1989 and now garners 81 percent of its current $17 billion in revenues supplying diabetes medicine and care products. The company estimates that it owns 46 percent of the world market and 36 percent of the US market for insulin; and 45 percent of the world market for "modern" or "new generation" insulin, which is delivered using new technologies and delivery mechanisms.

Unfortunately, diabetes as a disease continues to grow. Although diabetes is a complex disease for which the many treatments aren't easy to understand, it does break down into two "types" (really, three, if you include the rarer gestational diabetes occurring only in pregnant women): type 1, in which the pancreas fails to produce enough insulin (and regular insulin supplements are required), and type 2, a condition whereby cells fail to absorb insulin properly, often called "adult onset" diabetes. NVO estimates that 425 million people (about 6 percent of the world population) have diabetes of one type or another, that only about half of them have been diagnosed, and only 6 percent are in "good control" of their condition. That number is likely to grow to 629 million by 2045, according to the World Health Organization. On top of that, NVO estimates that 650 million live with obesity, which has a tendency to bring on diabetes. The company estimates that its products are used by about 25 million people worldwide today and plans to grow this to 40 million by 2020.

Major products include traditional human-based insulin and protein-related products for type 1 diabetes treatment, which are being replaced by higher-performance "modern" and "new generation" insulins. The company has reaped the benefits of several recently rolled out new-generation insulins. One is Tresiba, which lasts 42 hours or more and reduces the risk of hypoglycemia, now available in 76 countries and bringing in over $1 billion in annual revenue. Another treatment called Ryzodeg for both type

1 and type 2 diabetes is manufactured artificially. It is absorbed faster and lasts longer than traditional human insulin. Xultophy is another new type 2 diabetes and hypoglycemia treatment, now in 26 countries with over $200 million in revenue.

R&D investments are large for this type of company, and at 13 percent of sales, NVO is no exception. New for 2018 were Ozempic (semaglutide)—a once-weekly type 2 diabetes and obesity treatment now marketed in 11 countries with $275 million in sales. Fiasp, a fast-acting mealtime insulin, has gotten off to a slower start but it's early. Regulatory approval submission in 2019 for an orally administered insulin and GLP-1 peptide treatment for type 2 diabetes should give rise to another strong revenue generator. The pipeline is full across the company, with new treatments especially in the Obesity sector, which grew 60 percent last year, largely on the success of Saxenda, recently introduced and now available in 41 countries, bringing in $600 million a year with 51 percent growth. You can see the pattern and emphasis on new, more effective formulas and delivery systems (including new oral delivery systems) for diabetes, which to a degree replace "traditional" insulin and other treatments, which are typically approved and rolled out in non-FDA-controlled markets first. By the time they hit the US, they are both proven and more profitable.

We shouldn't ignore the 19 percent of Novo Nordisk devoted to diseases outside the diabetes space. The Obesity segment works hand in hand with the Diabetes segment, as the causes and treatments of both disorders have common roots. The Biopharmaceuticals segment targets hemophilia and other bleeding disorders, hormone-replacement therapies, and human growth hormone markets. The model is similar: pioneering approvals outside the US, then migrating them into US markets. About 51 percent of sales in total come from North America.

Financial Highlights, Fiscal Year 2018

Despite the strength of emerging new treatments and delivery systems, 2018 was a fairly soft year for Novo Nordisk. Total revenues declined about 5 percent, although a good part of this was currency, as the Danish crown depreciated almost 5 percent against the dollar. But there were some competitive and pricing pressures during the year, as well as higher new product launch and distribution costs, which hurt both sales and profits: Net income declined about 3.6 percent. Looking forward, the company is assuming a steady dollar, and with that a 5–6 percent growth rate in 2019 based again largely on new products; settling to a 3–5 percent growth in 2020. Aggressive share count reductions, favorable tax effects, and operating leverage as new drugs build volume will inject roughly 8–10 percent into per-share earnings in 2019 and 7–10 percent in 2020. Notably, the company has no long-term debt.

Reasons to Buy

Novo Nordisk continues to be an excellent long-term growth story. It is the closest thing to a "pure play" in the diabetes market, and it's an important player in obesity, growth disorder, coagulation (hemophilia), and hormone-replacement markets as well. The overall and unfortunate growth in these chronic diseases, particularly diabetes and obesity, will provide tailwinds for years to come. There is a lot of interest in new medications such as Saxenda that address obesity and diabetes simultaneously.

Steady revenues and profits from a traditional insulin treatment base fund new research and releases of more effective, more tailored, easier-to-use diabetes treatments. Despite some recent pricing pressures, we still feel very comfortable with this course, and the strong international footprint allows them to gain regulatory and market acceptance long before they enter the prized US market. Financials, too, continue to be excellent; NVO is a relatively less risky play in a dynamic and growing market.

Reasons for Caution

Once you're targeted as a "bad guy" in healthcare, it can take a long time to shake that notion. In 2016, NVO became a bit of a bad guy, being accused of predatory pricing—of course, the 32–35 percent net profit margins didn't help their cause. Some may see room for complaint, and a less aggressive stance on pricing and growth may rule for a while. Naturally, we are concerned about regulatory approvals, attempts to control prescription drug costs, and the potential aggressiveness of competitors, who could want their bigger slice of the lucrative diabetes market. Some regulatory bodies outside the US are holding prices to less-than-acceptable levels—the blockbuster Tresiba was taken off the market in Germany for a while, as an example. Finally, even though Novo presents itself well, it is in a complex business on a complex international stage; it continues to push our "buy businesses you understand" mantra to its limits.

SECTOR: Healthcare ❑ Beta coefficient: 0.95 ❑ 10-year compound earnings per-share growth: 19.0% ❑ 10-year compound dividends per-share growth: 27.0%

		2011	2012	2013	2014	2015	2016	2017	2018
Revenues (mil)		11,559	13,384	15,435	14,511	15,779	15,832	17,988	17,132
Net income (mil)		2,979	3,800	4,651	4,326	5,093	5,356	6,147	5,916
Earnings per share		1.04	1.38	1.73	1.65	1.98	2.11	2.48	2.44
Dividends per share		0.38	0.50	0.62	0.83	0.73	1.41	1.14	1.27
Cash flow per share		1.24	1.58	1.95	1.88	2.19	2.32	2.66	2.72
Price:	high	26.6	34.1	38.9	49.1	60.3	58.2	54.1	58.4
	low	18.9	22.8	29.9	36.6	41.7	30.9	32.8	41.2

Website: www.novonordisk.com

AGGRESSIVE GROWTH   NEW FOR 2020

Nutrien Ltd.

Ticker symbol: NTR (NYSE) ❑ Large Cap ❑ Value Line financial strength rating: A ❑ Current yield: 3.4% ❑ Dividend raises, past 10 years: NM

Company Profile

Well, we finally gave up. It wasn't easy. We gave up on one of our favorite selections, a company we added way back in 2013, in fact.

We liked the industry—nutrients mining for fertilizer production, specifically phosphates and potash in support of agriculture. "Strategic commodities" we called them—necessary for the production of food in an environment where the demand for food, especially quality food products, was ever growing as middle classes grew in emerging markets. There was only a handful of producers. They formed a small cartel to, shall we say, *influence* prices. The company sported excellent, informative, clear, and transparent corporate presentations and material—what more could you want?

The company was the Mosaic Company. We stuck through it thick and thin. But it got pretty thin back in 2015 when the rather oligopolistic fertilizer mining market got a whole lot less oligopolistic when producers in former Soviet Republics decided to flood the market with mined material to gain market share. This sent Mosaic's fortunes plummeting, resulting in a two-thirds share price haircut, a 90 percent dividend cut, and a struggle to make numbers in the face of weak pricing.

We still like the industry. We feel that at least one of our *100 Best Stocks* should be engaged in the food chain of food production. With Mosaic, however, we must admit we fell into a trap we've generally avoided. We've generally avoided mining and commodity producing shares all along because of the difficulty differentiating their products and because of the mining and commodity cycle. What's that? you ask. When the market is oversupplied, prices are low and profits suffer. When it is undersupplied, prices rise. But then what happens? Producers produce more in response to the high prices, and the cycle quickly reverses back to lower prices.

So, "sell when there's something better to buy." And we searched. We wanted to stay in the agricultural "food chain" but wanted to become less dependent on the fortunes of mining, and wanted to be more diversified as well—not just the two "P + K" commodities that Mosaic brought to market. We landed on Nutrien, a product of the early 2018 merger between retailer and farm services provider Agrium Inc. and potash miner Potash Corporation of Saskatchewan.

The result, Nutrien, brings to the table phosphate, potash, *and* a nitrogen-producing business. More than that, it brings a vast, 1,700-outlet, seven-country network of bulk distribution and retail outlets for all crop nutrients, seeds and seed solutions, crop protection (herbicides, insecticides, etc.), application services, financial services, and an advisory service with 3,300 agronomists and crop advisors helping farmers know what and when to plant and other key aspects of managing their farms. The retail outlet is known as Nutrien AG and is the largest *single* retail agricultural supplier in the world with 19 percent of the market (the aggregate of co-ops and small independent sellers total a larger amount). By EBITDA, the potash represents 38 percent, retail 28 percent, nitrogen 27 percent, and phosphate and sulfate 7 percent of the company's results. Within retail, crop protection provides 38 percent of the gross margin, crop nutrients 31 percent, seed 11 percent, services/other 17 percent, and merchandise 3 percent.

Financial Highlights, Fiscal Year 2018

It's hard to discern any clear trends for a company with two years of history, but it's worth sharing a few financial facts and looking at forward projections. During 2018 several divestitures were required to meet regulatory compliance, and there were a few acquisitions as well, including a US retailer, Van Horn, and Ruralco Holdings, one of Australia's leading agriservices businesses. The company has a "clear line of sight" on $600 million in operating synergies, and prices are improving in most major markets with the possible exception of nitrogen. For 2019 and 2020, revenues are projected to rise a fairly modest 3–5 percent annually, while cost savings, operating leverage, and margin expansion are expected to nourish earnings some 12–16 percent annually. The dividend was raised 43 percent in 2019, with 5–10 percent raises likely going forward, while the company has already retired some 7 percent of its shares since the merger and plans to continue moderate buybacks.

Reasons to Buy

As hard as it was to part with Mosaic, we do like the more diverse plate of services offered to farmers here, and we still like the fundamentals of the farm industry in the intermediate and long term. Nutrien has a strong, diverse, and well-embedded position in the distribution of an assortment of farm services, and we only expect it to become more well embedded as the brand becomes more well known. There is a lot of consolidation in the ag services sector, and Nutrien will figure into that via mergers and acquisitions—with only 19 percent of the market, the field is green for expansion. Generally, crop prices and farm incomes seem to be on a gentle rise in contrast to considerable variability over the past few years. In contrast to the mining cyclicity of Mosaic and the damage done to its dividend, Nutrien portends an environment of steadier cash flows, allowing for both a larger and more secure dividend.

Reasons for Caution

Of course, Nutrien is a miner too, and subject to some of the same ups and downs as Mosaic was. But mining is a far smaller portion of their business, and weakness in nutrient commodity prices can actually help out their retail business. That said, keep in mind that Nutrien is also impacted by ups and downs in crop prices like everyone else. Also, acquisitions of small, "tuck in" distributors are likely, with a certain amount of distraction and financial drag to follow. With this sort of company, it's best to think long term.

SECTOR: Materials ❑ Beta coefficient: NM ❑ 10-year compound earnings per-share growth: NM ❑ 10-year compound dividends per-share growth: NM

	2011	2012	2013	2014	2015	2016	2017	2018
Revenues (mil)	—	—	—	—	—	—	18,242	19,636
Net income (mil)	—	—	—	—	—	—	816	1,460
Earnings per share	—	—	—	—	—	—	1.27	2.34
Dividends per share	—	—	—	—	—	—	1.20	1.72
Cash flow per share	—	—	—	—	—	—	3.15	5.20
Price: high	—	—	—	—	—	—	—	59.0
low	—	—	—	—	—	—	—	40.4

Website: www.nutrien.com

AGGRESSIVE GROWTH

Oracle Corporation

Ticker symbol: ORCL (NYSE) ❑ Large Cap ❑ Value Line financial strength rating: A++ ❑ Current yield: 1.5% ❑ Dividend raises, past 10 years: 9

Company Profile

Founded in 1978 as the rather blandly named Software Development Laboratories, Oracle Corporation has since grown to become the second-largest software company in the world (by revenue) only behind Microsoft. The company's early entry into the then-new relational database market eventually led to an extended period of dominance for that flagship product (the Oracle Database) in the enterprise market. The company successfully leveraged this position with associated software and hardware products through acquisitions and internal development and now has a strong presence in both the middleware and applications space.

Oracle was one of the early proponents of cloud architecture before the name "cloud" became a catchall for any remotely run and managed software. As a consequence, today some of the company's strongest growth vectors are in what are becoming widely adopted IaaS, PaaS, and SaaS architectures (Infrastructure/Platform/Software as a Service). In this space, the customer doesn't own the tool or application but rather pays a fee to use it on a remote server. Increasingly, customers use a "hybrid" model, where some software resides in the cloud and other platform components reside on premises. The transition from traditional on-premises systems to the cloud has hindered sales somewhat over the past ten years as it has for most software vendors, but is becoming less of a factor as the company's cloud products gain traction.

The company owes its current product breadth to both internal development and an aggressive acquisition strategy, most significantly with the purchases of applications software provider PeopleSoft in 2004, hardware supplier Sun Microsystems in 2010, and e-commerce software specialist NetSuite in 2016. Acquisitions continue to be a focus for Oracle, with over $70 billion spent since 2006, and $12 billion spent in 2016 alone, mostly on small firms in the tool, applications, and security spaces. That said, 2018 acquisitions were "not significant individually or in the aggregate" according to the company's annual report.

Mainly through acquisitions, Oracle has become a premier provider of software applications for such widespread corporate tasks as human capital management (HCM, formerly "personnel" or "HR") and enterprise resource planning (ERP) in addition to its core database software business; currently they are transitioning database products to the cloud as well. Sales of these two applications alone advanced 25 percent last year to about $2.6 billion annually.

Financial Highlights, Fiscal Year 2018

Revenues in FY2018 (ending June 1) were up 5.2 percent, as currency headwinds subsided (52 percent of sales are overseas). As Oracle transitions to more of a cloud and hybrid and less of an on-premises business model, it has stopped giving detailed breakdowns of cloud and on-premises business; they have lumped the cloud and on-premises businesses together into a single "Cloud Services and License Support" segment comprising 82 percent of total revenues. Other segments include Hardware (leftover from the Sun Microsystems acquisition), 10 percent, and a Services segment at 8 percent. Revenues for the Cloud Services and License Support segment advanced 6.9 percent in FY2018, while Hardware declined 3.8 percent and services were roughly unchanged. FY2018 net income advanced 14.4 percent due mainly to scale (like most software providers, most of Oracle's costs are fixed) and lower effective tax rates. The long upgrade cycle for companies moving into the cloud and the resulting dampening effects on total sales as on-premises sales decrease will keep revenue advances slim at 0–3 percent annually, while earnings will advance in the 4–6 percent range per year. Oracle continues to buy shares back aggressively with an 8 percent share buyback in 2019 and more modest 1–2 percent buybacks annually thereafter; long term the company has bought back 30 percent of its float—1.5 billion shares—in the past 12 years. Dividends, while modest, are increasing at an increasing rate.

Reasons to Buy

Oracle is one of those rare beasts: a mature technology company that has pretty much become an industry standard. At the ripe old age of 41 years, Oracle is clearly in select company. The fact that they've been able to grow and remain at the head of the pack in an industry where it is commonplace for technological tidal shifts to eliminate entire classes of companies speaks to their robust market awareness, sound and aggressive acquisition strategy, and competent execution.

That said, this is a large company with a large presence in older, slow-growth businesses. For decades Oracle was a strong proponent of captive, in-house IT operations and sold software, hardware, and services into that segment quite successfully. As this model fades in favor of SaaS/PaaS and similar models that require less capital investment, Oracle is in the happy position of having a solid, high-margin revenue stream to fund the development of the replacement, all while retaining a loyal customer base reluctant to move to anything "too" new. Many of their competitors in this developing space are not as established or as well funded and so will need to be good, fast, and lucky, where Oracle really just has to be good. Displacing an existing Oracle "seat" (software installation) will require a long sales cycle and a compelling solution. Retaining an Oracle seat, however, simply requires a reasonable transition and a credible road map going forward; it has adapted well to the new computing model. A quick glance at Oracle's share price history does not stir the blood, but it has proven to be pretty defensive during market downturns; businesses will always need software. Additionally, Oracle has been successful evolving its platforms to the latest technologies; having platforms and strategies in place to cannibalize your own businesses is far preferable to having others eat it for you.

Reasons for Caution

Oracle would never admit to overpaying for some of their acquisitions, but it's clear in retrospect that some of their purchases have been driven less by the numbers and perhaps more by exuberance. The Sun acquisition, which we actually defended previously as a move to sell a bundled software and platform solution, has not turned out as well as hoped. In their cloud businesses, Oracle's IaaS infrastructure goes up against established IBM SoftLayer, Microsoft, and, more dauntingly, Amazon Web Services offerings. IaaS is inherently a lower-margin model, and the marketplace challenges will be significantly greater than in SaaS/PaaS. More broadly, the company must not become too complacent or play fast and loose with its existing installed base; its customer relationships are one of its chief advantages and "moats" against its rivals.

SECTOR: **Information Technology** ❑ **Beta coefficient: 1.05** ❑ **10-year compound earnings per-share growth: 10.5%** ❑ **10-year compound dividends per-share growth: 35.0%**

		2011	2012	2013	2014	2015	2016	2017	2018
Revenues (mil)		35,850	37,221	37,253	38,305	38,253	37,056	37,900	39,878
Net income (mil)		11,385	12,520	12,958	13,214	12,489	11,236	11,550	13,244
Earnings per share		2.22	2.46	2.68	2.87	2.77	2.61	2.74	3.13
Dividends per share		0.20	0.24	0.30	0.48	0.51	0.60	0.64	0.76
Cash flow per share		2.32	2.65	2.91	3.10	3.04	2.93	3.04	3.61
Price:	high	36.5	34.3	38.3	46.7	45.3	42.0	53.1	53.5
	low	24.7	25.3	29.9	35.4	35.1	33.1	38.3	42.4

Website: **www.oracle.com**

Ormat Technologies

Ticker symbol: ORA (NYSE) ◻ Mid Cap ◻ Value Line financial strength rating: C++ ◻ Current yield: 0.8% ◻ Dividend raises, past 10 years: 5

Company Profile

Ormat Technologies, a developer and operator of geothermal plants and maker of thermal power recovery products, is the largest geothermal energy pure play in North America. A renewed interest in baseline "green" power, combined with a growing need for electrification far from traditional grid-based solutions puts Ormat in a unique position as a provider of clean, always-on baseline electricity at the lowest operating cost of any solution. "Green energy you can rely on" is their apt slogan, highlighting their advantage over solar and wind-based solutions. The company operates in two primary business segments. The Electricity segment builds, owns, and operates geothermal power plants, selling the electricity mostly into the grid as a wholesale power generator. The Product segment sells power plant equipment utilizing their proprietary geothermal technology to geothermal operators and to industrial users for use in remote power generation and recovered energy applications. In 2018 the Electricity segment accounted for 71 percent of Ormat's revenue.

Ormat's total worldwide installed capacity is 910 megawatts, concentrated in 19 sites mainly in the states of Nevada and California, but including Hawaii, Idaho, Oregon, and Utah. The capacity of each of their geothermal plants tops out at about 35MW in the western United States, the Pacific Rim, and the Mediterranean and east Africa.

The Product segment has sold and built 150 power plants producing 2,200 megawatts in installations located around the world, including far-off locations such as Turkey, Ethiopia, and Indonesia as supported by the local geology. The power generation products are particularly attractive for harsh, remote locations as the technology requires very little in the way of management or maintenance. The company also produces REG—Recovered Energy Generation—units, which produce electricity from nearly any form of waste heat. The vast majority of these units are currently sold outside of the United States and are commonly used in gas pipeline compressor stations but are suited to any process that generates significant waste heat, including oil refineries. Finally, the company also participates in the Energy Management sector via its acquisition of Viridity in 2017. This segment contributed 1 percent of revenues in 2018.

The company owns over 100 patents on its efficient "binary" geothermal energy conversion process and related technologies. Their products do not require exotic manufacturing processes or materials, and the company builds almost all of its own products at its plants in Nevada and Israel.

Financial Highlights, Fiscal Year 2018

For FY2018, total revenues increased 3.8 percent over the previous year, with electricity segment revenues leading the way with a gain of 9.5 percent. Product segment revenues declined $23 million, or 10 percent, due in part to the long lead times of equipment and the timing of certain orders and shipments, rather than in a general decline in business levels. Power production in the consolidated plants grew 6.7 percent to 5.5 million MWh, accounting for 71 percent of total revenues. Earnings declined $37 million year over year largely due to a $14 million goodwill impairment charge in the Viridity acquisition, a $5 million termination fee of the Galena 2 PPA, decreases in the Product segment gross margin, and reduced revenues from the Puna plant, which had to be shut down due to a volcanic eruption (the current plan shows a return to full operation by the end of 2019). Additional expenses included interest expense associated with the acquisition in 2018 of US Geothermal and an increased income tax provision. The company raised approximately $260 million in financing for various projects, including a new 35MW facility in Honduras. The Product segment enters 2019 with a backlog of $217 million with an additional agreement for $60 million in the works.

Reasons to Buy

We've been watching Ormat for over eight years now and have seen the company transition from "green energy experiment" to an important niche player in the renewable energy market to the primary geothermal solution in the US and several other countries, with approximately 24 percent of the entire US market. Last year the company has moved into the "smart grid" environment with the acquisition of Viridity Energy, a privately held provider of software and consulting expertise in the fields of Capacity Demand Response and energy management and storage solutions. The company anticipates that the BESS market (Battery Energy Storage Systems, typically used for grid stabilization) will grow to $160 billion over the next ten years and that the Viridity technology will provide them with an early presence there. Their first project, a pair of 20MWh utility scale BESS systems based in New Jersey, has begun operations as a load-balancing system and will generate $7–$8 million annually. We also see this acquisition as a positive step for increasing Ormat's viability in the developing "microgrid" market, whereby traditional grid customers continue to rely on incumbent electrical supply for their backup and bulk needs, but tailor a solution that also employs renewables and peak capacity to reduce their overall cost and improve uptime. Microgrids have been employed in universities, small municipalities, military bases, and large industrial facilities to good effect, and Ormat's technology is a good fit in these scenarios.

Although Ormat is far less of a speculative play than it was when we first started covering its business, this sector still relies on governmental incentives for a significant chunk of its financial lifeblood. These incentives take the form of widely marketed long-term carbon credit swaps and carbon reduction mandates issued by both state and federal agencies. Global incentives are also taking shape, and now Australia, China, the EU, Germany, Japan, and the UK all have renewable portfolio standards of various types in place. Ormat sees these as the most important drivers for expansion of their existing power plants and new projects. The State of Nevada, long a friend of Ormat, may well lead the nation in clean energy implementation, recently passing legislation requiring the elimination of at least 800MW of coal-fired generating capacity by the end of 2019. Neighboring California has set very aggressive targets for renewable energy content of all sales—33 percent by 2020, 40 percent by 2024, and 60 percent by 2030. Hawaii, Oregon, and Utah have established similar programs with stringent renewable energy requirements as well. In addition, 24 other states, 3 territories, and the District of Columbia have established renewable energy goals.

These incentives are important for geothermal installations given their higher initial cost and their (often) remote locations. A geothermal plant will cost approximately $2,500 per kW of installed capacity versus $1,000 per kW for a gas turbine facility. Operating costs, however, are where the geothermal plant shines—generation costs are in the range of $0.01–$0.03 per kilowatt hour. Coal, the next cheapest alternative, yields costs of $0.02–$0.04 per kilowatt hour. The recent tax cuts provided a boon to Ormat in the form of highly accelerated bonus depreciation in year one of qualifying projects, increasing from 40 percent to 100 percent.

Geothermal plants are also extremely reliable, with 24/7 availability (a big differentiator from solar and wind power) and provide nearly 98 percent uptime, with very little maintenance and near zero environmental impact. Coal plants, on the other hand, average about 75 percent availability and come saddled with massive environmental costs rarely paid for by ratepayers. These geothermal plants are very good solutions for particular needs in particular locations, but they cannot be plopped down just anywhere as they require a source of geothermal heat. Fortunately, the Department of Energy estimates a large number of potential sites in the western United States. Developing nations without access to coal or oil but with geothermal resources can create low-cost baseline electrical capacity with appropriate levels of investment.

In all, Ormat remains well positioned with their geothermal business and has some exciting new opportunities in grid stabilization and microgrid developments.

Reasons for Caution

The US government has pulled out of the Paris Agreement on climate change. This is something of a blow to the renewables and low-carbon energy providers in the US but, as it turns out, many states and municipalities have already set their own agendas and are well into the implementation phase of plans to decrease their reliance on fossil fuels. Nonetheless, it remains to be seen what the effects of this policy change will be.

One of Ormat's larger customers (nearly 2 percent of revenues) is Pacific Gas and Electric, who filed for Chapter 11 bankruptcy protections in early 2019 as a result of a series of catastrophic wildfires. PG&E's account is current as of this writing, but the situation bears monitoring.

SECTOR: Energy ❑ Beta coefficient: 0.85 ❑ 10-year compound earnings per-share growth: 13.0% ❑ 10-year compound dividends per-share growth: 9.5%

	2011	2012	2013	2014	2015	2016	2017	2018
Revenues (mil)	437.0	514.4	533.2	559.5	594.6	662.6	692.8	719.3
Net income (mil)	(43.1)	(51.1)	37.3	54.2	119.6	93.9	156	98.9
Earnings per share	(.95)	(1.12)	0.81	1.18	2.43	1.87	3.06	1.92
Dividends per share	0.13	0.08	0.08	0.21	0.26	0.52	0.41	0.53
Cash flow per share	1.17	1.13	2.87	3.40	4.62	4.02	5.35	4.55
Price: high	31.2	22.2	28.3	30.5	40.9	53.9	66.5	70.7
low	14.1	16.0	18.8	24.0	25.9	32.2	51.4	45.8

Website: www.ormat.com

AGGRESSIVE GROWTH

Paychex, Inc.

Ticker symbol: PAYX (NASDAQ) ❑ Large Cap ❑ Value Line financial strength rating: A ❑ Current yield: 3.6% ❑ Dividend raises, past 10 years: 8

Company Profile

Paychex, Inc., provides payroll, human resources, and benefits outsourcing solutions for small- to medium-sized businesses with 10–200 employees. Founded in 1971, the company has more than 100 offices and serves over 650,000 clients in the United States as well as about 2,000 clients in Germany. Some 85 percent of its customers are the small- to medium-sized businesses previously mentioned; the company estimates that it pays one out of every 12 employees nationwide. The company has two sources of revenue: service revenue, paid by clients for services, and interest income on the funds held by Paychex for clients.

Paychex offers a one-stop shop portfolio of services and products including:

- Payroll processing
- Payroll tax administration services
- Employee payment services, including expense reporting, reimbursements, etc.
- Regulatory compliance services (new-hire reporting and garnishment processing)
- Retirement services administration
- Workers' compensation insurance services
- Health and benefits services
- Time and attendance solutions
- Medical deduction, state unemployment, and other HR services and products

About 60 percent of Paychex's revenue originates from payroll (service revenue plus interest income); the remaining 40 percent comes from its human resource services offerings. In addition to its website and direct sales force, the company uses its relationships with existing clients, CPAs, and banks for new client referrals and to grow the base of services used by existing clients. Approximately half of its new clients come via these referral sources.

Larger clients can choose to outsource their payroll and HR functions or to run them in-house using a Paychex platform. For those clients, the company offers what it calls "Paychex Flex," which can be run locally or on a web-hosted SaaS environment.

In addition to traditional payroll services, Paychex offers full-service HR outsourcing solutions; custom-built solutions including payroll, compliance, HR, and employee benefits sourcing and administration; outsourcing management; and even professionally trained onsite HR representatives. The company also manages retirement plans and other benefits, including pretax "cafeteria" plans, and has a subsidiary insurance agency offering property and casualty, workers' comp, health, and auto policies to an employer's employee base.

The company is the nation's number one provider of payroll services to small businesses (1–50 employees) and number two for midsized businesses (50–500 employees). The majority of these small business clients are in Professional Services, Healthcare, and Construction. About 41,000 of the 650,000 Payroll clients use the full Human Resource Services offering, with a total employee count of about 1.2 million, an increase of 12 percent over last year. The company has recently implemented web-based and mobile versions of its key products, adding to convenience and reducing paperwork for its clients, and has also added a suite of analytics to its HR offerings. Through the Retirement Services Group, the company administers 82,000 retirement plans, achieving the number one spot nationwide by number of plans.

As a payroll and benefits processor, the company holds significant short-term funds received from clients to pay out to employees—and earns interest on these funds while they are held. Low recent interest rates have held this revenue and profit source back, but as interest rates rise, this segment, while small, grew 26 percent last year to $63.5 million and is expected to grow about 10 percent a year.

Finally, during 2018 the company expanded its European footprint through the acquisition of the Lessor Group, a market-leading payroll and benefit provider, and purchased a large US-based HR service provider called Oasis. Much of last year's 45,000 employee growth to 650,000 is from the Lessor acquisition, while Oasis will give a lift to 2019 results and beyond.

Financial Highlights, Fiscal Year 2018

The economy appears healthy, and it appears that many of the policies of the Trump administration will help smaller domestic businesses, and this will help Paychex. The company should (1) add new clients, (2) sell more services to new and existing clients, (3) sell more to each client as the employee base rises, in addition to expanding its domestic and overseas footprint through acquisitions. This combination led to a 7 percent organic top-line gain (13 percent with the acquisition) and a 7 percent bottom-line gain in FY2018 as the mix and scale of the business improved. Favorable margin and mix trends should continue into FY2019 and beyond, with revenues continuing up 8–12 percent in total and about 6–7 percent organically and net profit up in the 10–12 percent range. About 56 percent of service revenue is payroll services, while HR services make up the other 44 percent. Interest income ("Interest on Funds Held for Clients" in company vernacular) should continue to give a nice upside lift in 2018 and especially 2019 but accounts for about 2 percent of total revenue. Notably, the company has no long-term debt and has been raising its dividend about 10 percent per year.

Reasons to Buy

A bet on Paychex is a bet on four things: (1) strength in the economy and employment, (2) the continued rise of "small" and independent businesses and contractors, (3) continued adoption of broader "one-stop" platform services, and (4) an increase in interest rates (so they can make money on the float). In the meantime, you get a decent yield, steady gains, steady dividend gains, and little downside risk if you own the stock.

Paychex's primary market is companies with fewer than 100 employees. The all-important small business segment has been strong since the Great Recession and is likely to get stronger with Trump's domestic business–friendly approach. Beyond that, the cost of switching and good client relationships has made for a loyal client base. We continue to think the trend to outsource payroll and HR activities will not only continue but will accelerate as easier Internet-based solutions come more into favor.

The company has been a rock-steady performer—conservatively run, well managed, and well financed. It isn't just a "service" company, it is an IT company with a lot of innovation in its DNA. Margins are significantly higher than its closest competitor, Automated Data Processing (ADP). It has carried no long-term debt although plans to take on a modest amount due to the Oasis acquisition and thus should have little difficulty funding the generous dividend, even at its current payout level of 80 percent of earnings. Fragmentation in the market and Paychex's extremely strong financial position will allow the company to continue to grow market share through acquisition. Finally, as short-term interest rates tick upward the company will once again be able to profit from the float (the company has $3–$4 billion of its customers' money held for payroll at any given time). This is one of the few stocks on our list that can tangibly benefit from *moderate* interest rate increases. We like that defensive characteristic.

Reasons for Caution

This company will always be vulnerable to economic swings, such as those brought on by large interest rate increases. The company's acquisitions of small payroll processors and human resource service providers make sense, as those acquisitions increase market share, but they do come with costs and risks.

SECTOR: Information Technology ▫ Beta coefficient: 1.00 ▫ 10-year compound earnings per-share growth: 7.5% ▫ 10-year compound dividends per-share growth: 12.5%

		2011	2012	2013	2014	2015	2016	2017	2018
Revenues (mil)		2,084	2,230	2,326	2,519	2,739	2,952	3,151	3,381
Net income (mil)		516	548	569	627	675	757	817	901
Earnings per share		1.42	1.51	1.56	1.71	1.85	2.09	2.25	2.49
Dividends per share		1.24	1.27	1.31	1.40	1.52	1.68	1.84	2.06
Cash flow per share		1.67	1.78	1.83	2.02	2.16	2.42	2.63	2.89
Price:	high	33.9	34.7	45.9	48.2	54.8	62.2	70.4	76.0
	low	25.1	29.1	31.5	39.8	41.6	45.8	54.2	59.4

Website: www.paychex.com

CONSERVATIVE GROWTH

The Procter & Gamble Company

Ticker symbol: PG (NYSE) ▫ Large Cap ▫ Value Line financial strength rating: A++ ▫ Current yield: 3.1% ▫ Dividend raises, past 10 years: 10

Company Profile

Last year, the legendary Procter & Gamble became the sole remaining broadline consumer home staples company on our *100 Best* list. Over the past three years we eliminated Clorox, Colgate-Palmolive, and Kimberly-Clark; however, this year we put Kimberly-Clark back on. Still, we feel the list is more nimble and reflective of the times. Did we make the right choices? Yes, indeed: Procter turned in a stellar performance, up 20 percent for the year, while the others pretty much flatlined. Procter stands out because of its relatively stronger brands, more profitable operations, and relatively successful adaptation to change, some of which came about through the 2016 proxy fight with Nelson Peltz's Trian investment fund.

Procter & Gamble dates back to 1837, when William Procter and James Gamble began making soap and candles from surplus animal fat from the stockyards in Cincinnati, Ohio. The company's first major product introduction took place in 1879 when it launched Ivory soap. Since then, P&G has continually created a host of blockbuster products, added some key acquisitions, exited the food business, and now downsized its brand list by over 100 brands—but still in total has some of the strongest, most recognizable consumer brands in the world.

P&G is a uniquely diversified consumer products company with a strong global presence. P&G markets its broad line of products to nearly 5 billion consumers in more than 180 countries.

The company is a recognized leader in the development, manufacturing, and marketing of quality laundry, cleaning, paper, personal care, and healthcare products.

To understand Procter, it's worth a look at how the company is organized:

- Beauty (19 percent of FY2018 sales, 23 percent of net earnings) includes shampoo, skin care, deodorant, hair care and color, and bar soap products, including such traditional brands as Head & Shoulders, Ivory soap, Safeguard, Secret, Pantene, Vidal Sassoon, Olay, and Old Spice.
- Grooming (10 percent, 14 percent) includes razors, blades, pre- and post-shave products, and other shaving products, including Braun, Gillette, Gillette Fusion, Gillette Mach3, and Prestobarba brands.
- Healthcare (12 percent, 13 percent) is made up of two subunits, Personal Healthcare and Oral Care. Personal Healthcare in turn includes gastrointestinal, respiratory, rapid diagnostics, and vitamins/minerals/supplements, and includes such brands as Vicks, Metamucil, Prilosec, and Pepto-Bismol. Oral Care includes the familiar Crest, Scope, and Oral-B brands among others.
- Fabric and Home Care (32 percent, 27 percent) covers many of the familiar laundry and cleaning brands—Tide, Dawn, Febreze, Downy, Bounce, Mr. Clean, Swiffer, and a handful created for international markets.
- Baby, Feminine, and Family Care (27 percent, 23 percent) markets mostly paper products like Puffs, Charmin, Pampers, Luvs, Bounty, Always, and Tampax into baby care, feminine care, adult incontinence, and family care markets.

Procter has always been a hallmark example of brand management and building intrinsic brand strength—that is, strength not from the company name but through the brand's own name and reputation. It is described as a "house of brands," not a "branded house," although we're starting to see the P&G name more prominently in its marketing and advertising. The company tells us that its 50 "Leadership Brands" are some of the world's most well-known household names, that 90 percent of its business comes from these 50 brands, and that 25 of them are billion-dollar businesses.

The company has a strong and growing international presence, with 56 percent of sales originating outside the US and Canada. The company also manufactures locally in its largest international markets, with on-the-ground operations in approximately 70 countries.

In an effort to become a "much simpler company," Procter has now completed its brand realignment, which entailed shrinking the portfolio from 166 brands down to just 65 by the end of 2017. Savings have come from everything from reducing manufacturing sites to organizational units to the number of legal entities and invoices produced. The remaining 65 brands account for approximately 85 percent of earlier FY2015 sales and 95 percent of pretax profit. The number of country/category combinations has dropped from 140 to 50, with new focus on everything from innovation to a reconfigured supply chain. In beauty parlance, it was a total makeover.

During FY2018 the company acquired the over-the-counter health-care business of Merck, which sells consumer healthcare products in mostly international markets and will add about $1 billion in revenues.

Financial Highlights, Fiscal Year 2018

FY2018 sales rose a modest 2.7 percent, but that is the first improvement in five years as brand cuts and soft demand cut into the top line. Volumes grew 2 percent, while "organic" sales grew 1 percent in dollar terms. Per-share earnings advanced 8 percent, further evidence of a successful "right-sizing" and trimming of dead branches and a healthy 2 percent share buyback. For 2019 Procter is looking for another 8–10 percent per-share earnings growth on a 1 percent revenue gain; for 2020, the company is looking for mid-single-digit advances in both revenues and earnings. Modest dividend increases and share buybacks should continue as the simplified business moves forward.

Reasons to Buy

Regardless of developments in the world economy, people will continue to shave, bathe, do laundry, and care for their babies, and P&G is the global leader in baby care, feminine care, fabric care, and shaving products. Everyone should consider at least one defensive play in their portfolio, and P&G continues to deserve a spot at the top of the list.

We like the company's new position on brand proliferation. More is not always better, particularly when each brand carries with it a not-insignificant SG&A and Marketing overhead. As the company continues to evolve its organizational structure, it has departed from its traditional model of managing brands as wholly separate businesses with brand-specific advertising budgets, product research labs, and so forth. Synergies from combining ads and ad strategies alone should reduce total costs across the company's many portfolios (to that point, they estimate a 50 percent reduction in advertising, PR, and other agencies). The business won't miss these brands all that much; focus, critical mass, simplicity, supply-chain efficiency, and profitability appear to be their strategic mainstays moving forward.

In short, we continue to like the mix of the company's long traditions and its current renaissance, its marketplace and financial strength; sure and steady dividend growth (the company has raised its dividend 63 straight years); and short- and long-term prospects.

Reasons for Caution

So much change so fast can be disruptive, and there's been a lot of it. The brand simplification has worked; it remains to be seen what influence Trian has, and there's always the chance that some bitter aftereffects of the proxy struggle might linger and poison the well with management and employees—but things seem okay so far. Competition is fierce in P&G's markets, and operational and marketing missteps can be painful.

Finally, rising commodity and logistics costs can negatively affect P&G. Some can be and have been passed on through price increases, but it's difficult to count on price increases for success in this sector.

SECTOR: Consumer Staples ▫ **Beta coefficient: 0.65** ▫ **10-year compound earnings per-share growth: 2.5%** ▫ **10-year compound dividends per-share growth: 7.5%**

	2011	2012	2013	2014	2015	2016	2017	2018
Revenues (mil)	82,559	83,680	85,500	83,062	76,279	65,299	65,058	66,832
Net income (mil)	11,797	11,344	11,869	12,220	11,535	10,441	10,733	11,205
Earnings per share	3.93	3.85	4.05	4.22	4.02	3.67	3.92	4.22
Dividends per share	1.97	2.14	2.29	2.45	2.59	2.66	2.70	2.79
Cash flow per share	5.21	5.20	5.33	5.57	5.31	4.97	5.21	5.52
Price: high	67.7	71.0	85.8	93.9	91.8	90.3	94.7	94.9
low	57.6	59.1	68.4	75.3	65.0	74.5	83.2	70.7

Website: www.pg.com

GROWTH AND INCOME

Prologis, Inc.

Ticker symbol: PLD (NYSE) ❑ Large Cap ❑ Value Line financial strength rating: B+ ❑ Current yield: 3.0% ❑ Dividend raises, past 10 years: 5

Company Profile

We like ordinary stocks: shares of prosperous, growing businesses. In addition to ordinary shares, we've come to like REITs—or real estate investment trusts—shares of specialized income-producing real estate portfolios. These specialized investments allow you to become a landlord and to collect (usually rising) rents. Beyond rents, at least with the REITs we prefer and choose, there is a good business sitting on top of the real estate that adds a measure of growth to the base rental income produced by the real estate.

Long averse to investment "products," we've been adding REITs for about six years because of strong fundamentals, healthy dividend income, and growth opportunities we see in those with particularly strong businesses accompanying the real estate ownership. Three years ago, in the context of the rising importance of supply-chain economics and execution to business in general and especially e-commerce, we added Prologis.

Prologis is a global leader in industrial logistics real estate across the Americas, Europe, and Asia. "Industrial logistics real estate" is mainly distribution warehouses and specialized facilities that store goods and prepare them for shipment, sometimes with some final assembly or value add, and are an integral component of the supply chain for many types of organizations. Major clients include third-party logistics providers, transportation companies, retail (including online), and manufacturers.

Prologis operates 3,690 properties (up from 3,232 in 2017) all across 19 countries on four continents, with about 60 percent of the square footage in the US (down from 64 percent), 23 percent in Europe, 7 percent in "other" Americas, and 10 percent in Asia. The company owns and operates most of these properties mainly as standard warehouses in industrial parks or near port or airport facilities, leasing them to large and small companies either in whole or in sections according to need. Prologis also develops custom partner solutions through their "Global Customer Solutions" business, which designs, builds, and operates custom distribution facilities for major accounts like Amazon, DHL, and others. In fact, their top ten customers accounted for 15.1 percent of the business (up from 12.4 percent last year); Amazon is the largest customer at 5.3 percent (4.7 percent last year) of "net effective rent," FedEx is second at 1.9 percent, and Home Depot is third at 1.8 percent. Overall, however, the customer base is quite diverse with 5,200 customers in all, and the top 25 customers account for 21.3 percent of the revenue. The overall location strategy is (1) to appeal to the needs of these top-tier logistics users and (2) to locate in relatively high-barrier-to-entry markets such as around larger cities, ports, and terminals.

Financial Highlights, Fiscal Year 2018

FY2018 was another strong year for the business, as occupancy ran strong and "releasing" spreads (the ratio of rent on new versus expiring leases, effectively, price increases) were also strong. Revenues rose 6.7 percent. Same-store revenues rose 3.7 percent while occupancy rates ticked down slightly from 97.3 percent to 97.2 percent—still a very strong figure. Net income was roughly flat—but only after a very strong 2017 compare; it was 25 percent ahead of 2016. Projections call for a 17–18 percent revenue rise in 2019, fueled partly by international expansion, followed by another 3–5 percent in 2020. Rent increases and expanded business will keep net income and funds from operation growing in the 3–5 percent range each year. Dividends should grow in the mid-single digits.

Reasons to Buy

The value proposition of modern, flexible logistics sites for today's organizations is strong, and particularly strong for e-commerce businesses—such as Amazon, as previously noted. More generally, the state of the art in supply-chain management has advanced significantly in just a few years, driven by e-commerce and just-in-time production management. As supply chains become more global, and as products become more customized and have shorter life cycles, as shipments get smaller, more numerous, and more likely to have an assembly and a "reverse" component, flexible logistics solutions become far more important. Also, e-commerce, because of its high shipment "granularity," requires about three times the space per dollar of revenue as brick-and-mortar warehouse operations. In short, current trends toward e-commerce and urbanization have driven changes in consumption and supply chain management, and Prologis is at the heart of that change.

Equally important is today's current business climate, with companies relying on back-end productivity rather than top-line growth to increase profits. Prologis sits right in the middle of this trend, with a solid base of real estate, skills to manage it, and skills to partner with major clients to deliver the right and often customized solution.

All major financial metrics are on a strong upward advance, occupancy levels are at an all-time high, pricing power is apparent, and steady dividend increases appear likely. We think, given the favorable supply/demand picture in this business, that Prologis's financial forecasts could be too conservative going forward; there is more upside than downside assuming continuing strong global e-commerce growth. Consistent with much of the REIT industry, share counts are on the rise as Prologis replaces debt with equity or uses equity to finance acquisitions. The current debt-to-equity ratio of 33 percent is very healthy for the industry. Also, if you are investing in this or any other REIT in an after-tax account (not a retirement account) know that new rules about so-called "pass through" income (Section 199 income) allow you to deduct 20 percent of the income from this REIT.

Reasons for Caution

We've picked four individual REITs now—in senior living, self-storage, cell phone towers—and now, logistics and warehousing—Prologis. Guess which one is most vulnerable to economic downturns. Prologis? Right. A protracted economic downturn would hurt this business more than many REITs (we have avoided shopping center and hospitality REITs altogether because in our view they're even more vulnerable). We should also note that e-commerce, the strongest growth vector, currently accounts for only about 13 percent of the business. As millennials shift their focus from goods to experiences, and as most sought-after goods get smaller (such as smartphones), the future global economy could simply require less physical space to operate.

SECTOR: Real Estate ◻ Beta coefficient: 1.00 ◻ 10-year compound earnings per-share growth: NM ◻ 10-year compound dividends per-share growth: NM

	2011	2012	2013	2014	2015	2016	2017	2018
Revenues (mil)	1,533	2,006	1,750	1,761	2,197	2,533	2,618	2,804
Net income (mil)	(153.4)	(102.4)	219.4	636.2	869.4	1,210	1,652	1,649
Funds from operations per share	1.10	1.19	1.65	1.88	2.23	2.57	2.81	3.03
Real estate owned per share	57.25	55.74	45.67	47.63	52.47	51.30	51.96	57.65
Dividends per share	1.12	1.12	1.12	1.32	1.52	1.68	1.76	1.92
Price: high	37.5	37.6	45.5	44.1	47.6	54.9	67.5	68.9
low	21.7	28.2	34.6	36.3	36.3	35.3	48.3	55.2

Website: www.prologis.com

Prudential Financial

Ticker symbol: PRU (NYSE) ❑ Large Cap ❑ Value Line financial strength rating: B++ ❑ Current yield: 4.4% ❑ Dividend raises, past 10 years: 10

Company Profile

"Own a Piece of the Rock" is one of the classic slogans of corporate America. We've all heard it so many times it's like a song you can't get out of your head; yet it's so familiar that you might well have forgotten the company it stands for. Oh yeah. Prudential. The Rock of Gibraltar in the picture. A trademarked symbol. Does it ring a bell? In choosing stocks for our *100 Best* list, we look for stability and safety. Yes, we look for a piece of the rock in every choice we make. But we also look for innovation and the sort of market leadership that leads to profitable growth. We usually do not look for financial stocks, as they are hard to understand and vulnerable to economic shock. But due to a rock-solid base plus some noteworthy innovations, we'll stick with Pru again for 2020.

Prudential began selling life insurance 143 years ago and has evolved this rather unsexy business into an insurance, asset management, and retirement powerhouse well positioned to handle not only your retirement planning needs but also those of major corporations—that's where a large innovation hinted at previously comes in. The company operates in four Divisions in the wake of a late 2017 reorganization:

* Workplace Solutions (20 percent of 2018 operating income) has within two segments: Retirement and Group Insurance. The Retirement segment provides administrative services and products including group annuities, structured investment products, and the pension risk transfer products (the innovation cited several times in this narrative). Currently the group serves some 20 million people; some 2,700 companies offer Group Insurance products.
* Individual Solutions (34 percent of income) contains Individual Annuities and Individual Life. The Annuities business "manufactures" and distributes individual variable, fixed, and fixed indexed annuities primarily to the "mass affluent" market for retirement income stabilization and supplement. The Individual Life subsegment is one of the industry's largest in this field. The group serves more than 5 million people.

- The Investment Management (15 percent of income) segment provides portfolio management and specific investment products such as mutual funds, which are both publicly and privately available. It has about $1.2 trillion in assets under management, making it one of the world's largest.
- International Insurance (51 percent of income) creates, modifies, and distributes life insurance, retirement, and related products outside the US through various channels. Important developed markets include Japan and Korea while emerging markets include Brazil and Chile.

The company currently operates in 47 countries. Unlike many such companies, international expansion is a major strategy; individuals and workers outside the US have significant needs for financial services as well.

The innovation we've been pretty excited about is now a ten-year-old initiative, now getting traction, to sell packaged corporate pension plans to employers of all types. When a company takes on a pension obligation, either willfully or as a consequence of a union negotiation or some such, it takes on a risk. The pension is a promise to pay a defined amount (hence "defined benefit"), and it's up to the company to pay this amount come whatever happens to its own resources and investments. Bottom line: The employer company takes on a lot of risk when it creates a pension program. Here's where Prudential comes in: Companies can transfer this risk to Prudential by paying Prudential a fee to take over, essentially buying an annuity to cover future pension obligations. Prudential takes on the risk of the employer for a fee. That's what insurers do. It's a new business that Prudential knows how to do and will realize economies from as it takes over in larger volumes from employer customers. Currently, the "book" is up to $100 billion in assets managed under this program, with some $12.6 billion taken in just last year.

We also applaud Pru's dedication to financial wellness and financial wellness education—rare in today's world of financial services providers who seem more interested in making their products confusing and requiring of explanation by expensive commissioned salespeople than straightforward and easy to grasp. Kudos to Pru's financial wellness research and their Prudential Pathways and LINK financial education programs, which have been adopted by 500 companies.

Further—and we don't often make much mention of this—Prudential has gone to great lengths to establish itself as a good corporate citizen and has a "trophy hall" of some 25 accolades received from major organizations for ethics, inclusiveness, and positive change, from the *Fortune* "Change the World" list to Ethisphere's "World's Most Ethical Companies" to Black Enterprise's

"Best Companies for Diversity" list. It's an impressive list, and if you're looking for a socially responsible investment, you've come to the right place.

Financial Highlights, Fiscal Year 2018

Lower fees and pricing in some segments and an end-of-year market sell-off were offset by a favorable product mix, higher interest rates, expense controls, and a strong performance from the new pension risk transfer business all leading to a pretty good year for Pru. Revenues (Premium plus Investment plus Other, or "Total Income") advanced about 8 percent; net profit also advanced about 8 percent. The company expects flat to slightly lower revenues in 2019 returning to current levels in 2020, but a 10 percent increase in profits over that time. Two to 3 percent buybacks are likely going forward with dividend increases in the 10 percent range typically—although management raised it a full 20 percent in early 2018.

Reasons to Buy

Prudential, long a stalwart of the sleepy life insurance business, has witnessed an accelerating transition toward the ever-greater need for retirement planning solutions both on the part of individuals and employer organizations. Annuities, long another fairly sleepy part of the business, are enjoying a resurgence as corporate and public pensions evolve away from full-coverage defined benefit plans; annuities are also becoming more acceptable and more easily used by financial advisors to round out financial plans as their roles and features are better tailored and better understood. Furthermore, pending federal legislation to allow greater use of annuities in individual 401(k) plans will help this business. The new pension risk transfer product "innovation" offers an exciting path to growth as more employers with traditional pension obligations come on board; Prudential is the market leader in this new growth opportunity. The international expansion also bodes well particularly as the dollar stabilizes. All of the businesses should fare well in a higher interest rate and less regulated environment. Finally, investor cash returns have been on the rise for years and should continue along that path.

Reasons for Caution

Hats off to you if you can understand this business! Like most financials it is hard to sort through the terminology and nuances of each business, and the financial statements are a puzzle. We're still not sure we got it.

There are some other risks here too: longevity (people living longer makes annuities less profitable) and general risks associated with the financial industry, mostly risks of complexity and greed we fell into back in 2008 and regulatory actions that can result from such events. We're breaking the "invest in things you understand" rule a bit here, but we do understand the idea of pension risk transfer and of annuities becoming a more important and more trusted retirement planning vehicle as pensions continue to go away and people become more responsible for their own retirement destinies.

SECTOR: Financials ❑ Beta coefficient: 1.30 ❑ 10-year compound earnings per-share growth: 8.5% ❑ 10-year compound dividends per-share growth: 11.0%

	2011	2012	2013	2014	2015	2016	2017	2018
Premium income (bil)	21.4	62.1	23.1	25.1	25.5	28.0	29.2	33.0
Total income (bil)	39.4	81.1	45.3	49.8	48.6	51.6	53.6	58.1
Net profit (bil)	3.1	3.0	4.8	4.2	4.5	3.9	4.7	5.0
Earnings per share	6.41	6.27	9.67	9.21	10.04	9.13	10.58	11.69
Dividends per share	1.45	1.60	1.73	2.17	2.44	2.80	3.00	3.60
Price: high	67.5	65.2	92.7	94.3	92.6	108.3	118.2	127.1
low	42.4	44.5	53.4	75.9	73.2	57.2	97.9	75.6

Website: www.prudential.com

GROWTH AND INCOME

Public Storage

Ticker symbol: PSA (NYSE) ❑ Large Cap ❑ Value Line financial strength rating: A+ ❑ Current yield: 3.8% ❑ Dividend raises, past 10 years: 9

Company Profile

You have stuff. We have stuff. We all have stuff. Stuff to store somewhere. Stuff from our families, stuff from our kids, stuff from our past. Collectibles, treasures, boats, RVs, and extra vehicles. Boxes, boxes, and more boxes. And we all need to store that stuff somewhere. But where? As more of us live in houses with smaller yards and devoid of basements, where? As more of us choose to rent rather than buy, where? As more of us, especially the younger millennials among us, choose to live closer to the centers of larger cities, where? As the retirees among us downsize, where? As the elderly give up their primary residences, where?

You get the idea. There is more personal stuff for most of us to store, and less space to do it. That's where Public Storage becomes a pretty good investment idea.

Public Storage is a real estate investment trust (REIT) owning and operating 2,429 self-storage properties (2,386 in 2017) in 38 states and another 232 facilities in seven countries in Europe (221 in 2017). The company has a 49 percent interest in Europe's "Shurgard," and also owns a 42 percent interest in another trust called PS Business Parks, which owns 103 rentable properties in six states. The company points out that, based on the number of tenants, it is one of the world's largest landlords. The slogan "We're in your neighborhood" also tells you something.

Most are probably familiar with the format—small, unfinished, generally not-climate-controlled lockers rentable on a month-to-month basis for personal and business use. They range in size from 25–400 square feet, and there are typically 350–750 storage spaces in each facility. Some include covered parking for vehicle, boat, and RV storage. On average the company gets about $1.24 per square foot per month—a rather handsome sum considering these units do not come with any of the finish or comfort of an apartment or even a home, which may rent for something similar per square foot depending on the market.

Not surprisingly, the largest concentrations are in California, Texas, and Florida (since these are centers for retirees and homes with no basements), and most are near a major US or European city. The three largest markets are New York, San Francisco, and Los Angeles. Branding in the US is "Public Storage"; in Europe it is "Shurgard." US self-storage revenues account for about 76 percent of the total; European self-storage accounts for about 6 percent, and the commercial business park business accounts for about 12 percent. The remaining "ancillary businesses" include selling supplies like locks for storage units and storage unit insurance.

The key strategies continue to be revenue and cost optimization, market-share growth in major markets, achieving scale to lower operating costs, and building brand recognition. The company has a centralized call center and a website to help market its product and facilitate transactions. Acquisitions are also an important part of the strategy; the current market is fragmented with PSA only owning 10–20 percent of the market at most, and good properties come up regularly. The company expects to grow its property base a steady 1–2 percent annually, but recognizes that development occurs in cycles, which they project may be coming to a top in 2019. One strategy they've embarked on is expanding space or redeveloping *existing* properties in more popular areas with high barriers to entry; the company already gets 71 percent of its revenue from the 20 largest metropolitan statistical areas in the US.

Our principle in owning REITs remains the same; we're not looking for just real estate, we want to own a good business that *just happens* to own a lot of real estate. REITs are typically good income producers as they are required by law to pay a substantial portion of their cash flow to investors. The accounting rules are different, and REIT investors should focus on funds from operations (FFO), which is analogous to operating income; net income figures have depreciation expenses deducted, which can vary in timing and not always be realistic. FFO supports the dividends paid to investors. Also, if you are investing in this or any other REIT in an after-tax account (not a retirement account) know that new rules about so-called "pass through" income (Section 199 income) allow you to deduct 20 percent of the income from this REIT.

Financial Highlights, Fiscal Year 2018

Higher rents were the primary driver of a moderate 3.2 percent increase in FY2018 revenues. Net income was up some 27 percent; however, some of this was due to new construction and realized gains on sale of certain assets; in fact, cost of operations for same-store facilities notched up 3 percent due to higher property taxes and other expenses. Occupancy rates ended 2018 at 92.6 percent, down a tick from 3.8 percent in 2017 but still strong given the relatively high turnover in this type of business. Realized rents rose 2.0 percent versus 3.0 percent in 2017 and 4.9 percent in 2016. Per-share FFO as a consequence of all these factors rose a moderate 7.7 percent. Forecasts call largely for more of the same, with revenues advancing 3–5 percent in each of the next two years. Per-share FFO and dividend increases should also be in the 3–5 percent range through 2020. Debt is a mere 13 percent of total capital, reflecting a strong and conservative capital structure.

Reasons to Buy

With REITs, our emphasis continues to be more on the business and less on real estate, and with Public Storage, we feel we've found a good business that happens to be based on real estate. PSA has the best brand and highest operating efficiency and profitability in the business, and the core business model and need for its product is sustained and growing—albeit more slowly of late. No matter how easy it is to sell stuff on Craigslist, it's also too easy to acquire stuff, and although millennials are more about "experiences" than "things," there will still be plenty of people in the habit of acquiring "stuff," and Lord knows there's plenty of stuff already out there. At the same time, real estate is trending away from large suburban McMansions with extra space and more toward city digs, patio homes, cluster homes, and the like. All point to strong, steady business prospects for providers of flexible storage solutions, and as PSA strengthens its brand and market-share foothold, more of that business will go its way.

Reasons for Caution

There is growing evidence that millennials and others are simply less about collecting "stuff" than their predecessors—ask any antique dealer and they'll tell you. Occupancy and rent growth are starting to slow, although at 54 percent net margin, the current business is plenty profitable. Also, any profitable business will attract competitors, and there is some evidence of overbuilding and competition in markets like Houston, Chicago, DC, and Denver, and new chains like Extra Space Storage are coming on line. That said, PSA has a pretty good lock on the tighter, more lucrative markets like Los Angeles, San Francisco, Seattle, and Portland with three to ten times the market share of the next competitor. This is a good, steady, profitable real estate business with high margins; that said, investors may have to become more patient about growth prospects.

SECTOR: Real Estate ▫ Beta coefficient: 0.70 ▫ 10-year compound FFO per-share growth: 7.5% ▫ 10-year compound dividends per-share growth: 13.5%

	2011	2012	2013	2014	2015	2016	2017	2018
Revenues (mil)	1,752	1,826	1,982	2,195	2,382	2,561	2,669	2,754
Net income (mil)	824	670	845	908	1,053	1,184	1,172	1,489
Funds from operations per share	5.93	6.31	7.53	7.98	8.79	9.70	9.70	10.45
Real estate owned per share	43.35	42.71	47.97	49.20	49.49	51.49	53.09	54.22
Dividends per share	3.65	4.40	5.15	5.60	6.50	7.30	8.00	8.00
Price: high	136.7	152.7	176.7	190.2	253.9	277.6	232.2	234.9
low	100.0	129.0	144.4	148.0	192.1	200.9	192.1	180.5

Website: www.publicstorage.com

AGGRESSIVE GROWTH

Qualcomm, Inc.

Ticker symbol: QCOM (NASDAQ) ❑ Large Cap ❑ Value Line financial strength rating: A++
❑ Current yield: 5.0% ❑ Dividend raises, past 10 years: 10

Company Profile

When a company is in the process of being acquired, and we think there's a pretty good chance of the acquisition going through, we typically remove it from the *100 Best Stocks* list. It doesn't make sense to present a company that, by the time you get the book and review it, is either gone or its fortunes as a going concern are soon to end. Voice and data communications platform and device maker Qualcomm was just such a company; it was well into the process of being acquired by Singapore-based communications device maker Broadcom, so we took it off the 2019 *100 Best* list. Then President Trump blocked the merger on national security grounds—Qualcomm is a big player in emerging 5G networks, and the idea of an Asian-based company controlling its destiny was unsettling. The merger came apart in mid-2018, and we're putting Qualcomm back on the list once again for 2020.

Qualcomm, based in surf-friendly San Diego, is a global leader in the development and commercialization of foundational technologies and products used in mobile devices and other wireless products and network equipment. It produces the hardware and related software that powers most of the high-end mobile web-surfing and web-accessing devices in use today. Smartphones lie at the center of the assortment of devices, but increasingly, medical devices, automobiles and other "Internet of Things (IoT)" devices connect to networks through Qualcomm devices.

Products include mainly integrated circuits and system software used in voice and data communications, networking, GPS, and other technologies. It also licenses most of the key technologies used in today's cell phone networks, including CDMA and LTE. Their Snapdragon processors are used in most of the "flagship" smartphones on the market, as well as many tablets. In addition to processors, the company also makes many of the modems and "front-end" hardware used at both ends of a cellular connection, as well as peripheral devices for Wi-Fi and Bluetooth transmission for personal computers.

The company is organized into three segments, two of which account for the majority of the revenue:

- Qualcomm CDMA Technology (76 percent of 2018 revenue) develops and supplies integrated circuits and software for wireless voice and data communications, networking, multimedia, and GPS products for mobile devices, tablets, laptops, handheld wireless computers, routers, broadband gateway equipment, automotive telematics, infotainment systems, and medical devices.
- Qualcomm Technology Licensing (23 percent) grants licenses and rights to utilize patents in CDMA, LTE, and 3G/4G/5G standards among others to OEM manufacturers such as Apple, Samsung, and others. This "passive income" part of the business, while generating only 23 percent of revenues, generates some 54 percent of earnings before taxes. A number of lawsuits have been filed against Qualcomm for alleged anticompetitive practices, including charging for the sale of a component and for a license to use the imbedded technology. The biggest complaint has been filed by Apple, which has in fact stopped making royalty payments on some technologies—a big reason for soft revenue and especially earnings performances in the past few years. Qualcomm has been winning some smaller cases, giving some promise for the outcome of the big one with Apple, and won a patent infringement suit against Apple as well. Meanwhile, some OEMs have started sourcing some components elsewhere or having them made to spec. The jury is still out, as it were.
- Qualcomm Strategic Initiatives makes strategic investments toward designing new products for voice and data communications often under contract or in cooperation with other companies in vertical industries such as automotive and healthcare.

Qualcomm also continues to invest heavily in the "Internet of Things." Their apt slogan: "We started by connecting the phone to the Internet; now we're connecting the Internet to everything else." In 2018 the company finally completed the acquisition of the large IoT chipmaker NXP.

Financial Highlights, Fiscal Year 2018
An unfavorable hardware mix and declining licensing revenues led to a moderate 2.2 percent revenue decline and a more significant 15 percent decline in net income in 2018. The conditions causing this hiccup will remain in place in 2019, with another 5 percent decline in revenues and another 13–15 percent decline in net income. However, these trends are expected to reverse in 2020 with a 2–5 percent net income gain on a 4–6 percent revenue gain. Of course, if the lawsuits are favorably resolved, QCOM could return to its

mid-decade glory more quickly. Projections into the early 2020s call for a 7–10 percent increase in net profit margins (to 22 percent, very healthy for this business) and a 20 percent sales increase—a rosy future when they clear the legal challenges. QCOM is an aggressive dividend raiser and a more aggressive share repurchaser; they are currently retiring 5–10 percent of their shares per year, and have reduced share counts some 35 percent in six years.

Reasons to Buy

If there's a word to describe Qualcomm's presence in the mobile market, it's "ubiquitous." Qualcomm's platform, voice, and data communications devices are used in the mobile products of over 90 manufacturers. In some cases, only the front-end parts are used. In many cases, however, the manufacturer will simply copy Qualcomm's whole product reference designs for particular price points and use them without modification. This minimizes the manufacturer's development cost and time to market, while absolutely maximizing Qualcomm's product content and revenue.

As the developer (or co-developer) of many of the technologies used in modern wireless communications, Qualcomm is a major beneficiary of all licensing activity associated with cellular communication. Every cell phone produced in at least the past ten years has come with Qualcomm IP, for which the manufacturer has been (or should have been) paying Qualcomm on a per-unit basis. We mention the licensing collections issue only because there has been a growing level of attention on a number of licensees that are under-reporting device sales in order to avoid payment of fees. Recent litigation has addressed this issue for the most part.

Qualcomm is a major presence in the growing mobile automotive market. In-car communication and data services have become extremely popular with consumers to the point where manufacturers are offering a range of those services either as standard equipment or options, even on their entry-level cars. Qualcomm's GPS and sensor technologies are already in wide use here, but plans for extended functionality in these applications hold promise for significant growth. We expect the growth of Apple's CarPlay, Android Auto, and other in-car data services to leverage strongly on Qualcomm's existing technology while, again, providing for licensing revenue regardless of the hardware employed.

Qualcomm is investing heavily in IoT. All of these interconnected devices use Bluetooth, near-field communication, or simple Wi-Fi to provide wireless, always-on connectivity, and all of these technologies are already in place and under further development at Qualcomm. The company's product line here includes technology for wearables, smart homes, healthcare, and other markets.

A dividend north of 5 percent and growing rings loudly in our ears, especially for a growing tech company. If Qualcomm can master its legal challenges, it's a definite winner; if not, it's still a solid player in a dynamic market.

Reasons for Caution

Competitive losses and signs of saturation in the upper-tier markets still plague QCOM, although licensing fees are still collected when competitors get design wins (at least in theory). The biggest issue facing the company currently is a lawsuit by Apple contesting QCOM's "unreasonable and costly" royalty rates. The company feels it will be able to resolve these disputes, but the headlines bear watching.

SECTOR: Information Technology □ Beta coefficient: 1.00 □ 10-year compound earnings per-share growth: 8.0% □ 10-year compound dividends per-share growth: 15.5%

	2011	2012	2013	2014	2015	2016	2017	2018
Revenues (mil)	14,957	19,121	24,866	26,487	25,277	23,507	23,235	22,732
Net income (mil)	5,407	6,463	7,911	9,032	7,461	6,653	6,386	5,443
Earnings per share	3.20	3.71	4.51	5.27	4.66	4.44	4.28	3.69
Dividends per share	0.81	0.93	1.20	1.54	1.80	2.02	2.20	2.38
Cash flow per share	3.85	4.31	5.30	6.10	5.81	5.48	5.32	5.75
Price: high	59.8	68.9	74.3	82.0	75.3	71.6	69.3	76.5
low	46.0	53.1	59.0	67.7	45.9	42.2	48.9	49.1

Website: www.qualcomm.com

AGGRESSIVE GROWTH

Quest Diagnostics, Inc.

Ticker symbol: DGX (NYSE) □ Large Cap □ Value Line financial strength rating: B++ □ Current yield: 2.4% □ Dividend raises, past 10 years: 8

Company Profile

If you have gone for any kind of medical test, either at the recommendation of a doctor or as required by an employer or insurance company, chances are pretty good you got that test in a lab operated by Quest Diagnostics. Quest is the world's leading provider of diagnostic testing, information, and services to support doctors, hospitals, and the care-giving process.

The company operates more than 2,250 labs and patient service centers including about 150 smaller "rapid-response" labs in the US and has facilities in India, Mexico, the UK, Ireland, and Sweden. It provides about 150 million lab test results a year and serves physicians, hospitals, employers, life and healthcare insurers, and other health facilities. The company has a logistics network including 3,750 courier vehicles and 25 aircraft and has some 20 *billion* test results from the past decade in its databases, a rich source for medical research data. Quest estimates that it serves more than half the hospitals and physicians in the United States and estimates that it "touches the lives" of 30 percent of all US adults each year.

The company offers diagnostic testing services covering pretty much the gamut of medical necessity in its testing facilities. It also offers a line of diagnostic kits, reagents, and devices to support its own labs, home and remote testing, and other labs. Employer drug testing is a big business. The company offers a series of "wellness and risk management services," including tests, exams, and record services for the insurance industry. The company also does tests and provides other support for clinical research and trials, and finally, through its information technology segment, it offers a Care360 platform to help physicians maintain charts and access data through its network, which has about 200,000 physicians enrolled. Mobile technology is another innovation front; the company has developed a mobile patient portal within Care360 known as "MyQuest" to help patients keep track of test results, schedule appointments and medications, and share information with physicians and other care providers. MyQuest was recently integrated into Apple Health to provide a complete and easy experience to track results, appointments, and other information online.

Other innovations include a new initiative called "Data Diagnostics," a tool delivering real-time analytics to the point of care suggesting possible conditions and additional tests to perform "to achieve better clinical and financial outcomes" in diagnosis, treatment, and utilization management. The company has also been a leader in developing so-called "moderate complexity" direct molecular testing procedures, where more complex diagnostic tests can be performed in "moderate complexity" environments—i.e., a "retail" lab format such as Quest operates. The company is a leader in "gene-based" and "esoteric" testing and has launched an assortment of molecular genetics tests supporting new trends in the health industry toward individualized medicine—medicine based on a patient's own unique gene makeup and characteristics. A new "ImmunoCAP" allergy test can identify hundreds of allergens with a single blood sample. And, in a bit of good news for all of us and especially our kids, the new "Quiggles" phlebotomy device uses an ice pack and vibration to make those blood draws more comfortable and less stressful. Finally, the company makes data and analysis available (anonymously, of course) to provide information on diagnostic trends for public health agencies. The Quest Diagnostics Drug Testing Index examines trends in workplace drug testing, and various reports and solutions are provided for everything from wellness management to risk assessment for the life insurance industry.

Financial Highlights, Fiscal Year 2018

Competition, changes in reimbursement rates, and the healthcare landscape (less exclusivity with certain healthcare plans, for example) has led to a bit of a flat spot in volumes and revenue growth: Revenues actually declined about 2.3 percent in 2018. Earnings, however, rose some 10.3 percent, alleviating our concerns about the company at least for the 2020 *100 Best* list. Revenues should return to 2017 levels in 2019, then rise 2–3 percent in 2020. Operating efficiencies and a small shift toward higher value tests will increase margins slightly by 2020, giving earnings about 5 percent higher than today's level. The company intends to return cash to shareholders through dividends, which are projected to rise in the 8–10 percent range annually with relatively steady share counts. We think these forecasts could be conservative as new tests and test packages become mainstream.

Reasons to Buy

People are becoming more health conscious, and an ever-greater emphasis on wellness and preventative care is likely to send more people for routine checkups, particularly if insurance carriers offer benefits (like free tests or lower coinsurance) to motivate such preventative care.

Even more, we're excited about the innovative new tests performed at the retail lab level for molecular-level and gene-based diagnostics, which bode well for the future; the company is advancing to higher, more profitable levels of the diagnostic food chain.

We're also fans of the "package" tests and of Quest's ancillary businesses—clinical trials, insurance qualifications, employer testing, and IT services—which all should do well in an environment favoring greater cost control and outsourcing of distinct services such as Quest provides. Finally, Quest has retired 30 percent of its shares in the past ten years.

Reasons for Caution

Continued pressure to contain healthcare costs will likely bring some additional malaise over the next few years. Offsetting that is the placement of more emphasis on preventative care, a Quest sweet spot. The path to sustained revenue growth seems to be the big question, and the company continues to work on answers. While we think acquisitions of smaller "bolt on" labs are inevitable (and strategically correct) we hope they don't go on to too much of an acquisition binge just to restart growth.

The competitive landscape continues to change as the healthcare industry evolves and new combinations are formed. There is an upside: They may become an acquisition target for a healthcare business trying to integrate vertically, such as CVS. The recent high share price could bring some high blood pressure; there are many moving parts here in a formerly staid industry.

SECTOR: Healthcare ❑ Beta coefficient: 0.95 ❑ 10-year compound earnings per-share growth: 6.5% ❑ 10-year compound dividends per-share growth: 16.0%

	2011	2012	2013	2014	2015	2016	2017	2018
Revenues (mil)	7,511	7,468	7,146	7,435	7,493	7,515	7,709	7,531
Net income (mil)	728	700	612	587	695	737	792	878
Earnings per share	4.53	4.43	4.00	4.10	4.77	5.15	5.67	6.31
Dividends per share	0.47	0.81	1.20	1.29	1.52	1.65	1.80	1.95
Cash flow per share	6.42	6.23	6.22	6.21	6.99	7.19	7.75	8.79
Price: high	61.2	64.9	64.1	68.5	89.0	93.6	113.0	116.5
low	45.1	53.3	52.5	50.5	60.1	59.7	90.1	78.9

Website: www.questdiagnostics.com

AGGRESSIVE GROWTH

ResMed, Inc.

Ticker symbol: RMD (NYSE) ❑ Large Cap ❑ Value Line financial strength rating: A ❑ Current yield: 1.6% ❑ Dividend raises, past 10 years: 6

Company Profile

Sleep disorders are a big deal among adult populations. Reading the clinical description of sleep disorders and their myriad causes could for some be a cure for such disorders, but suffice it to say (as ResMed does in its market analysis) that 26 percent of US adults age 30–70, or about 46 million people, have some form of sleep apnea—and few of them, as few as 4 percent out of the 26 percent, know they have it. That's where the story of ResMed begins, and it continues around the world: Another study estimated that one in four adults worldwide has some form of sleep apnea.

Perhaps you know someone using a CPAP (continuous positive airway pressure) machine to alleviate SDB (sleep-disordered breathing) or OSA (obstructive sleep apnea). As we age and tend to gain weight, these devices are becoming a more mainstream way for folks (and their partners) to get some much-needed sleep.

Formed in 1989, ResMed develops, manufactures, and distributes medical equipment for treating, diagnosing, and managing sleep-disordered breathing and other respiratory disorders. Products include diagnostic products, airflow generators, headgear, and other accessories. The original and still largest product line of CPAP machines delivers pressurized air through a mask during sleep to prevent collapse of tissue in the upper airway, a condition common in people with narrow upper airways and poor muscle tone—in many cases, people who are older and overweight. As the numbers suggest, a great many of the estimated 46 million with sleep apnea, who exhibit the typical symptoms of daytime sleepiness, snoring, hypertension, and irritability, have yet to be diagnosed.

CPAP machines and their cousins VPAP (variable positive airway pressure) and others were at one time massive, clunky machines restricting movement and very difficult to travel with. No more: The new machines are smaller, lighter, cheaper, and easier to use. We don't like solutions that are worse than the problem, and ResMed has turned the corner on that with the new machines; they're becoming more acceptable, less expensive, and more mainstream. We think the company's four-pronged strategy is a good one:

- Make the machines easier to deal with (and afford). This includes smaller, lighter machines, more comfortable masks, including pediatric and other special-needs masks, humidifiers, and other enhancements. The new AirMini CPAP machine, the smallest on the market, fits in the palm of your hand and brings CPAP to people who travel a lot, and the AirFit top-of-head mask is lighter and more comfortable.
- Increase clinical awareness and the rate of diagnosis. Get doctors and other clinicians to understand and recommend the solution.

- Expand into new applications including stroke, congestive heart failure, and COPD (Chronic Obstructive Pulmonary Disease) treatment.
- Expand internationally. The 2016 acquisition of Curative Medical gives ResMed access to the China market.

The company continues to execute effectively on all fronts.

The company markets its products in 120 countries, makes them in six countries outside the US, and invests about 7 percent of revenues in R&D. About 40 percent of sales come from outside the US.

ResMed continues to develop a holistic sleep management offering; a new "S+" noncontact sleep tracker is one new product example. The "AirMini" line of traveling CPAP machines described previously is another breakthrough. The "AirFit" line of masks adds a comfortable top-of-head design, like a headset, to the CPAP offering. The company continues to make small acquisitions to broaden its product line particularly into disease treatment and into new international markets. The 2016 acquisition of cloud software provider Brightree entered the company into the teleconnected post-acute home sleep disorder care market. A new cloud-connected platform known as AirView now has more than 8 million cloud-connected diagnostic and monitoring devices with more than 2 million of those receiving home monitoring. Predictive analytics are now making diagnostic use of the one billion nights of sleep data gathered by these cloud tools. Finally, consumables—mainly sleep masks—add a strong repeatable sales base and today comprise about 37 percent of sales.

The company is spreading further into adjacent markets and into technology, such as SaaS (Software as a Service, or cloud based) solutions for 24-hour centralized monitoring and management for sleep disorders and now other diseases such as COPD. A new "Mobi" portable miniature oxygen device allows COPD patients to "enjoy ResMed-quality oxygen therapy wherever they go."

Financial Highlights, Fiscal Year 2018

FY2018 sales rose 13 percent on robust sales of both new and existing devices and software and on acquisitions. Lower tax rates and operating efficiencies breathed 28 percent more life into earnings. New products and further improvements in product mix and efficiencies will bring a 16 percent net income rise in 2020 on a 12–13 percent revenue gain after a relatively more modest 2019. Dividends should grow steadily through the period, but significant buybacks are still not in the plans.

Reasons to Buy

We believe that the company's four-pronged strategy, previously outlined, is right on. As these machines, and the diagnosis of the condition they're designed for, become more mainstream, we expect more people in the market, lower prices, and reduced inconvenience. Software, size, and improved comfort technologies will all play a role in growing this market. All these things should open up larger and larger slices of the market for the company. We like the robust application of teleconnected medicine; it really makes sense in this space and can go a long way to reduce hospital admissions and overall healthcare costs.

Demographics are a plus too—as people get older and heavier, these machines will find more potential users. It's a niche business, and ResMed dominates the niche and is the only company solely focused on this market. While we tend not to rely on this in our selections, we feel the company has the earmarks of a good acquisition candidate for a larger provider of healthcare technology products.

Reasons for Caution

One of the bigger issues facing CPAP and related technologies is the eligibility for reimbursement or coverage through Medicare/Medicaid and through private insurers. The current landscape is a mixed bag: Many non-Medicare health insurance plans do not cover the machines (which range from about $600–$1,900 in price), and Medicare has driven payment rates down through competitive bidding and across-the-board cuts. That all said, this treatment is becoming more mainstream, and payer resistance is less than it used to be.

Too, the market is becoming more competitive, and there have been a few legal contests on intellectual property—most of which have gone ResMed's way so far. We continue to feel that ResMed's technology leadership, full-line offering, and experience in this market will prevail. Finally, a strong run-up in the stock price since early 2017 may leave some investors short of breath—choose entry points carefully.

SECTOR: Healthcare ❑ Beta coefficient: 0.90 ❑ 10-year compound earnings per-share growth: 15.0% ❑ 10-year compound dividends per-share growth: NM

	2011	2012	2013	2014	2015	2016	2017	2018
Revenues (mil)	1,243	1,368	1,514	1,555	1,679	1,839	2,067	2,342
Net income (mil)	227.0	254.9	307.1	345.4	352.9	352.4	366.0	474.1
Earnings per share	1.44	1.71	2.10	2.39	2.47	2.49	2.57	3.29
Dividends per share	—	—	0.68	1.00	1.12	1.20	1.32	1.40
Cash flow per share	1.96	2.40	2.71	2.99	3.03	3.12	3.36	3.45
Price: high	35.4	42.9	57.3	57.6	75.3	70.9	87.8	116.6
low	23.4	24.4	42.0	41.5	49.0	50.8	61.2	84.9

Website: www.resmed.com

CONSERVATIVE GROWTH

C.H. Robinson Worldwide, Inc.

Ticker symbol: CHRW (NASDAQ) ❑ Large Cap ❑ Value Line financial strength rating: A ❑ Current yield: 2.2% ❑ Dividend raises, past 10 years: 9

Company Profile

"We're the Original 3PL" proclaims the company website. "What's a 3PL?" "A third-party logistics provider." "Oh, good to know. Now what's that?"

The best way to explain is by example, and we have a good one here: C.H. Robinson Worldwide.

C.H. Robinson Worldwide, Inc., is one of the largest third-party logistics (3PL) providers in North America. The company provides bundled and "turnkey" freight transportation services and logistics solutions to companies of all sizes in a variety of industries. These customers are looking to outsource all or part of their logistics and supply-chain activities to gain expertise, efficient capacity utilization, and better pricing—hence the "third-party" logistics provider moniker.

C.H. Robinson is a non-asset-based provider, meaning it contracts with a network of 76,000 transportation carriers (mostly trucking firms but also railroads, intermodal operators, ship and air lines) and a network of warehousing, customs clearance operations, and other supply-chain components to provide a complete, flexible, and tailored solution to customers across and around the world. In addition to transportation, the company has a division called Robinson Fresh that provides sourcing services in the perishable food industry buying, selling, and marketing fresh fruits, vegetables, and other perishable items and transporting them to market—120 million cases annually for 2,000 growers. The fresh produce division accounts for about 13.5 percent of revenues, while "North American Surface Transportation," or "NAST," accounts for 67 percent of gross revenues and Global Forwarding (mostly ship and air) accounts for 15 percent. Other services, including consulting and other "Managed Services," account for the remaining 4 percent of revenues. About 70 percent of net revenues (gross less carrier payment) comes from trucking services.

In 2018, C.H. Robinson handled approximately 17.5 million shipments and worked with over 124,000 active customers. The customer base is diverse—manufacturing, food and beverage, retail, chemical, and automotive are the largest customer segments. The company has 285 offices across North and South America, Europe, and Asia.

The company has invested heavily in technology; its "Navisphere" single global technology "ecosystem" connects 150,000 customers, carriers, and suppliers and covers the entire "life cycle" of a shipment from notification to scheduling to delivery. Customers can track their shipments down to a single item; about 70 percent of Robinson's customer contacts come through this platform. The 2015 acquisition of electronic freight broker Freightquote added significant revenues and customer convenience especially in the LTL ("less than truckload") shipping market for smaller customers. Finally, Robinson's TMC division models your supply chain and applies analytics, predictive modeling, and network optimization as a consulting service.

Financial Highlights, Fiscal Year 2018

A strengthening economy, continuing marketplace emphasis on logistics as a competitive advantage, and a more favorable balance between trucking costs and trucking pricing helped to drive "gross" revenues up 11.8 percent in 2018 and the all-important "net" revenues up 14.2 percent. Why so important? Because gross includes the freight costs paid to third parties (trucking companies, railroads, etc.) while net is just the revenue leftover after paying the carrier bill. When "net" rises faster than "gross" that effectively shows that prices are rising faster than costs. Trucking costs, which had been driven higher by a mandated shift to onboard electronic logging devices and higher fuel prices, backed off in the latter part of the year. Net income rose almost 32 percent on the back of this pricing shift and lower tax rates. Top-line growth, margin expansion, and technology-based efficiencies should lead to profit increases in the mid-to-high single digits on revenue increases in the mid-single digits in 2019 and 2020. The company reiterated a stated goal to return 90 percent of net income to shareholders annually, foreshadowing continued dividend increases and capturing the fact that the company has bought back about 22 percent of its shares since 2011.

Reasons to Buy

The main idea behind C.H. Robinson is to provide businesses, large and small, with a flexible and scalable way to outsource their logistics operations, thus reducing poorly matched capacities and risks. (Do you, as operator of a private trucking fleet, ever have the right number of trucks? Nope—always too few or too many!)

A 3PL firm can also achieve efficiencies by combining loads for different customers. The company's value proposition for customers, in fact, is to "drive costs down," "improve efficiency," "mitigate risk," and "manage change." In today's fast-moving business world, products and supply chains change quickly, and companies have an increasing mandate to find ways to control costs and create supply-chain advantages. ("Accelerate Your Advantage" is one of their apt slogans.) As top-line improvements are hard to come by, services such as those offered by C.H. Robinson continue to make sense for an ever-increasing customer base. We like the way they do this with a minimal asset base—no trucks, ships, or trains of their own!

Traditionally, the company operated as a procurement, or forwarding, service for transportation services for its customers; today as much as anything else, it is a technology company deploying technology solutions to not only procure but also to manage and optimize the network. We like companies that deploy technology to create an advantage, particularly when it's an advantage for their customers. The strategy seems to be to become a fully integrated, technology-connected solution for firms shipping big stuff, just as FedEx and UPS have for firms shipping small stuff. The strong commitment to shareholder returns and the steady price related to the market add to the list of attractions.

Reasons for Caution

Shipping and transportation services are always cyclical and often volatile; in addition, large changes in fuel costs can be difficult to adjust to. Changes in transportation economics—such as those caused by fuel prices, shortages of truck drivers, environmental regulations, and the like—can disrupt supply-chain networks and be costly to comply with. Competition in the industry is fierce, but C.H. Robinson has a pretty strong lead in integrating its suppliers and customers, and even the 76,000 transportation suppliers stand to gain from the Robinson intermediary even if it crimps their own margins. The company is a "win-win" in the transportation and logistics market.

SECTOR: Transportation ❑ Beta coefficient: 0.85 ❑ 10-year compound earnings per-share growth: 9.0% ❑ 10-year compound dividends per-share growth: 12.0%

	2011	2012	2013	2014	2015	2016	2017	2018
Revenues (mil)	10,336	11,369	12,752	13,470	13,476	13,144	14,689	16,631
Net income (mil)	432	594	416	450	510	515	505	665
Earnings per share	2.82	3.67	2.65	3.05	3.51	3.59	3.57	4.73
Dividends per share	1.20	1.67	1.40	1.43	1.57	1.74	1.81	1.88
Cash flow per share	2.62	3.92	3.18	3.46	4.00	4.15	4.25	5.45
Price: high	82.8	71.8	67.9	77.5	76.2	77.9	89.9	101.2
low	62.3	50.8	53.7	50.2	59.7	60.3	63.4	78.8

Website: www.chrobinson.com

AGGRESSIVE GROWTH

Ross Stores, Inc.

Ticker symbol: ROST (NASDAQ) ❑ Large Cap ❑ Value Line financial strength rating: A ❑ Current yield: 1.1% ❑ Dividend raises, past 10 years: 10

Company Profile

The current retail transition to more of an online, "from the couch" approach has claimed a lot of retail victims recently, including Macy's from our *100 Best* list, and has forced us to evaluate whether the others have sufficient defenses against the Amazon threat. We have actually added a few that we felt did have some built-in protections from the Amazon threat—Home Depot and Target (returning last year) and Best Buy (returning this year). Amazon can't ship lumber and drywall, nor can it easily match Target's visual convenience nor Best Buy's in-home technology expertise. We examined Ross carefully, and once again it passes the test; it is unique enough in its shopping approach (Amazon is easier to shop when you know something specific you want, then look at the price; you go into a discounter like Ross looking at the prices, then deciding what you want) and its stores are enough of a destination for its current loyal shopper base that we think it can keep people coming to its bargain bins.

"Say Yes to Bargains" is the apt and timely motto of Ross Stores, the second-largest off-price retailer in the United States. Ross and its subsidiaries operate two chains of apparel and home accessories stores. As of 2018 the company operated a total of 1,717 stores, up from 1,622 in 2017, 1,553 in 2016, and 1,125 in 2011. Of that total, 1,480 were Ross Dress for Less locations in 38 states, DC, and Guam, and 267 were dd's DISCOUNTS stores in 18 states. Just under half the company's stores are located in three states—California, Florida, and Texas.

Both chains target value-conscious women and men between the ages of 18 and 54. Ross's target customers are primarily from middle-income households, while dd's DISCOUNTS target customers are typically from lower- to middle-income households. Merchandising, purchasing, pricing, and the locations of the stores are all aimed at these customer bases. Ross and dd's DISCOUNTS both offer first-quality, in-season, name-brand and designer apparel, accessories, and footwear for the family at savings typically in the 20–60 percent range off department store prices (at Ross) or 20–70 percent off (at dd's DISCOUNTS). The stores also offer discounted home fashions and housewares, educational toys and games, furniture and furniture accents, luggage, cookware, and at some stores jewelry.

Sales break down by category roughly as follows: 26 percent Ladies'; 26 percent Home Accents, Bed, and Bath; 14 percent for Men's; 13 percent for Accessories, Lingerie, Jewelry, and Fragrances; 13 percent for Shoes; and 8 percent Children's. The shopping demographic is 75–80 percent female, shopping for herself or other family members; the core customer averages about three store visits a month. Their market research also suggests that the average customer "wants"—not "needs"—a bargain; there are a number of frugal but fairly well-heeled customers looking for a brand at a good price.

Ross's strategy is to offer competitive values to target customers by offering a well-managed mix of inventory with a strong percentage of department store name brands and items of local and seasonal interest at attractive prices. The company plans to add 75 more Ross stores and 25 dd's DISCOUNTS stores again for 2019 (they added 95 in 2018) while closing or relocating about ten stores, and it plans to ultimately grow to about 2,400 Ross and 600 dd's DISCOUNTS stores, although probably not by the end of the decade as once thought.

Financial Highlights, Fiscal Year 2018

Store expansion and a 4 percent same-store sales gain led to a 6 percent 2018 sales gain in all, which would have been closer to 8 percent had the 2017 year not been 53 measured weeks. Operating margins fell about 0.9 percent however due to the extra week in 2017 and higher freight and wage costs. Net profit rose 24 percent anyway on the higher volumes and lower taxes, and per-share earnings grew 29 percent with a 4 percent share buyback.

FY2019 and FY2020 forecasts call for roughly 5 percent revenue gains annually with 1–2 percent same-store sales growth. Margins should stabilize as the company's across-the-board $11 minimum wage increase is already behind it. Net income is expected to rise in the 3–5 percent range each year. Healthy share buybacks should continue, keeping per-share earnings growth humming along in the 10–20 percent range.

Reasons to Buy

We had become a little tired of this story, which really got a boost from the now-faded Great Recession years. We saw revenue growth being driven mainly by store expansion, and profit growth attenuating. Did we also see that, with more disposable income, consumers may wander away? Did we see signs of too many stores? All might be warning signs of future trouble, and these give us a bit of fright every year. But we've stayed on this horse year after year for one big reason: profitability. Net profit margins—after taxes and everything else—run in the 9–10 percent range. Such a figure is not easy to find in the retail world.

The recession apparently helped Ross gain mainstream appeal across a wider set of customers. While some of those customers defected back to full-price retail stores as things improved, a greater number have shown that they will continue to shop at the stores. At the same time, the company was successful with operational changes begun years ago to improve merchandising and inventory management, which led to better stocking of a more favorable mix of goods and better inventory turnover. The higher store count has increased operating leverage as well—more volume through the same infrastructure and cost base. Nothing much is mentioned about international expansion, but we wonder if there too lies an opportunity.

Strong, defensible niche, moderate expansion, operational excellence, sustained shareholder returns; it's an attractive formula and the results speak for themselves as well as pointing to good management. And one more thing: We like how they present all of this to shareholders; their investor materials are easy to follow.

Reasons for Caution

E-commerce doesn't seem to have taken a bite out of Ross yet, but there's always that possibility, particularly with the advance of online promotional and coupon portals like Groupon. We still think the typical Ross shopper actually likes the "hunt" and is less likely to transition to couch-based shopping than most other shoppers. Another concern is that the company is dependent on the actions of others—mainly first-line apparel retailers—for its success. The availability of surplus inventories is high now as first-line retailers struggle…but who knows what lies ahead? We also remain concerned that the company still depends to a degree on store expansion, which carries its own risks, and could make supply bubbles and constraints hurt even more.

Finally, while Ross may be synonymous with bargains for shoppers, its share price has not followed suit for investors—the stock has been on a steady upward march for ten years. Look for "off price" bargains when picking up this one.

SECTOR: Retail ❑ Beta coefficient: 0.95 ❑ 10-year compound earnings per-share growth: 21.5% ❑ 10-year compound dividends per-share growth: 23.5%

	2011	2012	2013	2014	2015	2016	2017	2018
Revenues (mil)	8,608	9,721	10,230	11,042	11,940	12,867	14,135	14,984
Net income (mil)	657	787	837	925	1,021	1,118	1,282	1,588
Earnings per share	1.43	1.77	1.94	2.21	2.51	2.83	3.34	4.26
Dividends per share	0.24	0.30	0.36	0.40	0.47	0.54	0.64	0.90
Cash flow per share	1.81	2.21	2.44	2.79	3.22	3.62	4.20	5.21
Price: high	24.6	35.4	41.0	48.1	56.7	69.6	81.5	104.4
low	15.0	23.5	26.5	30.9	43.5	50.4	52.8	73.8

Website: www.rossstores.com

AGGRESSIVE GROWTH

RPM International, Inc.

Ticker symbol: RPM (NYSE) ❑ Large Cap ❑ Value Line financial strength rating: B+ ❑ Current yield: 2.4% ❑ Dividend raises, past 10 years: 10

Company Profile

Have you ever finished a piece of furniture or a wood floor with Varathane? Stained it with Watco? Caulked a bathtub or sink with DAP? Spray-painted a metal gate with Rust-Oleum? Primed bathroom walls with Zinsser primers before painting them? Glued a model airplane together with Testors? We have—and it seems like every time we do those little weekend warrior tasks around the house, we're using one of these products.

We wondered, Who makes and markets this stuff? Where do these well-established brands that seem to show up in every hardware store and home improvement center we go into come from? How did they become household names, even category-defining names like Kleenex? After a little digging, we came up with a company we'd never heard of. Sometimes that's a really good sign. A "house of brands," each with its own strength, image, and loyal following, can have more staying and growing power than a "branded house." Just ask anyone on the marketing team at Procter & Gamble.

Anyway, the company we found is in all likelihood one you've never heard of, based in Medina, Ohio—a town you've probably never heard of, either. "The Brands You Know and Trust" is their slogan, and the company is RPM International. RPM International makes and markets an assortment of specialty chemicals and coatings, targeted mostly to repair, maintenance, and replacement, for consumer and industrial markets.

Industrial markets? Indeed, only about a third (33 percent, actually) of RPM's sales come from the aforementioned "consumer" brands found in Home Depot and the like. The company also makes and markets a vast line of brands for industrial and construction use—sealants, chemicals, roofing systems, corrosion control coatings, marine paints and coatings, fluorescent pigments (you've probably heard of DayGlo, their line of fluorescent paints), powder coatings, fire coatings, and concrete waterproofing and repair products.

There are now 40 "Industrial" brands in all including brands such as Increte Systems, a maker of textured stamped concrete systems, or USL BridgeCare solutions, or Carboline corrosion control coatings; you get the idea. Product categories in this segment include construction sealants and chemicals, roofing systems, flooring systems, corrosion control coatings, fiberglass reinforced gratings, waterproofing coatings and sealants, concrete admixtures and repair products, and fireproofing coatings. Much of this is aimed at the preservation and corrosion protection of existing structures, which makes the company a strong play in the infrastructure reinvestment market. About 85 percent of the company's business comes from repair and maintenance, and about 15 percent comes from new construction. The Industrial segment accounts for 53 percent of the business, and many of its brands are made and sold in foreign markets. In fact, about 50 percent of Industrial business is overseas, while 85 percent of the consumer business originates in North America.

The "Consumer" segment includes categories such as caulks and sealants, primers, specialty paints, wood stains and finishes, rust-preventive paints, garage and basement floor coatings, deck and driveway coatings, and hobby and craft products. DAP, Rust-Oleum, SprayMate, Krud Kutter, Varathane, and Watco are among the 27 brands originating in this segment.

The "Specialty" segment produces DayGlo as well as other fluorescent pigments, specialty coatings for specialty powder and marine coatings, edible coatings, restoration and cleaning solutions, insulation, and concrete repair, with 20 brands and about 14 percent of RPM's business.

Not to beat the brand thing to death, but Rust-Oleum, Varathane, DAP, and Zinsser on the consumer side own number one positions in their respective markets, while eight industrial and specialty brands, including DayGlo, of course, but also Tremco in roofing, Stonhard in polymer flooring, and Carboline in corrosion control, own number one positions in their US markets.

The company has accumulated most of these brands through acquisitions of small specialty companies making single products or product lines in the "small chemical" space. Many of these small operators seek to be acquired by RPM; the resulting "conglomerate" has a bit of a Berkshire Hathaway feel with its stable of small, independently managed businesses. RPM has acquired 170+ companies in the past 30 years and 70 in the past decade. About 35 percent of sales are overseas.

Financial Highlights, Fiscal Year 2018

FY2018 sales growth rang in at 7.3 percent, about half of that due to acquisitions. US construction-related businesses such as roofing and flooring were strong but offset somewhat by weakness in the oil and gas industry and difficulties in specific markets such as Brazil. Higher raw material costs hurt gross margins, but net profit advanced 18 percent anyway due to reductions in SG&A and in tax rates. The outlook for 2019 calls for continued pain on the input cost front, with operating margins declining another 0.5 percent and net income dropping some 15 percent even as sales advance about 5 percent; the company is responding with efficiency measures, some of which eliminate duplication between the many business units, designed to save $290 million annually. As a result, earnings are expected to bounce back some 30–35 percent in 2020 on another 5 percent sales advance. Moderation in material cost increases will help further. Dividends should increase in the high-single-digit range, and about $1 billion has been earmarked for share buybacks.

Reasons to Buy

We always like premier brands in relatively simple, well-managed businesses, and RPM International seems to fit the model. The company presents itself well: Its website and investor materials are among the best and most informative we've encountered. From what we see, we like the straightforward qualities of the management team; it's one we'd want to work for. These factors alone wouldn't be enough to land RPM on our *100 Best* list; however, we also take notice of good businesses with good brands, marketplace position, and fundamentals. We also take notice of a company that has raised its dividend 45 straight years (and is proud of it), and we like the defensive nature of its repeat-purchase, mainly maintenance and repair, product lines. Finally, RPM should do well as infrastructure improvement programs take hold—this factor is still not really included in the forecasts.

Reasons for Caution

Clearly this has not been one of our best performers, and while we think patience may prevail, we do wonder how big the growth opportunity really is. We also wonder if the business is stretched a bit too thin and if consolidating some of those little subsidiaries to make stronger, more focused brands and to eliminate duplicate costs might make sense; the company seems to agree at least on the cost side. With so many acquisitions the chances of a failure grow—although the Berkshire model in place here does more good than bad in that respect. Raw material cost increases have always been a threat and have become a forefront issue to deal with.

SECTOR: Materials ❑ Beta coefficient: 1.10 ❑ 10-year compound earnings per-share growth: 5.5% ❑ 10-year compound dividends per-share growth: 5.5%

	2011	2012	2013	2014	2015	2016	2017	2018
Revenues (mil)	3,382	3,777	4,081	4,376	4,595	4,814	4,958	5,321
Net income (mil)	189	215	241	292	323	355	331	384
Earnings per share	1.45	1.65	1.83	2.18	2.38	2.63	2.47	2.92
Dividends per share	0.84	0.86	0.89	0.95	1.02	1.09	1.18	1.26
Cash flow per share	2.01	2.20	2.45	2.86	3.17	3.50	3.37	3.91
Price: high	26.0	29.6	41.6	52.0	51.4	55.9	56.5	68.1
low	17.2	23.0	29.1	37.6	40.1	36.8	47.9	46.4

Website: www.rpminc.com

Schnitzer Steel Industries, Inc.

Ticker symbol: SCHN (NASDAQ) ❑ Small Cap ❑ Value Line financial strength rating: B ❑ Current yield: 3.1% ❑ Dividend raises, past 10 years: 2

Company Profile

Here we come to one of our favorite Small Cap picks, one that has tantalized us for about six years now, at last breaking out of its slump in 2017 as commodity prices (finally!) firmed, then going back into a bit of one as China swooned and prices of certain metals began to fall again. Here we have a story of value waiting to be unlocked, as this company, more than many, embarked on a years-long efficiency program in response to the Great Recession, then carried those benefits forward into recovery. That is...if the recovery would last. Meanwhile, we collect our 3 percent dividends and wait...

Founded in 1946, Schnitzer Steel is mainly a collector and recycler of ferrous and nonferrous scrap, with smaller operations that collect, dismantle, and market auto and truck parts and a steel mill "mini mill" finished steel product business. There are two business segments: Auto and Metals Recycling (AMR) and Cascade Steel and Scrap (CSS).

The AMR business, which accounts for about 80 percent of Schnitzer's 2018 revenues, includes the Metals Recycling business (about 91 percent of AMR), which collects, recycles, processes, and brokers scrap steel and nonferrous metals to domestic and foreign markets—4.3 million tons of ferrous scrap metal and 636 million pounds of nonferrous metal in all. By revenues, 73 percent of 2018 revenues were ferrous (iron and steel), and 27 percent were nonferrous (dominated by copper and aluminum but also including stainless steel, nickel, brass, titanium, and lead, among others).

Larger scrap mills are located in Oregon; Washington; Oakland, California; and Massachusetts, with smaller mills in Rhode Island, Puerto Rico, Hawaii, and Alaska, all with adjacent deepwater ports, correctly suggesting an orientation toward international export of scrap metal for foreign mills. Indeed, that is true—some 61 percent of revenue comes from outside North America (which means trade wars don't matter that much so long as someone is buying foreign steel). The company operates 44 metals recycling facilities ("scrapyards," in popular vernacular) in 23 states, mostly on the coasts and in the south, 7 in Canada, and 5 in Puerto Rico. The operation adds value in part by sorting and shredding input scrap into homogenous materials well suited to the needs of downstream customers.

The Auto Parts business portion of the AMR segment (9 percent of that segment's revenues) operates 52 self-serve auto parts scrapyards and stores, some co-located with Metals Recycling facilities, in 16 states with a concentration in California under the "Pick-n-Pull" name. This operation processes about 350,000 cars annually. Inventories of scrapped autos and common parts from those autos are posted online and updated as new inventory is received.

The Cascade Steel and Scrap business (19 percent of total revenues) principally operates an electric arc furnace mini mill in McMinnville, Oregon, producing rebar, wire rod, merchant bar, and other specialty products, mainly for western US markets, of course from scrap steel available from the company's own Metals Recycling facilities. CSS operates the recycling facilities in Oregon and Washington that supply this mill while other recycling facilities operate under the AMR segment.

About 39 percent of revenue comes from North America, while the rest comes from Asia (44 percent), Europe (16 percent), and 1 percent each to Africa and South America. By country, the five largest "customer" countries are the US, Turkey, China, Bangladesh, and South Korea, which together account for 75 percent of total revenues.

Financial Highlights, Fiscal Year 2018

In 2017, average recycled ferrous selling prices finally surged ahead to $242 per ton in 2017, up from $196 in 2016 and $179 in 2015. That was pretty good, and 2018 was even better, with average ferrous prices averaging $317 per ton for the year. That and strong demand (3,708 million tons for the year versus 3,145 million in 2017 and 2,899 million in 2016) gave rise to a substantial boost in 2018 revenue and profitability: Profits rose some 254 percent on a 40 percent revenue gain. Nonferrous prices rose from 60 cents to 72 cents a pound over the same period, with shipments rising from 473,737 pounds in 2016 to 571,705 pounds in 2018. Those results certainly marked a return to health for Schnitzer, but unfortunately prices for nonferrous scrap faltered 19 percent in early 2019 due to China weakness, particularly in aluminum scrap. The most recent forecast calls for a 20 percent profit decline in 2019 on flat revenues if prices hold; 2020 looks better with a 16 percent net profit recovery on a 5–7 percent revenue gain. These figures should allow for modest dividend raises and share buybacks after years of no change.

Reasons to Buy

We continue to bet on strengthening steel and scrap prices and this company's strong focus and productivity track record in this industry. Scrap as a source of supply is much more flexible and environmentally sound and should lead the way as metals recover. We should also note that today's modern electric arc furnace mills such as those operated by Nucor are more cost-effective and flexible than traditional blast furnaces and tend to use scrap as the main input resource. Scrap is easier to source, more flexible, and more local than traditional iron ore inputs for these modern mills.

There are a lot of mom-and-pop scrap dealers around the world, but few have the size, operating leverage, and remarketing abilities of Schnitzer. The company is a strong and recognized brand in a fragmented and unbranded industry, offering advantages both on the sales and operational side. When prices and markets are soft, the company loses, but as we saw particularly in 2008, when markets are strong, the company does really, really well. Whether steel and other finished metal products are made domestically or imported, Schnitzer wins as a universal supplier. Schnitzer is well managed, adds a lot of value in a relatively non-value-add industry, and keeps its shareholders in mind.

Reasons for Caution

Schnitzer is still very sensitive to global steel and nonferrous metals markets and the ups and downs of pricing; as a consequence the stock has been more volatile over the years than we would typically like. While its size and marketing advantages serve it well in tough times, inventory is inventory, and the company can get caught with a lot of it purchased at higher prices if the markets don't move to its advantage. It does okay in bad economic climates, but the company is really a bet on recycling value add and on good times in global manufacturing. Global trade wars can shift the production landscape for metals and finished metals products, but scrap is the universal input so it doesn't matter too much who wins trade wars; that said it bears watching when countries like China move to limit recycled product imports as they have recently. If you buy in, you'll want to watch global steel and other metals prices. Also, while the company has a good track record, there are always some environmental risks and costs in this sort of business.

SECTOR: Industrials ❑ Beta coefficient: 1.45 ❑ 10-year compound earnings per-share growth: NM ❑ 10-year compound dividends per-share growth: 27.0%

	2011	2012	2013	2014	2015	2016	2017	2018
Revenues (mil)	3,459	3,341	2,621	2,544	1,915	1,352	1,688	2,365
Net income (mil)	119	30	(2.0)	5.1	(58.8)	(19.4)	44.9	113.9
Earnings per share	4.24	1.10	(0.07)	0.19	(2.25)	(0.66)	1.60	3.88
Dividends per share	0.20	0.41	0.75	0.75	0.75	0.75	0.75	0.75
Cash flow per share	7.08	4.28	3.05	3.19	0.23	1.32	3.50	6.13
Price: high	69.4	47.4	33.0	33.3	22.8	30.6	35.2	38.8
low	32.8	22.8	23.1	21.4	12.6	11.7	17.5	21.1

Website: www.schnitzersteel.com

AGGRESSIVE GROWTH

The Scotts Miracle-Gro Company

Ticker symbol: SMG (NYSE) ❑ Mid Cap ❑ Value Line financial strength rating: B++ ❑ Current yield: 2.7% ❑ Dividend raises, past 10 years: 9

Company Profile

Scotts Miracle-Gro, formerly Scotts Co., formerly O.M. Scott & Sons, is a 148-year-old provider of mostly packaged lawn- and garden-care products for consumer markets. Over the past three years the company has entered into the hydroponics supplies business through a series of small, targeted acquisitions. The new foray currently represents about 13 percent of revenues. More on that in a minute…

Originally a seed company, today SMG's lawn-care products include packaged, premixed fertilizers and combination fertilizer and weed-/pest-control products marketed mainly under the Scotts and Turf Builder brand names. The company also markets packaged grass seed and a line of individually packaged pest-/disease-control products mainly under the Ortho brand (acquired in 1997) and a line of specialty garden fertilizers and pest-control products under the Miracle-Gro name, acquired in 1995. The company also markets a line of consumer pest-control products and acts as the exclusive worldwide distributor (for Monsanto) for the Roundup brand of consumer weed-control products.

Scotts is a study in branding in an otherwise highly fragmented market. The attractive core brands of Scotts, Turf Builder, Miracle-Gro, and Ortho and Roundup take center stage in this business and in their respective markets. There are few nationally known brands in the lawn and garden maintenance sectors, and as such SMG's lines compete mainly with local and store brands for shelf space in regional chains like OSH and Tractor Supply. In the large national chains (Home Depot, Lowe's, etc.), SMG's best-known products are front and center.

Smaller but significant brands are Hyponex (bagged potting soil and manure), Weedol weed killers, Osmocote professional plant nutrients, and Fertiligene. The company's European and Australian brands were divested through sale in 2017 when SMG reorganized its International segment.

The vision is interesting: "To help people of all ages express themselves on their own piece of the earth." In addition to sounding pretty groovy, the message recognizes a demographic shift toward smaller, more urban gardening environments. In support of this vision, the company over the past four years has made acquisitions of just over $1 million for brands targeting hydroponics for personal and commercial growing operations. Though it isn't mentioned anywhere on their websites or in their financial reports, these products are primarily used in the rapidly legitimizing cannabis industry—a high-growth area (no pun intended).

People are also seeking organic gardening products in consumer packages; Scotts new line of organic Miracle-Gro products have begun to address this trend. Innovations also include new packaging to simplify the measurement and application and improve the safety of key products. We expect SMG to make additional brand acquisitions in the hydroponics market over the next two years.

Financial Highlights, Fiscal Year 2018

Sales overall for 2018 were up a scant 1 percent over 2017, with a $50 million decline in Consumer balanced by a $50 million increase at Hawthorne (the hydroponics brand) and an 8 percent increase in Other. The setbacks in Consumer were due to lower volumes and negative pricing impact. Hawthorne's 20 percent improvement was driven largely by acquisitions. The company in 2018 recognized several asset impairments, largely goodwill as a result of acquisitions, litigation provisions, and restructuring charges totaling $240 million which, while not negatively impacting operations going forward, were unusual one-time charges and are worth noting (approximately 20 percent of these charges were associated with the company's ongoing cost-reduction program). All of this results in a decline in net profit (on paper) of some 38 percent, so if you're reviewing SMG's numbers somewhere else, knowing the underlying causes should allay any resulting shock.

The company's typically strong cash-flow generation subsided a bit but can be expected to improve significantly following 2018's unique financial environment. Going forward, there are very encouraging numbers, particularly with Hawthorne now accounting for an increased percentage of SMG's total sales, an ongoing share buyback program, and continued support for a steadily increasing dividend. FY2019 looks to be a deeper shade of green.

Reasons to Buy

We continue to support SMG's refocusing on the North American market as we feel their brand strength there is a significant differentiator. The early numbers strongly suggest that exiting the European market and the reinvestment of that capital in the Hawthorne segment was the right move at the right time. Interestingly, the company retains some exposure to the European market in that several of their recent acquisitions are based in the Netherlands and established suppliers to the Dutch cut-flower and hydroponics markets.

The company's lawn-care and gardening products business is much healthier as a result of the recent pruning. Cost cutting has resulted in net margins which are, even though depressed last year, above the 2009–15 average, and FY2019 is projected to be one of the company's most profitable years ever.

The company has, over the past three years, acquired several hydroponics businesses, such as hardware manufacturers and growing media suppliers. We like the moves and are optimistic with regard to the prospects for strong growth in this segment. Players in this area have traditionally been small, localized businesses without access (in some cases) to traditional capital markets. SMG's national footprint and capital presence will provide these businesses (under its Hawthorne name) with a halo brand and the capability for faster growth. In June 2018 SMG took an even larger position in the industry through its $460 million acquisition of Sunlight Supply, the largest distributor of hydroponics products in the US (prior to this acquisition, Sunlight had been a nonexclusive distributor of SMG's products). The move came at something of a premium, but netted an already profitable business in an area of focus for SMG and created a significant distribution growth path for its supply partners. So far in 2019 Hawthorne's net sales are up 10 percent with the company on track for an expected $35 million increase in "synergies" from the Sunlight transaction and a full-year target of $60 million segment profit.

We understand that the hydroponics business may not be right for every investor and we would not presume to tell our readers what to think on this topic, but we do feel that a well-regulated, tax-paying cannabis industry is far preferable to what we've had nationwide over the past forty years. We think SMG is taking a business-savvy, prudent approach to an entry into what could be a tremendous market opportunity over the next decade.

Reasons for Caution

While big retailers have increasingly joined the Scotts bandwagon, they aren't the only brand in town, and the company does face some competition from less expensive house brands such as those sold at Ace Hardware, Home Depot, Lowe's, and elsewhere. Monsanto is running into some difficulty on the legal front, but at this time we do not foresee any impact to SMG's business levels as a distributor. Finally, the past decade of demographic shifts away from the suburbs, including downsizing and increases in renting versus owning, will continue to put pressure on the traditional bagged fertilizer and lawn goods business; Scotts' new products and services in new niches like hydroponics will keep the spreader moving forward here.

SECTOR: Materials ❑ Beta coefficient: 1.00 ❑ 10-year compound earnings per-share growth: 7.5% ❑ 10-year compound dividends per-share growth: 12.5%

	2011	2012	2013	2014	2015	2016	2017	2018
Revenues (mil)	2,835	2,826	2,819	2,841	3,017	2,836	2,642	2,663
Net income (mil)	121.9	113.2	161.2	165.4	158.7	253.8	197.8	127.6
Earnings per share	1.84	1.62	2.58	2.64	2.57	4.09	3.29	2.23
Dividends per share	.05	1.23	1.41	1.76	1.82	1.91	2.03	2.14
Cash flow per share	3.00	2.86	3.67	3.74	3.64	5.36	4.78	3.82
Price: high	60.8	55.9	62.6	64.0	72.3	98.8	108	110.1
low	40.0	35.5	42.0	52.4	58.1	62.2	81.5	58.0

Website: www.scottsmiraclegro.com

CONSERVATIVE GROWTH

Sealed Air

Ticker symbol: SEE (NYSE) ❑ Large Cap ❑ Value Line financial strength rating: B ❑ Current yield: 1.4% ❑ Dividend raises, past 10 years: 4

Company Profile

According to digital market researcher eMarketer, e-commerce sales are expected to grow almost 70 percent between 2018 and 2022—or about 14 percent compounded annually. And every one of these shipments requires the proper product and shipment packaging to make it work; the wrong package fails to protect the product, gives the customer a poor experience, and/or costs too much to pack and/or to ship—not to mention the environmental consequences. In short, packaging is becoming a key part of today's, and tomorrow's, never-leave-your-couch e-commerce ecosystem. It's the reasoning behind our quest to keep a product-packaging specialist on the 2020 *100 Best Stocks* list.

Now the remaining question was: Out of the six or seven large packaging suppliers to choose from, which one? We looked at several with an eye to which company had a significant presence in e-commerce—and more so, which company had the most innovative approach to improving e-commerce packaging. We arrived at packaging producer Sealed Air as the answer to add to the 2019 list, and so far, good things have come in Sealed Air packages.

We all know Sealed Air as the original makers of Bubble Wrap, that simple but effective cushioned wrapping material we all love to give to our kids to pop on Christmas morning.

Actually, Bubble Wrap is part of the Product Care segment within Sealed Air, which represents about 39 percent of Sealed Air's 2018 total revenue, while the larger portion of the business is represented by the Food Care segment, which represents the other 61 percent of volume. The e-commerce business lies within Product Care; as a consequence, not surprisingly, Product Care revenues grew 11 percent in 2018 while Food Care grew only 3 percent. About 49 percent of revenues come from outside the US.

So what's inside the package in each of these two segments? First, the Food Care division provides a broad range of products and integrated packaging systems to ship and store food products, minimizing contamination risk, improving shelf life, and improving merchandising and store display. These specialized packages, which you might see containing everything from your Thanksgiving turkey to packaged meats, vegetables, and pasta, are marketed under several brand names, "Cryovac" being the most prevalent. Focus is placed not just on the package but on the automation of the packaging process, bringing a complete solution for the producer supply chain.

Although we feel that the e-commerce boom will eventually spill over into this segment as better solutions are needed for the emerging food and meal home-delivery business, our e-commerce intrigue is really centered on the Product Care segment. The Product Care business exists to provide its customers with a "range of sustainable packaging solutions designed to reduce shipping and fulfillment costs, increase operational efficiency, reduce damage and enhance customer and brand experience." The largest customer sectors are e-commerce, general manufacturing, electronics, and transportation. Products include a range of packing materials and systems including the aforementioned Bubble Wrap but also AirCap cellular packaging, Cryovac shrink films, Instapak polyurethane foam systems, and others. More high-tech systems include "e-Cube," an automated high-velocity fulfillment solution that optimizes shipping box "cube" (to save shipping costs) and other bulk product packaging and storing systems that allow a shipper to pick and pull product ready to ship in its own container, bypassing a pack and ship process in a logistics operation.

What really sealed the deal (sorry) for us for Sealed Air was the 2017 announcement of a joint Packaging Innovation Center with UPS (another *100 Best* stock) in UPS's Louisville Supply Chain Solution's campus aimed specifically at "solving the packaging and shipping challenges of e-commerce retailers…by maximizing efficiency, minimizing waste, reducing shipping costs and increasing brand affinity." The joint effort, part of a larger strategic partnership between the two companies, puts specific focus on packaging innovation as part of supply-chain innovation. In part the new effort recognizes the need for performance—and customer experience benefits—for not only the specific product package but also for the secondary and tertiary packages that products are shipped in. With the vast increase in package volume moving through e-commerce channels and delivery vehicles, it's not hard to see the importance of this focus. For us, this effort and other innovation efforts (there are 41 packaging labs and design centers around the world) make Sealed Air stand out among the many packaging manufacturers.

Financial Highlights, Fiscal Year 2018

Food Care and Product Care reported 3 percent and 11 percent revenue gains, respectively, as noted previously, leading to a 6 percent revenue gain overall. Reported net profit was up 139 percent from a year depressed by the divestiture of its Diversey medical packaging operations, and still lagging behind better years past due to restructuring costs and higher input costs. Going forward the company expects sales gains in the 5–7 percent range for 2019 and in the 4–5 percent range in 2020; earnings should recover beyond previous years' levels on higher margins by 2019 with a full recovery and then some in net profit by 2020. Modest share repurchases after a healthy 8 percent repurchase in 2018 will help per-share earnings;

dividend raises are also projected to be modest but could surprise to the upside as cash flows are strong.

Reasons to Buy

As mentioned at the outset there are a number of integrated packaging providers at the doorstep of e-commerce; we chose Sealed Air because of its track record and callout of e-commerce as a strategic priority. We also think the food packaging business, while fairly mundane at present, could be a hidden card to play as local and centralized home food delivery become more prevalent. Aside from e-commerce, we think restructuring programs, innovation, and other efforts to bolster margins will help in this typically low-margin business.

Reasons for Caution

As a whole, the packaging industry is fairly mundane, as any employee of TV's Dunder Mifflin could tell you! It is competitive, and dynamic change and especially growth can be hard to come by. Second, while we're excited by the e-commerce opportunity, the entire Product Care group in which it lives still represents only 40 percent of the company. Input cost inflation could also pop Sealed Air's bubbles. So could its rather large debt load, which is targeted for improvement but currently far exceeds shareholder equity. Sealed Air has sold at roughly the same price for four years in a rising market—which can be taken as either a problem or an opportunity—we're clearly betting on both an improvement in business fundamentals and an improvement in the way the market perceives this company's fortunes.

SECTOR: Industrials ▫ Beta coefficient: 1.00 ▫ 10-year compound earnings per-share growth: -1.5% ▫ 10-year compound dividends per-share growth: 5.0%

	2011	2012	2013	2014	2015	2016	2017	2018
Revenues (mil)	5,641	7,648	7,691	7,750	7,031	6,778	4,461	4,733
Net income (mil)	243	200	263	258	335	486	63	150
Earnings per share	1.31	0.95	1.23	1.20	1.62	2.46	0.33	0.94
Dividends per share	0.52	0.52	0.52	0.52	0.52	0.61	0.64	0.64
Cash flow per share	2.25	2.59	2.77	2.49	2.80	3.62	1.25	1.81
Price: high	28.8	21.5	34.4	43.7	55.8	52.8	50.8	49.9
low	11.0	11.5	17.6	28.2	38.4	38.0	41.0	30.2

Website: www.sealedair.com

Siemens AG (ADR)

Ticker symbol: SIEGY ❑ Large Cap ❑ Value Line financial strength rating: A ❑ Current yield: 3.9% ❑ Dividend raises, past 10 years: 8

Company Profile

Operating under the slogan "Ingenuity for Life" and setting the benchmark to "electrify, automate and digitize the world around us," the $96 billion diversified industrial conglomerate known worldwide as Siemens continues to fascinate us. It fascinates us even though it's going through some complex organizational changes, lives in a difficult world of industrial conglomerates tainted by the collapse of GE, performed poorly in 2019, and is generally more complex and difficult to understand than we'd like. Why do we like Siemens? Quite simply, Siemens touches many industries and sectors of interest to us—infrastructure, healthcare, urban transportation, industrial automation, and alternative energy—with an assortment of technology-enhanced products and services. Smart investing implies investing "where the puck is going," and we think many of the businesses Siemens is active in are important and are laden with growth opportunity and that Siemens is positioning itself well to capitalize on it.

The company was founded in the late nineteenth century by Werner von Siemens, an early electrical engineering pioneer and inventor of the electric elevator. Siemens currently operates in six fully owned and operated product segments and two more "strategic" segments that are in various stages of spin-off with Siemens retaining a large share. First, the bad news:

- Power and Gas (15 percent of FY2018 revenues) supplies an assortment of products to the electric generation and the oil and gas production and transportation industries. Gas and steam turbines and other "heavy" power plant hardware of varying sizes are made by this operation. While the advent of alternative energy forms has cut into this business, they have recently introduced new large-scale and "decentral" power generation turbines. Still, revenues are down and profit margins have sunk from 10 to 3 percent. Notably GE has had big problems with this business too, but it's only 15 percent of Siemens's business.

- Energy Management (15 percent) is a leading global supplier of electrical grid hardware, solutions, and services "for the economical, reliable, and intelligent transmission and distribution of electric power," including high and low voltage and smart-grid solutions. FY2018 revenues were flat, but margins were up slightly.
- Digital Factory (16 percent) is one of the strongest and fastest-rising segments. It offers a portfolio of integrated hardware and software solutions to support product design processes and automate factories worldwide and to reduce their time to market. Mechanical drivers, digital controls, and design and operating software are applied to many vertical industries. Electronics design automation software maker Mentor Graphics was acquired in 2017.
- Process Industries and Drives (11 percent) offers a complete product, software, and solution portfolio to the handling of all kinds of material flows across many vertical businesses from cement, mining, and shipbuilding to food, beverages, and pharmaceuticals. This segment is experiencing modest growth.
- Mobility (11 percent) combines and sells a wide variety of products involved in passenger and freight rail transportation, including urban transportation infrastructure products, most notably so-called "light rail" transit cars; a large factory in Sacramento, California, produces these vehicles for the US and certain global markets. A recent attempt to merge this division with France's Alstom was blocked; what happens from here remains to be seen. Revenues, margins, and especially orders are on the rise.
- Building Technologies (8 percent) is the "world market leader" for safe, secure, and efficient buildings and infrastructures. Products include building automation technologies, HVAC controls, security, fire protection, and energy management products and services. "Steady state" for this segment.
- "Healthineers" (Healthcare—16 percent) is a world leader in medical imaging, laboratory diagnostics, therapy systems, hearing instruments, and clinical IT. In early 2018, this unit was spun off in an initial public offering, so it is no longer an operating segment. However, Siemens maintains ownership of 85 percent of the shares. It is the most profitable segment, with orders and revenues gaining slowly.
- Siemens Gamesa Renewable Energy, formerly Wind Power (11 percent), provides hardware, software, and services toward the creation of efficient onshore and offshore wind-power-generation facilities. The

relative size and importance of this segment increased with the 2017 acquisition of Spanish wind turbine manufacturer Gamesa.

By region, revenues break down as follows: Americas (27 percent), EMEA (excluding Germany—37 percent), Asia/Australia (22 percent), and Germany (14 percent).

Financial Highlights, Fiscal Year 2018

Currency translation effects are a major driver of the numbers you see in the following; the recent euro/US dollar conversion rate of 1.16 pales in comparison to the 1.46 rate back in 2009, hence results (and dividend payouts) look choppier than they really are. The assortment of acquisitions and divestitures also makes it hard to track results over time. Strength in the digital factory and healthcare businesses did not quite overcome the power segment's weakness and structural changes; revenues fell about 1.6 percent for 2018; earnings fell 3.8 percent due to slumping power and higher input costs. For FY2019, revenues are expected to rise 2–3 percent with a more robust 10–12 percent earnings rise; the company is expecting a good tailwind for their businesses as automation trends take hold; FY2020 forecasts call for an 8–10 percent net income gain on a similar rise in revenues, all with steady moderate dividend increases and buybacks.

Reasons to Buy

"Digitalization, Globalization, and Urbanization" are the three stated marketplace themes of this progressive leader in the world of industrial design and infrastructure. We believe as Siemens does that the world will be a more integrated industrial and distribution arena, more connected, more processes will be created and managed digitally, and that new and modern urban infrastructure will become increasingly important as urban populations grow. To those trends, the company brings new focus on added value in "digitalization, automation, and electrification" of the industrial and infrastructure space worldwide. We think this is a solid and very progressive—not to mention more profitable—position in comparison to most of today's industrial and infrastructure suppliers. The strategy seems right, and we think Siemens has already achieved world leadership in these areas. In fact, we classified the company under "Industrials" as a sector but could have easily justified classifying it as a "Technology" company. The world's factories, energy grids, transportation, and other infrastructure are all ripe for a major refresh, and Siemens will be right in the middle of it.

The company has made great progress to build and optimize its product portfolio going forward with these markets and principles in mind. We also like their refocus on "core" businesses and technologies such as industrial automation; as many conglomerates learned from rival GE this year, big is not always best. A more profitable business mix and cost efficiency measures are projected to increase gross and net margins moderately; as this occurs we expect moderately increasing shareholder returns over time.

Reasons for Caution

As the following numbers show, performance has been (and can be) choppy, not just because of currency but also exposure to economic cycles and slow-downs. Siemens makes capital equipment, and capital equipment is one of the first things to be cut out of customer budgets when the going gets tough. That said, recent Trump administration policies, cash repatriation, and a general sense that manufacturing and public infrastructure needs to be modernized should all help Siemens out. Finally—the usual warning about foreign-based companies—Siemens is harder to understand than a lot of US equivalents; it is complex, it operates differently, and it presents itself differently. That said, the company does a better-than-average job of explaining itself to potential investors on its website.

SECTOR: Industrials ☐ Beta coefficient: 1.10 ☐ 10-year compound earnings per-share growth: 6.5% ☐ 10-year compound dividends per-share growth: 8.0%

	2011	2012	2013	2014	2015	2016	2017	2018
Revenues (bil)	98.8	100.7	102.7	91.0	84.8	89.2	98.0	96.3
Net income (bil)	9.1	6.5	5.5	6.7	6.0	6.3	7.2	7.0
Earnings per share	5.19	3.67	3.26	3.91	3.53	3.60	4.27	3.98
Dividends per share	1.84	1.93	2.01	2.05	1.88	1.90	2.17	2.15
Cash flow per share	7.28	5.85	5.60	5.76	5.48	5.78	6.78	6.74
Price: high	73.4	55.4	69.6	69.0	57.5	62.1	79.4	77.2
low	42.4	38.9	49.3	51.6	43.9	43.3	60.1	54.2

Website: www.siemens.com

AGGRESSIVE GROWTH   NEW FOR **2020**

Skechers USA, Inc.

Ticker symbol: SKX (NYSE) ❑ Mid Cap ❑ Value Line financial strength rating: B++ ❑ Current yield: Nil ❑ Dividend raises, past 10 years: NA

Company Profile

"A highly agile, efficient and profitable global brand" touts the website of contemporary casual, active, and performance footwear maker Skechers USA. Indeed, Skechers shoes have a unique and innovative style, look, and comfort that we feel excels handily over the rest of the rather drab and dull shoe marketplace, and they have made a decently profitable and growing Mid Cap business out of it. Looking for a pair of fast casual shoes to wear to work, to the beach, and to the restaurant later on? One pair of shoes to take on that week-long vacation? Lightweight shoes that barely feel like they're on your feet and in many cases, slip on despite maintaining the look of a laced-up shoe? Look no further; get yourself a pair of Skechers.

In their words, Skechers seeks to "offer consumers a vast array of stylish and comfortable footwear that satisfies their active, casual, dress casual and athletic footwear needs." Their "core consumers" are "style-conscious men and women" attracted to "relevant brand image, fashion-forward designs and affordable product." We agree—for the most part, they look nice, are attractive, are affordable, and have appeal to all age groups. Skechers has also developed a set of "Skechers Kids" core styles targeted to children.

Skechers markets about 3,000 styles in total worldwide in 170 countries through 3,000+ Skechers stores (about 700 owned, the rest as wholesaler). About 56 percent of sales are international. The company maintains a number one market position in the US for walk, work, casual dress, and casual lifestyle shoes.

The company has three principal distribution channels:

- Domestic Wholesale sells to department stores, specialty stores, athletic shoe stores, independent retailers, and Internet retailers. Sales amounted to $1.26 billion, or about 27 percent of 2018 sales, with a gross margin of 35.9 percent, a five-year compound growth rate of 6 percent, and a 4.8 percent sales growth rate last year. This "legacy" channel keeps the Skechers brand going in about 2,300 stores across the US but is not a major growth vector.

- Direct to Consumer includes three company-owned retail formats: concept stores (in high-end malls, mostly), outlet stores, and warehouse outlet stores—and an online portal. As of early 2019 there were 113 concept stores, 170 factory outlets, and 187 warehouse outlet stores in the US and 134 concept stores, 78 factory outlets, and 10 warehouse stores internationally, with plans to open up to 80 new stores in 2019. Factory outlet stores are typically located in factory outlet malls and sell both current and discontinued or odd-sized merchandise, while warehouse stores are freestanding and focus on discontinued and odd-sized items. The presence of these outlets prevents the sale of distressed product to discounters, thereby preserving the brand image and making the most of this necessary part of the shoe business. US company-owned stores accounted for 29 percent of the business with a 58.8 percent gross margin, an 18 percent compound five-year annual sales growth, and 7.5 percent growth last year.
- International Wholesale sells product overseas into 2,300 stores through foreign distributors and direct to department store chains through subsidiaries in the Americas, Europe, and Japan and through joint ventures in other major countries in Asia and the Middle East; China, India, Israel, South Africa, and South Korea are large markets. International has been the growth star lately, with 44 percent of the business, a 46.7 percent gross margin, a 31 percent five-year compound growth rate, and 18.4 percent growth last year.

Like most shoe marketers, manufacturing is done by an assortment of contract manufacturers, mostly in Asia. Five manufacturers account for about 41 percent of the sourcing; the largest 12.8 percent of the sourcing.

Financial Highlights, Fiscal Year 2018

Bolstered by international direct and distributor sales, which together grew 18 percent, FY2018 revenues rose 11.5 percent overall, and would have been higher were it not for currency effects. Net income rose about 8 percent in total but some 68 percent not including some one-time items in 2017. The company continues to focus on international markets and on brand building through company-owned stores and online sales, and expects additional spend on a China distribution center, advertising, and a team of brand ambassadors including David Ortiz, Tony Romo, Sugar Ray Leonard, and Howie Long for men and Camila Cabello for women—this will take a chunk out of 2019 profits with a forecast of only a 3 percent gain on a 5.6 percent sales increase, but should widen out to a 10–12 percent gain in profits on an 8–10 percent sales increase in 2020. The company is in the late growth stages and has chosen not to pay a dividend or retire shares at this point, but forward projections call for more operating leverage and higher margins beyond 2020, which should bring strong results as the brand gains strength.

Reasons to Buy

We think Skechers has "got it right" in this otherwise fairly mundane industry. Of course, Nike (another *100 Best* stock) stands out for athletic footwear and for crossover casual footwear that still carries a hint of its athletic roots; Skechers on the other hand is aimed dead center at the casual market and may have matched Nike's success with this target. We like its three-tier distribution strategy, which is similar to Nike's as well. We recommend trying on a pair before hitting the buy button—if you haven't already.

Reasons for Caution

We're a bit concerned about the overlap in distribution strategies— although it seems in vogue for the shoe industry and the clothing industry in general. Direct sales probably cannibalize distributor sales, and while this tends to increase average margins, it can leave wholesale customers holding the bag and result in inventory problems down the road. The shoe business is notoriously difficult for having to maintain all the styles and sizes in stock, which can result in distressed sales later, which actually is a boon to coauthor Scott and his size 13 feet but can make for an ugly income statement and balance sheet—Skechers seems to manage their inventory pretty well.

SECTOR: Consumer Staples ◻ **Beta coefficient: 1.35** ◻ **10-year compound earnings per-share growth: 13.0%** ◻ **10-year compound dividends per-share growth: NA**

	2011	2012	2013	2014	2015	2016	2017	2018
Revenues (mil)	1,606	1,560	1,846	2,378	3,147	3,563	4,164	4,642
Net income (mil)	(51.4)	9.5	54.8	138.8	231.9	243.5	279.1	301.0
Earnings per share	(0.35)	0.06	0.36	0.91	1.50	1.57	1.78	1.92
Dividends per share	—	—	—	—	—	—	—	—
Cash flow per share	(0.12)	0.34	0.64	1.22	1.85	2.00	2.32	2.68
Price: high	7.9	7.5	11.6	21.6	54.5	34.3	28.9	43.1
low	3.9	3.7	5.7	8.8	18.4	18.8	22.3	21.4

Website: www.skx.com

The J.M. Smucker Company

Ticker symbol: SJM (NYSE) ❑ Large Cap ❑ Value Line financial strength rating: A++ ❑ Current yield: 2.9% ❑ Dividend raises, past 10 years: 10

Company Profile

"With a name like Smucker's, it has to be good!" This ad copy says it all about this eastern Ohio–based firm, a leading manufacturer of jams, jellies, and other processed foods for years. Thanks in part to divestitures from the Procter & Gamble food division and other companies, it has grown itself into a premier player in the packaged food industry. The 2015 acquisition of pet food makers Big Heart Pet Brands (Meow Mix, Milk-Bone, and others) and Ainsworth last year, signals further expansion into adjacent markets.

Smucker manufactures and markets products under its own name, as well as under a number of other household names such as Crisco, Folgers, Knudsen, Hungry Jack, Eagle, Carnation, Pillsbury, Jif (why not sell the peanut butter if they sell the jelly?), and, naturally, Goober (a combination of peanut butter and jelly in a single jar) and Uncrustables (why not just sell the whole sandwich?). The company also produces and distributes Dunkin' (formerly Dunkin' Donuts) coffee and produces an assortment of cooking oils, toppings, juices, and baking ingredients, and has recently acquired the Wesson cooking oil brand. The company has revitalized such brands as Folgers and Jif through improved marketing, channel relationships, and better focus on the packaging and delivery of these brands to the customer. In the coffee business, for example, Smucker's now offers custom blends, K-Cup offerings, etc., notably under the Dunkin' brand. The Café Bustelo brand targets Hispanic and millennial markets with edgy "experiential" marketing with pop-up cafés at music festivals and the like. "Coffee Served Your Way" is Smucker's motto, and there are new convenience packages for peanut butter, jelly, and other spreads as well—Jif To Go Dippers is but one example. Organic brands, most of which have been around for a while, include Santa Cruz Organic, Sahale Snacks, and truRoots brands, Smucker's Natural, Laura Scudder's, and a handful of others. New areas include fruit spreads, nut butters, and other organic baking materials, beverages, and snacks; they also produce a line of sugar-free, reduced-sugar, and sugar-alternative products. The Big Heart acquisition grew the total business by about a third, and Ainsworth added high-end meals and snacks to the mix. Healthy pet food is a big new market too—Nature's Recipe, Milk-Bone Grain Free Snacks, and Rachael Ray Nutrish Tasty Real Meal Treats all serve to expand this category. The company estimates that at least one of its products is found in 92 percent of all US households.

Overall, the company aims to sell the number one brand in the various markets it serves, and to develop on-trend or premium products in markets adjacent to these number one brands. An example is the "1850" series Folger coffee offering: an assortment of premium bagged coffees in retro classy 1850-style bags with bottled iced coffees and other products with the same look introduced in early 2018.

Smucker's is currently organized into four evenly split reporting segments, with major trademarks listed:

- US Retail Coffee (28 percent of revenues, 36 percent of profit)—Folgers, Dunkin', Café Bustelo
- US Retail Consumer Foods (27 percent, 28 percent)—Smucker's, Jif, Crisco, Pillsbury (under a 20-year license), Uncrustables
- US Retail Pet Foods (30 percent, 26 percent)—Meow Mix, Milk-Bone, Natural Balance, Kibbles 'n Bits, 9Lives, Pup-Peroni
- International and Away From Home (formerly Foodservice, 15 percent, 11 percent)—Folgers, Smucker's, Sweet'N Low, and Sugar in the Raw under license

Operations are centered in the US, Canada, and Europe, with about 10 percent of sales coming from outside the US with Canada representing more than 80 percent of that.

Even as a nearly $7.9 billion-a-year enterprise, the company still retains the feel of a family business, with brothers Mark and Richard Smucker sharing the CEO responsibilities as president and chairman, respectively. The Company Store and Café located just outside of Orrville, Ohio, is a national treasure and a classic case study in branding and brand image.

Financial Highlights, Fiscal Year 2018

Unfavorable pricing, high ingredient and logistics costs, and new product development across all businesses continued to hamper FY2018 performance as with many competitors, but 2019 appears to be better, at least for coffee and retail consumer brands. Pet foods continue to be weak. Total sales rose 6.5 percent, but much of that was from acquisitions, while earnings dropped just under 5 percent. New products, stronger marketing, lower taxes, and a strong economy should bring sales growth in the 1–3 percent range (without acquisitions) in 2019 and in the 2–3 percent range in 2020, while earnings should grow 4–6 percent through the period. Regular dividend raises in the mid- to high-single-digit range are likely.

Reasons to Buy

This is a very well-managed company with an excellent and lasting reputation in its markets. In recent years, it has a proven track record in buying and revitalizing key brands, the most prominent being former Procter & Gamble food brands, Sara Lee foodservice coffee and beverage brands, and a few International Multifoods brands. We expect this trend to continue. The company's aggressive moves into coffee and other beverages were well timed; it remains to be seen whether or when they can make the most of their Big Heart and Ainsworth pet food acquisitions, which were expected to leverage existing channels and bring a measure of stability, profitability, and growth to the table.

Profitability figures are both among the best for the relatively staid food industry with net profit margins exceeding 10 percent. The base for steady growth in cash flows and investor returns is well established over the long term. Steady and safe: Smucker is the ever-improving peanut butter and jelly sandwich of the investing landscape.

Reasons for Caution

The prepared-food business is very sensitive in the short term to competition as well as commodity costs. There is also the ever-present transition of the customer base to the millennial generation and tastes—do millennials eat peanut butter and jelly sandwiches? Smucker seems to have plenty on the drawing board in case they don't.

We do wonder if the company has strayed just a bit outside of its traditional feel-good, relatively healthy or at least wholesome, peanut-butter-and-jelly base. While you can't grow a business much on peanut butter and jelly alone, the venture into relatively lower-margined pet food may not fit with what has made Smucker's taste so good up to now.

SECTOR: Consumer Staples ▫ Beta coefficient: 0.70 ▫ 10-year compound earnings per-share growth: 8.5% ▫ 10-year compound dividends per-share growth: 10.0%

	2011	2012	2013	2014	2015	2016	2017	2018
Revenues (mil)	5,526	5,897	5,611	5,450	7,811	7,400	7,357	7,875
Net income (mil)	535.6	584	588	540	704	753	795	765
Earnings per share	4.73	5.37	5.64	5.30	5.89	6.45	6.97	6.70
Dividends per share	1.88	2.06	2.32	2.56	2.68	3.00	3.12	3.33
Cash flow per share	6.75	7.85	8.30	6.87	9.75	10.10	10.64	10.60
Price: high	80.3	89.4	114.7	107.1	125.3	157.3	143.7	133.4
low	61.2	70.5	86.5	87.1	97.3	117.4	99.6	91.3

Website: www.smuckers.com

CONSERVATIVE GROWTH

Southwest Airlines Co.

Ticker symbol: LUV (NYSE) ▫ Large Cap ▫ Value Line financial strength rating: A ▫ Current yield: 1.1% ▫ Dividend raises, past 10 years: 7

Company Profile

For years we were critical of the airline industry for its inability to control prices because of intense competition and to control costs largely comprised of fuel, airport, and unionized labor. These factors—and persistent losses—made airlines into poster children for the kinds of stocks we tend to avoid.

Now much of that has changed. Fuel costs have dropped and look to stay down for a while. Most airlines have, by design or by default, rationalized their route structures and capacity, necessitated by once-high fuel costs, airport constraints, and economic slowdowns. The rationalized capacity helps them better able to control both prices and costs. Now with a strong economy and more efficient aircraft to boot, airline outlooks are pretty bright across the board. For the seventh year in a row now we are choosing the best of the best—Southwest Airlines—for our *100 Best* list.

Southwest Airlines provides passenger air transport mainly in the United States and all within North America. In early 2019 the company served over 100 cities in 41 US states and serves all of the Top 50 US markets and now Hawaii. With the acquisition of AirTran, it also serves Mexico, Cuba, and eight other countries in Central America and the Caribbean. The company serves these markets almost exclusively with 706 Boeing 750 aircraft, the largest Boeing aircraft fleet in the world. Southwest continues to be the largest domestic air carrier in the United States, as measured by the number of domestic originating passengers boarded, with a leading market share of 23 percent. At 4,000 peak-season departures per day, the airline also originates the most flights. This should give an idea of their business model—low cost, shorter flights, and maximum passenger loads.

The business model is one of simplicity—no-frills aircraft, no first-class passenger cabin, limited interchange with other carriers, no onboard meals, simple boarding and seat assignment practices, direct sales over the Internet (over 80 percent of sales online), no baggage fees—all designed to provide steady and reliable transportation, with one of the best on-time performances in the industry, and to maximize asset utilization with minimal downtime, crew disruptions, and other upward influences on operating costs. The company has long used secondary airports—such as its original Love Field in Dallas instead of the massive DFW (giving rise to the ticker symbol LUV); Providence, Rhode Island, and Manchester, New Hampshire, to serve Boston and the New England area; Allentown, Pennsylvania, and East Islip, New York, to serve the New York/New Jersey area (though it now serves LaGuardia, too, if you want that choice); and Chicago Midway to reduce delays and costs. This strategy has worked well.

Southwest has successfully implemented initiatives to squeeze out some extra revenue without alienating the core passenger group, mostly business travelers. One such initiative is Business Select, which offers priority boarding, priority security, bonus frequent flyer credit, and a free beverage for a small upgrade fee. The company also sells early boarding as a stand-alone for a modest $30–$50 fee. But they continue to offer the basic two-bag limit free for now, a move we strenuously applaud. Southwest also produces more than $600 million in revenue annually from its Rapid Rewards loyalty point program through partnerships and sales of points. The program routinely wins "best of" awards in the industry.

New initiatives include a transition to newer Boeing 737 aircraft, including the Boeing 737-MAX 7 and MAX 8, 30 and 219 of which are on order, respectively (although the MAX series was grounded as of press time in 2019), and which can fly 500 miles farther than existing models opening up more international markets, and more 143-seat 747-700s and 175-seat 737-800s (typical older 737 models range from 117 to 132 seats). As of 2017 the entire fleet now consists of 737-700s, 737-800s, 737 MAX 7s, and 737 MAX 8s.

Financial Highlights, Fiscal Year 2018

Southwest had already been taxiing into position with operational improvements, capacity rationalization, the AirTran acquisition, and other market and efficiency gains. New aircraft, lower fuel prices, other small process improvements like single-engine taxiing, lighter seats, and "split scimitar winglets" on the wings have helped Southwest continue its best-in-class low cost structure. Cost per average seat mile (ASM) is about 8 cents, compared to a figure north of 12 cents for the "major" carriers. Fuel runs about 22–23 percent of operating expenses, down from the high 30s in 2008 through 2013.

FY2018 saw a rebound from the rather disappointing 2017 figures, which were weak from higher fuel prices and some wage increases. Lower fuel prices, an improved load factor (percentage of seats paid for and occupied, 83.4, up from around 80 a few years ago), better economics from flying larger, just-as-full planes, and tax cuts all led to a 13.6 percent gain in net income on a modest 3.8 percent rise in revenues. More of the same is in store for 2019 with a predicted profit gain in the 20 percent range on a 7–8 percent gain in revenues; net income starts to level off a bit in 2020 as revenues continue on the 7–8 percent per year climb, although this is likely to be attenuated somewhat in 2019 by the MAX series problems). Most of this income and cash flow is being returned to shareholders, with dividends rising at a 20 percent annual clip (still small in absolute terms but becoming more noteworthy) and buybacks in the 4–5 percent range. The company has retired 25 percent of its shares since 2010.

Reasons to Buy

The story remains much the same: Southwest continues to be the best player in an industry whose fundamentals have dramatically improved. The company continues to be the "envy" value proposition of the industry, and we continue to be surprised that no one else has been able to emulate it successfully—but at this point, even if they do, Southwest has a decades-long first-mover advantage.

The airline "gets it" that what customers want is no-hassle transportation at best-possible prices—and yes, no bag fees—and has been able to do that better than anyone else for years and is now extending its value proposition further for business travelers, who increasingly book their own fares and respond well to $15 priority boarding upgrades and other offers. Good management, efficient operation, and excellent marketing make it all possible. Financially, the company has earned a profit for 46 consecutive years—in the volatile airline industry we know no greater testimonial to good marketing and good management.

Reasons for Caution

Fuel prices will always be a wild card. The company has shown in the past that it can use hedges to manage fuel price shocks, and they've been doing a lot of that lately. More efficient aircraft mitigate the risk to a degree, but that said, there may also be some "lag" in customers getting used to flying the MAX series aircraft when they come back on line.

Generally, we fear anything that would move Southwest away from its core competencies—complacency in the short run, acquisitions in the longer term. The longer Southwest can stay Southwest, and avoid looking like other airlines, the better.

SECTOR: Transportation ❑ Beta coefficient: 1.15 ❑ 10-year compound earnings per-share growth: 18.5% ❑ 10-year compound dividends per-share growth: 35.0%

	2011	2012	2013	2014	2015	2016	2017	2018
Revenues (mil)	15,658	17,088	17,699	18,605	19,820	20,425	21,171	21,965
Net income (mil)	330	421	754	1,136	2,161	2,244	2,076	2,465
Earnings per share	0.42	0.58	1.05	1.64	3.27	3.55	3.41	4.29
Dividends per share	0.03	0.04	0.10	0.22	0.29	0.38	0.48	0.61
Cash flow per share	1.35	1.73	2.35	3.07	4.94	5.45	5.55	6.55
Price: high	13.9	10.6	19.0	43.2	51.3	51.3	67.0	66.5
low	7.1	7.8	10.4	18.8	31.4	34.0	48.7	44.3

Website: www.southwest.com

AGGRESSIVE GROWTH

Square, Inc.

Ticker symbol: SQ (NASDAQ) ❑ Large Cap ❑ Value Line financial strength rating: B ❑ Current yield: Nil ❑ Dividend raises, past 10 years: NA

Company Profile

"Economic Empowerment" is but one of many slogans carried by the small-biz financial hardware and software juggernaut well known for the shape of its flagship card-swipe tablet and phone adapter device. Founded in 2009 and headquartered in San Francisco, Square, Inc., provides payment and point-of-sale solutions in the US, Canada, Japan, and Australia (so far). The company's aptly named "cohesive commerce ecosystem" includes point-of-sale hardware and software that enables sellers to turn iOS and Android mobile and computing devices into payment and point-of-sale solutions, which in turn connect to other business management platforms provided by Square and others to not only accept payments but to run entire businesses. Hardware products include:

- Magstripe reader—the familiar white square-shaped attachment for mobile devices, which enables swiped transactions of magnetic stripe cards.
- Chip card reader—accepts EMV (Europay, MasterCard, Visa) chip cards and enables swiped transactions of magnetic stripe cards.
- Contactless and chip reader—accepts EMV chip cards and Near Field Communication payments from smartphones.
- Square Stand—enables an iPad to be used as a payment terminal or full point-of-sale solution.
- Square Register—a complete system combining hardware, point-of-sale software, and payments technology into a managed payment solution.

Software products include:

- Square Point of Sale software—operates inside the hardware to execute card- and smartphone-based transactions and allows merchants to use any of the hardware front ends or to enter a card number manually; it also provides analytics, employee and facility management tools, and vertical-market-specific tools such as for restaurants, retail, scheduling tools for service providers, etc. As an example, in mid-2018 Square launched "Square for Restaurants," a complete solution integrating point of sale throughout a restaurant with front-end and back-end processes including menu setup, ordering, tipping, tip and bill splitting, employee management, and performance tracking. It blends with the previously acquired "Caviar" app, which manages food pickup and delivery and carryout transactions.
- Cash App—a peer-to-peer payments system that accesses the general banking and financial system, allowing customers to electronically send, store, and spend money.
- Square Capital—a lending facility that provides loans to sellers based on real-time payment and point-of-sale data.

Additionally, the company provides an "Open Developer Platform": application programming interfaces (APIs) allowing programmers of business-specific or market-specific software to integrate Square app features into their platforms.

Recent additions include the Square Terminal, a portable all-in-one device as an alternative to traditional keypad terminals, and Square Installments, a credit facility allowing sellers to provide instant financing to make purchases. Beyond that, the company is in the process of going into the banking business, creating a wholly owned bank to offer loans, deposit accounts, credit lines, customer financing, and prepaid cards as a service residing behind the point-of-sale and business management software offerings. Clearly Square wants to be the "one-stop-shop" for all small and medium business transactional and financial needs.

This "commerce ecosystem" was originally designed to meet the commerce and transaction needs of small and often portable businesses, where the point of sale can be in a trade show, flea market, food court, or some other quasi-temporary setting, in addition to most home-based businesses. Increasingly, Square products are being adopted by sellers of all sizes as a substitute for the traditional cash register and point-of-sale card reader even where portability isn't a requirement due to their ease of use and access to other parts of the Square ecosystem. Sellers with annualized Gross Payment Volume (transactions times selling price) of more than $500K per year have risen from 3 percent to 24 percent of the mix; sellers between $125K and $500K have risen from 16 percent to 28 percent of the mix, leaving only 48 percent of the payment base in small sellers selling less than $125K per year.

The business model is largely transaction based, although the company does earn some income selling and renting equipment and through software subscriptions. Sellers are charged a per-transaction fee in the range of 3 percent (exact figures aren't disclosed in company documents); these transactions are then fed to an Acquiring Processor (usually associated with a bank), then to a Card Network (Visa, MasterCard, etc.) and its issuing bank. These entities charge fees, which essentially comprise cost of goods sold, totaling to about 2 percent of the transaction value; the resulting gross margin is about a third of the entire transaction revenue stream, or 1.07 percent of the total transaction value versus 1.06 percent in 2017 and 1.03 percent in 2016.

Financial Highlights, Fiscal Year 2018

Through Q3 2018 transaction volume was up 29 percent and total revenue projected for the year was up about 47 percent. Why such a big divergence between volume and revenue? The answer lies in the expanding base of services being made available and consumed by customers; acquisitions figured in as well. Transaction revenue represents about 74 percent of total revenue (down from 87 percent last year), giving an idea of the size and expansion of ancillary services. Square has never earned a profit but has finally turned cash-flow positive and is very close to breakeven on the operating earnings front (they have reported a couple of slimly profitably quarters based on one-time items). We expect the company to be in the black by the end of 2019 and to grow into profitability beyond that. The play here is purely on scale; more users and more transaction volume will absorb fixed costs and drop in a large part to the bottom line once scale is achieved. As Square customers use other parts of the ecosystem beyond the transaction capabilities, margins should increase as well.

Reasons to Buy

Square represents the first time in the history of *100 Best Stocks* that we've listed a company that has never made money and is still in the "cash burn" phase of its existence. To break that barrier, must it be that we see something big in this company? Indeed we do.

Square and its commerce ecosystem fit right into the land of the millennials. Buy something where you want to, when you want to, using the latest technology. Square enables business to happen the way you want it to—whether for the seller or the buyer. We like the value proposition of simplicity, flexibility, and tie-in with customized business platforms. The brand is already strong, and their efforts to promote the product resonate; they've become the go-to solution for small and many medium-sized businesses. International expansion is promising as well.

We've been conditioned by the success of Visa in its ability to live off of growing transaction volume and turning it into profit with a relatively minimal investment. We think Square will also reach critical mass and go far beyond, turning transaction fees into steadily increasing cash flows as volume builds. By 2020, it will have passed the critical breakeven point. When you mix in other parts of the ecosystem as revenue generators, the earning power grows further.

Reasons for Caution

Obviously there are inherent technology, marketplace, and financial risks in investing in a nascent business like Square. New competitors can emerge, taking the concept further and faster; or an established player like Visa or Apple could enter the fray (or, on the flip side, could buy Square!). As we write this, the share price bakes in a lot of our favorable expectations already and is quite volatile to boot. Although Square ventures pretty far from our normal *100 Best* comfort zone, we think it's a great way to plug a little leading-edge technology into your portfolio. Swipe carefully.

SECTOR: Information Technology ❑ Beta coefficient: 1.35 ❑ 10-year compound earnings per-share growth: NA ❑ 10-year compound dividends per-share growth: NA

	2011	2012	2013	2014	2015	2016	2017	2018
Revenues (mil)	—	—	—	—	1,267	1,709	2,214	3,270
Net income (mil)	—	—	—	—	(179.8)	(171.6)	(62.8)	(63.0)
Earnings per share	—	—	—	—	(1.24)	(0.50)	(0.17)	(0.16)
Dividends per share	—	—	—	—	—	—	—	—
Cash flow per share	—	—	—	—	(0.45)	(0.35)	(0.06)	(0.05)
Price: high	—	—	—	—	14.8	15.9	49.6	101.1
low	—	—	—	—	9.0	8.1	13.7	34.7

Website: www.squareup.com

AGGRESSIVE GROWTH

Starbucks Corporation

Ticker symbol: SBUX (NASDAQ) ❑ Large Cap ❑ Value Line financial strength rating: A++ ❑ Current yield: 2.2% ❑ Dividend raises, past 10 years: 8

Company Profile

Founded in 1985 in a modest storefront in downtown Seattle, Starbucks Corporation is the leading retailer, roaster, and brand of specialty coffee in the world. The company sells whole-bean coffees through its retailers, its specialty sales group, and supermarkets. The company delivers the "Starbucks Experience" more than 85 million times per week at more than 28,000 stores in 76 countries.

The Starbucks store footprint continues to expand. In the Americas there are now 9,768 company-owned stores (9,413 at the end of 2017) and 7,770 licensed stores (7,146 in 2017). In "CAP" (China/Asia-Pacific) there are 5,159 (3,070) company-owned and 3,371 (4,409) licensee stores; in EMEA (Europe, Middle East, and Africa) there are 490 (502) and 2,830 (2,472) stores respectively. In all it's a rich brew of 15,616 company-owned and 14,249 licensee stores worldwide. As you can see, the company recently converted hundreds of licensed stores to company owned in China. Retail coffee shop sales constitute about 90 percent of its revenue, up from 89 percent last year. About 80 percent of revenue originates in company-operated stores. Unlike many in the restaurant sector, the company does not franchise its stores—all are either company owned or operated by licensees in special venues such as airports, college campuses, and other places where access is restricted, and in foreign markets where it is necessary or advantageous.

The company continues to expand overseas, usually at first through partnerships and joint ventures; then sometimes through acquiring its partner. The FY2018 sales breakdown: 68 percent Americas, 4 percent Europe/Middle East/Africa, 18 percent China/Asia-Pacific, and 10 percent other segments and "channel development," which is largely made up of branded product sales through non-Starbucks retailers. The international footprint is getting deeper and wider: leading countries for store openings include South Korea (138), China (84), Mexico (76), Turkey (67), and Indonesia (56). The company continues to adjust its product portfolio beyond coffee. In 2017 Starbucks decided to sell its Tazo tea business and close its Teavana stores (Teavana premium teas will continue to be offered in Starbucks stores and sold into the grocery channel). Starbucks continues to offer Evolution Fresh juices, Ethos Water products, numerous food items, and specialty packages like "Via" and Keurig-compatible single-serve coffee packages and has added several cold beverages including Cold Brew and Iced Espresso to its menu. Finally, Starbucks has joint ventures with PepsiCo and Dreyer's to market bottled coffee drinks and coffee-flavored ice creams.

In 2018, the sum total revenue mix in company-operated stores was 74 percent beverages, 20 percent food, 2 percent packaged and single-serve coffees and teas, and 4 percent "other" including coffee-making equipment and other merchandise.

Starbucks continues to invest and expand its leadership in the deployment of technology. The popular "Mobile App" platform includes "Mobile Order and Pay," where users can order and pay for their drinks using smartphones, then subsequently arrive at locations to pick up their drinks. Naturally, the app acts as a conduit for a greater digital engagement, including a rewards program and expanded delivery services both in the US and in China. The company continues to add drive-thru locations as well. Speed of service remains a major objective. The company's retail goal continues to be the unique Starbucks experience, which the company defines as a third place beyond home and work. The "experience" is built upon superior customer service and a clean, well-maintained retail store that reflects the personality of the community in which it operates—all aimed at building loyalty and frequent repeat visits. The Mobile App enhances this experience, particularly in saving time waiting in line during busy periods.

The company also gets high marks for citizenship, continuing to offer health coverage, equity participation, and even college assistance for its 291,000 employees ("partners"). Commitments to hire veterans, military spouses, and more recently, Syrian refugees, are notable among a list of other commitments to community service and social issues of the day.

Financial Highlights, Fiscal Year 2018

Technology improvements, brand, optimized store locations, moderate expansion, and a strong economy all led to a 10 percent revenue gain on a 2 percent same-store sales gain, most of which was based on a higher average ticket per visit rather than higher traffic. Margins were down a bit due to unfavorable mix changes in the Americas, higher input costs, tech innovation costs, and the cost of converting to company-operated stores in China, offset somewhat by a favorable sale of Tazo. Net earnings were up 12 percent, and with a massive 8 percent share buyback, per-share earnings advanced almost 18 percent. Estimates call for a 5–7 percent top-line growth rate in both 2019 and 2020, with earnings growth tapering off into the 3–5 percent range as margins continue to shrink a bit; operational improvements should start to favorably impact margins beyond 2020. "Cream and sugar" comes in the form of dividend increases in the mid-double digits with continued active share buyback activity added in for good measure.

Reasons to Buy

After all these years, Starbucks is still a great story. The company's stores continue to be more than coffee shops and are really that "third place" where professionals, students, moms, and other prosperous folks will meet and dole out a few bucks for quality drinks. The "third place" aura creates a lot of the brand strength and, in our view, represents the company's true strength—well beyond the quality of the coffee itself and related products. The company has a steadily (and profitably) growing presence on the world stage. We believe the technology and experience improvements will be big both for customers and operations.

The company is well managed, has an extremely strong brand, has solid financials, and, once again, has a steady growth track record, and it is carving out an ever-stronger international footprint. Cash returns to investors are on the rise, and safety (as proxied by beta) has improved sharply from years ago. Starbucks offers both growth and, increasingly, cash returns and safety—a very nice brew for investors indeed.

Reasons for Caution

The biggest risk used to be overexpansion and cannibalization—which they've encountered and dealt with well in recent years but could reemerge as a trouble spot down the road. Competition from other mostly local premium coffee shops is growing. Despite operational and technology improvements, people still spend a lot of time in line at certain locations. Perhaps our biggest fear remains the temptation to expand too far into the food-service business, which could reduce margins, dilute the experience, and make the stores smell like a sandwich shop, far less appealing for most than the aroma of coffee. It also brings operational complexities, so we score the experience with food so far as mostly a success but continue to keep our eyes (and noses) open for signs of stress.

SECTOR: Restaurant ❑ Beta coefficient: 0.95 ❑ 10-year compound earnings per-share growth: 18.5% ❑ 10-year compound dividends per-share growth: NM

	2011	2012	2013	2014	2015	2016	2017	2018
Revenues (mil)	11,701	13,299	14,892	16,448	19,163	21,316	22,387	24,720
Net income (mil)	1,174	1,385	1,721	2,068	2,394	2,635	3,011	3,370
Earnings per share	0.76	0.90	1.13	1.36	1.58	1.91	2.06	2.42
Dividends per share	0.26	0.34	0.42	0.52	0.64	0.80	1.00	1.26
Cash flow per share	1.14	1.29	1.58	1.85	2.21	2.61	2.81	3.53
Price: high	23.3	31.0	41.3	42.1	64.0	61.8	64.9	69.0
low	15.4	21.5	26.3	34.0	39.3	50.8	52.6	47.4

Website: www.starbucks.com

AGGRESSIVE GROWTH

Stryker Corporation

Ticker symbol: SYK (NYSE) ❑ Large Cap ❑ Value Line financial strength rating: A++ ❑ Current yield: 1.2% ❑ Dividend increases, past 10 years: 9

Company Profile

Stryker Corporation was founded as the Orthopedic Frame Company in 1941 by Dr. Homer H. Stryker, a leading orthopedic surgeon and the inventor of several orthopedic products. The company now ranks as a dominant player in the global orthopedics industry with more than 59,000 products in its catalog and a strong innovation track record, with more than 6 percent of sales invested in R&D.

The Orthopaedics segment (that's how the company spells it) accounts for about 37 percent of 2018 sales and has a significant market share in such "spare parts" as artificial hips, prosthetic knees, implant products for other extremities, and trauma and recovery products. Within that group, knees are 34 percent of segment sales, hips are 27 percent, and "Trauma & Extremities" are another 32 percent of segment sales. An "Other" category accounts for 7 percent.

The MedSurg unit, about 44 percent of sales, develops, manufactures, and markets worldwide powered and computer-assisted and robotic surgical instruments, endoscopic surgical systems, hospital beds, and other patient care and handling equipment. Instruments (30 percent of segment sales), endoscopy (31 percent), and medical devices, including emergency devices (35 percent), are the largest contributors, and a new group called "Sustainability," which reprocesses and remanufactures certain medical devices, now contributes 4 percent.

The Neurotechnology & Spine segment, a large part of which was acquired from Boston Scientific in 2010, accounts for 18 percent of sales and sells spinal reconstructive and surgical equipment, neurovascular surgery equipment including stroke treatment, and a line of skull, brain surgery, and craniomaxillofacial products.

Stryker's revenue is split roughly 73/27 percent domestic and international. Stryker continues to be active on the acquisition front. Most are smaller "tuck-in" acquisitions intended to strengthen existing product lines. K2M adds a line of complex spine and minimally invasive spinal solutions; Entellus Medical adds a line of minimally invasive ear/nose/throat treatments; Invuity adds a line of single use photonics (lighting) solutions for intricate surgery; and SafeAir is a producer of products to safely evacuate surgical smoke.

Financial Highlights, Fiscal Year 2018
Helped along somewhat by acquisitions, FY2018 sales rose a bit over 9 percent, with healthy sales gains in all three businesses. Net earnings grew almost 13 percent as better product mix and scale, and tax cuts, strengthened both operating and net margins. Within these figures, Neurotechnology is the fastest-growing segment with a 22 percent growth rate during the year; the "Hips" segment was weakest with a 2.5 percent increase. Going forward, Stryker projects an 8–10 percent net income gain for FY2019 and a 6–8 percent revenue increase; for FY2020 the company expects similar results. Modest share buybacks will resume as the size of acquisitions has decreased; dividends should rise in the 5–10 percent range over the next few years.

Reasons to Buy

We continue to see Stryker as an innovative healthcare products ("med tech") company with relatively less-entrenched competition than many others, a strong presence in the orthopedic market, and a growing presence in surgical and neurological markets. This should allow it to capitalize on aging trends and a general economic recovery, which will induce more elective surgeries. Emerging markets, particularly China, present a good opportunity, and recent acquisitions should strengthen the portfolio and brand worldwide. Stryker has been a slow, steady, and very dependable grower over the years.

Reasons for Caution

Ongoing scrutiny of healthcare costs and a continuation of small acquisitions bring some risks to the company, but we don't think they are excessive. The future of the Affordable Care Act and its replacement, and new initiatives such as the Amazon/Berkshire/JPMorgan consortium to analyze healthcare cost and delivery models are other unknowns and concerns. While these bear watching, however, companies with stronger, more-dominated niches like Stryker stand to be relatively less affected. Another concern is today's reduced hospital census (that is, occupancy)—an industry-wide trend reflecting cost management and more effective outpatient treatments—the company makes a lot of hospital beds and similar products that might not do well in a major hospital shakeout.

Stryker makes fairly high-tech medical products and as such is exposed to legal, regulatory, and manufacturing risks, warranty expenses, and product recalls. While the dividend is increasing at a good pace, the yield could still be higher given the company's strong cash flow.

SECTOR: Healthcare ◻ Beta coefficient: 0.90 ◻ 10-year compound earnings per-share growth: 7.5% ◻ 10-year compound dividends per-share growth: 22.0%

	2011	2012	2013	2014	2015	2016	2017	2018
Revenues (mil)	8,307	8,656	9,021	9,675	9,946	11,325	12,144	13,601
Net income (mil)	1,448	1,298	1,006	960	1,439	1,647	1,853	2,779
Earnings per share	3.72	3.39	2.63	2.36	3.78	4.35	4.87	7.31
Dividends per share	0.72	0.85	1.10	1.26	1.42	1.52	1.70	1.88
Cash flow per share	5.08	4.69	4.01	3.94	5.44	6.15	6.65	9.35
Price: high	65.2	64.1	75.8	96.2	105.3	123.6	160.8	179.8
low	43.7	49.4	55.2	74.0	89.8	86.7	116.5	144.8

Website: www.stryker.com

CONSERVATIVE GROWTH

Sysco Corporation

Ticker symbol: SYY (NYSE) ❑ Large Cap ❑ Value Line financial strength rating: A+ ❑ Current yield: 2.3% ❑ Dividend raises, past 10 years: 10

Company Profile

Sysco is the leading marketer and distributor of food, food products, and related equipment and supplies to the US foodservice industry. The company distributes fresh and frozen meats, prepared entrées, vegetables, canned and dried foods, dairy products, beverages, and produce, as well as paper products, restaurant equipment and supplies, and cleaning supplies. The company might be familiar for its "institutional" number ten–sized cans of food found in many high-volume kitchens, but the product line and customer base are much larger, including many specialty and chain restaurants, lodges, hotels, hospitals, schools, and other distribution centers across the country. Restaurants account for about 62 percent of the 2018 business; healthcare (mainly hospitals and nursing homes) about 9 percent, education (schools and colleges) and government about 8 percent, travel and leisure (hotels and motels) and retail about 8 percent, and "other" categories make up the rest—about 13 percent. You see their lift-gated "bobtail" delivery trucks continuously, but you may not notice them delivering and unloading a pallet or two of goods at a time for a broad assortment of foodservice venues in your area. If you eat out at all, you've most likely consumed Sysco-distributed products.

Sysco has more than 600,000 customer locations and distributes over 400,000 products, including 41,000 under its own label. The company operates 330 distribution facilities in 13 countries and conducts business in more than 90 countries through company-owned facilities and joint ventures. From these centers, Sysco distributes 1.4 billion cases of food annually using a fleet of 13,400 delivery vehicles. The facilities include its 95 "Broadline" facilities, which supply independent and chain restaurants and other food-preparation facilities with a wide variety of food and non-food products. It has 11 hotel supply locations, 25 specialty produce facilities, 17 SYGMA distribution centers (specialized, high-volume centers supplying to certain chain restaurants), 27 custom-cutting meat locations, and two distributors specializing in the niche Asian foodservice market. There are 330 distribution facilities in all, 162 in the US, 68 in the UK,

38 in France, and 34 in Canada. The company has recently been adding healthier, non-GMO, sustainably sourced, and other such items into its menu, which should play well with foodservice customers expanding their menus in this direction.

The company also supplies the hotel industry with guest amenities, equipment, housekeeping supplies, room accessories, and textiles. By product type, the top five products are: 20 percent meat and frozen meals, 17 percent canned/dry, 15 percent frozen, 10 percent dairy, and 10 percent poultry, with produce, paper goods, seafood, beverages, janitorial products, and others making up the rest.

Sysco is by far the largest company in the domestic foodservice distribution industry; yet it only has about an 18 percent share of the $289 billion market. It has grown mainly through small "bolt-on" acquisitions in specialty food companies (such as seafood) or new geographies, for example buying the UK-based Brakes Group to become a leading foodservice provider in England, France, and Sweden in 2016. International operations also include Canada, Mexico, Costa Rica, the Bahamas, and Panama.

Financial Highlights, Fiscal Year 2018

Sysco did well in 2018. Sales rose 6.1 percent overall, with domestic sales up 5.4 percent and international sales up 8.5 percent. Case volume was up about 2 percent in the US, 0.8 percent of it was acquisitions; the rest is mostly price increases. Net income was up 11 percent even with input price increases and increased logistics costs, suggesting that most cost increases were successfully passed through to customers; lower taxes also helped. Revenues should move forward in the 3–4 percent range annually through 2020; net income, helped along by scale and international progress, is forecast to rise in the 8–10 percent range in 2019 and the 7–9 percent range in 2020. Healthy share buybacks will continue to keep per-share earnings rising at a higher rate; per-share earnings are forecast 20–25 percent higher by the end of 2020, while share counts will have dropped about 20 percent since 2015. Dividend raises should continue at a steady pace.

Reasons to Buy

Sysco continues to be a dominant player in a niche that won't go away anytime soon. The current foodservice environment is improving, and the company still has plenty to work on in the form of operational efficiencies, and now international expansion is added to the mix as a growth driver.

Sysco's recent investments in technology continue to bear fruit, and we like to see innovation in an industry not known for it. New analytics, routing optimization, and recycling initiatives are being applied to realize savings in people, fuel, and other costs; the effects are manifest in the profit margin improvement—from 2.0 percent to 2.7 percent since 2014 and on to 3.0 percent in 2020. The company is also working to become a total supplier for foodservice operations by adding technology tools to its offering; a new platform called "CAKE" manages point of sale, guest reservations, etc., while mobile apps make customer ordering easy. In sum, this is a steady and safe company with a pretty good track record for steady business, strong and enduring customer relationships, decent cash flow, and decent shareholder payouts.

Reasons for Caution

Although the trend is slowly reversing, the recession got many folks away from the habit of eating out, and many restaurants disappeared altogether during this period. Volatility in food and ingredient prices, and fuel costs too, can pressure margins; this is always a cause for concern especially as inflation appears ready to pick up a bit. We also now worry that new dining trends and tastes of the millennials and others will require more specialization in the restaurant market, something Sysco will need to adapt to at least to a degree (and has begun to).

As described previously, this is a low-margin business with not a lot of room for error. That said, Sysco, more than most, continues to be a "sleep at night" kind of investment.

SECTOR: Consumer Staples ◻ Beta coefficient: 0.70 ◻ 10-year compound earnings per-share growth: 5.0% ◻ 10-year compound dividends per-share growth: 6.0%

	2011	2012	2013	2014	2015	2016	2017	2018
Revenues (mil)	39,323	42,381	44,411	46,517	48,681	50,367	55,371	58,727
Net income (mil)	1,153	1,122	992	931	1,100	1,214	1,359	1,595
Earnings per share	1.96	1.90	1.67	1.58	1.84	2.10	2.48	3.01
Dividends per share	1.03	1.07	1.11	1.16	1.19	1.23	1.30	1.41
Cash flow per share	2.62	2.63	2.57	2.54	2.78	3.22	4.06	4.53
Price: high	32.6	32.4	43.4	41.2	42.0	57.1	62.8	76.0
low	25.1	27.0	30.5	34.1	35.4	38.8	48.8	56.0

Website: www.sysco.com

GROWTH AND INCOME

Target Corporation

Ticker symbol: TGT (NYSE) ❑ Large Cap ❑ S&P rating: A ❑ Value Line financial strength rating: A ❑ Current yield: 3.1% ❑ Dividend raises, past 10 years: 10

Company Profile

Target is a classic story (for us, anyway) of reacting, possibly overreacting, to short-term changes in the business context, i.e., the rapidly expanding competitive threat of Amazon and their tepid response to it. We got scared out of our boots by the notion that Amazon would eat Target's lunch (possibly even with brick-and-mortar outlets in the manner of Whole Foods)—the idea of a business earning sub–4 percent net profit margins competing with Amazon Prime scared us—and when Target said they were going to answer the threat by driving lower prices, we hung up. (How much do you have to lower prices to meet Amazon on their own turf? Certainly more than 4 percent.)

So we reluctantly removed Target from the 2018 *100 Best Stocks* list. We watched and listened, and lo and behold, they changed their tune. Instead of competing on price, they decided to take advantage of their competitive advantage: their store assets and the customer experience in the stores. Plans emerged to remodel stores, enhance merchandise offerings, build an omnichannel mechanism for customers to pick up ordered merchandise at a drive-up window without even leaving their cars, and expanding and enhancing Target.com. We liked the story, and back to the list they went for 2019. The stock returned 12.9 percent for the year, 16.5 percent including the dividend. Welcome back, Target.

Target is the nation's second-largest general merchandise retailer and specializes in general merchandise at a discount in a large-store format. The company now operates 1,844 stores in 50 states (Vermont finally got its first and only store last year), including 275 Super Targets with larger and more complete merchandise selections. The greatest concentration of Target stores is in California (15 percent), Texas (8 percent), and Florida (7 percent), with a combined total of about 30 percent of the stores. There is another concentration in the upper Midwest. Target positions itself against its main competitor, Walmart, as a more upscale and trend-conscious "cheap chic" alternative. The typical Target customer has a higher level of disposable income than that of Walmart, which the company courts by offering brand-name merchandise in addition to a series of 39 largely successful owned house brands such as Michael Graves, Market Pantry, Smith & Hawken, Fieldcrest, Room Essentials, and

Archer Farms. These brands generate about a third of Target's sales. The company's revenues come from retail exclusively; it sold its credit card operations to TD Bank in 2013 and its pharmacy business to CVS in 2015. Digital sales, a major strategic focus, grew some 36 percent and accounted for 7.1 percent of the total (vs. 5.5 percent in 2017) and have established Target as a legitimate player in the online retail world—with an experience and promotional accompaniment many feel to be better than Amazon. The company dropped its money-losing Canadian operations in 2015 and bought local same-day delivery provider Shipt in 2017.

The company is also investing domestically in its food lines, which now account for 20 percent of total sales. Food is sold in about 70 percent of stores. The total sales breakdown is 23 percent beauty and household essentials, 20 percent food and pet supplies, 20 percent apparel and accessories, 18 percent hardlines, and 19 percent home furnishings and décor.

Among its peers, Target enjoys a loyal, somewhat upscale customer base, which shops at Target for basic household items, clothing, electronics, furniture, and seasonal items on a fairly regular basis, in addition to the food and beverage operations. They are known for good taste and design in the products they sell. The shopping experience is usually a plus—quiet, clean stores, good quality and attractive merchandising, and name brands with in-house brands sprinkled throughout.

When it came time to repulse the Amazon threat, Target management started with its "compete on price" strategy, then changed to capitalize on their core strengths: design, convenience, and experience. The goal: Make Target "America's easiest place to shop, offering the most comprehensive suite of fulfillment choices and coast-to-coast network of any retailer in the industry."

The outcome: a $7 billion "next generation" store design, which was piloted on its flagship Minneapolis- and Houston-area stores. Elements of the design include separate entrances for pickup customers (often picking up what they ordered online) and for traditional "showroom" customers. The pickup entrance is staffed and has direct access to groceries and a beer and wine shop as well as merchandise pickup for online customers. It will have dedicated parking spaces; this format has been rolled out in about 1,000 stores and made 2 million deliveries last year.

A redesigned grocery department sports wooden floors, new display cases, and a vastly expanded assortment of fresh produce as well as quick grab-n-go meals. They updated 110 stores in 2017 and 300 each in 2018 and 2019. The company has seen a 2–4 percent sales lift in each of the remodeled stores. The company also plans to open 100 "small-format" stores in urban areas and college towns by the end of 2021. To accompany this initiative, Target has added a redesigned app, mobile wallet technology, and network-tethered store floor employees who can look up items, place orders, and handle checkout right on the sales floor.

As a final praiseworthy note about Target: They have been donating 5 percent of profits to local communities since 1946.

Financial Highlights, Fiscal Year 2018

Revitalized stores and a strong economy brought a 5.2 percent top line increase and that, combined with lower tax rates, brought an 11 percent profit gain, albeit on a soft 2017 comparison, but notable as the company was spending a lot on enhancements. Same-store sales were up just under 5 percent. For 2019 and 2020, revenue is projected to grow in the 3–4 percent range, with earnings gains in the 5–7 percent range each year. Gross margins, aided by merchandising strategies and home-grown products, should rise from the high 20s to the low 30 percent range. Modest share buybacks and low-single-digit dividend increases should accompany these business results for the next few years. Notably, the company continued to raise the dividend through each of its "crises" and through the Great Recession.

Reasons to Buy

After a 2013 credit card crisis, and now the online assault, we're pretty convinced this company can find its way through almost any storm. Target is well-managed and counts on its strengths in brand, customer loyalty, and its position in the marketplace.

In fact, Target remains a classic positioning success story. Customers understand and appreciate Target, and it has some of the highest customer satisfaction numbers in the industry. The company continues to take share away from specialty retailers in home lines, clothing, children's items, and other areas. People like the Target brand and associate it with well-managed stores and quality and good taste at a reasonable price with good locations. The strategy to transform a Target store into a "neighborhood fulfillment center"—a pickup and delivery point for goods in stock and goods ordered online—bodes well for store traffic and cross-selling opportunities, thus defusing the Amazon threat; Target wants its place in today's "from the couch" economy.

Better economic conditions and more spending on home and domestic goods should improve Target's market share. We continue to admit our mistake in Target's hasty removal and welcome its return.

Reasons for Caution

Target is up against some very tough competitors: Walmart, Costco, and others, and one cannot ignore the Internet's destructive effects on "brick and mortar" these days, even if the company operates one of the best online sites (www.target.com) out there. It looks like international expansion is off the table, at least for now. We still see some risk in the grocery business, as groceries are very low margin, and the company hasn't really figured out how to make the grocery offering complete with meats and fresh produce. From our personal observations, the grocery department seems pretty empty by comparison to other grocery stores and other parts of Target stores. Gross and operating margins may see some pressure from this business, depending on how valuable the generation of more frequent store visits turns out to be.

SECTOR: Retail ▫ Beta coefficient: 0.95 ▫ 10-year compound earnings per-share growth: 5.0% ▫ 10-year compound dividends per-share growth: 17.0%

	2011	2012	2013	2014	2015	2016	2017	2018
Revenues (mil)	69,865	73,301	72,596	72,618	73,785	69,496	71,879	75,356
Net income (mil)	2,829	2,925	2,060	2,734	2,978	2,920	2,592	2,871
Earnings per share	4.28	4.38	3.21	4.27	4.69	5.01	4.71	5.39
Dividends per share	1.10	1.32	1.58	1.90	2.16	2.32	2.48	2.52
Cash flow per share	7.46	7.82	6.77	7.60	8.62	9.38	8.84	9.84
Price: high	61.0	65.5	73.5	76.6	85.8	84.1	74.2	90.4
low	45.3	47.3	55.0	54.7	68.1	65.5	48.6	60.2

Website: www.target.com

AGGRESSIVE GROWTH

The Timken Company

Ticker symbol: TKR (NYSE) ▫ Mid Cap ▫ Value Line financial strength rating: B++ ▫ Current yield: 2.4% ▫ Dividend raises, past 10 years: 8

Company Profile

When you operate a 140-ton loaded railroad car, a giant windmill, a harvesting machine, or a rolling mill in a steel-fabricating plant, you have tremendous frictional forces to overcome, often in harsh environments, for long periods of operating time and with 100 percent reliability required. Without a dependable and efficient friction solution to these moving parts, they can overheat, fail, get out of alignment, and otherwise wreak havoc on your mobile system or stationary machine—not to mention make it cost more to operate. That's where premium-engineered, replaceable bearing assemblies come into play.

On rail cars, for instance, roller bearings—small, tapered, hardened steel bearings "rolling" between the rotating axle and the wheel housing—solved years of headaches (and fires and accidents) caused by oiled brass bearings. Years ago, roller bearings became mandatory for US railroad operation. Similar gains in performance, reliability, reduced friction, and cost came to other businesses and technologies; much the same sort of bearings are used in aircraft wheels, for instance. These specialized, high-value-add bearings—and now application-specific bearing assemblies and housings that hold them—are a critical manufactured and serviced component of most of today's mobile and many of today's stationary systems.

"Rolling Steady" is one apt slogan for Timken, the world's oldest, most established and focused, and largest producer of bearings and bearing products. Over time, they have evolved the product line from relatively simple tapered and ball bearings to a greater number of protected bearing assemblies, or "housed units," which enable solutions in harsher operating environments and create maintenance cost savings for the customer.

The company, after spinning off its steelmaking business in 2014, is made up of two business segments:

- Mobile Industries (51 percent of 2018 sales) offers bearings, bearing systems, seals, lubrication devices, and power transmission systems mainly to OEMs and operators of trucks, automobiles, rail cars and locomotives, rotor and fixed-wing aircraft, construction and mining machinery, and certain military items. There had been a separate Aerospace segment; it is now part of Mobile.
- Process Industries (49 percent of sales) supplies industrial bearings, bearing systems and assemblies, and power transmission components to OEMs and operators in metals, mining, cement, aggregates production, food processing, wind energy, turbine and oil drilling equipment, material handling equipment, and certain marine applications, among many applications. These are stationary machines without wheels, whereas Mobile mainly supports things with wheels (or rotors or wings).

The company is still adding to its portfolio of adjacent machinery and mechanical power transmission parts, including chains, belts, gear drives, couplings, brakes, sprockets, clutches, including sales but also service and reconditioning businesses. Like bearings, these are relatively mission-critical, high-value-add components with serviceable lives requiring replacement. In 2018 the company acquired a company called Cone Drive, a maker of precision gear drives, and Rollon, a maker of linear motion-based industrial automation machinery. Timken's strategy is to position as a single-source, branded, full-service vendor for such components. The diverse base of end markets includes Industrial Machinery (22 percent), Automotive (13 percent), Heavy Truck (9 percent), Agriculture/Turf (8 percent), Rail (8 percent), Aerospace (7 percent), Mining (6 percent), Construction (6 percent), and Renewable Energy (5 percent). About 54 percent of Timken's business originates in North America; EMEA (21 percent), Asia (18 percent), and Latin America (7 percent) make up the rest.

The product sales mix is about 72 percent bearings and related products and 28 percent power transmission products and services. About 56 percent of total sales come from OEMs (manufacturers of new products) while the rest come from the Distribution and End User channel (mainly replacement and maintenance uses)—suggesting a steady revenue stream after the initial sale. The company is actively involved in providing technical and consulting services to help end customers solve "friction and power transmission challenges."

Financial Highlights, Fiscal Year 2018

Strong end markets and favorable pricing and mix drove a 17 percent revenue gain in FY2018. About half of that was organic growth and half was acquisitions, and it also faced a 2 percent currency headwind. End-market demand was higher in almost all categories. Higher volumes drove higher margins, although this was somewhat offset by higher raw material costs ($5 million according to the company just for tariffs); tax cuts helped too, so net earnings rolled ahead some 58 percent. Favorable demand trends, again across most end-user markets, will butt up against some currency and input cost headwinds in 2019; the company expects 8–10 percent revenue growth (4–6 percent organic) and an 11 percent growth in net income. For 2020, the company is projecting another 8–10 percent growth in earnings on a 4–6 percent growth in revenue. The company has been paying dividends since its IPO in 1922 and raising them about 4 cents a year regularly.

Reasons to Buy

We like companies with strong brands and legacies that also happen to supply very key high-value-add components to a value chain. Timken offers such key components in several important value chains, and these components wear out and must be replaced periodically—they aren't just depending on new capital investment for business. In addition, they offer one-stop convenience on a variety of bearings and other "wear" components. It's a solid niche, and we like niches.

Timken's presentations drive this home—one highlights the rail car example where a given rail car has a 35-year life and requires bearing replacement every five years, bringing $800,000 in lifetime revenue to Timken for a 100-car train (or $8,000 per rail car for life for the million-and-a-half-plus of them out there if you'd prefer to look at it that way). Lifetime value calculations like this, spread across many industries, really bring Timken's value proposition home.

Timken has also grown market share, but there's still plenty of market to conquer. They have about 36 percent of the worldwide tapered roller bearing market but only 12 percent of the bearing market in general. These figures are up from 30 percent and 5 percent a few years ago—the numbers indicate both success and opportunity. Finally, the net profit margin of roughly 9–10 percent indicates a differentiated industry (not a commodity) and a strong market position.

Reasons for Caution

Economic cycles, of course, will affect Timken's fortunes, as will competition from foreign manufacturers mainly in China and other parts of Asia. We do like the spread of customers across many industries, however; they aren't overexposed to any one industry such as energy. Trade wars are the biggest current uncertainty; while they help end-product sales somewhat, they also drive up input costs and create some uncertainty for the whole business.

SECTOR: Industrials ▫ Beta coefficient: 1.40 ▫ 10-year compound earnings per-share growth: 2.5% ▫ 10-year compound dividends per-share growth: 5.5%

	2011	2012	2013	2014	2015	2016	2017	2018
Revenues (mil)	5,170	4,987	4,341	3,076	2,872	2,670	3,003	3,581
Net income (mil)	457	456	263	234	189	156	208	328
Earnings per share	4.59	4.66	2.74	2.55	2.21	1.97	2.63	4.18
Dividends per share	0.78	0.92	0.92	1.00	1.03	1.04	1.06	1.11
Cash flow per share	6.65	6.81	4.93	4.19	3.98	3.70	4.50	6.20
Price: high	57.8	57.9	64.4	69.5	43.6	41.2	53.1	55.7
low	30.2	32.6	47.7	37.6	26.4	22.2	40.1	34.0

Website: www.timken.com

AGGRESSIVE GROWTH

T-Mobile US, Inc.

Ticker symbol: TMUS (NASDAQ) ❑ Large Cap ❑ Value Line financial strength rating: B+
❑ Current yield: Nil ❑ Dividend raises, past 10 years: NA

Company Profile

T-Mobile is the third-largest US-based wireless network operator, with 82 million subscribers (Q2 2019). It trails only AT&T and Verizon in terms of customer base, but it is currently in negotiations to acquire Sprint, which (if successful) would give it the largest geographical coverage and customer base in the US. More on that later.

The company operates HSPA+/LTE networks in the US, (mostly) western Canada, and Mexico, with LTE coverage in the US for 99 percent of the population.

They have announced planned rollouts of 5G capability on compatible handsets in mid-2019 and have entered into a multiyear $3.5 billion contract with Nokia to provide end-to-end 5G technology and services.

Revenues in 2018 were from branded postpaid customers (65 percent), branded prepaid customers (30 percent), and wholesale bandwidth (5 percent). T-Mobile is majority owned by Deutsche Telekom (61 percent).

The history of wireless telecommunications in the US is the history of mergers, acquisitions, and spin-offs. This is true for no company more than T-Mobile, with all three of these transactions in its relatively brief lifespan, and with more likely to come. Formed as VoiceStream Wireless in 1994 as a subsidiary of Western Wireless, it was spun off in 1999 and two years later purchased by Deutsche Telekom AG. One year later it was renamed T-Mobile USA, and then in 2013 merged with Metro PCS. In the intervening years T-Mobile acquired no fewer than three other wireless carriers and was the target of an acquisition by AT&T, a bid later withdrawn after it became clear that the US Department of Justice would likely move to block the deal on anti-competitive grounds.

This brings us more or less to the present. As we go to press, a proposed merger between T-Mobile and Sprint is still under review at the DOJ with a decision due by early August. In addition, however, nine state attorneys general have joined in a filing to block the merger, also on uncompetitive grounds. This may prolong the closing of the deal well into the third quarter of 2019.

Financial Highlights, Fiscal Year 2018

Highlights for FY2018 include a 7 percent increase in branded postpaid revenues, a 7 percent increase in wholesale revenues, a 7 percent increase in equipment revenues…and an increase in overall revenues of 7 percent (the following table, while consistent in its treatment of revenue recognition from year to year, discounts the effect of certain tax adjustments reported by the company in 2017 and so reflects a larger increase in 2018). In short, a good year for T-Mobile, with significant gains in operating margin and net margin, as well as a 2 percent increase in net cash generation and a 60 percent increase in free cash flow.

Reasons to Buy

T-Mobile's revenue growth over the past four years is roughly 30 percent, while their earnings growth is roughly 300 percent. The Metro merger had some up-and-down effects on the trajectory of revenue and earnings; it's apparent that T-Mobile is on the right track and has integrated the Metro assets very well. This would bode well for the potential merger with Sprint, a company that offers a complementary set of technologies and spectrum to the portfolio currently in place at T-Mobile. Even without the Sprint merger, projections for T-Mobile's net margin are expected to grow another 50 percent by 2021.

Gaining new customers and holding on to the ones you have are a key measure for wireless carriers, and T-Mobile is doing well in this regard. In 2018 they increased their customer base by 10 percent and saw a further reduction in "churn" on creditworthy accounts of just 1 percent, a figure that has been trending downward for the past four years.

Though still in an early rollout phase, the company is bringing to market a bundled television product to compete with standard and premium cable television offerings. Called "TVision," it offers local and nationwide broadcasts, on-demand viewing, DVR functionality, 4K content, etc., for a flat rate of $90 per month. Although the product is in early pilot and is not likely to generate significant revenues in its first year, the growth opportunity is tantalizing, particularly considering the advent of a T-Mobile 5G network that would not require a cable drop or a truck roll to install the product. You would simply plug in the set-top box and configure it for wireless connection to the 5G network. This has potential to be a game-changer for Sprint if it is managed well.

T-Mobile calls itself the "Un-carrier," claiming (with some fairly solid data) that they provide superior customer service, which, I think we can all agree, is a bold claim for an industry that ranks right up with used-car dealerships in terms of customer satisfaction. This may be more of a reason to buy their phone rather than their stock, but if their documented low churn rates reflect the real-world experience…well, we all know it's cheaper to keep a customer than it is to buy a new one, especially with discounted service.

Reasons for Caution

Of course, the merger is today's elephant in the room, and its possible litigation at both the federal and state level. We've tried to write up the prospects for T-Mobile assuming the merger is not approved, so our caution is already discounted somewhat in this regard. Still, it needs to be mentioned and understood that there are serious impediments to this deal. Another concern, and not for just T-Mobile, is the delay in finalization and rollout of the 5G spec and compliant hardware. This is not a done deal either, but it most certainly will get done at some point in the future. Revenues anticipated in this rollout will be delayed possibly until the spec is complete. Consult with your local techie for an update.

SECTOR: Telecommunications Services ❑ Beta coefficient: 0.95 ❑ 10-year compound earnings per-share growth: NM ❑ 10-year compound dividends per-share growth: Nil

		2011	2012	2013	2014	2015	2016	2017	2018
Revenues (bil)		20.62	19.72	24.42	29.56	32.05	37.24	40.60	43.31
Net income (mil)		d4,718	d7,336	35.0	d273.8	733	934	1,919	2,888
Earnings per share		NMF	NMF	0.05	d0.32	0.82	1.08	2.14	3.36
Dividends per share		—	—	—	—	—	—	—	—
Cash flow per share		NMF	NMF	4.57	5.13	6.56	8.63	9.13	11.03
Price:	high	—	—	34.1	35.5	43.4	59.2	68.9	70.9
	low	—	—	16.0	24.3	26.5	33.2	54.6	55.1

Website: www.t-mobile.com

GROWTH AND INCOME

Total S.A. (ADR)

Ticker symbol: TOT (NYSE) ❑ Large Cap ❑ Value Line financial strength rating: A++ ❑ Current yield: 5.6% ❑ Dividend raises, past 10 years: 6

Company Profile

Total S.A. (S.A. is short for Société Anonyme, which is the French equivalent of "incorporated") is the sixth-largest international oil and gas company. Headquartered in France and primarily traded on the French CAC stock exchange, the company has operations in more than 130 countries. Total is vertically integrated with upstream operations engaged in oil and gas exploration and downstream operations engaged in refining and distribution of petroleum products; the company also has a chemicals and a solar subsidiary.

Upstream activities are geographically well diversified, with exploration occurring in 50 countries and production happening in 30 of them. As a deliberate strategy to spread risk, many of the E&P projects are done through partnerships—if you examine their major productive assets, in most cases they own a 20–50 percent share—not the whole operation.

The largest production regions are (in production-volume sequence for 2017): Europe and Central Asia, including the North Sea, Russia, and Azerbaijan (30 percent), the Middle East and North Africa (25 percent), the Americas (14 percent), and Asia Pacific (10 percent). Liquids (oil) account for about 52 percent of production, while natural gas is 48 percent. The company is a leader in the emerging liquefied natural gas (LNG) market for export. Downstream operations are also worldwide and centered in Europe. Operations include interests in 20 refineries worldwide, with 8 refineries and 72 percent of total refining capacity in Europe. There are also 20 petrochemical plants. Total also operates 16,630 service stations in 65 countries, mainly under the Total, Elf, and Elan names, again weighted toward Europe and North Africa. Total is the world's number two retailer outside of North America. The downstream presence is also growing in Asia-Pacific (including China), Latin America, and the Caribbean. The company now has a leading market presence in those regions.

Total also has ventures in alternative energy, notably solar. It owns a 57 percent interest in global solar leader SunPower, making it the number two solar operator in the world. Mainly through that venture it designs, manufactures, and distributes cells and solar panels ("upstream") and is active in designing, building, and operating large-scale solar plants ("downstream"). What is thought to be the world's largest solar plant, the Solar Star project, was brought online in the US in 2015; another large plant was brought on in Abu Dhabi in 2013. The company also bought a 23 percent stake in European wind power provider Eren. Another new subsidiary called Saft Groupe S.A. is in the stationary battery storage business. Long term, Total projects nonhydrocarbon energy sources to comprise 40 percent of total energy demand by the year 2035; the company is managing its energy portfolio accordingly.

By and large, Total used the recent cyclical low in energy prices as an opportunity to fine-tune, acquire, and produce from assets on several fronts. Production expanded holdings in the North Sea and Brazil and ramped up new operations in Congo and Kazakhstan, acquired an LNG business in Europe, expanded service station outlets in Mexico, and launched a new petrochemicals business in South Korea. The company is the first major to return to production in Iran. All told, Total bought $350 million and sold $2.1 billion in assets just during the fourth quarter of 2018.

Financial Highlights, Fiscal Year 2018

A modest recovery in oil prices (average $71/bbl versus $54/bbl in 2017), a favorable currency conversion rate, stronger natural gas prices ($4.96/MBtu versus $4.22), production increases (about 7 percent for the year), and strength in downstream operations led to a 23 percent gain in FY2018 revenues. That and various efficiency measures made for a 30 percent gain in reported net income. Forecasts call for a 14–15 percent revenue advance in 2019, based in part on production increases, followed by a 4–6 percent rise in 2020. Earnings will track ahead faster, growing 20 percent or a bit more in 2019 and 12–15 percent in 2020 although this may prove to be optimistic if oil prices fail to stay above $60/barrel. Investors should enjoy a modest mix of dividend increases, share buybacks, and debt reduction.

Reasons to Buy

Due to advantageous and diverse geographic positioning and effective management during the downturn, Total's recovery appeared sooner and stronger than most. We like their branding and dominance in the key worldwide markets they serve. They seem to manage their business well both for the short and long term; long-term prospects are bright, persistent and growing cash returns beyond what's given in current forecasts.

Reasons for Caution

The downsides are pretty much still the same. Risks still come from (1) oil prices, (2) dollar versus euro fluctuations, and (3) international tensions. More aggression on Russia's part, both militarily and economically, would add risk to a situation already destabilized by the usual Middle East tensions and European economic uncertainties. Finally, the company took on long-term debt to get it through the down cycle, albeit less than some of its competitors.

More generally, we remain cautious on investing in foreign companies because of differences in management style and accounting rules; they aren't necessarily bad but are difficult to understand and follow. Company information is hard to sift through; the website is mainly a collection of PR pieces—what tangible business information they have is presented in too much detail and is hard to mine for the important stuff. Antiquated European pension rules and other labor practices could also be a disadvantage, as could recent isolationist movements. Total has a bit more risk than some of the other majors; however, we still think there is safety in diversity and that the rewards outweigh the risks.

SECTOR: Energy ❑ Beta coefficient: 1.25 ❑ 10-year compound earnings per-share growth: -9.0% ❑ 10-year compound dividends per-share growth: 2.0%

	2011	2012	2013	2014	2015	2016	2017	2018
Revenues (bil)	216	234	228	212	143	128	149	184
Net income (bil)	15.9	15.9	14.2	12.8	5.1	6.1	8.5	11.1
Earnings per share	7.05	7.01	6.28	5.63	2.19	2.52	3.36	4.24
Dividends per share	3.12	2.98	3.10	3.21	2.73	2.70	2.72	2.96
Cash flow per share	11.37	12.46	11.57	10.90	9.76	8.07	9.72	9.61
Price: high	64.4	57.1	62.4	74.2	55.9	51.4	57.1	65.7
low	40.0	41.8	45.9	48.4	40.9	39.1	48.2	49.7

Website: www.total.com

AGGRESSIVE GROWTH

Trex Company, Inc.

Ticker symbol: TREX (NYSE) ❑ Mid Cap ❑ Value Line financial strength rating: B+ ❑ Current yield: Nil ❑ Dividend raises, past 10 years: NA

Company Profile

"Engineering what's next in outdoor living" is the apt slogan of Trex, the world's largest manufacturer of composite wood decking. Composite deck boards and related materials are milled from a composite of mostly recycled sawdust and polyethylene, 95 percent recycled, in fact. Its "Wood-Polymer" lumber provides the appearance of wood (or better) and its benefits without the need of maintenance in the form of protective sealants—it is weatherproof and maintains its look for life.

The products, all manufactured in the United States, include decking, fencing, railings, stairwell materials, trim, steel framing, outdoor furniture, and outdoor lighting materials, mainly for residential but increasingly for commercial and public sector (i.e., parks, etc.) use. The three decking product lines, roughly representing good, better, and best, include Trex Select, Trex Enhance, and Trex Transcend and provide several color and texture appearance options from gray weathered pine to Brazilian ipe. A new line just introduced, called Trex Enhance Basics, brings a more moderately priced option to market at about twice the cost of conventional stained lumber and designed to compete head on with pressure-treated lumber. This is a good thing since higher-end Trex lines can cost three to five times as much as conventional lumber and stain. The company has also expanded its line of railings, fencing, and deck accessories such as lighting and has a line of deck furniture, e.g., Adirondack chairs, as well, made from their composite material.

Trex has traditionally been marketed through about 3,000 traditional lumber yards and building products dealers; over the years it has stepped up its presence, both in scale and brand presence, in the building products superstores, namely Home Depot, Lowe's, and similar retailers. It is now stocked in some 6,700 locations worldwide. The informative website helps not only with product selection but with deck design and dealer and contractor selection.

The 2017 acquisition of commercial architectural and stadium railing manufacturer SC Companies in mid-2017 gives Trex a stronger commercial presence and a greater opportunity to sell decking products into commercial accounts and projects.

Financial Highlights, Fiscal Year 2018

Mix together brand recognition, market-share growth, quality and process improvements, and wider distribution with a manufacturing process hungry for volume to make the most of fixed costs and you get what we call "scale" or "operating leverage" and thus significantly higher gross margins. Higher gross margins on higher sales is a powerful formula for success. So it continues to go for Trex, which has grown volume 39 percent in the past three years (not including about 10 percent from the SC acquisition) and grown gross margins almost 10 points along the way, from 36 percent to 46.1 percent for the residential business, which represents about 90 percent of the total. The commercial business lags these margins a bit but is expected to catch up.

For 2018 sales rose 21 percent but closer to 9 percent without SC. Net income, helped along by SC, improved margins, and lower taxes, advanced 41 percent. Sales and profit gains may taper a bit in 2019, especially profits as the cost of launching the new Trex Enhance line will come into play; the company expects an 11 percent earnings gain on a 9–11 percent sales increase. Favorable trends in the remodel construction space, market-share gains from wood, international expansion, and other factors are expected to bring a 13–15 percent earnings gain on a roughly 10 percent sales increase in 2020. Trex has a likeable tendency to underpromise and overdeliver; we think these estimates might be somewhat understated. It does appear that dividends will be "nil" for some time, but modest buybacks are likely. Notably, Trex has no long-term debt.

Reasons to Buy

What attracts us to Trex is not only the beauty and resilience of these products for both new and replacement construction but also the fact that Trex is not only taking market share from other composite decking manufacturers, it is also taking share from the much larger traditional lumber market as appearance, maintenance, and now commodity pricing for lumber play a role in the choice. Yet it still only has 17 percent of the market versus wood, offering considerable opportunity—the company estimates every 1 percent market share taken from conventional wood is worth about $50 million in Trex sales. The new lower price point should speed this up considerably.

Moreover, beyond the obvious consideration for outdoor living spaces on new construction, there were millions of decks built in the 1970s, 1980s, and 1990s well in need of replacement. According to the company, repair and remodeling projects are expected to grow 5.15 percent by the end of 2019. If that wasn't enough, the trend toward building attractive and useful outdoor living spaces continues to grow (again according to Trex, 34 percent of home improvement spending is on exterior improvements). These trends all provide substantial tailwinds for Trex. Finally, we like the transformation of inexpensive recycled materials into a high-value-add product with a strong brand—which by the way is becoming more prominent in the nation's large home improvement stores and is starting to gain traction overseas as well. Growing market, great brand, improved margins, cash flow and operating leverage, zero debt, recycled material: What's not to like?

Reasons for Caution

The main thing not to like is the price of the stock, which has been on a run perhaps more than commensurate to the business. A slowdown even to a more modest growth rate could hurt. The stock is a bit volatile and tends to pull back whenever there is bad news on the housing industry (which doesn't affect the company as much as one might think since a lot of its business is in replacement). We're only sorry we didn't bring this one to you sooner.

SECTOR: Materials ❑ Beta coefficient: 1.35 ❑ 10-year compound earnings per-share growth: 60.0% ❑ 10-year compound dividends per-share growth: NA

	2011	2012	2013	2014	2015	2016	2017	2018
Revenues (mil)	267	307	344	392	441	480	565	684
Net income (mil)	(5.6)	26.6	48.2	41.5	48.1	67.8	95.1	134
Earnings per share	(0.07)	0.39	0.70	0.64	0.76	1.15	1.61	2.28
Dividends per share	—	—	—	—	—	—	—	—
Cash flow per share	0.20	0.64	0.96	0.97	1.01	1.40	1.90	2.58
Price: high	8.5	10.2	20.8	22.4	28.9	36.1	59.3	90.7
low	3.6	5.7	9.5	12.6	15.9	15.6	30.8	50.7

Website: www.trex.com

CONSERVATIVE GROWTH

Union Pacific Corporation

Ticker symbol: UNP (NYSE) ❑ Large Cap ❑ Value Line financial strength rating: A++ ❑ Current yield: 2.1% ❑ Dividend raises, past 10 years: 10

Company Profile

Union Pacific has been a familiar name and logo in the railroad business since its inception during the Civil War. With about 32,000 miles of track covering 23 states in the western two-thirds of the US, today's Union Pacific Railroad, the primary subsidiary of the Union Pacific Corporation, describes itself as "America's Premier Railroad Franchise." The route system is anchored by Gulf Coast and West Coast ports and areas in between and has coordinated schedules and gateways with other lines in the eastern US, Canada, and Mexico.

With 10,000 customers, a large number in today's era of trainload-sized shipments, UNP has a more diversified customer and revenue mix than the other rail companies, including the other three of the "big four" railroads:

Burlington Northern Santa Fe, Norfolk Southern, and CSX. The company has reorganized its traffic and revenue mix reporting into four categories:

• Premium (31 percent of revenue) includes general merchandise, intermodal and automotive (finished cars and parts).
• Industrial (27 percent) includes construction materials, forest products, industrial chemicals, plastics, paper and packaging products, metals, ores, lime, cement, salt, and waste.
• Agricultural (21 percent) includes grains, fertilizers, food and beverage products.
• Energy (21 percent) includes coal, oil, propane and LPG, and sand (mainly for "fracking" production).

This regrouping more closely reflects the balance of the business, particularly as large commodity bases such as coal decline; no point in reporting it separately. As coal declines, the company is putting more emphasis on diversifying the traffic base and recapturing smaller single-car shipments, mostly of manufactured goods, once given up to truckers. New trucking rules requiring time of service logging technology for trucks has put a tailwind behind this shift, as has a shortage of drivers and an across-the-board increase in truck rates.

Union Pacific has long been an innovator in railroad technology, including motive power, communications and technology automation, physical plant, community relations, and marketing. Improved volumes and efficiencies dropped the operating ratio to an all-time best of 62.7—that is, variable costs are 62.7 percent of revenues—best in the industry and despite a sometimes costly network congestion due in part to the strong economy at the beginning of the year. By comparison, this closely watched ratio was 62.8 in 2017, 63.5 in 2016, 63.1 in 2015, 63.5 in 2014, 65.0 in 2013, 67.8 in 2012, and 70.6 in 2011—you get the idea. A low operating ratio allows a solid contribution to the substantial fixed costs of owning and running a railroad. This success has translated to continued strong operating margins, which of course have helped earnings and cash flows and in turn have funded physical plant improvements and shareholder returns over time.

Like operational "rival" (they don't serve the same markets) *100 Best* stock Norfolk Southern, UP has started to implement the operational principle called Precision Scheduled Railroading, where movements are scheduled down to the carload to optimize efficiency, keep cars and trains moving, and serve customers better and with more transparency. Like NS, UP states a goal to drive the operating ratio down to 60 as early as the end of 2020; as of early

2019 they had already removed 1,200 locomotives and 30,000 freight cars from the network.

The company also invests in marketing and community relations. One example is the mostly steam-powered "Heritage Fleet" program, through which the company operates excursion trains with vintage equipment on selected lines. Literally thousands of people (and current and prospective customers) gather trackside in every town along the way as these beautiful trains roll through. The company recently restored and ran a "Big Boy" 4-8-8-4 steam locomotive, the largest ever used in regular service (of course, for the UP originally) for the Golden Spike sesquicentennial in May 2019. Such public relations efforts show an extraordinary measure of pride and an appreciation for heritage and community. We continue to applaud this effort, as do tens of thousands of trackside spectators and thousands of UP customers.

Financial Highlights, Fiscal Year 2018

After an initial slow period due to inventory buildups and system congestion, 2018 ended on a solid note. Shipments were up 5 percent, revenues rose 7.5 percent, and per-share earnings were up a full 37 percent. Favorable traffic mix, volume, operating efficiencies, and tax cuts (which benefit high-fixed-costs outfits like railroads in particular) all played a part. Operational improvements and a continued strong economy will keep the train on the track for a 7–8 percent earnings growth on a 3–5 percent growth in revenues in 2019, with an 8–10 percent earnings growth on a similar revenue advance in 2020, assuming no derailments in the economy. A very aggressive buy-back plan retiring some 55 million shares by 2020 will help advance per-share earnings even faster; dividends are slated to grow in the double-digit range annually as well (the dividend was raised 23 percent last year).

Reasons to Buy

Put simply, this company has performed well even in bad times and has also returned plenty of cash to shareholders. After hitting some slow orders in 2016 and early 2018, it seems on track to emerge stronger than ever.

UNP is an extraordinarily well-managed company and has become more efficient and at the same time more user friendly to its customers and to the general public. The company continues to make gains at the expense of the trucking industry, and new short- and long-distance intermodal services move higher-valued goods more quickly and cost effectively; we see a steady shift toward this business especially as the new trucking economics and rules take effect. A continuing recovery in the energy and other commodity and basic materials industries will also help. The company has a solid and diverse traffic base and continues to have a good brand and reputation in the industry, and Precision Scheduled Railroading will help on the operational side. The company got an early start expanding and modernizing its physical plant and technology base; that has paid off well and will continue to do so.

Reasons for Caution

No doubt, some of their coal, and to a lesser extent, oil, traffic has shifted away forever. Railroads are chiefly a commodity-hauling business, and when commodities are down, they suffer. The company has had to adjust and execute well both in marketing and operations to backfill this lost volume; traffic once lost is hard to get back. More recently, trade barriers have cut into traffic, although it may just be a timing thing, as imports surged prior to the recent tariffs; traffic may recover once inventories are depleted.

Railroads are and will always be economically sensitive because of commodity revenue and their high-fixed-cost structure. They also have significant headline risk—a single event like a derailment or spill can put them in a bad public eye or worse, tangle them up in regulation, lawsuits, and unplanned costs. Regulation and mandates for Positive Train Control and other safety features are expensive. Longer-term factors also include effects from new Trump administration trade policies, which could hurt import and some export traffic if left in place as they are.

Railroads will always struggle to put the right amount of capacity on the ground—too little causes service problems and delays; too much eats into profits. It is difficult to manage these ups and downs, but Precision Scheduled Railroading should help better utilize capacity.

SECTOR: Transportation ◻ Beta coefficient: 1.15 ◻ 10-year compound earnings per-share growth: 15.0% ◻ 10-year compound dividends per-share growth: 22.0%

		2011	2012	2013	2014	2015	2016	2017	2018
Revenues (mil)		19,557	20,926	21,953	23,988	21,813	19,941	21,240	22,832
Net income (mil)		3,292	3,943	4,388	5,180	4,702	4,233	4,638	5,968
Earnings per share		3.36	4.14	4.71	5.75	5.41	5.07	5.80	7.93
Dividends per share		0.97	1.25	1.48	1.91	2.20	2.26	2.48	3.06
Cash flow per share		5.11	6.07	6.76	8.02	7.91	7.69	8.60	11.20
Price:	high	53.9	64.6	84.1	123.6	124.5	106.6	136.3	165.6
	low	38.9	52.0	63.7	82.5	74.8	67.1	101.1	121.2

Website: www.up.com

UnitedHealth Group, Inc.

Ticker symbol: UNH (NYSE) ❑ Large Cap ❑ Value Line financial strength rating: A++ ❑ Current yield: 1.2% ❑ Dividend raises, past 10 years: 9

Company Profile

UnitedHealth Group is the parent company of a number of health insurers and service organizations. It is the largest publicly traded health insurance company in the United States, with $226 billion in revenue reported in 2018, a number five US company ranking on the *Fortune* 500 list (up from six last year), and a membership in the Dow Jones Industrial Average.

The company operates in two major business segments: UnitedHealthcare (health insurance and benefits) and Optum (health services), which, combined, touch about 78 million people worldwide in 50 US states and 125 countries globally.

UnitedHealthcare provides traditional and Medicare-based health benefit and insurance plans for individuals and employers, covering approximately 27 million individuals, with about 400 national employer accounts and 200,000 other smaller employer accounts. The company estimates that it serves more than half of the *Fortune* 100 companies list. The company, mainly through this unit, has been an active acquirer of other familiar healthcare and insurance brands over the years. The UnitedHealthcare insurance business in total accounts for 64 percent of FY2017 revenues and 53 percent of profits.

The UnitedHealthcare business unit actively markets traditional individual and employee health plans ("Employer & Individual"), which account for about 30 percent of the UnitedHealthcare-branded insurance products. Even larger at 41 percent today is the senior and military market ("Medicare & Retirement"), with a growing assortment of Medicare Advantage, Medicare Part D, and Medicare supplement plans (Medicare premiums alone represents 30 percent of UNH's total consolidated revenues). The recently added TRICARE insurance program for active and retired military is a large contributor to this subsegment. The rest of the insurance unit is made up by Community & State (23 percent, programs for economically disadvantaged, mainly Medicaid) and Global (5 percent).

Beyond the insurance business lies the large and rapidly growing health services businesses, marketed under the Optum brand umbrella. At just over $100 million in revenue annually, this segment is far and away big enough to be a separate company and is a rapidly growing and increasingly important part of the overall UNH business offering.

Optum delivers these health services through three separate businesses. OptumHealth is an operating "information and technology–based health population management solution," deploying mostly remote telesupport for well care, mental health, ongoing disease management, and substance abuse programs to 93 million individuals. The OptumRx business is a pharmacy-benefits provider serving 65 million customers and a network of 67,000 pharmacies and other outlets with about 600 million prescriptions annually, while OptumInsight is a management information, analytics, and process-improvement arm providing an assortment of services for health plans, physicians, hospitals, and life science research. Of the total Optum-branded business of $101 billion (36 percent of total company revenue and 9 percent ahead of FY2017), Rx accounts for the lion's share at $69 billion, while OptumHealth, which grew 22 percent again in FY2018, weighs in at $24 billion and OptumInsight at $9 billion with 10 percent annual growth. Although these numbers may seem small in the context of UNH's total $226 billion annual revenue footprint, they are sizeable businesses when looked at individually; all would be sizeable and significant stand-alone businesses. The Optum umbrella brand is gaining in prominence and even has its own web presence at www.optum.com.

UnitedHealth Group has been a leader in process, delivery, and cost improvement and a recognized innovator in the industry. ("The Future of Digital Health Care" is one of their slogans.) The company has moved aggressively to offer tools to manage and contain costs in the healthcare system, mostly through the Optum business. The company sits on top of a mountain of healthcare data and is putting it to good use and has emerged as a leader in developing remote and preventative care models.

UNH's experience and participation in the Affordable Care Act has been curtailed substantially—from 34 to 3 states in 2017—citing costs and mounting losses. At the same time, they're increasing participation in Medicare and Medicaid in particular. The company is known for making quick decisions to enter and exit specific markets and businesses.

Financial Highlights, Fiscal Year 2018

Price increases, market-share gains, membership gains, and growth across both the insurance and the Optum businesses led to a 12.5 percent total revenue gain for FY2018; a strong compare versus 2017 in part because of the 2017 near exit of the ACA business. Moderating healthcare costs, scale in the Optum businesses, and tax changes helped to ring up another substantial 30 percent gain in net income. Revenues are forecast ahead 8–10 percent in 2019 and a similar amount in 2020; net earnings, with no new tax changes, should also forge ahead 8–10 percent in 2019, rising to 12–15 percent in 2020. Dividend-growth prospects are equally healthy (in fact, a 20 percent raise last year), and share repurchases, while slowing some, should chip in as well.

Reasons to Buy

This bellwether company is one of the most solid, diverse, and innovative enterprises in the health insurance industry. Health insurers are doing a better job of understanding and managing their businesses through utilization management and other initiatives instead of just passing costs on; these initiatives are bearing fruit. As well, the scale of UNH's operation gives it tremendous leverage when negotiating for the services of healthcare providers.

Meanwhile, like CVS/Aetna, UNH brings a fair amount of innovation to the marketplace, primarily through its Optum offerings. We like its initiatives to make use of its own "big data" with analytics; the size of its database and the tools it possesses can deliver efficiency improvements, and even slight efficiency improvements can help the bottom line substantially.

Reasons for Caution

With the merger of Aetna and CVS, the healthcare cost investigation and consortium being launched by Amazon, Berkshire Hathaway, and JPMorgan Chase, and other possible mergers and acquisitions, the once-stable healthcare payer and provider landscape is suddenly starting to shift; we don't know where this ends. UNH already has a pharmacy benefits operation (OptumRx) so isn't likely to grow in this direction—but who knows which way the winds blow; the company could still pull off a large acquisition somewhere in this space, and it's difficult to predict how these acquisitions will work out in the end. UNH may feel compelled to follow suit, and whether they do or not, competition is likely to strengthen. The company is vulnerable to shifts in public opinion and to new regulation (and pulling in almost $12.5 billion in annual profit doesn't help). Finally, while probably justified based on performance, the stock has made new highs in most of the last year and could correct on bad news or a large acquisition.

SECTOR: Healthcare ❑ Beta coefficient: 1.00 ❑ 10-year compound earnings per-share growth: 12.5% ❑ 10-year compound dividends per-share growth: 58.0%

	2011	2012	2013	2014	2015	2016	2017	2018
Revenues (bil)	101.9	110.6	122.5	130.5	157.1	184.8	201.2	226.2
Net income (mil)	5,142	5,526	5,625	5,619	5,947	7,792	9,928	12,654
Earnings per share	4.73	5.28	5.50	5.70	6.15	8.05	10.07	12.87
Dividends per share	0.61	0.80	1.05	1.41	1.88	2.38	2.88	3.45
Cash flow per share	5.86	6.67	7.09	7.44	7.88	10.34	12.55	15.71
Price: high	53.5	60.8	75.9	104.0	126.2	164.0	231.6	287.9
low	36.4	49.8	51.4	69.6	95.0	107.5	156.1	208.5

Website: www.unitedhealthgroup.com

CONSERVATIVE GROWTH

United Parcel Service, Inc.

Ticker symbol: UPS (NYSE) ❑ Large cap ❑ Value Line financial strength rating: A ❑ Current yield: 3.5% ❑ Dividend raises, past 10 years: 10

Company Profile

UPS is the world's largest integrated ground and air package delivery carrier. Over the years, UPS and rival FedEx have converged on the same business from different directions—FedEx being an air company getting more into the ground business; UPS being a ground business taking to the air. That convergence is now nearly complete. Both companies continue to build international capabilities, invest in technology to track shipments, and provide logistics services beyond a basic assortment of transportation services. UPS derives just over 62 percent of revenues from US package operations, 20 percent from international package operations, and 18 percent from Supply Chain & Freight, an assortment of bundled logistics and supply-chain services and solutions. Of the 63 percent US package operations, about 72 percent of that is ground, 18 percent is next-day air, and the rest "deferred" (two days or longer) air.

The company operates 568 aircraft and 119,000 ground vehicles ("package cars"), most of the familiar brown variety. They serve more than 10 million shipping customers in 220 countries with an assortment of priority to deferred services, with 154,000 domestic and international entry points including 41,000 drop boxes, 1,000 customer service centers, and 5,000 independently owned "UPS Store" (formerly "Mail Boxes Etc.")

storefronts. The company delivered 21 million packages per day worldwide in 2018.

Once thought to be old-fashioned and averse to innovation, the company has invested in sophisticated package-tracking systems and links for customers to tie into them. An example is My Choice, which allows a customer to control the timing and destination of deliveries mid-service—by smartphone if they choose—so no more waiting half a day at home for a delivery that might come anytime (hallelujah!). The service, which is now used by over 51 million recipients, is a nice perk for a consumer waiting for an e-commerce shipment as well as a savings for the company, avoiding multiple delivery attempts and possible door-front theft. The company also offers specialized logistics services for vertical markets, such as the auto industry "Autogistics" and the healthcare industry, retail, high tech, and more. Other new services include UPS Worldwide Express Freight Midday, offering a 12 p.m. to 2 p.m. delivery commit time from all 71 origin countries to 35 destination countries for urgent palletized shipments over 150 pounds, typically one to three days with customs clearance included.

The company has embarked on numerous revenue- and cost-optimization campaigns, among them a detailed analysis of the cost drivers for their businesses. As an example, they found that one mile saved in their Small Package Pickup & Delivery business across all delivery routes saves $50 million per year; one minute saved would save $14.6 million per year, and one minute of idle time reduced would save $515K. The company continues to use analytics to predict and optimize route selection and other aspects of the delivery network. The first phase of "Orion," dubbed as the "world's largest operations research project," is now complete. The company opened 22 new US facilities including 5 new "superhubs" in 2018. These initiatives, now all comprising the "UPS Smart Logistics Network," will be crucial to maintaining service and margins as the industry evolves to a higher percentage of single-package to single-address shipments with the e-commerce surge, while traditional users require ever more flexible logistics solutions.

Financial Highlights, Fiscal Year 2018

Despite the persistent shift toward e-commerce, which presents challenges to margins and thus profits, UPS delivered a solid 2018 performance. Rising volumes and higher prices led to a 7.9 percent revenue gain; earnings, helped along by stronger pricing, scale, automation, and the tax cuts, rose 23 percent after an anemic 2017 performance. Looking forward, e-commerce and other volume gains will keep annual revenue growth in the 5–7 percent range through 2020, with operational efficiencies and selective price increases ("yield management") driving a modest 3–4 percent 2019 profit advance, then a healthier 8–10 percent profit increase in 2020. Dividend growth is healthy; the dividend has been raised 48 consecutive years—notable in the up-and-down transportation industry.

Reasons to Buy

The "fastest ship in the shipping business" continues to also be one of the most stable; UPS continues to position itself as the standard logistics provider of the world. The mainstay businesses are cyclical but sound; the emerging e-commerce business is gaining critical mass (volumes rising to the point of optimal efficiency) and will lead to better capacity utilization overall. In general, we applaud the use of technology to get "details" right on the operational front.

We are also fans of its logistics and supply-chain management businesses and the many innovations in that space, as the push for many customers to optimize this part of their business will lead them to UPS's front door.

Finally, the continued ability to raise prices enough not to just cover cost increases but also to boost profits tells us that demand is strong and getting stronger, and that UPS is positioned well to capitalize on that demand. "Big Brown" has many tailwinds at its back.

Reasons for Caution

Competition in this industry is fierce. The Postal Service is getting more aggressive in marketing its small-package and logistics services as it sees the writing on the wall for traditional mail services, and rival FedEx has made gains on UPS's traditional turf with their ground and freight services and their SmartPost program (see FedEx, another *100 Best* stock). Also of note is Amazon getting into the freight business itself; they have started acquiring aircraft and other assets. We think they would have far to go to displace the well-established supply-chain network of a UPS or a FedEx, but their actions (or threat) could force price concessions, and Amazon has been known to be surprisingly successful when attacking adjacent markets (like cloud computing). Labor relations and pension funding both bear watching. Of course, fuel prices are a wild card, and have already turned back upward a little.

SECTOR: Transportation ❑ Beta coefficient: 0.95 ❑ 10-year compound earnings per-share growth: 4.0% ❑ 10-year compound dividends per-share growth: 7.5%

	2011	2012	2013	2014	2015	2016	2017	2018
Revenues (mil)	53,105	54,127	55,438	58,232	58,363	60,906	65,872	71,861
Net income (mil)	4,213	4,389	4,372	4,389	4,923	5,104	5,259	6,301
Earnings per share	4.25	4.53	4.61	4.75	5.43	5.75	6.01	7.24
Dividends per share	2.08	2.28	2.48	2.68	2.92	3.12	3.32	3.64
Cash flow per share	6.60	6.90	6.75	6.97	7.81	8.36	8.65	9.89
Price: high	77.0	84.9	105.4	113.1	114.4	120.4	125.2	135.5
low	60.7	75.0	75.0	93.2	93.6	87.3	102.1	89.9

Website: www.ups.com

AGGRESSIVE GROWTH

Valero Energy Corporation

Ticker symbol: VLO (NYSE) ❑ Large Cap ❑ Value Line financial strength rating: A+ ❑ Current yield: 4.2% ❑ Dividend raises, past 10 years: 9

Company Profile

Valero Energy is the world's second-largest independent oil refiner behind Phillips 66. The company owns 15 refineries and distributes primarily through a network of 7,400 retail combined gasoline stations and convenience stores throughout the United States (5,700 outlets), the UK and Ireland (900), and Canada (800). Most of these sales are under Valero's formerly owned retail brand names, which include the Valero brand itself but also Ultramar, Shamrock, Diamond Shamrock, and Beacon brands. The company owns the names and supplies the product, but in 2013 the company spun off the retail operations themselves into an independent public company called CST Brands. These outlets are located in all but four US states and the eastern half of Canada. Aside from unlocking capital and increasing focus on refining, the separation of these businesses allows more refining sales to other channels and allows the retailers to source from their lowest-cost supplier—improving the performance of both.

Most of the 15 Valero refineries are located in the United States, centered in the South and on the Texas Gulf Coast (70 percent of total capacity) with others in Memphis, Oklahoma, and on the West Coast. Others are located in Quebec and Wales in the UK. The refining operations produce the full gamut of hydrocarbon products: gasoline, jet fuel, diesel, asphalt, propane, base oils, solvents, aromatics, natural gas liquids, sulfur, hydrogen, middle distillates, and special fuel blends to meet California Air Resources Board requirements. The company markets these products where the refineries are located, plus in the Caribbean and in Ireland.

Valero is strictly focused on downstream operations—now just the refining portion, no longer retail—and owns no oil wells or production facilities. Instead, they purchase a variety of feedstocks on the open market and can adjust those purchases to market conditions while using contracts and hedging tools to manage input prices to a degree—and rail transport along with existing pipelines to get it to the refinery. About half of feedstocks are purchased under contracts, with the other half on the spot market. Most of these refineries are legacy operations and have been in place for many years, as far back as 1908. The company has invested heavily in upgrading these refineries to improve capacity, efficiency, and environmental compliance and in recent years has grown its refinery mechanical availability rate to 96.9 percent and total availability excluding scheduled shutdowns to 99 percent. Actual throughput capacity utilization was 96 percent—an excellent figure after the hurricane-plagued 2017.

The company continues to develop its US logistics capabilities with the strategic goal of sourcing as much crude as it can flexibly from the least expensive sources. The emphasis has shifted from building out its railcar fleet a few years ago to developing and hooking into various pipeline projects to bring US crude into its refineries. Far more crude originates today in the US; the company now imports about half the amount of crude that it did back in 2006. With much of its refining capacity on the Gulf Coast, the company was a large importer of Venezuelan crude but has replaced that with other sources. Logistics are more complicated as crude has begun to head in all directions with strengthened US production and overseas disruptions, but Valero hasn't seen many critical bottlenecks or cost increases as a result so far.

Bulk sales to other retail outlets, commercial distributors, and large-end customers like airlines and railroads are also important. The company also owns and operates 14 ethanol plants in the US Midwest, producing and shipping 1.4 billion gallons per year and a 50 percent interest in a 10,500 barrels-per-day renewable diesel plant.

Financial Highlights, Fiscal Year 2018

Strong demand, favorable spot crude prices, refinery improvements, and new pipelines led to a record earnings performance on a near-record revenue rate. Total sales rose 24 percent while earnings, helped along by the previously noted factors plus lower tax rates and a soft 2017 comparison, pumped up some 41 percent and an even more impressive 47 percent on a per-share basis. Moderating retail and crude prices are predicted to keep revenues largely unchanged through 2020 but earnings, driven by operational and logistics efficiencies, should advance 6–8 percent each year.

In this sort of business, refining margins and throughput and the cash generated from that are most important; the company manages that margin and cash flow very carefully. Cash flows approaching $15 per share are expected to lead to continued strong dividend increases and active share buybacks (the company has bought back 25 percent of its float since 2010). While the dividend raise pace may slow some, Valero continues to be one of our strongest dividend aggressors.

Reasons to Buy

The profitability of this business, like other refining businesses, depends on the supply and cost of feedstocks and the wholesale and retail prices of finished products. In addition, the availability of refining capacity is also a factor; when markets get tight, it is extremely difficult to put another refinery on the ground to handle demand. These two factors can work together very favorably for Valero—lower input costs, no new competition—it's an oligopolistic dream and should bode well for profits for years to come, especially in today's new world of crude oil (over)abundance.

Flexibility is a key part of Valero's strategy. Rail transport has been providing excellent flexibility; now a more relaxed regulatory view of pipelines has energized their extension and operation. Valero will make the best of both worlds to bring in crude at the lowest overall cost and is ahead of its competitors in its ability to do so. Finally, one cannot overlook the commitment to cash returns to shareholders in the form of dividends.

Reasons for Caution

The refining business is inherently volatile (no pun intended!) and complex, and what may appear today as an advantageous input and output pricing profile might disappear in a minute. Indeed, refined products are in a glut too, making future prices uncertain, and the recent allowance of crude exports makes less oil available in Valero's own backyard.

Gross, operating, and net margins can become very thin, typically in the 1–2 percent range—although much of Valero's recent success is due to breaking out of that range into the low 3 percent range, helped along by the tax law—but that is still pretty thin and vulnerable to changing business conditions. Refiners also endure the headline risk of refinery mishaps, a few of which have already come Valero's way in recent years. Finally, the recent liberalization of environmental constraints on pipelines could come to an end if the Trump administration begins to lose its influence in Washington.

SECTOR: Energy ❑ Beta coefficient: 1.20 ❑ 10-year compound earnings per-share growth: -2.5% ❑ 10-year compound dividends per-share growth: 21.5%

	2011	2012	2013	2014	2015	2016	2017	2018
Revenues (bil)	125.1	138.3	138.1	130.8	87.8	75.7	94.0	117.0
Net income (mil)	2,097	2,083	2,395	3,630	3,990	2,289	2,200	3,122
Earnings per share	3.69	3.75	4.37	6.85	7.99	4.94	4.96	7.29
Dividends per share	0.30	0.65	0.85	1.05	1.70	2.40	2.80	3.20
Cash flow per share	6.52	6.60	7.65	10.47	12.25	9.25	9.50	12.35
Price: high	31.1	34.5	50.5	59.7	73.9	72.5	93.2	127.0
low	16.4	16.1	33.0	42.5	43.4	45.9	60.7	68.6

Website: www.valero.com

AGGRESSIVE GROWTH

Valmont Industries, Inc.

Ticker symbol: VMI (NYSE) ❑ Mid Cap ❑ Value Line financial strength rating: A ❑ Current yield: 1.1% ❑ Dividend raises, past 10 years: 7

Company Profile

Valmont Industries was founded in 1946 as a supplier of irrigation products and became one of the classic postwar industrial success stories, growing along with the need for increased farm output. It was an early pioneer of the center-pivot irrigation system, which enabled much of that growth and now dominates the high-yield agricultural business. These irrigation machines remain a mainstay of this most profitable product line, but the company has expanded on that core expertise in galvanized metal to make such familiar infrastructure items as light poles, cell phone towers and other utility structures, and those familiar high-tension electric towers that crisscross the landscape. As well, it provides such galvanizing services to other product manufacturers.

From the following product line summary, you'll get a good idea how Valmont plays in important areas of infrastructure and agriculture:

- Engineered Support Structure products (35 percent of FY2018 revenues, 17 percent of operating income)—Lighting poles, including decorative lighting poles, guard rails, sign structures, towers, and other metal structures used in lighting, communications, roadway safety, wireless phone carriers, and other applications. Also includes products for the energy and mining industries including tubing and piping products, conveyance systems, grinding products, grates and screens for separation, windmill towers, and parts and products for human access like walkways and stair structures. Telecommunications towers are part of this business, and the shift to wireless and especially 5G networks will drive growth. Products are available as standard designs and engineered for custom applications as needed for industrial, commercial, and residential applications. If you've ever sat at a stoplight and wondered how a single cantilevered arm could support four 400-pound traffic signals, these are the folks to ask.
- Utility Support Structures (31 percent, 32 percent)—This segment produces the very large concrete and steel substations and electric transmission support towers used by electric utilities. This segment also includes offshore structures, once part of a separate Energy and Mining segment. We like this unit's prospects as utility infrastructure is replaced and modernized in the interest of grid efficiency, and now, aesthetic and environmental sensibility—replacing traditional wood utility poles is part of this.
- Irrigation (23 percent, 35 percent)—Under the Valley brand name, Valmont produces a wide range of equipment, including gravity and drip products, as well as its center-pivot designs, which can service up to 500 acres from a single machine. Valmont also sells its irrigation controllers to other manufacturers.
- Coatings (10 percent, 16 percent)—Developed as an adjunct to its other metal products businesses, the coatings business now provides services such as galvanizing, electroplating, powder coating, and anodizing to industrial customers throughout the company's operating areas.

The company is a market leader in a number of infrastructure segments including irrigation, power transmission poles, highway infrastructure, and certain coated products. In 2018 the company made several small but significant acquisitions, including Convert Italia, a provider of solar trackers; CSP, a New Zealand steel-coatings operation; Derit, a zinc galvanizer and manufacturer of steel lattice structures; Irrigation Components International, an irrigation supplier; Torrent, a high-pressure water and air components supplier; and Walpar, a manufacturer of overhead highway structures.

Financial Highlights, Fiscal Year 2018

Several headwinds in the form of increased material and transportation costs, soft global sales in utility structures and irrigation, tariff uncertainties, low farm incomes, and soft business in China led to a flat sales year in 2018; however, lower tax rates led to an 8 percent gain in net income. For 2019 and especially 2020, the company looks to improved business especially in transportation and telecommunications structures (5G especially) and electric grid replacement to drive stronger revenues: 5–7 percent higher in 2019 and 2–3 percent 2020 with earnings up 5–7 percent in both years. The company has stated long-term goals of 5–10 percent revenue growth and per-share earnings growth exceeding 10 percent. Modest buybacks will reduce the already-low share count (22 million shares) while the dividend may remain unchanged for the next couple of years as the company pays down long-term debt.

Reasons to Buy

We remain attracted to—and loyal to—the fundamental strengths of Valmont and its core businesses, and in particular their niche strength and strategic importance to the interests of agriculture, water conservation, and infrastructure.

As much as anything we continue to view Valmont as a key infrastructure play. America's infrastructure needs to be replaced and much of it upgraded, as does infrastructure in much of the developed world. As for the less-developed world, that infrastructure needs to be built in the first place. We think, long term, that Valmont is in the right place to capture a decent share of this replacement business, including electric utility infrastructure—which in particular may be moving away from the traditional wooden telephone pole (as it has in most of the rest of the world) and as more aesthetic high-tension power poles come into favor. Wireless networking infrastructure will become a more important part of this business. The original irrigation business should also do well in the long term as global food consumption increases and as agriculture, farmland, and farm commodity prices eventually strengthen—and as droughts in key "ag" markets persist. The company's continued emphasis on growth into new geographies should pay dividends as India and China build more infrastructure and adopt more modern agricultural methods. We also like the relatively simple, straightforward nature of this business and the way the company presents itself online and in shareholder documents.

Reasons for Caution

Of course, the infrastructure "boom" may be drawn out over time as capital investment and government funding address other priorities. The relatively small size and deep, large-scale manufacturing infrastructure of a company like Valmont makes it more vulnerable to cyclical weakness—although steadier public sector demand mitigates that somewhat. Raw materials costs and tariffs have gotten in the way but may become less of a factor. Valmont presents plenty of long-term opportunity in our view, but that doesn't come without some risk.

SECTOR: Industrials ❑ Beta coefficient: 1.05 ❑ 10-year compound earnings per-share growth: 7.0% ❑ 10-year compound dividends per-share growth: 13.5%

	2011	2012	2013	2014	2015	2016	2017	2018
Revenues (mil)	2,661	3,029	3,304	3,123	2,619	2,523	2,746	2,757
Net income (mil)	158.0	234.1	278.5	184.0	40.0	173.2	158.2	170.4
Earnings per share	5.97	8.75	10.35	7.09	1.71	7.63	6.95	7.59
Cash flow per share	8.80	11.40	13.27	11.39	5.74	11.35	10.71	11.54
Dividends per share	0.72	0.88	0.98	1.38	1.50	1.50	1.50	1.50
Price: high	116.0	141.2	164.9	163.2	129.1	156.0	176.4	171.5
low	73.0	90.2	129.0	116.7	92.3	96.5	136.0	103.0

Website: www.valmont.com

GROWTH AND INCOME

NEW FOR 2020

Vanguard Real Estate Index Fund Shares ETF

Ticker symbol: VNQ (NYSE Arca) ❑ Large Cap ❑ Value Line financial strength rating: NA ❑ Current yield: 4.0% ❑ Dividend raises, past 10 years: 9

Company Profile

This year, we decided to shake things up a bit. We added 17 new or returning stocks for the 2020 campaign—a new record in the 11 years we've been creating this book. We added an IPO stock—a brand new, untested company—Beyond Meat. We also took the considerably less radical step of adding back some old favorites that got us here, favorites we may have left too soon like Kimberly-Clark and AT&T, while finally cleaning the slate of some other "faves" we probably hung on to for too long, like Mosaic and Perrigo. And here, we are about to take another step into the beyond, by adding an Exchange-Traded Fund to our *100 Best Stocks* list!

No, we aren't changing the title—nor the purpose—of our book. Our book is still about individual stocks in individual companies for you to choose as a prescient, value-conscious investor. It's about individual stocks for an actively and deliberately chosen part of your portfolio, picked to try to beat the averages and to beat the performance of so-called "passive" funds that are all the rage today. It's about choosing just the good, not the bad and the ugly, in a particular industry, index, or grouping of stocks.

We offer this ETF with a purpose. It is not offered as an alternative to investing in individual stocks; we still think individual stock investing is the only clear path to beating the averages. But often when we invest in individual stocks, we don't see enough good opportunities to become fully invested. Prices are too high. Questions swirl about the economy and the timing of the next recession. You're going on a four-week Himalayan trek and won't have the time or ability to watch your stock portfolio. Sometimes you simply need to *park* cash. But you want to park it in a lot somewhere that pays a decent return while you wait. It is for that situation that we choose Vanguard REIT ETF—as a place to park cash while waiting for a better opportunity, while still collecting about 4 percent in "rent" for your parked sum.

Vanguard REIT ETF is, simply, a fund of funds. It is a fund that owns about 186 REITs; each REIT itself is a basket of real estate holdings. According to Vanguard, itself one of the premier providers of low-cost, simple, efficient ETFs, the Vanguard REIT ETF "seeks to provide a high level of income and moderate long-term capital appreciation by tracking the performance of the MSCI US Investable Market Real Estate 25/50 Index that measures the performance of publicly traded equity REITs and other real estate-related investments."

Financial Highlights, Fiscal Year 2018

Since this is an Exchange-Traded Fund, not a company or a stock, we will dispense with the typical evaluation of financial results and projections. We prefer to share a few statistics that characterize the fund:

- Total assets under management: $33.6 billion. VNQ is not a "top 10" fund in size, but comes in the next group. As ETFs go, this is a large fund.
- Number of holdings: 186. VNQ is well diversified, but within the category of real estate. It is a pure play in real estate, and holds REITs of all types—residential, apartment, office, retail, healthcare, logistics, storage, data center, communications, and others. We should also note that VNQ's holdings are virtually 100 percent US-based.

- Expense Ratio: 0.12 percent. This means that for every $1,000 you have invested, the fund manager collects $1.20 in fees annually for managing the fund—or $120 per year for $100,000 managed. This is low but still is a consideration when choosing an ETF or any other investment product to invest in.

What's under the Hood

As of mid-2019, the top 10 holdings represent 36.6 percent of the portfolio:

- American Tower—7.42 percent
- Simon Property Group—4.70 percent
- Crown Castle—4.51 percent
- Prologis—4.12 percent
- Equinix—3.38 percent
- Public Storage—3.06 percent
- Welltower—2.48 percent
- Equity Residential—2.41 percent
- AvalonBay Communities—2.39 percent
- Digital Realty Trust—2.13 percent

Reasons to Buy

For years, people have asked us where they should "park" investible cash while waiting for better entry points for individual companies. We like the idea of parking "surplus" capital somewhere where we can collect rent for a while. More often than not, especially in today's paltry interest rate environment, we've been suggesting VNQ. VNQ provides safety (extensive diversification within the different types of REITs, relative price stability), decent returns (3.5–4 percent consistently), and liquidity (as an ETF, easy and cheap to buy and sell). You may have noticed that four of the top 10 holdings (previously noted) are individual members of the *100 Best Stocks* list—Crown Castle, Prologis, Public Storage, and Welltower—so there is some consistency between this fund's holdings and what we think are good ideas in this space. VNQ has performed well, with $10,000 invested in 2008 being worth over $38,000 today with dividends reinvested, and with an average 8.7 percent annual return over the life of the fund. VNQ is a reliable place to park to get current return while awaiting sharper individual stock opportunities—or for a steady foundational segment of your portfolio—or to keep locked away while you're on safari.

Reasons for Caution

Even with the diversification within the REIT space, the REIT space itself is subject to a degree of interest rate risk; that is, if rates rise, the rental revenue streams and thus the REIT yields look relatively less attractive—so REITs can and will change in value as interest rates fluctuate. While we noted the "congruence" between their top 10 holdings and our four individual REIT holdings, we also note that, as a diversified REIT fund, they also own REITs in what we consider more risky real estate spaces in today's environment; for instance, their number two holding is Simon Property Group, which owns a lot of retail properties that may be prone to struggle over the next few years. Finally, the "annual turnover ratio"—the percent of the portfolio that is sold and replaced every year—is a relatively high 24 percent; this could generate some taxable capital gains income in taxable accounts. We would have expected a more long-term approach to its holdings. Bottom line: There are downsides and risk to any investment; the trick is to know what they are, keep your eyes open, and learn to trust the intermediaries who are managing your money.

SECTOR: Real Estate ❑ Beta coefficient: 0.95 ❑ 10-year compound earnings per-share growth: NM ❑ 10-year compound dividends per-share growth: NM

		2011	2012	2013	2014	2015	2016	2017	2018
Dividends per share		2.05	2.19	2.20	2.91	3.12	3.98	3.51	3.53
Price:	high	63.3	67.6	78.9	83.7	89.3	92.9	84.5	83.7
	low	57.1	57.0	63.4	64.1	71.7	70.9	80.0	71.1

Website: https://investor.vanguard.com/etf/profile/VNQ

AGGRESSIVE GROWTH

Visa, Inc.

Ticker symbol: V (NYSE) ❑ Large Cap ❑ Value Line financial strength rating: A++ ❑ Current yield: 0.8% ❑ Dividend raises, past 10 years: 10

Company Profile

If we wrote about a company with a 50 percent net profit margin and a global brand that was in the business of collecting small fees on every one of the 34 billion of transactions worldwide (totaling in dollars about $11.2 trillion in 2018); a company that required almost no capital expenditures, plant, equipment, or inventory; a company that brought almost $1.2 million per employee in net profit (few companies return even that much per employee in net revenue; the company refers to this as "people light and technology heavy"); a company growing per-share earnings 20–30 percent a year; a company with a time-tested business model and absolutely zero long-term debt until recently (to fund the acquisition of its European counterpart)— would you believe that it existed? No. It must be a dream.

But it's all true, in fact. Founded in 1958 but not taken public until 2008, the Visa emblem has traditionally appeared on a majority of the world's credit cards—and now debit cards. In fact, there are about 3.3 *billion* such cards accepted at 54 million–plus merchant locations about 500 million times per day in 200 countries worldwide. According to BrandZ's 2018 Top 100 Most Valuable Global Brands Study, Visa is the number seven brand worldwide.

Visa operates the world's largest retail electronic payment network, providing processing services, payment platforms, and fraud-detection services for credit, debit, and commercial payments. The company also operates one of the largest global ATM networks with its Plus and Interlink brands. In total, the company processes 182 billion transactions per year (which works out to about 5.8 transactions *per second*) in 160 currencies and estimates that it can process about 11 times that amount in a peak scenario—65,000 transactions per second—while being operational 99.999999 percent of the time!

For years, Visa has been synonymous with credit and credit cards, but in recent years it has become more of a digital currency company, stitching together consumers, retailers, banks, and other businesses in a giant global network. Really, Visa is a global payments technology business that not only develops and supplies the technology but also collects fees upon its use.

The shift from traditional cash and check forms of payment to debit cards and other digital forms has been growing at about a 12 percent annual rate, driven by the security and convenience of these transactions as well as a shift away from consumer debt to more "paid for today" debit transactions. Debit transactions now account for more than half the company's overall business volume, albeit at a small penalty, as average transaction sizes are smaller.

The company is an active innovator, with several initiatives in what it calls an "evolving payments ecosystem" and in network security. Mobile payment and mobile wallet innovations include "V.me" and "payWave" licensed products, and, not surprisingly in light of recent news events, the company is also working on new payment and card security initiatives. A new "token" offering allows one-time issued numbers to replace credit card numbers for certain types of transactions in the interest of security. Visa Digital Solutions is a catch-all effort to allow other organizations to imbed payment services and authentication technologies in other processes. The company is also very active in fraud prevention and into mining data to help merchants grow their businesses with a new techy-sounding "Visa Threat Intelligence" fusion platform to monitor and control security threats. Some 60 percent of Visa's revenue now comes from outside the US, far more than its rivals and providing the company's strongest growth driver at present.

Financial Highlights, Fiscal Year 2018

A robust global economy and increased use of digital payment methods drove an 11 percent worldwide transaction volume gain and an across-the-board gain in transaction dollar volumes: up 9.6 percent in the US, 8.3 percent in Canada, 7.4 percent in Europe, 9.2 percent in Latin America, 7.1 percent in Asia Pacific, and 8.4 percent in Central Europe, Middle East, and Africa. This led to a 12 percent revenue gain and a 50 percent (!) net profit gain for 2018 driven in part by sharply lower tax rates. Current projections call for revenue growth in the 10–12 percent range through 2020 with steady margins and gains in net and per-share earnings in the 20 percent range. The company continues to repurchase shares at about a 1–3 percent annual rate and has already retired a third of its float since going public in 2008.

Reasons to Buy

"A Network that Connects the World" stands up as Visa's corporate mantra. Simply, it's hard to come up with a better business model—a company that develops and sells the network and collects fees every time it's used. "Financial Inclusion" is another slogan, as they expand globally to provide payment technologies for everyone everywhere. It would be like Microsoft collecting fees every time a file is created and saved or an email platform charging fees for every message. Visa is in a great position to not only capitalize on overall world economic growth, as most companies should be, but also to capitalize on a shift in this growth toward electronic and mobile payments. Even as debt-conscious consumers pull back on using credit cards, debit card usage continues to advance. This reinforces one of Visa's big strengths—unlike most other financial services businesses, Visa is relatively immune to downturns, as it makes its money by processing payments, not by extending credit. On the growth side, the company is expanding its footprint in emerging markets, and there is plenty of innovation opportunity in this business. Overall, while Visa has traditional competitors (MasterCard, American Express, Discover) and new competitors like Square, it continues to have the strongest franchise, technology leadership, and pricing power at its back. Its volumes are double its nearest competitor—MasterCard.

Reasons for Caution

The company has pricing power, but as with many companies that do, that power has come under government, merchant, and public scrutiny; the company must tread lightly or face possible consequences. Litigation and regulatory actions have presented some occasional headline and profit risk and may be construed as a threat to the franchise—perhaps if it sounds too good to be true, it may be. But even after some legal and regulatory bumps, Visa has emerged rock solid. Competition from new technologies like Square—and who knows, Bitcoin and other cryptocurrencies?—lurks in the wings, but especially in the case of Bitcoin, we don't think they pose a threat as of now.

Finally, with the steady success, good entry points have been very hard to find.

SECTOR: Financials ❑ Beta coefficient: 0.95 ❑ 10-year compound earnings per-share growth: 20.0% ❑ 10-year compound dividends per-share growth: 23.0%

	2011	2012	2013	2014	2015	2016	2017	2018
Revenues (mil)	9,188	10,421	11,776	12,702	13,880	15,082	18,358	20,609
Net income (mil)	3,650	4,203	4,980	5,438	6,238	5,991	6,699	10,301
Earnings per share	1.25	1.55	1.90	2.27	2.62	2.84	3.48	4.42
Dividends per share	0.15	0.22	0.33	0.42	0.50	0.59	0.69	0.88
Cash flow per share	1.39	1.67	2.05	2.44	2.82	3.07	3.75	4.72
Price: high	25.9	38.1	55.7	67.3	81.0	84.0	114.0	151.6
low	16.9	24.6	38.5	48.7	60.0	65.1	78.5	111.0

Website: www.corporate.visa.com

GROWTH AND INCOME

Waste Management, Inc.

Ticker symbol: WM (NYSE) ❑ Large Cap ❑ Value Line financial strength rating: A ❑ Current yield: 2.1% ❑ Dividend raises, past 10 years: 10

Company Profile

You may refer to it as a "garbage company" if you want—we won't take offense. Waste Management continues to be the largest and steadiest hand in the North American solid waste disposal industry. In their own words, "North America's leading provider of comprehensive waste management environmental services"; supporting this claim, they serve some 20 million municipal, commercial, and industrial customers in the US and Canada and handle about 114 million tons of waste annually, from which about 13 million tons is recycled. Like most large waste firms, WM has grown over time by assembling smaller, more local companies into a nationally branded and highly scaled operation with a notable amount of innovation on several fronts in the core business and especially in material recovery—translation, recycling.

The business is divided into three segments:

- Collection, which accounts for 54 percent of 2018 business, includes the standard dumpster and garbage truck operations. The company has about 600 collection operations, many of which have long-term contracts with municipalities and businesses. About 41 percent of the collection business is commercial, 26 percent residential, 28 percent industrial, and 5 percent other. For the industry, WM is considered an innovator even in its traditional collection operations; examples include the Bagster small-scale disposal units now sold through retail home-improvement outlets and 6,500 collection trucks converted to natural gas (some of which the company produces from waste; in 25 locations the company even sells waste-to-gas fuel to outside customers). The company perceives itself as a world-class logistics company (and why not?) and has equipped its trucks with the latest in onboard computers, centralized dispatching, and routing processes, reducing collection costs as much as 1 percent per year.
- Landfill (20 percent of revenues). The company operates 244 landfills across North America, servicing its own collection operations and other collection service providers. Among these sites, there are 127 landfill-gas-to-energy conversion projects producing fuel for electricity generation. There are also five active hazardous waste landfills and one underground hazardous waste facility.
- Transfer, Recycling, and Other (26 percent). These operations perform specialized material recovery and processing into useful commodities. There are 305 transfer stations set up for the collection of various forms of waste, including medical, recyclables, compact fluorescent (CFL), and e-waste. The company has also pioneered single-stream recycling, where physical and optical sorting technologies sort out unseparated recyclable materials. Single-streaming has greatly increased recycling rates in municipalities where it is used and provides a steady revenue stream in recovered

paper, glass, metals, etc., for the company. WM also further refines these materials into industrial inputs, e.g., glass or plastic feedstocks in certain colors. In total there are 61 traditional and 44 "single-stream" operations, recycling some 13 million tons of commodities annually today. Despite the strategic importance of recycling and the new technologies applied, volumes and pricing have retreated as global demand has waned, in part due to new regulations imposed by China on the import of recyclable material. Recycling prices dropped about 8 percent in 2017, but the company has worked since mainly on recycled material quality to make it suitable for domestic and other markets; recycled material revenue rose 9 percent in the fourth quarter 2018 after being down most of the year.

Financial Highlights, Fiscal Year 2018

Revenues advanced 3 percent overall, with a 4.8 percent gain in the collection and disposal business offset by the aforementioned weakness in recycling resulting from lower prices. The strong revenue showing was driven both by volume and price. Net income was up a much stronger 27 percent based on cost efficiencies, lower administrative expenses, and tax cuts. For 2019 the company projects a far more modest 3 percent earnings rise on a 4 percent revenue gain; for 2020 it projects a more robust 8–10 percent earnings growth on a 4–6 percent revenue rise. A rebound in recycled material prices could bring still better income results. Dividend increases in the 10 percent range annually and modest buybacks should continue coming down the conveyor belt.

Reasons to Buy

WM is the strongest and most entrenched player in a business that isn't going away anytime soon. "Strategic" waste collection, particularly with the high-value-add material recovery operations that have become a key part of WM's business, is not only here to stay but also will only become more important to residential, industrial, and municipal customers as time goes on. Although China closed its market to most recyclable materials, disrupting the market considerably, the current rebound in commodity prices foretells better recycling yields; we feel the "sweet spot" in this business is yet to come.

WM exhibits a lot of innovation in an industry not particularly known for it. WM's performance has indeed improved as operational improvements and lower fuel costs have taken effect and material yields have increased.

Regulation and regulatory compliance has always been a big deal for WM, but relaxed regulation likely in the Trump administration may reduce this burden, and now the tax cuts will help too.

Reasons for Caution

WM does rely on acquisitions for a lot of its growth—over half a billion worth in 2018 alone. In this business, that might not be so bad, for existing companies have captive markets and disposal facilities and can likely benefit from proven management processes and reduced overhead costs. As we've seen, the recycling operations, while cool and sexy, aren't always as profitable as one would think. A lot depends on trade policies and the price of "new" materials. Additionally, any waste company runs the risk of going afoul of environmental regulations; WM has largely steered clear of trouble thus far (and has indeed been voted in as a "world's most ethical company" for the past 11 years by the Ethisphere Institute—the only entry in the "environmental services" category), but there are no guarantees.

SECTOR: Business Services ❑ Beta coefficient: 0.70 ❑ 10-year compound earnings per-share growth: 5.0% ❑ 10-year compound dividends per-share growth: 6.0%

	2011	2012	2013	2014	2015	2016	2017	2018
Revenues (mil)	13,375	13,649	13,983	13,996	12,961	13,609	14,485	14,914
Net income (mil)	1,007	968	1,008	1,155	1,153	1,295	1,425	1,813
Earnings per share	2.14	2.08	2.15	2.48	2.53	2.91	3.22	4.20
Dividends per share	1.36	1.42	1.46	1.50	1.54	1.64	1.70	1.86
Cash flow per share	4.85	4.88	5.04	5.34	5.36	5.90	6.45	7.75
Price: high	36.7	36.3	46.4	51.9	55.9	71.8	86.9	95.5
low	27.8	30.8	33.7	40.3	45.9	50.4	69.0	78.4

Website: www.wm.com

GROWTH AND INCOME

Welltower, Inc.

Ticker symbol: WELL (NYSE) ❑ Large Cap ❑ Value Line financial strength rating: A++ ❑ Current yield: 4.5% ❑ Dividend raises, past 10 years: 9

Company Profile

Welltower, our first real estate investment trust (REIT) choice added six years ago in 2014, invests primarily in senior living, medical care, and medical office properties mainly in the US but also in Canada and the UK. The business—and we think it's a good business, not just a real estate portfolio—operates in three primary business segments. The first and largest by number of facilities is referred to as the Seniors Housing "triple-net" segment and is involved primarily in owning senior housing properties, including independent, continuing care, and assisted living facilities, and leasing them to qualified operators like Sunrise Senior Living, Revera, and Brookdale Senior Living in return for a steady income stream. This segment currently owns 659 properties in the US containing 66,470 units in 37 states but is concentrated in high-cost urban areas mostly on the coasts and contributes about 20 percent of revenues and 43 percent of net operating income. There are now also 61 facilities in the UK and 6 facilities in Canada.

The second, fastest-growing, and largest by revenue segment is the Seniors Housing Operating segment, which actually operates some of the facilities owned by the REIT and others owned by third parties. It operates 500 properties in 35 states, 110 in Canada, and 54 in the UK and contributes about 72 percent of revenues and 40 percent of net operating income. The third major segment is Outpatient Medical, which owns and sometimes operates 280 outpatient medical centers in 36 states, contributing about 12 percent of revenues and 17 percent to net operating income.

The company sold its last hospital and its life sciences facilities in 2015 and 2016 and has been repositioning its portfolio to focus more on more lucrative Seniors Housing and on outpatient medical and health system facilities, now the newest trend in the health space, while continuing to downsize its hospital and post-acute care (skilled nursing facilities, etc.). This has led to an ongoing campaign to "recycle capital," that is, to sell certain properties and acquire others—which affected short-term 2018 performance negatively. Seniors Housing, which was once just 40 percent of Welltower's revenue and 69 percent private pay (versus Medicare, etc.) is now 72 percent of revenue and 95 percent private pay. This is a more lucrative business, especially when the seniors can afford a more upscale existence on their own. In total, Welltower owns and/or operates some 1,510 properties in three countries, housing some 210,000 residents, and supporting 16 million annual outpatient visits.

Welltower employs a conscious and stated strategy of being in markets with high barriers to entry and with a more upscale, affluent retiree base—this is part of why we feel it is a good business, not just a real estate play. Markets such as Boston, New Jersey, Seattle, and major coastal California cities are territories for Welltower. The top five markets are New York, Philadelphia, Los Angeles, Boston, and greater London. A recent study concluded that 68–73 percent of seniors wanted to stay in their same city in the top ten markets in the US.

The average revenue per occupied room in the seniors operating segment is $6,784 per month, some 41 percent higher than the national senior housing industry average. In the markets in which WELL operates senior housing, the cost of the average single-family home runs 154 percent higher than the national average, and household incomes are 52 percent higher. Seventy-nine percent of facilities are in the 25 most affluent US metropolitan areas. FY2018 occupancy rates are 84.9 percent in the seniors housing triple-net segment (85.8 percent last year), 87.2 percent in the seniors housing operating (87.3 percent last year), and 93.1 percent in the medical facilities segments (93.7 percent last year). The facilities are newer, more attractive, and desirable, as a trip through the company's website at www.welltower.com will show.

The strategy and focus are to "differentiate" and to provide an "infrastructure platform that emphasizes wellness and connectivity across the continuum of care"—or pleasant, well-appointed alternatives to the traditional facilities usually offered to both healthy and less healthy seniors.

REITs, obviously, play on the real estate market, and in the Welltower case, in the high-value-add REIT segment of healthcare. You're also investing in the aging population, which is expected to grow 40 percent by 2024 against a 9.1 percent growth in the population as a whole. With Welltower, you're also investing in the ability and willingness of more affluent segments of the elderly population to spend for a pleasant retirement.

REITs are typically good income producers, as they are required by law to pay a substantial portion of their cash flow to investors. The accounting rules are different, and REIT investors should focus on funds from operations (FFO), which is analogous to operating income; net income figures have depreciation expenses deducted, which can vary in timing and not always be realistic. FFO support the dividends paid to investors. And now, with the new Section 199 provision of the 2017 Tax Cuts and Jobs Act, REIT income is considered "pass through" so 20 percent of it is deductible for those of you owning WELL in after-tax accounts.

Financial Highlights, Fiscal Year 2018

For the second year in a row, portfolio transitions and a slightly weaker occupancy rate in the triple-net and outpatient care portions of the business led to slightly softer results. Per-share FFO dropped just under 4 percent (although some of that was due to an increase in share count) on a 9 percent revenue gain. The company expects 5–7 percent revenue gains going forward into 2019 and 2020 with net income finally ticking upward with 4–6 percent FFO/share gains. The company suspended its first dividend raise in years (not the entire dividend) in early 2018 and stood pat in early 2019.

Reasons to Buy

Welltower continues to be a solid, income-oriented way to play the steady growth and trends of the healthcare industry and the aging demographic. Rents—and rent growth—are better than average, and its income payout is stable and typically growing. Longer term, the company estimates that senior housing rent growth will exceed inflation by 1.7 percent, that the US population over 75 years of age will grow some 86 percent over the next 20 years, and the 85+ population will double—all factors supporting a healthy growth story in the seniors housing business. Strong growth in outpatient medical procedures and services will help that segment too.

Some 95 percent of revenues were estimated to be derived from private pay sources in 2018, up from 93 percent in 2017, and 83 percent in 2014. With the concentration on private-pay services, Welltower will avoid some of the exposure to Medicare utilization management initiatives and related cutbacks that many others in the sector are exposed to—and an improving economy will only help further. We like, and most in the industry agree, the expansion into the UK, which positions them well for other fertile pastures overseas.

In sum, despite recent change, Welltower offers a good combination of high yield and safety with a modest long-term growth kicker mixed in for good measure.

Reasons for Caution

Because of their differences from ordinary corporations, it may be difficult to understand this investment, particularly the financial performance of REITs, especially a complex REIT such as this one, which has both traditional property investments and operating company investments. The 10-K Annual Report is overly complicated and one of the worst we've seen, but their investor presentations are helpful.

There is some evidence of competitive pressure and oversupply in the seniors real estate market, but we feel confident that Welltower is playing in the stronger, more exclusive niches and wisely not taking on the "mass market" players head to head. One could also question, going forward, whether retirees will be as well-heeled as they are today, with deterioration in retirement savings and increased costs. Finally, there is increasing sensitivity to rising interest rates; the modest underlying growth and high yield makes the stock act more like a bond than a stock much of the time.

SECTOR: Healthcare ❑ Beta coefficient: 0.65 ❑ 10-year compound FFO per-share growth: 2.5% ❑ 10-year compound dividends per-share growth: 2.5%

	2011	2012	2013	2014	2015	2016	2017	2018
Revenues (mil)	1,421	1,822	2,880	3,344	3,858	4,281	4,316	4,701
Net income (mil)	156	295	93	505	884	1,078	513	805
Funds from operations per share	3.41	3.52	3.80	4.13	4.38	4.55	4.21	4.03
Real estate owned per share	72.5	66.9	74.9	69.5	75.8	73.3	70.4	74.1
Dividends per share	2.84	2.96	3.06	3.18	3.30	3.44	3.48	3.48
Price: high	55.2	62.8	80.1	78.2	84.9	80.2	78.2	74.8
low	41.0	52.4	52.4	52.9	58.2	52.8	63.1	49.6

Website: www.welltower.com

CONSERVATIVE GROWTH

Whirlpool Corporation

Ticker symbol: WHR (NYSE) ❑ Large Cap ❑ Value Line financial strength rating: A+ ❑ Current yield: 3.4% ❑ Dividend raises, past 10 years: 8

Company Profile

Whirlpool is the world's leading home appliance manufacturer in a $120 billion global industry. The company manufactures appliances under familiar and recognized brand names in all major home appliance categories including fabric care (laundry), cooking, refrigeration, dishwashers, water filtration, and garage organization. Familiar brand names include Whirlpool, Maytag, Hotpoint, KitchenAid, Amana, JennAir, Gladiator, and international names Bauknecht, Brastemp, Indesit, and Consul. But beyond selling familiar appliances as steel boxes in all sizes and shapes, the company is moving fast-forward into the era of the "connected kitchen" and "smart home" with "connected appliances" that connect to the Internet or smartphone and can respond to voice commands either directly or through smart devices such as Google Home. Not only do these products respond to commands but they can also execute cook times, temperatures, and actions in accordance with stored or online recipes. The possibilities are endless and represent a pretty exciting application of today's Internet of Things (IoT) concept.

The Whirlpool brand itself is the number one global appliance brand and is either number one or number two across all four major world geographic regions. The company is the leading appliance manufacturer in seven of the world's ten largest countries. Products are found in 97 million homes worldwide. Six brands within the branded house generate over $1 billion in annual sales. Based on FY2018 sales, the product breakdown is about 29 percent refrigerators and freezers, 28 percent fabric care, 18 percent home cooking appliances, and 24 percent "other." About 46 percent of Whirlpool's sales come from outside North America: 22 percent in Europe/Middle East/Africa, 17 percent in Latin America, and 7 percent in Asia. Major investments in overseas brands include: Europe's Indesit (another billion-dollar brand) and China's Hefei Sanyo. The acquisition strategy keys on adjacent businesses, many to open or gain critical mass in international markets. Whirlpool estimates that through its acquisitions it now has access to 90 percent of the world's consumers.

In an industry not traditionally known for innovation, Whirlpool has striven to be an innovation leader in its industry ("Innovation at the Pace of Life" is one slogan). This has manifested itself both in new products, product platforms, and contemporary styling within those platforms; and in manufacturing and supply-chain efficiencies, such as a global platform design for local manufacture of washing machine products, recalling similar achievements in the auto industry. Such gains are key in this competitive, price-sensitive industry. Customer experience and customer-focused innovation are key strategic areas, especially with the incorporation of today's technologies ("Win the Digital Consumer Journey" is their mantra). The company also has initiatives to build lifetime brand loyalty and product quality, improve water and energy efficiency and quietness of operation, and add more interesting and decorative colors to some of its products. "Be the best kitchen and laundry company, in constant pursuit of improving life at home" states their vision better than most.

Overall, the strategy is to expand the business through innovation, brand strength, and geographic coverage; then to expand margins through supply-chain and cost-structure efficiency.

Financial Highlights, Fiscal Year 2018

For several years the company has ridden the coattails of an improving economy, an improved replacement cycle for old units, improved demand for today's more efficient appliances, and operational improvements. FY2018, following on 2017 was a bit of an off year, as tariffs and stronger commodity pricing hurt bottom line results while a bit of a flattening in new and existing home sales dented the top line. The company has been vocal in declaring that 2018 tariffs increased its costs by $300 million. Some, but not all, was offset by price increases and cost saving initiatives. Anyway, sales dropped about 1 percent while earnings dropped a little less than 1 percent; however, due to an enormous 10 percent share buyback, per-share earnings were up 10 percent. (We applaud the aggressive buyback when the share prices were a bargain in late 2018.) The company forecasts relatively flat earnings and sales over the next two years, which we feel is conservative as new product designs and technology enhancements should, in our opinion, speed up the appliance replacement cycle.

Reasons to Buy

Long a dull, boring business, Whirlpool has made shopping for an appliance more interesting and has profited handsomely from its efforts. If you shop for an appliance today—take washers and dryers, for example—they work better, they're more energy efficient, they use less water, and are more technology enabled. In short, they're better products, and guess what: They're higher priced and more profitable for the manufacturers too. Operational improvements, higher product value add, and a gradual increase in premium brands have driven operating and net margins substantially higher. We continue to like the way the company wrings ever more profit out of a modestly growing or even flat sales base.

Now as the economy and employment strengthen globally, Whirlpool is in a particularly good position to capitalize on these tailwinds. More than most, Whirlpool used the Great Recession and ensuing recovery as a wake-up call and an opportunity to streamline its businesses and to put some real strategic thought into how to drive its brand assortment and international portfolio to achieve better results. We think investors may tie too much of Whirlpool's fortunes to the level of *new* home construction—while it is a factor, replacement in existing homes appears a bigger success driver.

The company continues to innovate toward better and more connected products and internal processes. Long term, "smart" appliances will deliver better experiences, more energy-efficient results, and take center stage. Bottom line: Whirlpool has ever more to compete on than just price.

In addition, the company is building critical mass in overseas markets. Cash flows and investor returns are solid and rising as the company focuses on margin expansion and cash flow. More than most, the management team is a plus with a recognizable pragmatic and strategic approach to managing this business. And the shares have been cheap for a while at under ten times earnings and five times cash flow with a strong dividend and buyback profile. Even with a few headwinds Whirlpool shares should come out clean in the wash.

Reasons for Caution

By nature, the appliance business is highly competitive and cyclical. Many higher-income consumers have been opting for fancier, more expensive foreign brands, like Bosch and LG, a trend that could hurt if it continues. We believe that Whirlpool is countering this trend by adding elegance, advertising, and channel support for its top-tier brands and products—as well as a few "foreign" brands of its own. Trade wars look to bring a mixed blessing at this point; the company "won" some price protection on foreign "dumping" of laundry and other products—but tariffs on steel, aluminum, and other raw materials raise costs; it is difficult to predict the dynamics of just how the recent trade instability will affect WHR.

SECTOR: Consumer Durables ◻ Beta coefficient: 1.20 ◻ 10-year compound earnings per-share growth: 7.0% ◻ 10-year compound dividends per-share growth: 8.5%

		2011	2012	2013	2014	2015	2016	2017	2018
Revenues (mil)		18,666	18,143	18,768	19,872	20,891	20,718	21,253	21,037
Net income (mil)		699	559	810	907	987	1,085	1,025	1,018
Earnings per share		8.95	7.05	10.03	11.39	12.38	14.08	13.78	15.16
Dividends per share		1.93	2.00	2.38	2.88	3.45	3.90	4.30	4.55
Cash flow per share		16.54	14.05	17.53	18.80	21.43	23.51	23.65	26.00
Price:	high	92.3	104.2	159.2	196.7	217.1	194.1	203.0	187.5
	low	45.2	47.7	101.7	124.4	140.5	123.5	158.8	99.4

Website: www.whirlpoolcorp.com

AGGRESSIVE GROWTH

Zebra Technologies Corp.

Ticker symbol: ZBRA (NASDAQ) ◻ Large Cap ◻ Value Line financial strength rating: B++ ◻ Current yield: Nil ◻ Dividend raises, past 10 years: NA

Company Profile

Ever wondered in today's e-commerce world how those millions and millions of small packages actually get to their destination? In one or two days? With a minimum of number of errors? And how, if you don't like what came in that package, the very act of wanding a single barcode sets in motion a process that takes the merchandise off your hands, ships it to the right place, and credits your account immediately? Well, suffice it to say, it's all modern logistics, and Zebra Technologies supplies a lot of the stuff that makes modern logistics work together with today's logistics systems.

"Capture Your Edge," hails the principal website of Zebra Technologies. Originally established way back in 1969 in Lincolnshire, Illinois, as Data Specialties Incorporated, Zebra has grown organically and through more than a dozen acquisitions to become a leading provider of barcode reading, tracking, and labeling systems. Their most recent significant acquisition, the 2014 purchase of Motorola Mobility Solutions, also gave them a major presence in the RFID (Radio Frequency Identification, a system that reads small embedded chips on pallets and other moving things), mobile computing, and data capture services. The combined businesses bring to market what are known as AIDC products, an industry acronym for Automatic Identification and Data Capture. The "market" is becoming known by the rather interesting catchphrase "enterprise asset intelligence." Know what you have and where you have it, and be able to apply real time intelligence to making its next move.

The company reports business in two segments: AIT (Asset Intelligence and Tracking, about 32 percent of the business), which consists of the bulk of the existing product line prior to the Motorola acquisition, and EVM (Enterprise Visibility and Mobility, about 68 percent of the business), which represents the businesses that came in the acquisition, including RFID technologies, wireless handheld readers, mobile computing, and software tools. In 2018 the company acquired Xplore, a maker of rugged tablets for on-site asset tracking and management. As of FY2018 the company has largely completed its "One Zebra" program, the goal of which was to integrate what were fairly distinct but complementary businesses under one management structure and gain efficiencies where possible.

The bulk of their sales are in hardware platforms, including barcode scanners and imagers, mobile computers and tablets, RFID readers, and mobile and fixed specialty printers. They also sell supplies and accessories to support the hardware, as well as software platforms employed in device tracking and data analytics. End users of Zebra's products include businesses engaged in retailing and e-commerce, transportation and logistics, manufacturing, and healthcare. Nearly 50 percent of the products are sold through distribution, with downstream VARs ("value-added resellers"), independent software vendors, and systems integrators reselling a customized package/product to the end user. On the Zebra website you can see applications for tracking everything from cardiac patients to shopping carts.

The company's mobile computing platforms are widely supported in a multitude of applications, including federal and state government and civilian agencies, military, law enforcement, education, and public health. Applications are in place for material inspection, code enforcement, identity management, and healthcare analytics, to name a few. The list is deep and broad. Lastly, Zebra also sells subscription services for software and hardware support, as well as in-house custom development services for applications or hardware not available in their standard line.

The company provides products and services in over 180 countries, with 114 facilities and approximately 7,000 employees. About 52 percent of sales are overseas.

Financial Highlights, Fiscal Year 2018
Sales advanced 13.3 percent in FY2018, 11.1 percent "organically" without the Xplore acquisition and currency adjustments. Gross margin improved 1 percent and net margin (which includes tax change effects) advanced a full 4 percent, leading the way to a 57 percent increase in net earnings. Projections for FY2019 call for a 4–7 percent increase in net sales, with a moderating but still-healthy 11–13 percent gain in net earnings. For 2020, the company projects similar revenue and earnings growth.

Reasons to Buy
If there's anything to be learned from the Amazonification (new word, copyright *100 Best Stocks*) of the North American retail business, it's the value of smart logistics. By providing reliable, predictable, and verifiable delivery of goods to consumers, Amazon was able to win over most of those customers who were not initially persuaded simply by a marginally lower price. Now, obviously, order fulfillment is only part of Amazon's automation and logistics story, but our takeaway for the purposes of understanding Zebra's possibilities is that the appropriate application of intelligence can be a significant differentiator in endeavors even as mundane as knowing where a box is, because that box represents value. This is where Zebra lives. They provide the tools (the picks and shovels, a model we love) to help many different types of businesses gain an understanding of how value flows (or doesn't flow) through their organization on its way to a customer. It's all part of enterprise asset management, and enterprise asset management

is one of the new frontiers of winning against one's competitors, especially in today's highly distributed, fast-flowing e-commerce world.

The technology isn't particularly new or sexy—bar codes have been with us since the 1970s. But we like how Zebra has integrated the offering across several types of products and across hardware and software. Their traditional barcode and printer products (AIT) are still the industry standard in many applications, and the EVM segment brings wireless data capture and automated tracking, mobile computing, and services to support real-time applications. They have a strong partner ecosystem, global presence, and a solid brand. Why we find this company attractive now is not so much that they're discovering large new markets, it's that large markets are moving toward them.

Reasons for Caution

The Motorola Mobility business did not come cheap. Although the acquisition closed in 2014, Zebra is still carrying some $2.1 billion in total debt attributable to the purchase on its books. The debt itself has run about 70 percent of capital recently, but the company has made a priority of reducing it, to the tune of $2 billion of the original $3.1 billion paid off by the end of 2019. With cost reductions and strong cash flow, the company could easily pay it down to zero in the next few years and initiate some decent dividends and share buybacks. Much of that and the company's general success has been factored into the stock price; look for good buy points, but we doubt this zebra will change its stripes much anytime soon.

SECTOR: **Information Technology** ❑ Beta coefficient: 1.40 ❑ 10-year compound earnings per-share growth: 17.5% ❑ 10-year compound dividends per-share growth: NA

		2011	2012	2013	2014	2015	2016	2017	2018
Revenues (mil)		984	996	1,038	1,671	3,652	3,574	3,722	4,218
Net income (mil)		130	131	134	128	277	293	379	598
Earnings per share		2.40	2.53	2.63	2.49	5.31	5.60	7.05	11.01
Dividends per share		—	—	—	—	—	—	—	—
Cash flow per share		2.96	3.09	3.30	4.05	11.45	11.29	12.06	14.35
Price:	high	44.5	41.9	55.2	86.0	119.5	88.0	117.4	184.8
	low	28.2	31.8	40.0	52.6	63.9	46.1	81.0	102.8

Website: www.zebra.com

The 100 Best Stocks to Buy in 2020

Index of Stocks by Company Name (*New for 2020)

Company	Symbol	Category	Sector
3M	MMM	Conservative Growth	Industrials
—A—			
Abbott Labs	ABT	Growth and Income	Healthcare
AbbVie	ABBV	Aggressive Growth	Healthcare
Allstate	ALL	Conservative Growth	Financials
Amazon	AMZN	Aggressive Growth	Retail
Analog Devices	ADI	Aggressive Growth	Information Technology
Apple	AAPL	Aggressive Growth	Consumer Discretionary
Aptiv	APTV	Aggressive Growth	Industrials
Archer Daniels Midland	ADM	Conservative Growth	Consumer Staples
*AT&T	T	Growth and Income	Telecommunications Services
—B—			
Becton, Dickinson	BDX	Conservative Growth	Healthcare
*Best Buy	BBY	Aggressive Growth	Retail
*Beyond Meat	BYND	Aggressive Growth	Consumer Staples
*BlackRock	BLK	Growth and Income	Financials
Boeing	BA	Aggressive Growth	Industrials
—C—			
CarMax	KMX	Aggressive Growth	Retail
Carnival Corporation	CCL	Aggressive Growth	Consumer Discretionary
CenterPoint Energy	CNP	Growth and Income	Utilities
Chemed	CHE	Aggressive Growth	Healthcare
*Chemours	CC	Aggressive Growth	Materials
Chevron	CVX	Growth and Income	Energy
Coca-Cola	KO	Conservative Growth	Consumer Discretionary
Columbia Sportswear	COLM	Aggressive Growth	Consumer Staples
Comcast	CMCSA	Conservative Growth	Telecommunications Services
*Compass Holdings	CODI	Growth and Income	Financials
ConocoPhillips	COP	Growth and Income	Energy
Corning	GLW	Aggressive Growth	Information Technology
Costco Wholesale	COST	Aggressive Growth	Retail
*Crown Castle	CCI	Growth and Income	Real Estate
CVS Health	CVS	Conservative Growth	Retail

Index of Stocks by Company Name (continued)

Index of Stocks by Company Name (continued)

Index of Stocks by Company Name (continued)

Currently Available from Value Line for Individual Investors

The Value Line Investment Survey®
The signature publication from Value Line is one of the most highly regarded comprehensive investment research resources. Published weekly, it tracks 1,700+ stocks in more than 90 industries and ranks stocks for Safety™ as well as appreciation potential.

The Value Line Investment Survey®—Small & Mid-Cap
The Small & Mid-Cap Survey applies Value Line's data and analysis protocols to an additional approximately 1,700 companies with market values from less than $1 billion up to $5 billion.

The Value Line Investment Survey®—Smart Investor
This Internet version of The Value Line Investment Survey tracks approximately 1,700 stocks and offers sorting functions and custom alerts.

The Value Line Investment Survey®—Savvy Investor
The Internet counterpart of the preceding three Surveys, Savvy Investor includes every one of our nearly 3,400 stock reports plus updates during Stock Exchange hours.

The Value Line® 600
Provides stock reports from The Value Line Investment Survey on 600 large actively traded and widely held US exchange-listed corporations, including many foreign first, spanning more than 90 industries.

Value Line Select®
Once a month, subscribers receive a detailed report by Value Line, recommending the one stock that has the best upside and risk/reward ratio.

Value Line Select®: Dividend Income & Growth
A monthly, in-depth report recommending one dividend-paying stock, along with our views on numerous alternate selections.

The Value Line Special Situations Service®
The Value Line Special Situations Service is designed for those seeking investment ideas in the small-cap arena. Both aggressive and conservative selections appear monthly.

Value Line Select®: ETFs recommends one Exchange-Traded Fund each month, building on the industry expertise of Value Line staff.
A special 14-day trial of The Value Line Investment Survey—Smart Investor is available to individual investors with the code "100STOCKS" at www.valueline.com/100STOCKS.
551 Fifth Avenue, 3rd FL, New York, NY 10176
www.valueline.com
1-800-VALUELINE